LANDMARK ESS
RHETORIC AND FEMINISM

"Feminism" and "rhetoric" have not always been overlapping terms. While neglected as subjects of scholarly interest for centuries, women were nonetheless developing rhetorical practices and traditions all along. In recent decades women writers, speakers, and feminist scholars have recovered and forged new theories of and practices for feminist rhetoric. These women have struggled to see, re-shape, and re-deploy the rhetorical tradition in ways that not only admit but embrace and celebrate women and feminist understandings to the benefit of all people. This volume is the culmination of much of the work done by those scholars.

Edited by leading experts in field, Cheryl Glenn and Andrea A. Lunsford, *Landmark Essays on Rhetoric and Feminism* earns its significance in several key ways: it includes work done by scholars from departments of communication, English, and writing studies as well as a variety of public intellectuals; it traces a series of encounters between rhetoric and feminism during the last three decades; and it highlights five themes that represent the history of encounters between rhetoric and feminism including (1) recovery and recuperation, (2) methods and methodologies, (3) practices and performances, (4) pedagogical applications and implications, and (5) new theories and histories.

Cheryl Glenn is Liberal Arts Research Professor of English and Women's Studies at The Pennsylvania State University.

Andrea A. Lunsford is Louise Hewlett Nixon Professor of English, Emerita and former Director of the Program in Writing and Rhetoric at Stanford University.

THE LANDMARK ESSAYS SERIES

Landmark Essays is a series of anthologies providing ready access to key rhetorical studies in a wide variety of fields. The classic articles and chapters that are fundamental to every subject are often the most difficult to obtain, and almost impossible to find arranged together for research or for classroom use. This series solves that problem.

Each book encompasses a dozen or more of the most significant published studies in a particular field, and includes an index and bibliography for further study.

Series Editors:
James J. Murphy
Krista Radcliffe

Landmark Essays on Rhetoric and Feminism: 1973–2000
Edited by Cheryl Glenn,
Andrea Lunsford

Landmark Essays on Speech and Writing
Edited by Peter Elbow

Landmark Essays on Basic Writing
Edited by Kay Halasek, Nels P. Highberg

Landmark Essays on ESL Writing
Edited by Tony Silva, Paul Kei Matsuda

Landmark Essays on Rhetoric and Literature
Edited by Craig Kallendorf

Landmark Essays on Contemporary Rhetoric
Edited by Thomas B. Farrell

Landmark Essays on Aristotelian Rhetoric
Edited by Richard L. Enos, Lois P. Agnew

Landmark Essays on Bakhtin, Rhetoric, and Writing
Edited by Frank Farmer

Landmark Essays on Rhetoric and the Environment
Edited by Craig Waddell

Landmark Essays on Rhetoric of Science: Case Studies
Edited by Randy Allen Harris

Landmark Essays on Advanced Composition
Edited by Gary A. Olson, Julie Drew

Landmark Essays on Writing Centers
Edited by Christina Murphy, Joe Law

Landmark Essays on Rhetorical Invention in Writing
Edited by Richard E. Young, Yameng Liu

Landmark Essays on Writing Process
Edited by Sondra Perl

Landmark Essays on Writing Across the Curriculum
Edited by Charles Bazerman,
David R. Russell

Landmark Essays on Rhetorical Criticism
Edited by Thomas W. Benson

Landmark Essays on Voice and Writing
Edited by Peter Elbow

Landmark Essays on Classical Greek Rhetoric
Edited by A. Edward Schiappa

Landmark Essays on Kenneth Burke
Edited by Barry Brummett

Landmark Essays on American Public Address
Edited by Martin Medhurst

LANDMARK

ESSAYS ON RHETORIC AND FEMINISM

1973–2000

Edited by

CHERYL GLENN AND ANDREA A. LUNSFORD

Routledge
Taylor & Francis Group

NEW YORK AND LONDON

First published 2015
by Routledge
711 Third Avenue, New York, NY 10017

and by Routledge
2 Park Square, Milton Park, Abingdon, Oxon, OX14 4RN

Routledge is an imprint of the Taylor & Francis Group, an informa business

A catalogue record has been requested for this book.

Library of Congress Cataloging in Publication Data
Landmark essays on rhetoric and feminism : 1973–2000 / Cheryl Glenn
& Andrea A. Lunsford.
    pages cm.—(Landmark essays series)
  Includes bibliographical references and index.
  1. Rhetoric—Social aspects.   2. Feminism and literature.
  3. Women—Language.   4. Feminist theory.   I. Glenn, Cheryl, editor.
  II. Lunsford, Andrea A., 1942– editor.
  P301.5.S63L36 2015
  808—dc23   2014009698

ISBN: [978-0-415-64214-9] (hbk)
ISBN: [978-0-415-64215-6] (pbk)
ISBN: [978-0-203-76652-1] (ebk)

Typeset in Minion
by Keystroke, Station Road, Codsall, Wolverhampton

Printed and bound in the United States of America by Publishers Graphics,
LLC on sustainably sourced paper.

For Helen, Audrey, Imogen, and Lila
—to whom we entrust the future

CONTENTS

Acknowledgments   *ix*

Andrea A. Lunsford and Cheryl Glenn, Introduction:
On Rhetoric and Feminism: Forging Alliances   1

SECTION 1
INTRODUCTORY MOVES   17

  1 Karlyn Kohrs Campbell, "The Rhetoric of Women's Liberation:
     An Oxymoron" (1973)   19
  2 Cheris Kramer, "Women's Speech: Separate but Unequal?" (1974)   34

SECTION 2
RECOVERY AND RECUPERATION   47

  3 Barbara Biesecker, "Coming to Terms with Recent Attempts to
     Write Women into the History of Rhetoric" (1992)   49
  4 Cheryl Glenn, "sex, lies, and manuscript: Refiguring Aspasia in
     the History of Rhetoric" (1994)   66
  5 Shirley Wilson Logan, "Black Women on the Speaker's Platform
     (1832–1899)" (1997)   84

SECTION 3
METHODS AND METHODOLOGIES   103

  6 Susan C. Jarratt, "Speaking to the Past: Feminist Historiography
     in Rhetoric" (1990)   105
  7 Jacqueline Jones Royster, "When the First Voice You Hear Is Not
     Your Own" (1996)   122
  8 Patricia Bizzell, "Feminist Methods of Research in the History
     of Rhetoric: What Difference Do They Make?" (2000)   133

SECTION 4
PRACTICES AND PERFORMANCES   145

  9 Audre Lorde, "The Transformation of Silence into Language
     and Action" (1978)   147

10   Gloria Anzaldúa, "How to Tame a Wild Tongue" (1999)   150
11   Andrea A. Lunsford, "On Reclaiming Rhetorica" (1995)   159

SECTION 5
PEDAGOGICAL APPLICATIONS AND IMPLICATIONS   **165**

12   Elizabeth A. Flynn, "Composing as a Woman" (1988)   167
13   Dale M. Bauer, "The Other 'F' Word: The Feminist in the
     Classroom" (1990)   180
14   Madeleine R. Grumet, "Voice: The Search for a Feminist
     Rhetoric for Educational Studies" (1990)   192

SECTION 6
NEW THEORIES AND HISTORIES   **199**

15   Sally Miller Gearhart, "The Womanization of Rhetoric" (1979)   201
16   Sonja K. Foss and Cindy L. Griffin, "Beyond Persuasion:
     A Proposal for an Invitational Rhetoric" (1995)   209
17   Lisa Ede, Cheryl Glenn, and Andrea A. Lunsford "Border
     Crossings: Intersections of Rhetoric and Feminism" (1995)   228

Index   257

ACKNOWLEDGMENTS

We are fortunate indeed to have had the opportunity to gather these landmark essays in rhetoric and feminisms from 1973 to 2000. Working on this project has renewed our appreciation for all the women rhetors, all the feminists, all the powerful, public women who have come before.

The caryatid on our cover is a case in point. Since ancient times, women like this graceful female figure—who literally held up the Erectheion—have long upheld cultural values as well. Thus, the caryatid stands as strong, resolute testimony to the essential contributions of women to any society. Long may they all stand to remind us of their presence and their ongoing influence.

Akin to caryatids are the contemporary scholars whose voices speak from the pages of this book: we and countless others have been challenged and inspired by the example they have set in leading to greater understanding of rhetorical performance and theory and to the role women have played in both. And beyond these pages, we honor the voices of women rhetors and feminists throughout the ages, whose wisdom and perseverance set the stage for so much rhetorical work being done today.

Finally and most immediately, we are grateful to James J. Murphy and Krista Ratcliffe for inviting us to contribute to the renewed Landmark Series. Jerry and Krista's advice and support have been gifts indeed, as have Routledge and editor Ross Wagenhofer. Ross entered the scene late and heroically pulled our project together with efficiency, good humor, and inimitable professionalism. Deepest thanks to all.

Cheryl Glenn and Andrea A. Lunsford

ON RHETORIC
AND FEMINISM:
FORGING ALLIANCES
Andrea A. Lunsford and Cheryl Glenn

Editors' Note: *As these authors move through three distinct stages (or waves) of feminism, they demonstrate the alliances that feminists have forged with rhetoric as both public performance and scholarly subject. From earliest recorded time until now, feminist rhetors have been ignored, nearly erased, challenged, and discounted by historians and rhetorical scholars alike. This introduction provides a chronology of feminist rhetorical interventions (political, public, and scholarly), spanning from Enheduanna (ca. 2300) to Leymah Gbowee, Tawakkol Karman, and Ellen Johnson Sirleaf, winners of the 2011 Nobel Peace Prize.*

> This is my letter to the World
> that never wrote to Me.
>
> —Emily Dickinson, "This Is My Letter to the World"

Rhetoric. Feminism. For millennia, these words seemed to have little in common. In fact, rhetoric seemed to have no connection to women, much less feminism. Traditional histories of rhetoric by Thomas Conley, Edward P. J. Corbett, W. S. Howell, George Kennedy, and James J. Murphy make no mention of women's participation in or contributions to rhetorical history and practice. With its roots in western traditions of masculinist, agonistic, public, political discourse, rhetoric seemed to offer little room for the women who followed its practices and no recognition of those who employed rhetoric in different ways, in different scenes, and toward different ends. Indeed, rhetoric's long-held focus on the crucial importance of persuasion, dominance, and winning served to discourage women and other subaltern groups from its study and practice.

Neglected as subjects of scholarly interest, women were nonetheless developing rhetorical practices and traditions all along, with evidence of their accomplishments appearing in the ancient compositions of Enheduanna (ca. 2300 BCE), Sappho (ca. 530 BCE), and Aspasia (ca. 450 BCE). But for thousands of years, such women-inflected practices, even those displayed by powerful, public women (Queen Elizabeth I [1533–1603 CE] comes to mind), went unrecognized by men (from Aristotle through George Kennedy), who were all the while writing and recording the western rhetorical tradition. Little wonder, then, that activists in the early waves of feminism focused on political concerns, giving scant consideration to rhetorical studies.

Indeed, American first-wave feminists concentrated on the right to vote, to participate fully as U.S. citizens, a step that would lead to ongoing participation in the public sphere. In 1848, a small group of suffragists, including Elizabeth Cady Stanton and Lucretia Mott, gathered at the first Women's Rights Convention in Seneca Falls, New York to collaborate on their Declaration of Sentiments, which listed eighteen rights in the U.S. Declaration of Independence that men—but not women—enjoyed. Those rights included speaking in public, testifying in court, preaching from a pulpit, pursuing education, and entering into professions—all rights that would afford women opportunities to display their rhetorical abilities. During the seventy-two years it took for U.S. women to finally win the right to vote (guaranteed by the 1920 Nineteenth Amendment), first-wave feminists rallied around issues of voting rights, abolition of slavery, and patriotism in both the Civil War and what would eventually be called World War I. Throughout those decades, activist women continued to develop skills in speaking up and out on the lecture circuit, organizing public meetings and composing and gathering petitions, the only legal means of political expression open to women at the time. But despite the fact that each of these efforts constituted a rhetorical practice, these early feminists were not seen as writers, rhetors, or orators whose powerful public words and actions were worthy of attention and study.

During the second wave of feminism (roughly from the 1950s through the 1980s), activists were once again employing rhetorical power publicly, yet they still were not considered to be rhetors. Bella Abzug, Susan Brownmiller, Mary Daly, Andrea Dworkin, Marilyn French, Betty Friedan, Carolyn Heilbrun, Maxine Hong Kingston, Barbara Jordan, Audrey Lorde, Adrienne Rich, Gloria Steinem—and many others—were all writing and speaking publicly, politically, and very persuasively, but yet they were not considered part of, let alone crucial to, the rhetoric community. Nevertheless, these feminists were on the move, extending the activist work of their foremothers by working for the Civil Rights, Black Power, Student, and AntiVietnam war movements. Calling for rights that went far beyond the right to vote, these second-wave feminists addressed and resisted the male domination of contemporary political movements, whenever and wherever they could. Motivated by systemic power relations that continued to render women and other so-called minority groups subordinate, these feminists campaigned on a Pro-Woman/Women's Liberation platform to promote women's right to participate fully and equally in cultural, political, legal, and personal affairs.

The publication of such works as *The Feminine Mystique* (Friedan 1963); *Toward a Recognition of Androgyny* (Heilbrun, 1964); *The Dialectic of Sex: The Case for Feminist Revolution* (Firestone 1970); *Our Bodies, Our Selves* (Boston Women's Health 1971); *Titters* (Stillman and Beatts 1976); *The Cancer Journals* (Lorde 1980); *This Bridge Called my Back* (Anzaldúa 1984), and many others all contributed to the rhetorical power of feminists and to transformative societal changes. Feminists during the time worked to reconsider the sexual division of labor; to fight for equal pay for equal work; to attend and graduate from professional schools in large numbers; and to control their own bodies in terms of safety and reproduction. In addition, the cultural expectation of heterosexuality was rigorously questioned, opening up a space for lesbian identity.

Despite the cultural advances created by second-wave feminism, the movement was not an unmitigated success. The activists had not achieved a crucial goal, the passing of the Equal Rights Amendment (which is yet to pass!). Moreover, the mostly unremitting focus of second-wave feminism on the concerns of white, middle-class, heterosexual women exasperated so-called others (nonwhite, working-poor, lesbian, bisexual, nonwestern) who wanted to participate in collective action. Despite second-wave's sometimes sincere gestures of inclusivity, these others justifiably considered themselves and their issues neglected by an otherwise cooperative movement that could have easily leveraged their concerns as rallying points. This difficult and deeply regrettable situation, illustrated in Audre Lorde's "Open Letter to Mary Daly," demonstrated once again the degree to which the personal is political.

Over the course of more than 150 years, then, U.S. feminists have actively used public persuasive language—that is to say, rhetoric—to invite men and women into the movement, to inform the public about sociocultural ills and possibilities, and to persuade legislators to underscore equality under the law. Only when second-wave feminism sparked a scholarly interest in Women's Studies, however, did feminists officially stake a claim in academia, where they initiated women-centered courses across the disciplines. And as more feminists took up studies of rhetoric in English, communications, and linguistics, they began questioning its very foundations. Where were the women? How can their exclusion be accounted for? How could rhetoric be related to "women's liberation?"

One of the earliest rhetoric scholars to take up such questions was Karlyn Kohrs Campbell, whose 1973 *Quarterly Journal of Speech* essay "The Rhetoric of Women's Liberation: An Oxymoron" opens this volume. Following a thorough-going critique that demonstrates the systematic exclusion of women's voices and argues that feminism must get the attention of the academy before it could consider, much less generate, a concept such as feminist rhetoric, Campbell concludes that "women's liberation" as a movement is baffling because it has no program nor offers no clear answer to the question "What do women want?" She goes on to argue that women want what all people want: "dignity, respect, the right to self-determination, to develop their potentials as individuals"(29). But achieving such a goal will be difficult or impossible given the infinite variability of what "liberation" means to each person. What all these women share, however, as Campbell wryly notes, is "the paradox of having to 'fight an enemy who has outposts in your head'"(29). Campbell's recognition of the dangers of essentialism and of the difficulty of bringing feminism and rhetoric together in any mutually productive way set the stage for a generation of work, as did Cheris Kramer (Cheris Kramarae) in her 1974 *Quarterly Journal of Speech* "Woman's Speech: Separate but Unequal." This landmark essay also demonstrates the degree to which women as speakers have been silenced or ignored in the field of communications and strikes another blow against essentialist thinking by insisting that scholars must not lump all women together. Her detailed examination of the way women speak and her hypothesis that there are "systems of co-occurring, sex-linked, linguistic signals in the United States"(34) set off a volley of important research on women's ways of communicating.

By the time feminism's third wave was cresting, scholars in rhetoric—inspired by the work of such pioneers as Campbell and Kramer—began to mount serious challenges to the masculinist foundations of the western rhetorical tradition and to seek out ways to forge productive alliances between feminism and rhetoric. In particular, feminist scholars in both English and Communications argued that feminist rhetoricians must pursue several means of bringing about social, academic, and political change, including (1) recovery and recuperation, (2) methods and methodologies, (3) practices and performances, (4) pedagogical applications and implications, and (5) new theories and histories.

These are the categories we have chosen to organize this first volume of landmark essays on rhetoric and feminism. Focusing on these five goals allows us to highlight some of the efforts that have been made to bring feminism and rhetoric into alliance with one another in the United States. The first goal—recovery and recuperation—proved fundamental to achieving all the other feminist/rhetorical goals, and in this landmark volume we highlight three particularly generative essays: Barbara Biesecker's "Coming to Terms with Recent Attempts to Write Women into the History of Rhetoric" (1992); Cheryl Glenn's "sex, lies, and manuscript: Refiguring Aspasia in the History of Rhetoric" (1994); and Shirley Wilson Logan's "Black Women on the Speaker's Platform, 1832–1899" (1997).

Biesecker's 1992 assessment of attempts to write women into the history of rhetoric lay down a gauntlet for feminist historiographers of rhetoric. Arguing that work like Campbell's in *Man Cannot Speak for Her* (1989)—important as this two-volume work was in establishing women's presence in the history of rhetoric—ran the risk of achieving only "female tokenism," that is, simply adding a few exemplary women to the traditionally all-male canon. Acknowledging Campbell's work as a definite "landmark," Biesecker still worries that adding women is not enough, and she links that effort to what she calls the "affirmative action" approach, which she says merely perpetuates "cultural supremacy" (51). In the same way, adding women to the traditional canon may expand the list of so-called great works, but "the criteria for determining that list need not change" (51). In her essay, Biesecker rejects not only the all-male canon but a major premise on which it rests: individualism, arguing that Campbell's work does little to "undo the ideology of individualism that is the condition of possibility for the emergence of the received history of Rhetoric" (52). She turns, later in the essay, to Derrida's and Foucault's postmodern insights to deconstruct the radical individual she sees at the heart of rhetorical history and to demonstrate how a blending of their work can offer a theory of subjectivity to guide feminist rhetoric. Rather than a "stir and mix" approach to adding women, Biesecker calls for a gender-sensitive history of rhetoric that would acknowledge and address the "formidable difference between and amongst women, and, thus, address the real fact that different women . . . are constrained by different rhetorical constraints (62). This essay generated a spirited and much-cited debate between Biesecker and Campbell, with Campbell insisting that her approach does not neglect collaborative or collectivist women's efforts, which must, however, be placed in relationship to exemplary individual achievement. While most scholars view this debate as arriving at a stalemate, Biesecker's work continues to be foundational in its demonstration that feminist rhetorical scholars must expand their definitions of terms like "rhetor" and "rhetorical success" and that we must take great care to question not only the surface features of the rhetorical tradition (who's in and who's out of it) but the assumptions on which such a process of selection exists.

In many ways, Cheryl Glenn's "sex, Lies, and Manuscript: Refiguring Aspasia in the History of Rhetoric" (1994) addresses Biesecker's concerns, striking at the foundations of masculinist rhetoric and turning the work of male historians and theorists against them. Early in this essay, Glenn refers directly to Biesecker's challenge to "forge a new storying of our tradition that circumvents the veiled cultural supremacy operative in mainstream histories of Rhetoric" (67). This Braddock Award-winning essay mounts a spirited challenge to the dominant stories told about Western rhetoric and in doing so does much work of recovery and recuperation. Focusing on Aspasia of Miletus, Glenn reviews what is known of this remarkable woman and rereads what others have written about her, including Plato, Xenophon, Cicero, Athenaeus, and Plutarch, in ways that uncover and celebrate Aspasia's accomplishments and influence and refigure her not as "self-indulgent, licentious, immoral" but as a powerful and assertive rhetor (70) who was thoroughly trained in sophistic theory and perfectly capable of writing Pericles's famous funeral oration. In spite of Aspasia's prowess, Glenn acknowledges that her voice was muted, since she spoke "only through men" and since she was "quickly appropriated by males" (77).

Glenn's landmark essay goes a long way toward allowing us to hear Aspasia's voice coming to us down through the centuries, and thus recovering and recuperating her for us. Indeed, this essay helped spawn a new wave of feminist investigations that responded to Glenn's call "to look backwards at all the unquestioned scholarship that has come before" in order to "write a more inclusive history of rhetoric" that will rechart "the plains, valleys, and borders of rhetoric, and [account] for all the pockets of as-yet-unaccounted-for-activity" (78).

Shirley Wilson Logan's 1997 "Black Women on the Speaker's Platform (1832–1899)," which rounds out this section on recovery and recuperation, does much of the work of recharting that Glenn called for three years earlier. In fact, Logan's life work has been to recover and celebrate the powerful rhetorical practices and activities of Black women during the nineteenth century. She has led the way in introducing African American rhetors to students of rhetoric around the world, first in her ground-breaking collection *With Pen and Voice: A Critical Anthology of African American Women* (1995) and later with her critically acclaimed *"We Are Coming": The Persuasive Discourse of Nineteenth-Century African American Women* (1999).

Like Biesecker and Glenn, Logan seeks to shine the rhetorical spotlight on Black women's contributions to public discourse throughout the nineteenth century, demonstrating the degree to which these women "participated in history largely through their rhetorical activities" (99). Brilliant and powerful speakers such as Maria Stewart, Mary Ann Shadd Cary, Frances Ellen Watkins Harper, Mary Church Terrell, Sarah Parker Remond, Maria Miller, Isabella Baumfree (Sojourner Truth), Lucy Wilmot Smith, Ida B. Wells, Victoria Earle Matthews, Fannie Barrier Williams, Anna Julia

Cooper, Lucy Laney, and others—figures the rhetorical community knew almost nothing of—came to life in Logan's writings and engaged a new generation of scholars in studying their speeches and writings. As Logan concludes, "The activities of the women discussed ... illustrate the ranges of issues brought to public attention by women using oratory to effect change" (99). Her groundbreaking work on these pioneering African American orators perfectly illustrates the motto of The Women's Era Club: "Make the world better."

Feminist scholars who have sought to recover and recuperate women rhetors have consistently argued that such work is a key beginning point, one that must be accompanied or followed by bringing revisioned, repurposed, and new methods to bear. The landmark essays in the second section of this volume, then, focus on the issue of methods and methodologies and on how such methods can most appropriately illuminate the contributions of women. Susan Jarratt's 1990 "Speaking to the Past: Feminist Historiography in Rhetoric" begins by questioning the received goal of "objectivity" in historical research, arguing that historiography is a social practice through and through and that the goals of feminist historians of rhetoric must aim not only to provide as much accuracy as possible but, most importantly, to "create histories aimed at a more just future" (60). In this essay, Jarratt proposes to embody a "normative ethics," that is an "ethical way of acting, to be argued about, refuted, or taken up by other members of my social group" (106).

Jarratt opens her essay by noting how slow feminism and rhetoric and writing studies have been to come into alliance with one another and arguing that in establishing such an alliance, scholars must not only write women into the traditional history of rhetoric but also to produce "gendered readings of male-authored texts" (108), two goals she sees as complementary and deeply connected. In the remainder of her essay, Jarratt articulates and addresses a key concern: "How to do a history informed by poststructural analysis of the way difference constructs language—i.e., a gendered analysis—but responsive to women's desire to 'find' themselves in history" (110). In pursuing this goal, Jarratt uses the insights of Adrienne Rich, Linda Alcoff, Gayatri Spivak, and Nancy Hartsock with regard to positionality and standpoint theory to focus on methods that are grounded in space and place, location and representation. As illustration, she shows gendered analyses can reveal "what is reflected, adjusted, distorted, or completely absent" from the discourse about public speech in ancient Greece (116), using work by classicists Gerda Lerner, Froma Zeitlin, and Page duBois that has effectively put such gendered methodologies in play. Reading traditional sources in terms of gender in ways that show them to be constitutive of social relations could also lead, Jarratt argues, to study of "forms of women's speech performed during the religious festivals" that stood in radical contrast to the "rational" discourse of traditional rhetoric and philosophy (118). In addition to presenting positionality, standpoint theory, and gendered readings as methods for feminist scholars of rhetoric, Jarratt makes another influential move, one toward pedagogy. She concludes this landmark essay by calling on feminist scholars to ask students "to write their multiple selves—gendered, racial, classed—into history, creating narratives not in a unique voice but in polylog with past and future selves and others, singular accounts intertextualized with histories recent and distant" (118–19).

This turn to pedagogy and to collaborative, collective constructions of multiple selves offers yet another fruitful method for feminists to consider.

A focus on voice and voices echoes powerfully in Jacqueline Jones Royster's oft-cited and reprinted essay, "When the First Voice You Hear Is Not Your Own," which was first presented as her Chair's address to the 1995 meeting of the Conference on College Composition and Communication. Royster agrees with Jarratt about the importance of location and representation to a feminist rhetorical project, opening with a ringing acknowledgment that "'subject' position really is everything" (122). Royster, like Jarratt, rejects "objectivity" as a goal of rhetorical history, preferring to adopt subjectivity as a defining and instructional value. In this landmark essay, she sets forth just what adopting such a value means, in terms of privileging experiential data, stories, and emotional connection as feminist methods.

Insisting that "theories and practices should be transformed" to include "voicing as a phenomenon that is constructed and expressed visually and orally, and as a phenomenon that has import also in being a thing heard, perceived, and reconstructed" (123), Royster presents three stories or scenes drawn from her own experiences as an African American woman and scholar. Each story reveals the need to leave behind narrow and exclusive ways of looking at history and rather to embrace a self-conscious method of inquiry that rests on the knowledge that members of our communities and even our ancestors are observing what we do and say and how we act. These methods, based on inclusivity, respect, listening, and ethical conduct, are ones that will lead scholars and historians to honor all of the voices with which their subjects speak, setting those subjects into the most full and compelling context available to them.

Like other essays in this volume, Royster's has acted as a stone dropped in water, whose ripples extend ever outward to affect others. Her recognition and valuing of experiential evidence and of the multiple voices with which rhetors write, speak, and act lead her to say that we miss a critical method if we simply "talk and talk back" (130). We need to do these things, Royster argues, but we need, in our lives and in our research, to know when to listen and, more important, how to listen and to translate that listening "into language and action" (130). The goal of such methods, she argues, is to create "better practices so that we can exchange perspectives, negotiate meaning, and create understanding with the intent of being in a good position to cooperate, when, like now, cooperation is absolutely necessary" (130). Royster's focus on voicings and voices, on ethical practice, on personal commitment, on reciprocity and listening, and on the full embodiment of subjectivity are congruent with what has become a powerful set of methods for conducting feminist rhetorical inquiries.

The second section of this first volume of *Landmark Essays in Feminism and Rhetoric* concludes with Patricia Bizzell's "Feminist Methods of Research in the History of Rhetoric: What Difference Do They Make?" After reviewing the work she and Bruce Herzberg did in preparing the first edition of *The Rhetorical Tradition* and then revising that volume a decade later, Bizzell shows how feminist research during that period allowed her to increase the number of women represented in this important anthology, from the "not too many women" of volume one to including at least one woman in every section of the text, and often more than one, in the second edition. She goes on to summarize and then critique Xin Liu Gale's response to Cheryl Glenn and Susan Jarratt's work on Aspasia. Gale finds Glenn and Jarratt's readings deeply problematic, arguing that these authors are guilty of "twisting" the male texts that refer to Aspasia to "suit" their own feminist ends. In short, Gale complains that these scholars are not objective; rather she sees them as "passionate" and full of "personal truth" that is untrustworthy. Gale contrasts Glenn and Jarratt's readings to those of Madeline Henry, who meets Gale's standards of objectivity and is, therefore, the more trusted critic and historian. (These essays are featured in Volume 2 of this work).

Bizzell finds the heart of Gale's problem with the work of Jarratt and Glenn in her suspicion of their "expressions of feelings of solidarity" (139) with their subject, with feminist communities and with the emotional valence of their work. What Gale really objects to, Bizzell supposes, are feminist values in general and rhetorical ethos in particular—and the methods that such values entail. And this brings Bizzell to the major point of her essay: we need, she says, "more discussion of the part played in the setting of scholarly research agendas and the constructing of scholarly arguments by our emotions about our research topics—or subjects—and our imagined readers" (139). The remainder of this landmark essay shows the way that researchers such as Christine Mason Sutherland, Vicki Tolar Collins, and especially Jacqueline Jones Royster address this issue, noting that "it is to Royster that we owe our most thorough theorizing of the role of emotions in feminist research to date" (140). In an astute analysis of the methods Royster employs in *Traces of a Stream* and in her work with the scholarly journal *SAGE*, Bizzell sketches in the role that personal connection, multiple and shared identities, and care play in what Royster calls an "afrafeminist methodo- logy" (141). Understanding that negotiation and cross-questioning are imperative to an inclusive rhetorical history (and indeed to the survival of the planet), Royster's "afrafeminist" methods include careful analysis, acknowledgment of passionate attach- ment, attention to ethical action, and commitment to social responsibility (142). (Readers of this volume will recognize these methods as those Royster and Gesa Kirsch went on to develop in their groundbreaking *Feminist Rhetorical Practices*, which will feature in Volume 2 of this work.) In summing up the progress made on establishing feminist methods of scholarship and in articulating the connections among researchers and disciplinary frameworks, Patricia Bizzell offers us another landmark essay concerning methods and methodologies most useful for feminist rhetorical projects.

As this introduction indicates, women's rhetorical "Practices and Performances" were discounted if not overlooked altogether for millennia. Not until late twentieth- century scholars paused to analyze women's use of spoken and written words, did those scholars begin to understand what exactly women were doing, how they were doing it, where and why they were using language purposefully and often persuasively. What had once been considered background noise or public nuisance was translated into bona fide women's rhetorical practices and performances. As the three landmark essays in this third section illustrate, women's rhetorical displays have often been distinguished by their acknowledgment of their marginalization, their physical bodies, and the risk of speaking out itself. In addition, women's rhetorical performances often demonstrate various options for delivering a message, including recursiveness and repetition, silence, listening, collaboration, invitation, and translingualism.

For instance, Andre Lorde's "Transformation of Silence into Language and Action," which first appeared in a 1978 issue of *Sinister Wisdom*, speaks directly to the fear of those who are systematically silenced: if they speak out, they be "bruised or misunderstood" (128). Lorde urges the marginalized to follow her example, to overcome their fear and translate their long-standing silence into language, even action. The threat of cancer, the reality of her own mortality had become the best reasons for her to speak the truth, regardless of her "fear of contempt, of censure, or some judgment, . . . of annihilation" (148). After all, she argues, vulnerability can also be the "greatest strength." Her rhetorical performance was, by her own accord, a "bridge" to fearlessness, to mobilization.

In 1987, Gloria E. Anzaldúa broke new ground with the publication of *Borderlands/ La Frontera*, a translingual, hybrid narrative celebrating the words and actions of working-class, multilingual women living in the United States. "How to Tame a Wild Tongue" shows readers how powerful, political prose can also be playful and pedagogical. Anzaldúa taps multiple methods of development (narrative, exemplification, argument, definition, description, cause and effect, and so on) to develop her argument that her language, her "wild tongue" is both legitimate and political. "If you really want to hurt me, talk badly about my language. Ethnic identity is twin skin to linguistic identity—I am my language" (154). She traces the domination of brown-skinned Spanish speakers by white-skinned English speakers, people no better than her own but privileged by their race and language. And she upends that privilege, proving repeatedly the authority of her tongue, her wild tongue: "Until I can take pride in my language, I cannot take pride in myself" (154). Rhetoric, long the domain of the aristocratic, the rich and educated, can be inhabited by those considered to be "others," the working poor, the uneducated, the otherwise disenfranchised.

In her introduction to the landmark *Reclaiming Rhetorica: Women in the Rhetorical Tradition* (1995), Andrea Lunsford sketches an outline of the emerging field of feminist rhetoric, reflecting the rich and complex range of subjects in the essay collection. A kaleidoscopic series of women's rhetorical practices are cumulatively demonstrated by Aspasia, Diotima, Margery Kempe, Christine de Pisan, Mary Astell, Mary Wollstonecraft, Margaret Fuller, Ida B. Wells, Sojourner Truth, Laura Riding Jackson, Suzanne K. Langer, Louise Rosenblatt, and Julia Kristeva. Each of these women uses different means within different scenes of rhetoric: "some are deliberately learned and used the conventions of scholarly rhetoric," while others, "self-taught and working within the context of strong religious and political communities, spoke and wrote with deep conviction shaped through conscious rhetorical technique" (162). A few of these women were recognized as rhetors during their lives, but most of them were recognized as making contributions to theory or practice much later. A recovery project, to be sure, *Reclaiming Rhetorica* recovers and reclaims pivotal moments in the history of women's rhetoric. It also exemplifies the collaborative, mutually supportive spirit of a truly feminist scholarly enterprise.

The landmark essays in our fourth category, "Pedagogical Applications and Implications," realize the goals, methods, and findings of feminist rhetorical scholarship. Elizabeth A. Flynn's 1988 "Composing as a Woman" connects such scholarship with the field of composition, rendering apparent the feminist underpinnings of writing studies, what with the reversing of "traditional hierarchies by privileging private expression over public transition, process rather than product" (168), and coaching over judging students. This feminist foundation enables writing instructors to identify and value the differences between traditional and untraditional processes and products of writing, between the moral and intellectual development of male and female writers, and about gender differences of all kinds. Flynn's essay illuminates the potential of female experience to feed powerful writing.

When Dale Bauer's 1990 "The Other 'F' Word: The Feminist in the Classroom" first appeared, it created a stir, for she was one of the earliest feminist rhetors to call out the prejudice against the word itself. Bauer speaks to the resistance, even refusal that results from any measure (no matter how slight) of feminist awareness in the classroom. After all, as her students write, "Feminism is an important issue in society—but a very controversial one. It needs to be confronted on a personal basis, not in the classroom" (180). Bauer's students are not alone: people of all ages, in all walks of life continue to believe that feminism is important only when the discrimination is obvious, public, and felt personally, either by them or someone they love. Otherwise, the politics of feminism should be private, invisible, silent—nothing to contaminate the delivery of truth in a classroom. Bauer's students see little intellectual or academic value in feminism, nothing that can (or should) shape decision-making policy, collective moral and ethical rhetoric, or political commitment. Because any measure of understanding, appreciation, and identification with feminism is a rhetorical passage, Bauer chronicles some explicit pedagogical moves for easing the passage.

Madeleine R. Grumet's 1990 "Voice: The Search for a Feminist Rhetoric for Educational Studies" celebrates the power of "voice," purposeful, self-conscious voice to establish personal agency, rhetorical power, intellectual independence. Evoking the influential research findings of Carol Gilligan, whose conception of a "different voice" helped scholars and professionals across the nation appreciate the differences between the moral development of male and female subjects, Grumet uses voice not only as a marker to differentiate her work from that of her male colleagues but also as a way to express her ambivalence as she joined the procession of educated men. For her, then, "voice carried with it the promise of cultural transformation, as it announced resistance to a distant, universalist knowledge," and "generated collective action" (193). Grumet draws on the use of women's and men's voices (and voice overs) in academia, film, and educational research. Pertinent to her argument is the "voice-over of educational research" (194), which is dominated by allegedly objective discourse, such as quantitative measures and statistical analyses that "obscure individual experience" (194), most often that of females, the poor, the otherwise marginalized. Grumet argues for the use of three voices, then, one that contextualizes the utterance, another that narrativizes it, and a third that interprets it according to context and telling. "What is essential is that all three voices usher from one speaker and that each becomes a location through which the other is heard. None is privileged" (191).

The final section of our collection looks forward to "New Theories and Histories," with three foundational essays that, to a twenty-first-century sensibility, could be considered "vintage." Sally Miller Gearheart's 1979 "Womanization of Rhetoric" works to dislodge the long-held notion that the act of persuasion equates with the act of winning, the condition of being right. For Gearheart, any act of persuasion is an act of violence, one that works to disempower the "other." Even our teaching runs the gamut from condescension to coercion. Therefore, her goal is to reject the "conquest/conversion" (201) model of interaction and develop "new forms of relationships which allow for wholeness in the individual and differences among people and entities" (207). The results would be a feeling of equality, possibility, empowerment, and willingness to consider other ways of being in the world. She emphasizes listening, productive silence, mutual respect, and the creation of an atmosphere of collectivity—a womanization of rhetoric.

Sonja K. Foss and Cindy L. Griffin transport us "Beyond Persuasion: A Proposal for Invitational Rhetoric" (1995), based in part on Gearheart's groundbreaking work. Foss and Griffin also ask us to rethink the transactional goal of rhetoric from that of persuasion (over another) to mutual understanding. After all, the authors write, traditional rhetoric is rooted in the "power of the rhetor over others" and a devaluation of the "lives and perspectives of those others" (210). For them, such is the rhetoric of patriarchy, which could be enriched and improved with the use of an alternative, feminist rhetoric. Based on the basic feminist principles of "equality, immanent value, and self-determination" (211), feminist rhetoric is "invitational," an invitation to "understanding" as a means to create a relationship rooted in those basic feminist values. When rhetor and audience alike are committed to mutual respect, appreciation, openness, and understanding; when they speak and listen to each other; when they create an atmosphere of productive deliberation, then any change that occurs is the "result of new understanding and insights gained in the exchange of ideas" (213). No longer is the change a result of the "persuasive interactions of traditional rhetoric" in which the rhetor establishes "power and control over the audience" (213). Foss and Griffin's essay holds extraordinary rhetorical vision while simultaneously enacting the theory itself, for theirs is an invitational essay.

The last essay in our collection, Lisa Ede, Cheryl Glenn, and Andrea Lunsford's 1995 "Border Crossing: Intersections of Rhetoric and Feminism," was the first feminist essay to appear in *Rhetorica: A Journal of the History of Rhetoric*, the publication of the International Society for the History of Rhetoric. In "Border Crossings," the authors demonstrate ways that the two disciplines interanimate each other whenever they come into contact. Rhetoric offers feminism a "theorized space" for thinking about and organizing effective communication, while feminism offers rhetoric a "politicized space" for discussing such values as bridging difference, inclusion, and empowerment. To illuminate their points, the authors take on the challenge of rereading traditional rhetorical categories (invention, arrangement, style, memory, and delivery) in order to articulate the heretofore unspoken relationships between rhetoric and feminism. In the course of juxtaposing their resistant readings of those rhetorical canons alongside underappreciated feminist rhetorical displays, they find delivery to be of the greatest importance. The opportunities afforded by new technologies of communication, many of which are decoupled from traditional, hegemonic print texts, reveal traditions of oral, performative, and embodied rhetorics that have previously been repressed by print culture. Resistant readings of canonical rhetorical texts, categories, and concepts together with challenges to traditions of arrangement, style, delivery, and application have worked to help feminist rhetoricians create and sustain a new hybrid discipline.

As we hope our introduction demonstrates, women writers and speakers and feminist scholars have, for decades now, been forging theories and practices of feminist rhetoric, rhetoric that is conceptualized, arranged, and delivered in numerous, alternative, and sometimes resistant ways. These women have struggled re-see, re-shape, and re-deploy the rhetorical tradition in ways that not only admit but embrace and celebrate women as well as feminist understandings, understandings that we firmly believe are beneficial for all human beings. After all, feminist rhetorical principles of invitation, inclusion, and full representation give us access to alternative perspectives, the kind of knowledge that feeds our process of intellectual and moral growth.

Has this work been successful? Yes. But the advances remain modest at best, even as we continue to cull piles of publications for a collection of *Landmark Essays in Rhetoric and Feminism 2: 2000–*. As we continue to work on these volumes, women around the world are being beaten, raped, tortured, murdered, and otherwise violated apace. We believe this violence is related to the age-old agonistic base of the rhetorical tradition, with its reliance on combat, on dominance, and on winner-takes-all. That this traditional understanding of rhetoric is still too often accepted without critique is completely unacceptable.

And yet such violence also can serve, as it has over millennia, as the exigence for women to respond rhetorically, but in a markedly different and completely performative, embodied way. Consider the work women perform on International Women's Day (March 8th). All around the world—from Santa Fe, New Mexico to Cape Town, South Africa and from Antarctica to Hiroshima, Japan—women celebrate the day with antiwar protests. They meet in groups large enough to create artistic shapes with their naked bodies, which they form into the international peace sign or into letters that spell out "PEACE," "PAZ," "NO WAR," or "WHY?" These women then document and circulate their message. (Go to www.baringwitness.org to see what we mean.) Another rhetorically significant feature of their protests is their silence. Inspired by the tradition of worldwide nonviolent demonstrations, these women cast off the old paradigm of public, verbalized, well-armored aggression to inhabit, instead, a new paradigm of public silence in all its human vulnerability. They make the papers, the newscasts, the Webpages—as well as their shared point, their rhetoric of community.

Using silence to foster community effort is not new, even though it is rarely thought of in those terms. Ever since Lysistrata and the coalition of women from Sparta, Thebes, and Athens closed their bodies to their warring men, nonviolent, nonverbal protest has provided a vibrant alternative to verbal and physical combat. The Dalai Lama, Martin Luther King, Jr., Aung San Sui Kyi, Mahatma Gandhi, and many others have followed along that same pathway, closing their mouths in order to draw attention to their situations and invite understanding and exchange.

Given that our talkative western culture pays such homage to speaking out, being heard, verbal prowess, eloquence, and persuasion, it comes as no surprise that positive, productive silence has long been overlooked as a source of rhetorical power. What we refer to here as positive silence (see Glenn, *Unspoken*), Ratcliffe refers to as "rhetorical listening" (see *Rhetorical Listening*), a "stance of openness that a person may choose to assume in relation to any person, text, or culture" (2005: xiii). Feminist rhetoricians are drawn to a stance of openness, which declares a vulnerability not unlike that of the naked antiwar protesters and antiwar journalists (see Lunsford and Rosenblatt 2011). The overarching purpose of productive silence and rhetorical listening, closely aligned rhetorical positions, is to transcend self-interested intent (long the preferred stance of rhetors). To do so is to anticipate the other person's interest—the first move toward mutual receptivity and understanding and a purposeful departure from the traditional rhetorical ideal of mastery over another. Thus, positive silence and listening (which we expand upon in Volume 2) reveal the already existing grounds for feminist rhetorical negotiation of reciprocity and collaboration.

We should note that in their use of silence, women are creating a *performative rhetoric*, one that is not bound to written texts that for too long failed to address the gender-based violence rooted in a worldwide culture of denial of women's rights. We might point to Code Pink, a women-initiated grassroots network that has spread to 150 communities around the world; their work is grounded in the body, in performance, and in the ludic. Or we could note the work of Women in Black, inspired by the anti-apartheid Black Sash in South Africa and the Madres de la Plaza de Mayo in Argentina. Since 1988, this movement has spread across the globe, with large groups in the U.K., the U.S., Europe, South America, Australia, New Zealand, Canada, Bahrain, Egypt, India, Japan, Mexico, and Turkey. And we could cite Liberia's Women in White, the first Christian/ Muslim alliance that grew into the Liberian Mass Action for Peace, a nonviolent women's movement that helped end Charles Taylor's dictatorship and the war there. In fall, 2011, Ellen Johnson Sirleaf, the president of Liberia, Leymah Gbowee, a prominent Liberian peace activist, and Yemeni pro-democracy campaigner Tawakkol Karman were awarded the Nobel Peace Prize in recognition of their nonviolent struggle for women's safety and women's rights. For decades, they have performed a rhetoric of peace and justice.

In short, feminists today are attempting to build an alternative to traditional agonistic rhetoric through their strategic use of speech, silence, and resistance guided by nonviolent principles, a thoroughly feminist rhetoric that can account for embodied, performed rhetorical practices. What will such a rhetoric entail? At the very least, it will focus not only on the written but also on the performed (whether virtual or "real"), not on linearity but on webbed connection and collaboration; not on consumers of knowledge, art, and craft but on active, mutually informing producers of the same; not on winning at all costs but on *understanding* and working together. Such a rhetoric and the multiple practices it will evoke, render, and embody can help women and men, disenfranchised and powerful alike, in the U.S. and everywhere, break the links between traditional rhetoric and dis/empowerment, between power and violence. Such a rhetoric of invitation, listening, and empathy can transform the rhetorical tradition from one of persuasion, control, and discipline (on the part of the rhetor) to one of inherent worth, equality, and empowered action (for rhetor and audience alike). Rhetors using such a rhetoric will be embodying/performing rhetoric in ways that will reject combat and dominance in favor of sharing perspectives, understandings, and power. These are the goals an interanimating connection between rhetoric and feminism can—and must—achieve. After all, feminists and traditionalists, the subaltern and powerful, men and women, are all the same species: we are all human beings, humans with an innate capacity for language and the ability to care about one another, to work together, to change.

The feminist rhetorical essays we include in this collection support our belief that rhetoric is an endlessly pliable human art, one that always has the potential to be used toward *eudaimonia*, the greatest good for all of us human beings. Such feminist interventions into traditional rhetorical principles provide opportunities for new ways of being rhetorical, of showing respect, making commitments, sharing power, and distinguishing ourselves as human. Achieving these goals is the new—and ongoing— work of feminism and rhetoric.

References

Aristotle. *The Rhetoric and Poetics of Aristotle.* Trans. W. Rhys Roberts and Ingram Bywater. New York: Modern Library, 1984. Print.

Daly, Mary. *Websters' First New Intergalactic Wickedary of the English Language.* Boston: Beacon, 1989. Print.

Dickinson, Emily. "Tell all the truth but tell it slant." *Dickinson: Selected Poems and Commentaries.* Helen Vendler. Cambridge: Harvard UP, 2010. 431. Print.

Dworkin, Andrea. *Intercourse.* New York: Free Press-Simon & Schuster, 1987. Print.

——. *Pornography: Men Possessing Women.* New York: Putnam, 1979. Print.

Firestone, Shulamith. *The Dialectic of Sex: The Case for Feminist Revolution.* New York: William Morrow, 1970. Print.

Foss, Karen A., Sonja K. Foss, and Cindy Griffin. *Feminist Rhetorical Theories.* Sage Publications, 1999. Print.

Foss, Sonja, and Cindy L. Griffin. "Beyond Persuasion: A Proposal for an Invitational Rhetoric." *Communication Monographs,* 62 (March), 1995.

Friedan, Betty. *The Feminine Mystique.* New York: Norton, 1963. Print.

Fuller, Margaret. *The Portable Margaret Fuller.* Ed. Mary Kelley. New York: Viking, 1994. Print.

Gilligan, Carol. *Joining the Resistance.* Cambridge, UK: Polity, 2011. Print.

Glenn, Cheryl. *Rhetoric Retold: Regendering the Tradition from Antiquity Through the Renaissance.* Carbondale: Southern Illinois UP, 1997. Print.

——. *Unspoken: A Rhetoric of Silence.* Carbondale: Southern Illinois UP, 2004. Print.

Heilbrun, Carolyn. *Toward a Recognition of Androgyny.* New York: Knopf, 1964. Print.

Logan, Shirley Wilson. *"We Are Coming": The Persuasive Discourse of Nineteenth-Century Black Women.* Carbondale: Southern Illinois UP, 1999. Print.

Lorde, Audre. *The Cancer Journals.* 1980. San Francisco: Aunt Lute Books, 1995. Print.

——. "Learning from the 60s." *Sister Outsider:* 134–44. Print.

——. "An Open Letter to Mary Daly." *Sister Outsider.* 60–71. Print

——. "The Master's Tools Will Never Dismantle the Master's House." *Sister Outsider.* 110–13. Print.

——. *Sister Outsider: Essays and Speeches.* Berkeley: The Crossing Press, 1984. Print.

——. "Uses of Erotic: The Erotic as Power." In *Sister Outsider.* 53–59. Print.

Lunsford, Andrea, ed. *Reclaiming Rhetorica.* Pittsburgh: U of Pittsburgh P, 1995. Print.

Lunsford, Andrea A., and Adam Rosenblatt. "'Down a Road and into an Awful Silence': Graphic Listening in Joe Sacco's Comics Journalism." *Silence and Listening as Rhetorical Arts.* Eds. Cheryl Glenn and Krista Ratcliffe. Carbondale: Southern Illinois UP, 2011. 130–46. Print.

The Norton Anthology of Rhetoric and Writing. Eds. Andrea A. Lunsford, and Susan Jarratt. New York, Norton: Forthcoming. Print.

Our Bodies, Ourselves: A Book for and by Women. Boston: Boston Women's Health Book Collective, 1971. Print.

Ratcliffe, Krista. *Rhetorical Listening: Identification, Gender, Whiteness.* Carbondale: Southern Illinois UP, 2005. Print.

Royster, Jacqueline Jones. *Traces of a Stream: Literacy and Social Change Among African American Women.* Pittsburgh: U of Pittsburgh P, 2000. Print.

Sappho. *Sappho: A New Translation.* Trans. Mary Barnard. Berkeley: U of California P, 1958. Print.

Steinem, Gloria. *Outrageous Acts and Everyday Rebellions.* New York: New American Library, 1983. Print.

Stillman, Deanne, and Anne P. Beatts, ed. *Titters: The First Collection of Humor by Women.* Springfield, OH: Collier, 1976. Print.

SECTION 1

INTRODUCTORY MOVES

1.
THE RHETORIC OF WOMEN'S LIBERATION: AN OXYMORON
Karlyn Kohrs Campbell

Editors' Note: *One of the earliest scholars to examine the nexus of women, liberation, and rhetoric and to consider the difficulties of bringing feminism and rhetoric together in any mutually productive way, this author argues that feminism must take hold in the academy before any concept, let alone practice, of "feminist rhetoric" can be generated and realized. This landmark essay set the stage for a generation of scholarship.*

Whatever the phrase "women's liberation" means, it cannot, as yet, be used to refer to a cohesive historical-political movement. No clearly defined program or set of policies unifies the small, frequently transitory groups that compose it, nor is there much evidence of organizational unity and cooperation.[1] At this point in time, it has produced only minor changes in American society,[2] although it has made the issues with which it is associated major topics of concern and controversy. As some liberation advocates admit, it is a "state of mind" rather than a movement. Its major manifestation has been rhetorical, and as such, it merits rhetorical analysis.

Because any attempt to define a rhetorical movement or genre is beset by difficulties, and because of the unusual status of women's liberation I have briefly described, I wish to state explicitly two presuppositions informing what follows. First, I reject historical and socio-psychological definitions of movements as the basis for rhetorical criticism on the grounds that they do not, in fact, isolate a genre of *rhetoric* or a distinctive body of *rhetorical* acts.[3] The criteria defining a rhetorical movement must be rhetorical; in Aristotelian terminology, such criteria might arise from the relatively distinctive use or interpretation of the canons and modes of proof. However, rather than employing any codified critical scheme, I propose to treat two general categories— substance and style. In my judgment, the rhetoric of women's liberation (or any other body of discourses) merits *separate* critical treatment if, and only if, the symbolic acts of which it is composed can be shown to be distinctive on both substantive and stylistic grounds. Second, I presume that the style and substance of a genre of rhetoric are interdependent.[4] Stylistic choices are deeply influenced by subject-matter and context,[5] and issues are formulated and shaped by stylistic strategies.[6] The central argument of this essay is that the rhetoric of women's liberation is a distinctive genre because it evinces unique *rhetorical* qualities that are a fusion of substantive and stylistic features.

Karlyn Kohrs Campbell, "The Rhetoric of Women's Liberation: An Oxymoron." *QJS* 59. Feb. 1973: 74–86.

Distinctive Substantive Features

At first glance, demands for legal, economic, and social equality for women would seem to be a reiteration, in a slightly modified form, of arguments already familiar from the protest rhetoric of students and blacks. However, on closer examination, the fact that equality is being demanded *for women* alters the rhetorical picture drastically. Feminist advocacy unearths tensions woven deep into the fabric of our society and provokes an unusually intense and profound "rhetoric of moral conflict."[7] The sex role requirements for women contradict the dominant values of American culture—self-reliance, achievement, and independence.[8] Unlike most other groups, the social status of women is defined primarily by birth, and their social position is at odds with fundamental democratic values.[9] In fact, insofar as the role of rhetor entails qualities of self-reliance, self-confidence, and independence, *its very assumption is a violation* of *the female role*. Consequently, feminist rhetoric is substantively unique by definition, because no matter how traditional its argumentation, how justificatory its form, how discursive its method, or how scholarly its style, it attacks the entire psychosocial reality, the most fundamental values, of the cultural context in which it occurs. As illustration, consider the apparently moderate, reformist demands by feminists for legal, economic, and social equality—demands ostensibly based on the shared value of equality. (As presented here, each of these demands is a condensed version of arguments from highly traditional discourses by contemporary liberationists.)

The demand for legal equality arises out of a conflict in values. Women are not equal to men in the sight of the law. In 1874, the Supreme Court ruled that "some citizens could be denied rights which others had," specifically, that "the 'equal protection' clause of the Fourteenth Amendment did not give women equal rights with men," and reaffirmed this decision in 1961, stating that "the Fourteenth Amendment prohibits any arbitrary class legislation, except that based on sex."[10] The legal inferiority of women is most apparent in marriage laws. The core of these laws is that spouses have reciprocal—not equal—rights and duties. The husband must maintain the wife and children, but the amount of support beyond subsistence is at his discretion. In return, the wife is legally required to do the domestic chores, provide marital companionship, and sexual consortium but has no claim for direct compensation for any of the services rendered. Fundamentally, marriage is a property relationship. In the nine community property states, the husband is considered the head of the "community," and so long as he is capable of managing it, the wife, acting alone, cannot contract debts chargeable to it. In Texas and Nevada, the husband can even dispose of the property without his wife's consent, property that includes the income of a working wife. The forty-one common law states do not recognize the economic contribution of a wife who works only in the home. She has no right to an allowance, wages, or income of any sort, nor can she claim joint ownership upon divorce. In addition, every married woman's surname is legally that of her husband, and no court will uphold her right to go by another name.[11]

It seems to me that any audience of such argumentation confronts a moral dilemma. The listener must either admit that this is not a society based on the value of equality or make the overt assertion that women are special or inferior beings who merit discriminatory treatment.[12]

The argument for economic equality follows a similar pattern. Based on median income, it is a greater economic disadvantage to be female than to be black or poorly educated (of course, any combination of these spells economic disaster). Although half of the states have equal pay laws, dual pay scales are the rule. These cannot be justified economically because, married or single, the majority of women who work do so out of economic necessity, and some forty percent of families with incomes below the poverty level are headed by women. Occupationally, women are proportionately more disadvantaged today than they were in 1940, and the gap between male and female income steadily increases.[13] It might seem that these data merely indicate a discrepancy between law and practice—at least the value is embodied in some laws—although separating values and behavior is somewhat problematic. However, both law and practice have made women economically unequal. For example, so long as the law, as well as common practice, gives the husband a right to the domestic services of his wife, a woman must perform the equivalent of two jobs in order to hold one outside the home.[14] Once again, the audience of such argumentation confronts a moral dilemma.

The most overt challenge to cultural values appears in the demand for social or sexual equality, that we dispense forever with the notion that "men are male *humans* whereas women are human *females,*"[15] a notion enshrined in the familiar phrase, "I now pronounce you *man* and wife." An obvious reason for abolishing such distinctions is that they lead to cultural values for men as men and women as wives. Success for men is defined as instrumental, productive labor in the outside world whereas "wives" are confined to "woman's place"—child care and domestic labor in the home.[16] As long as these concepts determine "masculinity" and "femininity," the woman who strives for the kind of success defined as the exclusive domain of the male is inhibited by norms prescribing her "role" and must pay a heavy price for her deviance. Those who have done research on achievement motivation in women conclude that: "Even when legal and educational barriers to achievement are removed, the motive to avoid success will continue to inhibit women from doing 'too well'—thereby risking the possibility of being socially rejected as 'unfeminine' or 'castrating.'"[17] and "The girl who maintains qualities of independence and active striving (achievement-orientation) necessary for intellectual mastery defies the conventions of sex appropriate behavior and must pay a price, *a price in anxiety.*"[18] As long as education and socialization cause women to be "unsexed" by success whereas men are "unsexed" by failure, women cannot compete on equal terms or develop their individual potentials. No values, however, are more deeply engrained than those defining "masculinity" and "femininity." The fundamental conflict in values is evident.

Once their consequences and implications are understood, these apparently moderate, reformist demands are rightly seen as revolutionary and radical in the extreme. They threaten the institutions of marriage and the family and norms governing child-rearing and male–female roles. To meet them would require major, even revolutionary, social change.[19] It should be emphasized, however, that these arguments are drawn from discourses that could not be termed confrontative, alienating, or radical in any ordinary sense. In form, style, structure, and supporting materials, they would meet the demands of the strictest Aristotelian critic. Yet they are substantively unique, inevitably radical, because they attack the fundamental values underlying this culture. The option to be moderate and reformist is simply not available to women's liberation advocates.

Distinctive Stylistic Features

As a rhetoric of intense moral conflict, it would be surprising indeed if distinctive stylistic features did not appear as strategic adaptations to a difficult rhetorical situation.[20] I propose to treat "stylistic features" rather broadly, electing to view women's liberation as a persuasive campaign. In addition to the linguistic features usually considered, the stylistic features of a persuasive campaign include, in my view, characteristic modes of rhetorical interaction, typical ways of structuring the relationships among participants in a rhetorical transaction, and emphasis on particular forms of argument, proof, and evidence. The rhetoric of women's liberation is distinctive stylistically in rejecting certain traditional concepts of the rhetorical process—as persuasion of the many by an expert or leader, as adjustment or adaptation to audience norms, and as directed toward inducing acceptance of a specific program or a commitment to group action. This rather "anti-rhetorical" style is chosen on substantive grounds because rhetorical transactions with these features encourage submissiveness and passivity in the audience[21]—qualities at odds with a fundamental goal of feminist advocacy—self-determination. The paradigm that highlights the distinctive stylistic features of women's liberation is "consciousness raising," a mode of interaction or a type of rhetorical transaction uniquely adapted to the rhetorical problem of feminist advocacy.

The rhetorical problem may be summarized as follows: women are divided from one another by almost all the usual sources of identification—age, education, income, ethnic origin, even geography. In addition, counter-persuasive forces are pervasive and potent—nearly all spend their lives in close proximity to and under the control of males—fathers, husbands, employers, etc. Women also have very negative self-concepts, so negative, in fact, that it is difficult to view them as an audience, i.e., persons who see themselves as potential agents of change. When asked to select adjectives to describe themselves, they select such terms as "uncertain, anxious, nervous, hasty, careless, fearful, dull, childish, helpless, sorry, timid, clumsy, stupid, silly, and domestic … understanding, tender, sympathetic, pure, generous, affectionate, loving, moral, kind, grateful, and patient."[22] If a persuasive campaign directed to this audience is to be effective, it must transcend alienation to create "sisterhood," modify self-concepts to create a sense of autonomy, and speak to women in terms of private, concrete, individual experience, because women have little, if any, publicly shared experience. The substantive problem of the absence of shared values remains: when women become part of an audience for liberation rhetoric, they violate the norms governing sex appropriate behavior.

In its paradigmatic form, "consciousness raising" involves meetings of small, leaderless groups in which each person is encouraged to express her personal feelings and experiences. There is no leader, rhetor, or expert. All participate and lead; all are considered expert. The goal is to make the personal political: to create awareness (through shared experiences) that what were thought to be personal deficiencies and individual problems are common and shared, a result of their position as women. The participants seek to understand and interpret their lives as women, but there is no "message," no "party line." Individuals are encouraged to dissent, to find their own truths. If action is suggested, no group commitment is made; each must decide whether, and if so which, action is suitable for her.[23] The stylistic features heightened in this kind of transaction are characteristic of the rhetoric as a whole: affirmation of the affective, of the validity of personal experience, of the necessity for self-exposure and self-criticism, of the value of dialogue, and of the goal of autonomous, individual decision making. These stylistic features are very similar to those Maurice Natanson has described as characteristic of "genuine argumentation":

> What is at issue, really, in the risking of the self in genuine argument is the immediacy of the self's world of feeling, attitude, and the total subtle range of its affective and conative sensibility. . . . I open myself to the viable possibility that the consequence of an argument may be to make me *see* something of the structure of my immediate world . . . the personal and immediate domain of individual experience. . . .
>
> . . . feeling is a way of meaning as much as thinking is a way of formulating. Privacy is a means of establishing a world, and what genuine argument to persuade does is to publicize that privacy. The metaphor leads us to suggest that risking the self in argument is inviting a stranger to the interior familiarity of our home.[24]

Even a cursory reading of the numerous anthologies of women's liberation rhetoric will serve to confirm that the stylistic features I have indicated are characteristic. Particularly salient examples include Elizabeth Janeway's *Man's World; Woman's Place,* "The Demise of the Dancing Dog,"[25] "The Politics of Housework,"[26] *A Room of One's Own,*[27] and "Cutting Loose."[28] The conclusion of the last essay cited will serve as a model:

> The true dramatic conclusion of this narrative should be the dissolution of my marriage; there is a part of me which believes that you cannot fight a sexist system while acknowledging your need for the love of a man. . . . But in the end my husband and I did not divorce. . . . Instead I raged against him for many months and joined the Woman's Liberation Movement, and thought a great deal about myself, and about whether my problems were truly all women's problems, and decided that some of them were and that some of them were not. My sexual rage was the most powerful single emotion of my life, and the feminist analysis has become for me, as I think it will for most women of my generation, as significant an intellectual tool as Marxism was for generations of radicals. But it does not answer every question. . . . I would be lying if I said that my anger had taught me how to live. But my life has changed because of it. I think I am becoming in many small ways a woman who takes no shit. I am no longer submissive, no longer seductive. . . .
>
> My husband and I have to some degree worked out our differences. . . . But my hatred lies within me and between us, not wholly a personal hatred, but not entirely political either. And I wonder always whether it is possible to define myself as a feminist revolutionary and

still remain in any sense a wife. There are moments when I still worry that he will leave me, that he will come to need a woman less preoccupied with her own rights, and when I worry about that I also fear that no man will ever love me again, that no man could ever love a woman who is angry. And that fear is a great source of trouble to me, for it means that in certain fundamental ways I have not changed at all.

I would like to be cold and clear and selfish, to demand satisfaction for my needs, to compel respect rather than affection. And yet there are moments, and perhaps there always will be, when I fall back upon the old cop-outs. . . . Why should I work when my husband can support me, why should I be a human being when I can get away with being a child?

Women's liberation is finally only personal. It is hard to fight an enemy who has outposts in your head.[29]

This essay, the other works I have cited here, and the bulk of women's liberation rhetoric stand at the farthest remove from traditional models of rhetorical discourse, judged by the stylistic features I have discussed. This author, Sally Kempton, invites us into the interiority of her self, disclosing the inner dynamics of her feelings and the specific form that the problem of liberation takes in her life. In a rhetorically atypical fashion, she honors her feelings of fear, anger, hatred, and need for love and admits both her own ambivalence and the limits of her own experience as a norm for others. She is self-conscious and self-critical, cognizant of the inconsistencies in her life and of the temptation to "cop out," aware of both the psychic security and the psychic destruction inherent in the female role. She is tentatively describing and affirming the beginnings of a new identity and, in so doing, sets up a dialogue with other women in a similar position that permits the essay to perform the ego-functions that Richard Gregg has described.[30] The essay asks for the participation of the reader, not only in sharing the author's life as an example of the problems of growing up female in this society, but in a general process of self-scrutiny in which each person looks at the dynamics of the problems of liberation in her own life. The goal of the work is a process, not a particular belief or policy; she explicitly states that her problems are not those of all women and that a feminist analysis is not a blueprint for living. Most importantly, however, the essay exemplifies "risking the self" in its most poignant sense. The Sally Kempton we meet in the essay has been masochistic, manipulative, an exploiter of the female role and of men, weak, murderous, vengeful and castrating, lazy and selfish. The risk involved in such brutal honesty is that she will be rejected as neurotic, bitchy, crazy, in short, as not being a "good" woman, and more importantly, as *not like us.* The risk may lead to alienation or to sisterhood. By example, she asks other women to confront themselves, recognize their own ambivalence, and face their own participation and collaboration in the roles and processes that have such devastating effects on both men and women. Although an essay, this work has all the distinctive stylistic features of the "consciousness raising" paradigm.

Although the distinctive stylistic features of women's liberation are most apparent in the small group processes of consciousness raising, they are not confined to small group interactions. The features I have listed are equally present in essays, speeches, and other discourses completely divorced from the small group setting. In addition, I would argue that although these stylistic features show certain affinities for qualities associated with psychotherapeutic interaction, they are rhetorical rather than expressive and public and political rather than private and personal. The presumption of most psychotherapy is that the origins of and solutions to one's problems are personal;[31] the feminist analysis presumes that it is the social structure and the definition of the female role that generate the problems that individual women experience in their personal lives. As a consequence, solutions must be structural, not merely personal, and analysis must move from personal experience and feeling to illuminate a common condition that all women experience and share.

Finally, women's liberation rhetoric is characterized by the use of confrontative, non-adjustive strategies designed to "violate the reality structure."[32] These strategies not only attack the psycho-social reality of the culture, but violate the norms of decorum, morality, and "femininity" of the women addressed. Essays on frigidity and orgasm,[33] essays by prostitutes and lesbians,[34] personal accounts of promiscuity and masochism,[35] and essays attacking romantic love and urging man-hating as a necessary stage in liberation[36] "violate the reality structure" by close analysis of tabooed subjects, by treating "social outcasts" as "sisters" and credible sources, and by attacking areas of belief with great mythic power. Two specific linguistic techniques, "attack metaphors" and symbolic reversals, also seem to be characteristic. "Attack metaphors" mix matrices in order to reveal the "nonconscious ideology"[37] of sexism in language and belief, or they attempt to shock through a kind of "perspective by incongruity."[38] Some examples are: "Was Lurleen Wallace *Governess* of Alabama?" A drawing of Rodin's "Thinker" as a female. "Trust in God; She will provide."[39] "Prostitutes are the only honest women because they charge for their services, rather than submitting to a marriage contract which forces them to work for life without pay."[40] "If you think you are emancipated, you might consider the idea of tasting your menstrual blood—if it makes you sick, you've got a long way to go, baby."[41] Or this analogy:

> Suppose that a white male college student decided to room or set up a bachelor apartment with a black male friend. Surely the typical white student would not blithely assume that his black roommate was to handle all the domestic chores. Nor would his conscience allow him to do so even in the unlikely event that his roommate would say: "No, that's okay. I like doing housework. I'd be happy to do it. . . ." But change this hypothetical black roommate to a female marriage partner, and somehow the student's conscience goes to sleep.[42]

Symbolic reversals transform devil terms society has applied to women into god terms and always exploit the power and fear lurking in these terms as potential sources of strength. "The Bitch Manifesto" argues that liberated women are bitches—aggressive, confident, strong.[43] W.I.T.C.H., the Women's International Terrorist Conspiracy from Hell, says, in effect, "You think we're dangerous, creatures of the devil, witches? You're right! And we're going to hex you!"[44] Some feminists have argued that the lesbian is the paradigm of the liberated female;[45] others have described an androgynous role.[46] This type of reversal has, of course, appeared in other protest rhetorics, particularly in the affirmation that "black is beautiful!" But systematic reversals of traditional female roles, given the mystique associated with concepts of wife, mother, and loving sex partner, make these reversals especially disturbing and poignant. Quite evidently, they are attempts at the radical affirmation of new identities for women.[47]

The distinctive stylistic features of women's liberation rhetoric are a result of strategic adaptation to an acute rhetorical problem. Women's liberation is characterized by rhetorical interactions that emphasize affective proofs and personal testimony, participation and dialogue, self-revelation and self-criticism, the goal of autonomous decision making through self-persuasion, and the strategic use of techniques for "violating the reality structure." I conclude that, on stylistic grounds, women's liberation is a separate genre of rhetoric.

The Interdependence of Substantive and Stylistic Features

The rhetorical acts I have treated in the preceding section, particularly as illustrated by the excerpt from an essay by Sally Kempton, may seem to be a far cry from the works cited earlier demanding legal, economic, and social equality. However, I believe that all of these rhetorical acts are integral parts of a single genre, a conclusion I shall defend by examining the interdependent character of the substantive and stylistic features of the various discourses already discussed.

Essays such as that of Sally Kempton are the necessary counterparts of works articulating demands for equality. In fact, such discourses spell out the meaning and consequences of present conditions of inequity and the implications of equality in concrete, personal, affective terms. They complete the genre and are essential to its success as a persuasive campaign. In the first section, I argued that demands for equality for women "attack the entire psycho-social reality." That phrase may conceal the fact that such an attack is an attack on the *self* and on the roles and relationships in which women, and men too, have found their identities traditionally. The effect of such an argument is described by Natanson, "When an argument hurts me, cuts me, or cleanses and liberates me it is not because a particular stratum or segment of my world view is shaken up or jarred free but because *I* am wounded or enlivened— *I* in my particularity, and that means in my existential immediacy: feelings, pride, love, and sullenness, the world of my actuality as I live it."[48] The only effective response to the sensation of being threatened existentially is a rhetorical act that treats the personal, emotional, and concrete directly and explicitly, that is dialogic and participatory, that speaks from personal experience to personal experience. Consequently, the rhetoric of women's liberation includes numerous essays discussing the personal experiences of women in many differing circumstances—black women, welfare mothers, older women, factory workers, high school girls, journalists, unwed mothers, lawyers, secretaries, and so forth. Each attempts to describe concretely the personal experience of inequality in a particular situation and/or what liberation might mean in a particular case. Rhetorically, these essays function to translate public demands into personal experience and to treat threats and fears in concrete, affective terms.

Conversely, more traditional discourses arguing for equality are an essential counterpart to these more personal statements. As a process, consciousness raising requires that the personal be transcended by moving toward the structural, that the individual be transcended by moving toward the political. The works treating legal, economic, and social inequality provide the structural analyses and empirical data that permit women to generalize from their individual experiences to the conditions of women in this society. Unless such transcendence occurs, there is no persuasive campaign, no rhetoric in any public sense, only the very limited realm of therapeutic, small group interaction.

The interrelationship between the personal and the political is central to a conception of women's liberation as a genre of rhetoric. All of the issues of women's liberation are simultaneously personal and political. Ultimately, this interrelationship rests on the caste status of women, the basis of the moral conflict this rhetoric generates and intensifies. Feminists believe that sharing personal experience is liberating, i.e., raises consciousness, because all women, whatever their differences in age, education, income, etc., share a common condition, a radical form of "consubstantiality" that is the genesis of the peculiar kind of identification they call "sisterhood." Some unusual rhetorical transactions seem to confirm this analysis. "Speak-outs" on rape, abortion, and orgasm are mass meetings in which women share extremely personal and very negatively valued experiences. These events are difficult to explain without postulating a radical form of identification that permits such painful self-revelation. Similarly, "self-help clinics" in which women learn how to examine their cervixes and look at the cervixes of other women for purposes of comparison seem to require extreme identification and trust. Feminists would argue that "sisterhood is powerful" because it grows out of the recognition of pervasive, common experience of special caste status, the most radical and profound basis for cooperation and identification.

This feminist analysis also serves to explain the persuasive intent in "violating the reality structure." From this point of view, women in American society are always in a vortex of contradiction and paradox. On the one hand, they have been, for the most part, effectively socialized into traditional roles and values, as research into their achievement motivation and self-images confirms. On the other hand, "femininity" is in direct conflict with the most fundamental values of this society—a fact which makes women extremely vulnerable to attacks on the "reality structure." Hence, they argue, violations of norms may shock initially, but ultimately they will be recognized as articulating the contradictions inherent in "the female role." The violation of these norms is obvious in discourses such as that of Sally Kempton; it is merely less obvious in seemingly traditional and moderate works.

Conclusion

I conclude, then, that women's liberation is a unified, separate genre of rhetoric with distinctive substantive-stylistic features. Perhaps it is the only genuinely *radical* rhetoric on the contemporary American scene. Only the oxymoron, the figure of paradox and contradiction, can be its metaphor. Never is the paradoxical character of women's liberation more apparent than when it is compared to conventional or familiar definitions of rhetoric, analyses of rhetorical situations, and descriptions of rhetorical movements.

Traditional or familiar definitions of persuasion do not satisfactorily account for the rhetoric of women's liberation. In relation to such definitions, feminist advocacy wavers between the rhetorical and the non-rhetorical, the persuasive and the non-persuasive. Rhetoric is usually defined as dealing with public issues, structural analyses, and social action, yet women's liberation emphasizes acts concerned with personal exigences and private, concrete experience, and its goal is frequently limited to particular, autonomous action by individuals. The view that persuasion is an enthymematic adaptation to audience norms and values is confounded by rhetoric which seeks to persuade by "violating the reality structure" of those toward whom it is directed.

Nor are available analyses of rhetorical situations satisfactory when applied to the rhetoric of women's liberation. Parke Burgess' valuable and provocative discussion of certain rhetorical situations as consisting of two or more sets of conflicting moral demands[49] and Thomas Olbricht's insightful distinction between rhetorical acts occurring in the context of a shared value and those occurring in its absence[50] do not adequately explicate the situation in which feminists find themselves. And the reason is simply that the rhetoric of women's liberation appeals to *what are said to be* shared moral values, but forces recognition that those values are *not* shared, thereby creating the most intense of moral conflicts. Lloyd Bitzer's more specific analysis of the rhetorical situation as consisting of "one controlling exigence which functions as the organizing principle" (an exigence being "an imperfection marked by urgency" that "is capable of positive modification"), an audience made up "only of those persons who are capable of being influenced by discourse and of being mediators of change," and of constraints that can limit "decision and action needed to modify the exigence"[51]—this more specific analysis is also unsatisfactory. In women's liberation there are dual and conflicting exigences not solely of the public sort, and thus women's liberation rhetoric is a dialectic between discourses that deal with public, structural problems and the particularly significant statements of personal experience and feeling which extend beyond the traditional boundaries of rhetorical acts. A public exigence is, of course, present, but what is unavoidable and characteristic of this rhetoric is the accompanying and conflicting personal exigence. The concept of the audience does not account for a situation in which the audience must be *created under the special conditions* surrounding women's liberation. Lastly, the notion of constraints seems inadequate to a genre in which to act as a mediator of change, either as rhetor or audience member, is itself the most significant constraint inhibiting decision or action—a constraint that requires the violation of cultural norms and risks alienation no matter how traditional or reformist the rhetorical appeal may be.

And, similarly, nearly all descriptions of rhetorical movements prove unsatisfactory. Leland Griffin's early essay on the rhetoric of historical movements creates three important problems: he defines movements as occurring "at some time in the past"; he says members of movements "make efforts to alter their environment"; and he advises the student of rhetoric to focus on "the pattern of public discussion."[52] The first problem is that the critic is prevented from examining a contemporary movement and is forced to make sharp chronological distinctions between earlier efforts for liberation and contemporary feminist advocacy; the second problem is that once again the critic's attention is diverted from efforts to change the self, highly significant in the liberation movement, and shifted toward efforts to change the environment; and the third is a related deflection of critical concern from personal, consciousness-raising processes to public discussion. Herbert Simons' view of "a leader-centered conception of persuasion in social movements" defines a movement "as an uninstitutionalized collectivity that mobilizes for action to implement a program for the reconstitution of social norms or values."[53] As I have pointed out, leader-centered theories cannot be applied profitably to the feminist movement. Further, women's liberation is not characterized by a *program* that mobilzes feminist advocates to reconstitute social norms and values. Dan Hahn and Ruth Gonchar's idea of a movement as "socially shared activities and beliefs directed toward the demand for change in some aspect of the social order"[54] is unsuitable because it overlooks the extremely important elements of the personal exigence that require change in the self. There are, however, two recent statements describing rhetorical movements that are appropriate for women's liberation. Griffin's later essay describing a dramatistic framework for the development of movements has been applied insightfully to the inception period of contemporary women's liberation.[55] What makes this description applicable is that it recognizes a variety of symbolic acts, the role of drama and conflict, and the essentially moral or value-related character of rhetorical movements.[56] Also, Robert Cathcart's formulation, again a dramatistic one, is appropriate because it emphasizes *"dialectical enjoinment in the moral arena"* and the *"dialectical tension growing out of moral conflict."*[57]

And so I choose the oxymoron as a label, a metaphor, for the rhetoric of women's liberation. It is a genre without a rhetor, a rhetoric in search of an audience, that transforms traditional argumentation into confrontation, that "persuades" by "violating the reality structure" but that presumes a consubstantiality so radical that it permits the most intimate of identifications. It is a "movement" that eschews leadership, organizational cohesion, and the transactions typical of mass persuasion. Finally, of course, women's liberation is baffling because it has no program, because there is no clear answer to the recurring question, "What do women want?" On one level, the answer is simple; they want what every person wants—dignity, respect, the right to self-determination, to develop their potentials as individuals. But on another level, there is no answer—not even in feminist rhetoric. While there are legal and legislative changes on which most feminists agree (although the hierarchy of priorities differs), whatever liberation is, it will be something different for each woman as liberty is something different for each person. What each woman shares, however, is the paradox of having "to fight an enemy who has outposts in your head."

Ms. Campbell is Associate Professor of Rhetoric at the State University of New York at Binghamton.

Notes

1 A partial list of the numerous groups involved in women's liberation and an analysis of them is available in Julie Ellis, *Revolt of the Second Sex* (New York: Lancer Books, 1970), pp. 21–81. A similar list and an analysis emphasizing disunity, leadership problems, and policy conflicts is found in Edythe Cudlipp, *Understanding Women's Liberation* (New York: Paperback Library, 1971), pp. 129–170, 214–220. As she indicates, more radical groups have expelled members for the tendency to attract personal media attention, used "counters" to prevent domination of meetings by more articulate members; and rejected programs, specific policies, and coherent group action (pp. 146–147, 166, 214–215). The most optimistic estimate of the size of the movement is made by Charlotte Bunch-Weeks who says there are "perhaps 100,000 women in over 400 cities." ("A Broom of One's Own: Notes on the Women's Liberation Program," *The New Women,* ed. Joanne Cooke, Charlotte Bunch-Weeks and Robin Morgan [1970; rpt. Greenwich, Conn.: Fawcett Publications, 1971], p. 186.) Even if true, this compares unfavorably with the conservative League of Women Voters with 160,000 members (Cudlipp, p. 42) and the National Council of Women representing organizations with some 23 million members whose leadership has taken an extremely anti-liberationist stance. (See Lacey Fesburgh, "Traditional Groups Prefer to Ignore Women's Lib," *New York Times,* 26 Aug. 1970, p. 44.)

2 Ti-Grace Atkinson said: "There is no movement. Movement means going some place, and the movement is not going anywhere. It hasn't accomplished anything." Gloria Steinenn concurred: "In terms of real power—economic and political—we are still just beginning. But the consciousness, the awareness—that will never be the same." ("Women's Liberation Revisited," *Time,* 20 Mar. 1972, pp. 30, 31.) Polls do not seem to indicate marked attitude changes among American women. (See, for example, *Good Housekeeping,* Mar. 1971, pp. 34–38, and Carol Tavris, "Woman and Man," *Psychology Today,* Mar. 1972, pp. 57–64, 82–85.)

3 An excellent critique of both historical and socio-psychological definition of movements as the basis for rhetorical criticism has been made by Robert S. Cathcart in "New Approaches to the Study of Movements: Defining Movements Rhetorically," *Western Speech,* 36 (Spr. 1972), 82–88.

4 A particularly apt illustration of this point of view is Richard Hofstadter's "The Paranoid Style in American Politics," *The Paranoid Style in American Politics and Other Essays* (New York: Knopf, 1965), pp. 3–40. Similarly, the exhortative and argumentative genres developed by Edwin Black are defined on both substantive and stylistic grounds in *Rhetorical Criticism: A Study in Method* (New York: Macmillan, 1965), pp. 132–177.

5 The interrelationship of moral demands and strategic choices is argued by Parke G. Burgess in "The Rhetoric of Moral Conflict: Two Critical Dimensions," *QJS,* 56 (Apr. 1970), 120–130.

6 The notion that style is a token of ideology is the central concept in Edwin Black's "The Second Persona," *QJS,* 56 (Apr. 1970), 109–119.

7 See Burgess, *op. cit.* and "The Rhetoric of Black Power: A Moral Demand?" *QJS,* 54 (Apr. 1968), 122–133.

8 See Matina S. Horner, "Femininity and Successful Achievement: A Basic Inconsistency," *Roles Women Play: Readings Toward Women's Liberation,* ed. Michele Hoffnung Garskof (Belmont, Calif.: Brooks/Cole, 1971), pp. 105–108.

9 "Woman's role, looked at from this point of view, is archaic. This is not necessarily a bad thing, but it does make woman's position rather peculiar: it is a survival. In the old world, where one was born into a class and a region and often into an occupation, the fact that one was also sex-typed simply added one more attribute to those which every child learned he or she possessed. Now to be told, in Erik Erikson's words, that one is 'never not-a-woman' comes as rather more of a shock. This is especially true for American women because of the way in which the American ethos has honored the ideas of liberty and individual choice . . . woman's traditional role *in itself* is opposed to a significant aspect of our culture. It is more than restricting, because it involves women in the kind of conflict with their surroundings that no decision and no action open to them can be trusted to resolve." (Elizabeth Janeway, *Man's World; Woman's Place: A Study in Social Mythology* [New York: William Morrow, 1971], p. 99.)

10 Jo Freeman, "The Building of the Gilded Cage," *The Second Wave,* 1 (Spr. 1971), 33.

11 *Ibid.*, 8–9.

12 Judicial opinions upholding discriminatory legislation make this quite evident. "That woman's physical structure and the performance of maternal functions place her at a disadvantage in the struggle for subsistence is obvious ... the physical well-being of woman becomes an object of public interest and care in order to preserve the strength and vigor of the race ... looking at it from the viewpoint of the effort to maintain an independent position in life, she is not upon an equality ... she is properly placed in a class by herself.... The reason ... rests in the inherent difference between the two sexes, and in the different functions in life which they perform." (Muller v. Oregon, 208 U.S. 412 [1908], at 421–423.) This and similar judicial opinions are cited by Diane B. Schulder, "Does the Law Oppress Women?" *Sisterhood is Powerful*, ed. Robin Morgan (New York: Vintage Books, 1970), pp. 139–157.

13 Ellis, pp. 103–111. See also Caroline Bird, with Sara Welles Briller, *Born Female: The High Cost of Keeping Women Down* (1968; rpt. New York: Pocket Books, 1971), particularly pp. 61–83.

14 "The Chase Manhattan Bank estimated a U.S. woman's hours spent at housework at 99.6 per week." (Juliet Mitchell, "Women: The Longest Revolution [excerpt]," *Liberation Now!* ed. Deborah Babcox and Madeline Belkin [New York: Dell, 1971], p. 250.) See also Ann Crittenden Scott, "The Value of Housework," *Ms.*, July 1972, pp. 56–59.

15 Aileen S. Kraditor, *Up From the Pedestal. Selected Writings in the History of American Feminism* (Chicago: Quadrangle Books, 1968), p. 24.

16 The concepts underlying "woman's place" serve to explain the position that women hold outside the home in the economic sphere: "Are there any principles that explain the meanderings of the sex boundaries? One is the idea that women should work inside and men outside. Another earmarks service work for women and profit-making for men. Other rules reserve work with machinery, work carrying prestige, and the top job to men. Most sex boundaries can be explained on the basis of one or another of these three rules." (Bird, p. 72.)

17 Horner, p. 121.

18 From E. E. Maccoby, "Woman's Intellect," *The Potential of Woman,* ed. S. M. Farber and R. H. L. Wilson (New York: McGraw-Hill, 1963), pp. 24–39; cited in Horner, p. 106.

19 In the economic sphere alone, such changes would be far-reaching. "Equal access to jobs outside the home, while one of the preconditions for women's liberation, will not in itself be sufficient to give equality for women. Society must begin to take responsibility for children; the economic dependence of women and children on the husband-father must be ended. The other work that goes on in the home must also be changed—communal eating places and laundries for example. When such work is moved into the public sector, then the material basis for discrimination against women will be gone." (Margaret Benston, "The Political Economy of Women's Liberation," *Roles Women Play*, pp. 200–201.)

20 The individual elements described here did not originate with women's liberation. Consciousness raising has its roots in the "witnessing" of American revivalism and was an important persuasive strategy in the revolution on mainland China. Both the ancient Cynics and the modern Yippies have used violations of the reality structure as persuasive techniques (see Theodore Otto Windt, Jr., "The Diatribe: Last Resort for Protest," *QJS*, 58 [Feb. 1972], 1–14), and this notion is central to the purposes of agit-prop theatre, demonstrations, and acts of civil disobedience. Concepts of leaderless persuasion appear in Yippie documents and in the unstructured character of sensitivity groups. Finally, the idea that contradiction and alienation lead to altered consciousness and revolution has its origins in Marxian theory. It is the combination of these elements in women's liberation that is distinctive stylistically. As in a metaphor, the separate elements may be familiar; it is the fusion that is original.

21 The most explicit statement of the notion that audiences are "feminine" and rhetors or orators are "masculine" appears in the rhetorical theory of Adolf Hitler and the National Socialist Party in Germany. See Kenneth Burke, "The Rhetoric of Hitler's 'Battle,'" *The Philosophy of Literary Form* (1941; rpt. New York: Vintage Books, 1957), p. 167.

22 Jo Freeman, "The Social Construction of the Second Sex," *Roles Women Play*, p. 124.

23 The nature of consciousness raising is described in Susan Brownmiller, "Sisterhood is Powerful" and June Arnold, "Consciousness-Raising," *Women's Liberation: Blueprint for the Future*, ed.

Stookie Stambler (New York: Ace Books, 1970), pp. 141–161; Charlotte Bunch-Weeks, pp. 185–197; Carole Hanisch, "The Personal is Political," Kathie Sarachild, "A Program for Feminist 'Consciousness Raising,'" Irene Peslikis, "Resistances to Consciousness," Jennifer Gardner, "False Consciousness," and Pamela Kearon, "Man-Hating," in *Notes from the Second Year: Women's Liberation, Major Writings of the Radical Feminists,* ed. Shulamith Firestone and Anne Koedt (New York: By the Editors, 1970), pp. 76–86.

24 Maurice Natanson, "The Claims of Immediacy," *Philosophy, Rhetoric and Argumenta*tion, ed. Maurice Natanson and Henry W. Johnstone, Jr. (University Park: Pennsylvania State Univ. Press, 1965), pp. 15, 16.

25 Cynthia Ozick, "The Demise of the Dancing Dog," *The New Women,* pp. 28–42.

26 Redstockings, "The Politics of Housework," *Liberation Now!,* pp. 110–115. Note that in this, as in other cases, authorship is assigned to a group rather than an individual.

27 Virginia Woolf, *A Room of One's Own* (New York: Harbinger, 1929).

28 Sally Kempton, "Cutting Loose," *Liberation Now!,* pp. 39–55. This essay was originally published in *Esquire,* July 1970, pp. 53–57.

29 *Ibid,* pp. 54–55.

30 Richard B. Gregg, "The Ego-Function of the Rhetoric of Protest," *Philosophy & Rhetoric,* 4 (Spr. 1971), 71–91. The essay is discussed specifically on pp. 80–81.

31 Granted, there are humanistic or existential psychological theorists who argue that social or outer reality must be changed fully as often as psychic or inner reality. See, for example, Thomas S. Szasz, *The Myth of Mental Illness* (1961; rpt. New York: Dell, 1961), R. D. Laing and A. Esterson, *Sanity, Madness, and the Fami*ly (1964; rpt. New York: Basic Books, 1971), and William H. Grier and Price M. Cobbs, *Black Rage* (New York: Basic Books, 1968). However, the vast majority of psychological approaches assumes that the social order is, at least relatively, unalterable and that it is the personal realm that must be changed. See, for example, Sigmund Freud, A *General Introduction to Psychoanalysis,* trans. Joan Riviere (1924; rpt, New York: Washington Square Press, 1960), Wilhelm Stekel, *Technique of Analytical Psychotherapy,* trans. Eden and Cedar Paul (London: William Brown, 1950), Carl A. Whitaker and Thomas P. Malone, *The Roots of Psychotherapy* (New York: Blakiston, 1953), and Carl R. Rogers, *Client-Centered Therapy* (Boston: Houghton Mifflin, 1951).

32 This phrase originates with the loose coalition of radical groups called the Female Liberation Movement (Ellis, p. 55). See also Pamela Kearon, "Power as a Function of the Group," *Notes from the Second Year,* pp. 108–110.

33 See, for example, Anne Koedt, "The Myth of the Vaginal Orgasm," *Liberation Now!,* pp. 311–320; Susan Lydon, "The Politics of Orgasm," and Mary Jane Sherfey, M.D., "A Theory on Female Sexuality," *Sisterhood is Powerful,* pp. 197–205, 220–230.

34 See, for example, Radicalesbians, "The Woman-Identified Woman," *Liberation Now!,* pp. 287–293; Ellen Strong, "The Hooker," Gene Damon, "The Least of These: The Minority Whose Screams Haven't Yet Been Heard," and Martha Shelley, "Notes of a Radical Lesbian," *Sisterhood is Powerful,* pp, 289–311; Del Martin and Phyllis Lyon, "The Realities of Lesbianism," *The New Women,* pp. 99–109.

35 Sally Kempton's essay is perhaps the most vivid example of this type. See also Judith Ann, "The Secretarial Proletariat," and Zoe Moss, "It Hurts to be Alive and Obsolete: The Ageing Woman," *Sisterhood is Powerful,* pp. 86–100, 170–175.

36 See Shulamith Firestone, "Love," and Pamela Kearon, "Man-Hating," *Notes from the Second Year,* pp. 16–27, 83–86.

37 This term originates with Sandra L. Bem and Daryl J. Bem, "Training the Woman to Know Her Place: The Power of a Nonconcious Ideology," *Roles Women Play,* pp. 84–96.

38 This phrase originates with Kenneth Burke and is the title of Part II of *Permanence and Change,* 2nd rev. ed. (Indianapolis: Bobbs-Merrill, 1965).

39 Emmeline G. Pankhurst, cited by Ellis, p. 19.

40 Ti-Grace Atkinson, cited by Charles Winick and Paul M. Kinsie, "Prostitutes," *Psychology Today,* Feb. 1972, p. 57.

41 Germaine Greer, *The Female Eunuch* (New York: McGraw-Hill, 1970), p. 42.

42 Bern and Bem, pp. 94–95.

43 Joreen, "The Bitch Manifesto," *Notes from the Second Year*, pp. 5–9.

44 "WITCH Documents," *Sisterhood is Powerful*, pp. 538–553.

45 See, for example, Martha Shelley, "Notes of a Radical Lesbian," *Sisterhood is Powerful*, pp. 306–311. Paralleling this are the negative views of some radical groups toward heterosexual love and marriage. See "The Feminists: A Political Organization to Annihilate Sex Roles," *Notes from the Second Year*, pp. 114–118.

46 See, for example, Caroline Bird, "On Being Born Female," *Vital Speeches of the Day*, 15 Nov. 1968, pp. 88–91. This argument is also made negatively by denying that, as yet, there is any satisfactory basis for determining what differences, if any, there are between males and females. See, for example, Naomi Weisstein, "Psychology Constructs the Female, or the Fantasy Life of the Male Psychologist," *Roles Women Play*, pp. 68–83.

47 Elizabeth Janeway makes a very telling critique of many of these attempts. She argues that the roles of shrew, witch, and bitch are simple reversals of the positively valued and socially accepted roles of women. The shrew is the negative counterpart of the public role of the wife whose function is to charm and to evince honor and respect for her husband before others; the witch is the negative role of the good mother—capricious, unresponsive, and threatening; the bitch is the reversal of the private role of wife—instead of being comforting, loving, and serious, she is selfish, teasing, emasculating. The point she is making is that these are not new, creative roles, merely reversals of existing, socially defined roles. (Pp. 119–123, 126–127, 199–201.)

48 Natanson, pp. 15–16.

49 Parke G. Burgess, "The Rhetoric of Moral Conflict: Two Critical Dimensions."

50 Thomas H. Olbricht, "The Self as a Philosophical Ground of Rhetoric," *Pennsylvania Speech Annual*, 21 (Sept. 1964), 28–36.

51 Lloyd F. Bitzer, "The Rhetorical Situation," *Philosophy & Rhetoric*, 1 (Jan. 1968), 6–8.

52 Leland M. Griffin, "The Rhetoric of Historical Movements," *QJS*, 38 (Apr. 1952), 184–185.

53 Herbert W. Simons, "Requirements, Problems, and Strategies: A Theory of Persuasion for Social Movements," *QJS*, 56 (Feb. 1970), 3.

54 Dan F. Hahn and Ruth M. Gonchar, "Studying Social Movements: A Rhetorical Methodology," *Speech Teacher*, 20 (Jan. 1971), 44, cited from Joseph R. Gusfield, ed., *Protest, Reform, and Revolt: A Reader in Social Movements* (New York: Wiley, 1970), p. 2.

55 Brenda Robinson Hancock, "Affirmation by Negation in the Women's Liberation Movement," *QJS*, 58 (Oct. 1972), 264–271.

56 Leland M. Griffin, "A Dramatistic Theory of the Rhetoric of Movements," *Critical Responses to Kenneth Burke*, ed. William H. Rueckert (Minneapolis: Univ. of Minnesota Press, 1969), p. 456.

57 Robert S. Cathcart, p. 87.

2.
WOMEN'S SPEECH: SEPARATE BUT UNEQUAL?
Cheris Kramer

Editors' Note: *This foundational essay demonstrates the degree to which women as speakers have been silenced or ignored in the field of communication and strikes another blow against essentialist thinking by insisting that scholars (male and female alike) not lump all women together. This essay sparked a volley of influential research on women's ways of communicating.*

In generalizing about sex differences, Margaret Mead says that although societies differ in the way traits are assigned to men and women, all cultures set up societal norms for the sexes which go beyond the biological differences.[1] There continues to be disagreement, of course, on which behavioral differences are caused by cultural influence and which by biological characteristics. For researchers in speech and linguistics, however, the first task is to search for possible differences in the ways men and women speak.

Although there have recently been published a number of articles dealing with sexism in the English language (for example, the use of the dominant "he" meaning either male or female), there has been relatively little concern about the ways men and women use the English language differently. The sex role differences, so important to our culture, seem to have been largely ignored in communication research.

We need to consider not only the possibility of differences in grammatical, phonological, and semantic aspects, but also possible differences in the verbal skills, instrumental use of language, and the relationship of non-verbal uses to verbal behavior. We need to ask if there are differences between the sexes in their linguistic competence. Do women control some speech structures or vocabulary that men lack or vice versa? We need to ask if there are differences in linguistic performance. Are there syntactic structures, vocabulary, phonological rules that, say, women might know but not use while men both know and use?

This paper will consider the evidence for there being systems of co-occurring, sex-linked, linguistic signals in the United States.[2] There are, of course, very important implications of such a finding for future linguistic research. Discussion of possible reasons for sex-related differences in speech will be limited; the emphasis will be on, first, what type of research in linguistic sex contrasts has been done and then on relevant material in folk-linguistics (with suggestions of further areas of study).

Cheris Kramer, "Women's Speech: Separate but Unequal?" *QJS* 60. 1974: 14–24.

It has been easier to see the differences of language between the sexes in other cultures than in our own. For example, Furley says that sex contrasts in language usage are common among primitive tribes (though such contrasts are, he says, "barely discernible in the familiar languages of Europe"). He reports differences in phonetics, grammar, and vocabulary found in tribes in Siberia, Bengal, Bolivia, the United States (Indians), and the Lesser Antilles. There is, he writes, "linguistic evidence that in at least some scattered instances, the existence of these distinctions is associated with an assertion of masculine superiority."[3] Haas indicates that differences in the language spoken by men and women are common to many cultures. Although differences in grammar have been noticed, most differences seem to be either of vocabulary or of pronunciation.[4]

Frazer writes about the special speech used by the women of the Caffres of South Africa. A Caffre wife must not pronounce the names of her father-in-law or the names of her mate's male relations in the ascending line, or words which contain a syllable of any of those names. In the case of the Caffres, avoiding the emphatic syllable contained in many male names means that many words used by the women have a syllable changed and at times the entire words. Frazer's source states that the Caffres call this language "Ukuteta Kwabafazi" ("women's speech"). Restrictions are evidently often imposed on the males of a tribe also.[5]

Jespersen warns that differing lists of words restricted to either men or women do not necessarily make different languages. In his chapter "The Woman," he quotes Rochefort speaking of his experiences in the seventeenth century among the Caribbeans: "The men have a great many expressions peculiar to them, which the women understand but never pronounce themselves. On the other hand, the women have words and phrases which the men never use, or they would be laughed to scorn. Thus it happens that in their conversations it often seems as if women had another language than the men."[6] Rochefort is saying that these systems are exclusive. There are categorical differences. Women have words which the men *never* use. However, in the United States many differences appear to be a matter of context and frequency; for example: women perhaps know but do not use swear or curse words in the same context or with the same frequency as men. By the same token, women seem to use such words as "pretty," "cute," "lovely," and "oh dear" in contexts and in frequencies that differ from men.

In a 1969 article Shuy reviewed some of the small amount of research which had been done on women's speech in the United States. He mentions a Detroit study by Shuy himself, Wolfram, and Riley, that found clear sex differences in frequency of a linguistic feature. For example, males used "-in" (in place of "-ing") 62.2 per cent of the time compared to only 28.9 per cent of the time by females. (In a New England study, Fischer found that girls used "-ing" more frequently, while boys used "-in" more frequently.[7]) Shuy also reported that Wolfram in his work with Black English found that black females "have fewer *f, t* or Ø realizations of *th*. . . . Females come closer than males at approximating the norm." Black females show greater tendency toward norms in their grammar, also, especially black females of the lower middle class.[8]

Labov also found that lower middle class New York women have a more extreme pattern of hypercorrection than men in the same class.[9] Levine and Crockett found in a study of one American community that it was primarily the middle class women who led the community toward the national speech norms.[10] Trudgill found the same type of sex differentiation for speakers of urban British English. His study demonstrated that "women informants ... use forms associated with the prestige standard more frequently than men." His study also discovered that male speakers place a high value on working class nonstandard speech. He offers several possible reasons for the finding that the women are more likely to use forms considered correct: (1) The subordinate position of women in English and American societies makes it "more necessary for women to secure their social status linguistically"; and (2) While men can be rated socially on what they *do*, women may be rated primarily on how they *appear*—so their speech is more important.[11]

Another study discovered, in tests involving boys and girls, that even when there is no difference in articulatory mechanism size, the sex of the speaker can be accurately identified from his or her speech. The researchers offered some possible reasons for this finding, one of which was:

> If there is no average difference in articulatory mechanism size, the differences we have observed could arise from differential use of the anatomy. The children could be learning culturally determined patterns that are viewed as appropriate for each sex. Within the limit of his anatomy, a speaker could change the format pattern by pronouncing vowels with phonetic variations, or by changing the configuration of the lips. . . . Spreading the lips will shorten the vocal tract, and raise the formants. The characteristic way some women have of talking and smiling at the same time would have just this effect.[12]

Goldberg conducted an experiment which found that women college students are predisposed to value the scholarly writings of men in their professional fields over the writing of women in the same fields.[13]

Kester found that in a mixed group of people it is the men who talk much more than the women. She found that men interrupt women more often than women interrupt men.[14] In a study involving a verbal task, Wood concluded that men tended to use more words than women in responding to a given stimulus.[15]

Another study, done by Shuy, Baratz, and Wolfram in 1969, tested men's and women's subjective reactions to language performance, and found only an insignificant difference in men's and women's ability to identify the race of speakers heard on tape. Considering that his earlier study (that I have mentioned) had shown clear sex contrasts in language use, with women using the prestige forms more often than men, Shuy found the results of this later study surprising. He gives several possible reasons for the evidence that subjective reactions and performance in speech are asymmetrical, including the disappointing final one that "women continue to be one of the mysteries of the universe" (Shuy, pp. 12–14). This reaction in itself offers a possible reason that so little research has been done. Firestone calls such a reaction part of an "exaggeration process" that provides for stereotyping of women as a peculiar type of human being that cannot be understood or treated by the laws that govern mankind, i.e., males.[16]

I could find few other studies dealing with linguistic sex contrasts in English. There have been some published papers on the ratio of male to female stutterers. There is general agreement that there are more male stutterers than female. Here again, there is disagreement about whether biological or social factors are working. Some scholars have found evidence that stuttering is a hereditary trait but recent studies indicate that a male is more likely to stutter than a female because our culture places more importance on speech fluency in males than speech fluency in females. Conscious of the pressure on him to speak well, the male feels more insecure about his speech.[17]

A number of publications deal with sex-related differences in comprehension and retention of oral messages. Although early studies found that males comprehend more than females in tests using oral messages, a recent study did not find this result. The authors of the recent study conclude that the inconsistent findings of this type of research "demonstrate that the role of sex in communication has not been clearly defined. Further research should provide added insight into the role of sex in influencing communication effects, a problem which no researcher employing both males and females in communication research can ignore."[18]

Experiments dealing with possible sex-related differences in comprehension of compressed speech and in persuasibility show the same conflict in results.[19] There is evidently some factor or factors which have not been controlled in these tests.

I have mentioned, then, some of the few types of research projects which have been designed to find sex-related differences in speech. This is not to say that there has been no other word on the subject. The next section of my paper will try to pull together what can be called the folk-linguistics (using Hoenigswald's term)[20] of women's speech. Much can be said about the popular beliefs of what constitutes women's speech. These beliefs are not always articulated as beliefs, but from a reading of etiquette manuals, speech books, cartoons, and novels, a stereotype of the woman as having particular characteristics of speech will emerge. Sometimes belief is confused with fact. While researching this paper I became aware that there seems to be a conflict not only between what women's speech really is like and what people think women's speech really is like, but also between what people think women's speech is like and what they think it should be like.

Females are cautioned against talking too much. *The New Seventeen Book of Etiquette and Young Living* described in a 1972 *New Yorker* advertisement as "AN IDEAL GRADUATION GIFT" ("social confidence for girls starts here") gives the "basic rules of conduct" for young girls who are interested in learning to "fit in." The book makes reference to a "survey of opinions" collected from boys. Some of these opinions, given as support for guidelines for girls, mention speech: "I hate girls who can't stop talking." "I like a girl who talks—but not a whole lot." "I like girls who listen to me without interrupting and who pay attention." The editor adds some comments in support of the boys' opinions: "Concentrate on the other person. Ask questions to draw him out. He'll love talking about himself." "Everybody loves to hear praise, and boys in particular." "Any male is happy to be the source of information."[21]

Girls are not *supposed* to talk as much as men. Perhaps a "talkative" woman is one who does talk as much as a man. A number of experiments suggest themselves. The total amount of talking time could be measured for men and women in a variety of situations. (In one study women have been found to have a higher word count than men when giving descriptions of verbal displays. The experiment tested only one subject at a time; there were no interruptions.[22]) Here are several focal ideas for other possible experiments: Does the ratio of men to women in a group make a difference in the relative verbosity of members of the two sexes? Is there a difference in the rate at which men and women produce words and sentences? Is there a difference in the number of times men and women in a group speak? And corresponding to this, is there a difference in the time of individual speeches? How much talking can a woman do before she is labelled "talkative"? This last question might involve a study of the types of sentence construction used, the volume of the voice, and the topics of speech.

Jespersen cites proof from literature to support his discussion of the way women frequently leave sentences, especially exclamatory sentences, unfinished. "Well, I never"; "I must say!" (p. 251).

It may be that women ask more questions. In an article on the role of men and women as represented in children's books, Marjorie U'Ren is quoted on the fictional mother. "She enters a scene only to place a cake on the table and then disappears. Or she plays foil to her husband by setting him up for his line. It is mother who asks, 'What shall we do?' and by doing so invites a speech from father."[23] Do women indeed use more questions and fewer declarative sentences than men? Is this one way of showing subordination, submission to men?

Lakoff thinks women do use the tag-question formation more than men. A tag, in Lakoff's words, is "midway between an outright statement and a yes–no question: it is less assertive than the former, but more confident than the latter."[24] It is used when a speaker does not have full confidence in his or her statement. Instead of a firm declaration, the speaker asks for confirmation, and by being less decisive the speaker leaves himself or herself an out. He or she is willing to be persuaded otherwise. "This speech convention is terrible, isn't it?" "That law was poorly drafted, don't you think?"

Lakoff hears another question that has much the same effect. Even if the woman is asked a question for which she alone holds the information, she can turn her answer into a question. Lakoff gives this example: "(A) When will dinner be ready? (B) Oh . . . around six o'clock . . . ?" (p. 56). Here, intonation rather than sentence structure has the woman indicate subordination and uncertainty.

I have heard other ways that women, perhaps more than men, have of avoiding stating an opinion directly. "I kinda like that house." If someone points out to her the garage is too small and the fireplace mislocated, she can change her mind without too much difficulty or fear of embarrassment. "That dress is rather pretty." The qualifier gives her an out. Do women actually use tag-questions more than men? Do their declarative sentences contain more qualifiers? In what situations? On what topics?

Lakoff finds a relationship between the tag-question and the tag-order. Women, she says, are more likely to compound a request (pp. 56–57). "Will you help me with these groceries, please?" is more polite than "Come help me" (and politeness, Lakoff believes, is a characteristic of women's speech); and the longer request stated as a question leaves a stronger possibility of a negative response. I have seen no empirical studies which deal with this possible difference in men's and women's speech.

Another technique women might use to talk without seeming to do much talking is to lower the volume and pitch of their speech. We all know that at least in cartoons and novels whenever a number of women gather the resulting talk will be loud and high-pitched. In fact, such gatherings are often called "hen sessions" and the speech is then called a "cackle." Do women change volume and pitch, depending on the situation and the ratio of men and women present?

Pitch level depends upon the length, tension, and weight of the vocal cords. Women's cords are, in general, shorter, lighter, and stretched more tightly than men's. Pitch level is higher. Again, there seems to be a discrepancy between what really is and what is prescribed. The very fact that etiquette books warn women to avoid loud, high-pitched speaking indicates that performance does not always match the stated norms.[25]

In an article entitled "Down With Sexist Upbringing," Pogrebin recognizes high pitch as a stereotyped attribute of females, closely associated with other undesirable, but feminine, traits. She writes, "Even Sesame Street, despite its noble educational intentions, teaches role rigidity along with the letters of the alphabet. . . . Boy monsters are brave and gruff. Girl monsters are high-pitched and timid."[26] The pitch of the female voice, which is usually higher because of the given physical traits of the vocal cords, is associated with the undesirable trait of timidness.

The higher-pitched voice is not associated in people's minds with serious topics. Mannes quotes a broadcaster giving a reason why in the United States so few women are employed as reporters by television networks: "As a whole, people don't like to hear women's voices telling them serious things."[27] Qualities other than pitch alone are evidently involved here; a handbook for announcers states that although women were employed by stations during the war, they were not retained once men were once again available, because "often the higher-pitched female voices could not hold listeners' attention for any length of time, while the lower-pitched voices were frequently vehicles for an overly polished, ultra-sophisticated delivery that sounded phoney." According to the handbook, "Women's delivery . . . is lacking in the authority needed for a convincing newscast."[28]

Serious news, then, is not expected from females. It would be interesting to discover if women dislike hearing women's voices over radio and television to the same degree that men dislike hearing women's voices. Do the relatively few women who do have broadcasting jobs change their pitch and volume for their performances on the air to a greater degree than do male broadcasters? What kind of female voices are hired for broadcasting jobs? At what age does this preference for the male voice begin? And in what situations other than broadcasting? Dillard in writing about the use of peer recordings of speech to teach Standard English to speakers of Black English states: "Sex-grading has to be taken into account: will little boys be willing to learn seriously from records made by little girls, or by boys who impress them as being 'sissies'?"[29] Note that he is not worried about girls being willing to learn "seriously" from records made by boys.

It would be interesting to see if female speech patterns once found in a variety of situations in which women are in the subordinate positions are found in situations in which a woman speaks from some base of power. Perhaps the male–female division remains the most important consideration. One woman executive "in a top governmental position" has been quoted as saying, "I always try to remember that . . . this is a man's world, and when I have big problems to discuss I work with them in such a manner that the first thing I know they're telling *me* their ideas, which are just exactly what I've been talking about . . . but in a roundabout way through the backdoor . . . it's *their* idea."[30]

This quotation is not of recent date. It would be interesting to try to discover the present speech habits of female executives. If, as our literature suggests, women learn to control their speech to help convey an impression that they are living in the background, does the woman who has obtained a position of some power alongside or over men have these techniques perfected? Or, alternatively, has she other characteristics of speaking which have aided her in obtaining a position of power?

The material presented on the preceding pages indicates that there are many experiments to be run using the larger hypothesis that women's speech reflects the stereotyped roles of male and female in our society, i.e., women in a subservient, nurturing position in a male-dominated world. The tag-question, the relatively large number of questions asked, the intonation which makes a declarative sentence a question, the compounding of requests, the concern with unobtrusive pitch and volume, the triviality of subjects discussed over the air, the roundabout way of declaring ideas—all aspects of female speech, if they do indeed exist (for what I have been reporting is largely folk linguistics) for a significant segment of the female population, would indicate one way in which the sex roles are maintained.

There appear to be a number of other differences in the speech of men and women that do not seem as neatly categorized according to dominant–dominated characteristics.

Women are said to have a greater intonational range. "It is generally thought that women have more extremes of high and low intonation than do men and that there are some intonation patterns, impressionistically the 'whining, questioning, helpless' patterns, which are used predominantly by women" (Eble, p. 10).

There is some evidence—at least in jokes and novels—of a syntactic looseness in women's speech. (This is of course in comparison with men's speech.) Jespersen writes of the "greater rapidity of female thought" and of the "superior readiness of speech of women"—indicating that the talk is done without much thought. (He offers material from a number of novels written by men as partial proof.) Sentences are not completed, he attests, and women are prone to jump from one idea to another (pp. 250–53). Ellmann writes of the stereotyped formlessness of women's speech as it is represented in the writing of such men as Joyce, Sartre, Mailer, and Hemingway. Molly Bloom and so many women who followed her in literary history have just let it all flow out.[31] The same looseness is illustrated in a *Saturday Review* cartoon (30 Oct., 1971, p. 56) in which a mini-skirted co-ed is saying in class to her professor (male):

> If we don't know how big the whole universe is, then I don't see how we could be sure how big anything in it is either, like the whole thing might not be any bigger than maybe an orange would be if it weren't in the universe, I mean, so I don't think we ought to get too

uptight about any of it because it might be really sort of small and unimportant after all, and until we find out that everything isn't just some kind of specks and things, why maybe who needs it?

Jespersen states that the women can answer and talk more quickly because their vocabulary is more limited and more central—that is, women share a common vocabulary while men show more individuality in word choice. If Jespersen's book of 1922 seems to be referred to here an inordinately large number of times it is because he was a prolific and respected writer on language (selections from his books are still anthologized) and because he wrote one of the very few studies available on women's speech. The statements that he makes about women's speech have not been proved or disproved. The support he uses is largely taken from literature.

"Everyone knows that the vocabulary of women differs considerably from that of men," wrote Greenough and Kittredge back in 1901.[32] Yet one finds very little mention of this supposedly obvious difference. There is surprisingly little interest in linguistic literature even about the use of curse words. Jespersen declares that "there can be no doubt that women exercise a great and universal influence on linguistic development through their instinctive shrinking from coarse and gross expressions and their preference for refined and (in certain spheres) veiled and indirect expressions" (p. 246). Instinctive, he says. Firestone offers another explanation for this particular difference in the vocabulary of men and women: "As for the double standard about cursing: A man is allowed to blaspheme the world because it belongs to him to damn—but the same curse out of the mouth of a woman or a minor, i.e., an incomplete 'man' to whom the world does not yet belong, is considered presumptuous, and thus an impropriety or worse" (p. 100).

Men have a further claim to slang words in general. Flexner writes, in the preface to the *Dictionary of American Slang:*

> In my work on this dictionary, I was constantly aware that most American slang is created and used by males. Many types of slang words—including the taboo and strongly derogatory ones, those referring to sex, women, work, money, whiskey, politics, transportation, sports, and the like—refer primarily to male endeavor and interest. The majority of entries in this dictionary could be label[ed] "primarily masculine use . . ." Men also tend to avoid words that sound feminine or weak. Thus there are sexual differences in even the standard vocabularies of men and women.[33]

In her paradigm of terms for "prostitute," Stanley analyzed two hundred words ("not by any means an exhaustive list") used by men to refer to women who sell themselves or who give themselves away.[34]

This creation and use of slang is considered a healthy activity. According to Jespersen, "Men will certainly with great justice object that there is a danger of the language becoming languid and insipid if we are to content ourselves with women's expressions, and that vigour and vividness count for something" (p. 247). Eric Partridge writes about the "vivid expressiveness" and "vigorous ingenuity" expressed by the creation of the more than 1,200 English synonyms for the word "fuck." He says the words "bear witness to the fertility of English and to the enthusiastic English participation in the universal fascination of the creative act" (Stanley, p. 6).

The fascination of the act may be universal, but in this country it is not to be spoken about by girls. Here is *The New Seventeen* on people who use "those four letter words": "Boys find it especially repugnant when girls use these words. One boy described girls who use profanity as having nothing better to say" (p. 106).

This material indicates that there is at least one major restriction on what women are supposed to say. Of course, women often object to the slang used by men. But, after all, "Boys will be boys." (Have you ever heard "Girls will be girls"?) There does seem to be a feeling that there is something instinctive—or should be something instinctive—about the way men use coarse expressions and the way women avoid them.

Reik mentions what he thinks are differences in the ways men and women use the *same* words. A word such as "sex," "love," or "home" might have different connotations for the two sexes.[35] These differences could conceivably be found by the use of semantic differential tests.

A number of sources I consulted for this paper indicated that women do not use the same adjectives as men do, or they are used in different contexts or with different frequency. Native speakers will recognize "nice," "pretty," "darling," "charming," "sweet," "lovely," "cute," and "precious," as being words of approval used more frequently by women. As one male student in my speech class said, "If I heard a guy say something was 'cute,' I'd wonder about him." That is, his masculinity would be in question.

I found little mention of the use of adverbs in women's speech, although Jespersen says there are greater differences in the way the sexes use the adverb than the way they use the adjective—and he quotes Lord Chesterfield to prove it (p. 249). (Chesterfield objected to the extensive use of "vastly," which he said women used to mean anything.) Several sources, including Jespersen, mentioned the use of hyperbole in women's speech, especially the intensive "*so.*" Lakoff suggests that the heavily stressed "*so*" can be used like the tag-question to avoid full commitment to a statement. She feels that men use the intensive "*so*" most easily when the sentence is unemotional or nonsubjective (p. 3n), as in "That car is so beautiful." Since being emphatic is not seemingly a characteristic of women's speech, it would be useful to determine in what situations and with what topics women do use the intensive "*so.*" It might be that it is used in cases where agreement with another speaker is being made. Or where disagreement is unlikely.

Hyperbole perhaps is not a characteristic peculiar to women's speech. Flexner (p. xii) writes than men enjoy using hyperbole in slang. He continues: "Under many situations, men do not see or care to express fine shades of meaning: a girl is either a knockout or a dog." (At the end of this paragraph Flexner says that men like to make themselves the active doer, to use the transitive verb. Here is another syntax pattern to check.)

What I have discussed thus far has been primarily concerned with spoken words. There is some evidence that there are thought to be parallel differences in the written work of men and women. I have already mentioned a study involving the way scholarly writing by women is viewed by college women. Ellmann, in writing about fiction, states the stereotyped dichotomy: the masculine mode of writing contains the properties of reason and knowledge, the feminine mode of writing states feelings and intuitions (p. 158). Ellmann calls this dichotomy "unreal." Reason and knowledge, feelings and intuitions are difficult things to test for, based as they are on a culture's idea of what is real. But perhaps there are lesser tests to run. For example, is the dialogue different for the sexes in the novels? And do women writers treat the dialogue differently? Much of the support Jespersen used for his chapter on the speech of women consisted of dialogue taken from novels by male writers. Does this dialogue correspond with what is actually said by women and men? A female novelist, George Eliot, used Dorothea's speech (in *Middlemarch*) to indicate changes in Dorothea's feeling of self-assurance as she falls under the dominance of her husband. Her use of intensifying adverbs, for example, persists, but she loses her ability to use figurative speech—or she refrains from using it. As she is unable to get positive responses from her husband, she stops trying to gain agreement by means of her former method of using negatives ("Will you not now do . . ." [which seems a feminine, that is, a submissive construction to begin with]), and starts asking rhetorical questions for which no agreement is required. In her loneliness she uses much hyperbole—to herself. This analysis, by Derek Oldfield,[36] provides an interesting look at the ways a female novelist made a woman use her speech to indicate subordination—so that she was able to still use speech as an outlet.

Poetry, letter-writing, and reporting in the media would be other areas of communication to study. Can the written work of women be recognized by subject, sentence structure, or word choice, or by a combination of these features of formal communication?

This paper has stressed the fact that women as speakers have been largely ignored in communication research, but that there is a sizable amount of information that can be called folk-view: how people think women speak or how people think women should speak. Although these beliefs will make useful bases for hypotheses for research, it must be realized that women are individuals. Researchers interested in studying the speech of women as women (not as part of the category termed "man"—said to be an inclusive term but all too often actually meaning "male") must be careful not to make the error of grouping all women together. Labov and Basil Bernstein have made linguistics conscious of the necessity of recognizing the socio-economic status of speakers. The origin and race of women speakers might be important factors which bring diversity into the larger category of "women's speech." Age may be another important interacting factor—as religion might be.[37]

Margaret Mead has suggested that we need to try to disabuse our minds of assuming stereotypes to be fact and rather to begin asking some "open-ended exploratory questions" about males and females in our society (pp. 135–136). This paper suggests that some of these questions might be derived from those very stereotypes, the folk linguistics of speech that exist in our society.

Ms. Kramer *is Instructor of Speech Communication at the University of Illinois. This essay is a revised version of a paper which was presented at the annual meeting of the International Communication Association in Montreal, April 25–28, 1973.*

Notes

1 Margaret Mead, *Male and Female* (New York: William Marrow, 1949), p. 8.
2 Wayne Dickerson has suggested that the term "genderlects" be used to describe such systems. Braij Kachru has suggested "sexlects."
3 Paul Furley, "Men's and Women's Languages," *The American Catholic Sociological Review*, 5 (Oct. 1944), 218–23.
4 Mary R. Haas, "Men's and Women's Speech in Koasati," in *Language in Culture and Society*, ed. Dell Hymes (New York: Harper & Row, 1964), pp. 230–231.
5 J. G. Frazer, *The Golden Bough*, I (London: Macmillan, 1900), 404–441.
6 Otto Jespersen, *Language: Its Nature, Development, and Origin* (London: Allen & Unwin, 1922), p. 237.
7 John L. Fischer, "Social Influences on the Choice of a Linguistic Variant," in *Language in Culture and Society*, p. 484.
8 Roger Shuy, "Sex as a Factor in Sociolinguistic Research," Center for Applied Linguistics, Washington, D.C., 1969. (Mimeographed.)
9 William Labov, *The Social Stratification of English in New York City* (Washington, D.C.: Center for Applied Linguistics, 1966), pp. 310–314.
10 Lewis Levine and Harry J. Crockett, Jr., "Speech Variation in a Piedmont Community: Postvocalic r," in *Explorations in Sociolinguistics*, ed. Stanley Lieberson (The Hague: Mouton, 1966), pp. 76–98, *passim*.
11 Peter Trudgill, "Sex, Covert Prestige, and Linguistic Change in the Urban British English of Norwich," *Language in Society*, 1 (Oct. 1972), 179–195.
12 Jacqueline Sachs, Philip Lieberman, and Donna Erickson, "Anatomical and Cultural Determinants of Male and Female Speech," in *Language Attitudes: Current Trends and Prospects*, ed. Roger Shuy and Ralph Fasold (Washington, D.C.: Georgetown Univ. Press, 1973), pp. 74–84.
13 Philip Goldberg, "Are Women Prejudiced against Woman?" *Trans-action*, 5 (Apr. 1968), 28–30.
14 Judy Kester, mentioned in "In Other Words," *Chicago Sun-Times*, 7 May 1972. Another comment on this subject is made by Connie E. Eble, "How the Speech of Some Is More Equal than Others," Univ. of North Carolina (mimeographed).
15 Marion Wood, "The Influence of Sex and Knowledge of Communication Effectiveness on Spontaneous Speech," *Word*, 22 (Apr.–Aug.–Dec. 1966), 112–137.
16 Shulamith Firestone, *The Dialectic of Sex* (New York: William Morrow, 1970), p. 100.
17 See Ronald Goldman, "Cultural Influences on the Sex Ratio in the Incidence of Stuttering," *American Anthropologist*, 69 (Feb. 1967), 78–81.
18 Robert Kibler, Larry Barker, and Donald Cegala, "Effect of Sex on Comprehension and Retention," *Speech Monographs*, 37 (Nov. 1970), 287–292.
19 Sally McCracken, "Comprehension for Immediate Recall of Time-Compressed Speech as a Function of the Sex and Level of Activation of the Listener" (abstract), *Speech Monographs*, 36 (Aug. 1969), 308–309. Robert N. Bostrom and Alan P. Kemp, "Type of Speech, Sex of Speaker, and Sex of Subject as Factors Influencing Persuasion," *Central States Speech Journal*, 20 (Win. 1969), 245–251.
20 Henry M. Hoenigswald, "A Proposal for the Study of Folk-Linguistics," in *Sociolinguistics*, ed. William Bright (The Hague: Mouton, 1966), pp. 16–20.
21 Enid Haupt, *The New Seventeen Book of Etiquette and Young Living* (New York: David McKay, 1970), pp. 101–102.
22 Meredith D. Gall, Amos K. Hobby, and Kenneth H. Craik, "Non-Linguistic Factors in Oral Language Productivity," *Perceptual and Motor Skills*, 29 (Dec. 1969), 871–874.
23 Mary Ritchie Key, "The Role of Male and Female in Children's Books—Dispelling All Doubt," *Wilson Library Bulletin*, 46 (Oct. 1971), 170.
24 Robin Lakoff, "Language and Woman's Place," *Language in Society*, 2 (Apr. 1973), 54.
25 See Emily Post, *Etiquette* (New York: Funk & Wagnalls, 1960), pp. 39–40; and Haupt, p. 104.
26 Letty Cottin Pogrebin, "Down with Sexist Upbringing," *Ms*, Spr. 1972, p. 28.

27 Marya Mannes, "Women Are Equal, But—," in *Current Thinking and Writing,* ed. Joseph Bachelor, Ralph Henry, and Rachel Salisbury (New York: Appleton–Century–Crofts, 1969), p. 25.

28 Quoted by Mary Ritchie Key, "Linguistic Behavior of Male and Female," *Linguistics,* 88 (15 Aug. 1972), 19.

29 J. L. Dillard, "The Validity of Black English," *Intellectual Digest,* Dec. 1972, p. 42,

30 Margaret Cussler, *The Woman Executive* (New York: Harcourt, Brace, & World, 1958), p. 67.

31 Mary Ellmann, *Thinking about Women* (New York: Harcourt, Brace & World, 1968).

32 James B. Greenough and George L. Kittredge, *Words and Their Ways in English Speech* (1901; rpt. New York: Macmillan, 1914).

33 Stuart Flexner, "Preface" to the *Dictionary of American Slang* (New York: Crowell, 1960), p. xii.

34 Julia Stanley, "The Semantic Features of the Machismo Ethic in English," University of Georgia, 1972. (Mimeographed.)

35 Theodor Reik, "Men and Women Speak Different Languages," *Psychoanalysis,* 2 (Spr.–Sum. 1954), 15.

36 "The Language of the Novel," in *Middlemarch: Critical Approaches to the Novel,* ed. Barbara Hardy (New York: Oxford Univ. Press, 1967), pp. 63–86, *passim.*

37 This suggestion was made by Fred Hilpert.

SECTION 2

RECOVERY AND RECUPERATION

3.
COMING TO TERMS WITH RECENT ATTEMPTS TO WRITE WOMEN INTO THE HISTORY OF RHETORIC
Barbara Biesecker

Editors' Note: *This author lays down the gauntlet for feminist historiographers of rhetoric. Recognizing the value of recovering and recuperating female rhetorical figures, the author cautions scholars that the feminist rhetorical reclamation project must move beyond "female tokenism" into redefinitions of "rhetor" and "rhetorical success" as we interrogate the assumptions of a rhetorical "tradition."*

An increasing number of rhetorical critics and theorists have begun to renegotiate their relationship to the history of the discipline.[1] Indeed, many of us have found it necessary to question some of our discipline's most basic theoretical assumptions as we have understood that the rhetorical histories that emerge out of and are shaped by those assumptions have consequences both for the practices of our professional everyday lives and for the lives of our students.[2] Here I think two examples will suffice. The first example is an extract taken from Gerard Hauser's *Introduction to Rhetorical Theory*, a book that deserves serious attention for many reasons, not the least of which is that it is currently being used by many teachers for the express purpose of initiating undergraduate and graduate students to the discipline. The second extract is pulled from the first volume of Karlyn Kohrs Campbell's *Man Cannot Speak for Her.* I have chosen to use this source as I am persuaded that the intent of Campbell's volumes is to supplement, if not to subvert, the received tradition that Hauser's work represents.

Selection One:

> The Greeks developed public deliberation, or the practice of rhetoric as the means to achieving cooperation.... Every citizen might raise his voice confident that his views would be weighed in the whole process of assembly deliberation. The program of public deliberation did not establish a class of leaders blessed with special authority to make decisions, nor did it single out a special group whose opinions were esteemed as inherently superior in worth ... In the democratic assembly, many voices were heard. Each spoke as a partisan.[3]

Barbara Biesecker, "Coming to Terms with Recent Attempts to Write Women into the History of Rhetoric." *Philosophy & Rhetoric* 25 (1992): 140–61.

Selection Two:

> Men have an ancient and honorable rhetorical history. Their speeches and writings, from
> antiquity to the present, are studied and analyzed by historians and rhetoricians. . . . Women
> have no parallel rhetorical history. Indeed, for much of their history women have been
> prohibited from speaking, a prohibition reinforced by such powerful cultural authorities as
> Homer, Aristotle, and Scripture. . . . As a rhetorical critic I want to restore one segment of
> the history of women.[4]

As feminists, we cannot not want to be on the side of Campbell's revisionist history.
It is a carefully documented narrative that makes all-too-visible the ideological agenda
at work in Hauser's seemingly transparent and natural history of Rhetoric. By exposing
the manner in which decidedly male experiences have been made to stand in for the
history of Rhetoric as such, Campbell manages to bring the discipline and our own
self-understandings to crisis. Indeed, having read Campbell's book, we cannot but be
compelled to rethink our roles both in and outside the classroom, as Hauser's implicit
claim—that the glory of our origins that is also our end justifies our contemporary
practices—is radically undone.

Of course, Campbell is not alone in her attempt to refigure the history of the discipline. As Carole Spitzack and Kathryn Carter have recently pointed out,[5] and as Karen
Foss and Sonja Foss writing before them would agree,[6] recent critical essays seeking to
discredit the myth that "Man" is Rhetoric's hero by writing women into its history find
precedence in a relatively prodigious past. Yet even as we congratulate these critics for
having taken a decisive step toward eradicating decades of cultural misrepresentation,
we must also, Spitzack and Carter point out, caution against the potentially debilitating
consequence of their work: female tokenism. Adrienne Rich, speaking to the students
of Smith College in 1979, framed the problem of female tokenism in the following way:

> There's a false power which masculine society offers to a few women who "think like men"
> on condition that they use it to maintain things as they are. This is the meaning of female
> tokenism: the power withheld from the vast majority of women is offered to few, so that it
> may appear that any truly qualified woman can gain access to leadership, recognition, and
> reward; hence that justice based on merits actually prevails. The token woman is encour-
> aged to see herself as different from most other women, as exceptionally talented and
> deserving; and to separate herself from the wider female condition; and she is perceived by
> "ordinary" women as separate also: perhaps even as stronger than themselves.[7]

Like Rich, Spitzack and Carter argue that the project of situating "great women speakers" alongside their better-known male counterparts cuts two ways. On the one hand,
the inclusion of a few great women "lends richness and balance to research practices"
in the discipline; on the other hand, such projects "can easily support the presumption
that the *majority* of women cannot rival male accomplishments."[8] That is to say, even
as they recognize the importance of writing women's contributions into the history of
Rhetoric, thereby acknowledging the simple fact that women were not mere spectators
of but vital participants in an oratorical tradition, Spitzack and Carter refuse to cover

over what they understand to be the concomitant risk entailed in such an enterprise. While providing a heritage that potentially enables women to "seize and control their own creative resources,"[9] the inclusion of particular texts spoken by women serve, albeit unwittingly, to perpetuate the damaging fiction that most women simply do not have what it takes to play the public, rhetorical game.

While I agree with Spitzack and Carter that one must move with caution against female tokenism, I am also compelled to wonder at what point circumspection leads to silence, stagnation, and inactivity. Is it not the case that at a certain cultural-historical juncture one must risk the potentially dangerous side-effects of female tokenism so as to instate to their rightful place women's rhetorical achievements? Doesn't the mere inclusion of women's texts in the rhetorical canon make a difference—by destabilizing the subject of rhetorical history that up to this point has been exclusively male, by challenging the suggestion that masculinity and subjectivity are co-extensive notions? Should we not take our chances given that, as Teresa de Laurentis put it, a "'room of one's own' may not avail women's intellection if the texts one has in it are written in the languages of male tradition"?[10]

To all of these questions I must respond with a "yes and no." But I respond with a "yes and no" neither because I wish to occupy the safe middle ground of a dialectical sublation, nor because I am seeking to take refuge in a less than rigorous deconstructionist dodge. I say "yes and no" because I want to underscore yet another effect of attempts to insert "great women speakers" into the official record we call the canon, an effect that utterly escapes our detection as we weigh only the risks of female tokenism.

I think it is important to notice that recent attempts to render the discipline more equitable by supplementing the canon with texts spoken by women have something like a relationship with what only a few decades ago was coined as affirmative action.[11] In the socioeconomic sphere, of course, affirmative action is the institutionally sanctioned and insured measure through which a history of injustice is to be rectified. Specific structural mechanisms are set in place to provide equal opportunity to members of disadvantaged or marginal groups. Transposed to the cultural sphere and, more particularly, to the classroom, affirmative action translates into a three-pronged imperative: new knowledges must be read, taught, and learned. In quite practical terms, this means that course syllabi, comprehensives lists and curriculum requirements must all be revised. Yet when this strategy (useful as it may be in the social sphere) is made to operate in the cultural sphere, the project misfires. Why do I say that the project misfires since, as I noted earlier, thanks to pioneer feminist projects, a gender difference does seem to be challenging the identity of the field and history of Rhetoric?

What I find objectionable in the affirmative action approach to the production and distribution of knowledges—an approach not unrelated to, but, in fact, one of the conditions of female tokenism—is its underhanded perpetuation of "cultural supremacy." When deployed in the cultural sphere, affirmative action signifies nothing less than the power of the center to affirm certain voices and to discount others.[12] Despite its ostensible purpose—to move toward multiculturalism by adding new items to an ever-expanding list of "great works," the affirmative action agenda conserves the putative authority of the center by granting it license to continue to produce official explanations by the designation of what is and what is not worthy of inclusion. Thus, even as the list of "great works" expands over time, the criteria for determining that list need not change. Indeed, for the most part the criteria have remained firmly in place.

This line of thinking compels us to raise a question that the strategy of inclusion does not: What are the criteria against which any particular rhetorical discourse is measured in order to grant or deny its place in the canon? One way into this question is to recognize that the rhetorical canon is a system of cultural representation whose present form is predicated on and celebrates the individual. It is a list of proper names signifying the exceptional accomplishments of particular individuals over time: from Gorgias, Isocrates, Cicero, and Augustine to John Winthrop, Jonathan Edwards, Susan B. Anthony, and Martin Luther King. To each of these proper names corresponds a text or set of texts, and between them is marked a certain kind of originating function that wins the individual membership in a distinguished ensemble of individuals. But what is the problem with a criterion that applies equally to all, a criterion that purportedly crosses lines of gender, race, and class and asks only that an individual, any individual, "generate rhetorical works of extraordinary power and appeal"?[13] Nothing less than the fact that a system of cultural representation that coheres around the individual subject, that is both master of her- or himself and of her or his discourse, is not politically disinterested. Already entailed in the valorization of the individual is a mechanics of exclusion that fences out a vast array of collective rhetorical practices to which there belongs no proper name. The exaltation of individual rhetorical actions is secured by way of the devaluing of collective rhetorical practices which, one cannot fail to note, have been the most common form of women's intervention in the public sphere. In short, the danger in taking an affirmative action approach to the history of Rhetoric is that while we may have managed to insert some women into the canon (and, again, this is no small thing), we will have not yet begun to challenge the underlying logic of canon formation and the uses to which it has been put that have written the rhetorical contributions of collective women into oblivion.

Karlyn Campbell's most recent, and I think landmark, attempt is not immune to such a critique. To be sure, like her predecessors, she plots her revisionist history around the model of the individual speaking subject. Effective rhetorical discourse, that is to say rhetoric worthy of inclusion in the canon, is the outcome of strategic choices made among available techniques of persuasion on the part of an autonomous individual. Indeed, in organizing her book as a series of cameo appearances by extraordinary women who, "on occasion, found symbolic means of responding" so as to "show that the artistry of this rhetoric generated enduring monuments to human thought and creativity,"[14] Campbell's revisionist history of Rhetoric resolidifies rather than undoes the ideology of individualism that is the condition of possibility for the emergence of the received history of Rhetoric.

So far I have suggested that we must be vigilant against the desire to interpret all gestures toward inclusion as inherently revolutionary or *necessarily* disruptive of the status quo. More specifically, I have tried to argue that a feminist rewriting of the history of Rhetoric that founds itself on the mandate to secure a place in the canon for "great women speakers" is simply not enough. The mere accumulation of texts does not guarantee that our ways of knowing will change when the grounds for their inclusion and, likewise, our way of deciphering them, remain the same. But if a decidedly feminist revisionary history of Rhetoric hinges at least in part on our articulating an alternative to the ideology of individualism that has up until now enabled the discipline to identify "the great works," what criterion should take its place?

It is interesting that, if Karlyn Campbell's most recent work from which I draw my representative generalization marks a certain orthodoxy and ultimately disabling cultural politics operative in the field, it is her earliest work in this area that gestures toward an alternative. In 1973, Campbell published her now famous article entitled "The Rhetoric of Women's Liberation: An Oxymoron."[15] One of the most striking features of this early essay is the way in which it begins to challenge the presumed wisdom and general applicability of traditional theoretical models and customary modes of rhetorical understanding. By taking concrete instances of women's liberation discourse (however narrowly conceived) as her point of departure, Campbell attempts to cut loose from the prevailing tendency on the part of critics to posit rhetorical categories on an a priori basis. Campbell's boldest stroke takes the form of an explicit and seemingly uncompromising challenge to Lloyd Bitzer's theorization of the audience. Given the history of the disenfranchisement of women, Campbell argues persuasively, "it is difficult to view them as an audience, i.e., as persons who see themselves as potential agents of change;"[16] unlike other rhetorics, rhetorics directed toward the liberation of women must take as their point of departure "the radical affirmation of new identities."[17]

A sensitivity to the constraints that the grafting of theoretical models onto specific discourses imposes on rhetorical analysis is what gives Campbell's essay its critical edge. Yet it is an edge that has been blunted by the force of the tradition within which it was produced: though she identifies the limits of Bitzer's conceptualization of audience by reopening the question of (female) identity and subjectivity, her uncritical mobilization of the concept-metaphor "consciousness raising" as the paradigmatic expression of the rhetoric of women's liberation marks the essay's complicity with precisely those normative theorizations that it seeks to oppose. Taken quite literally, "consciousness raising" signifies the project of bringing to the surface something that is hidden, the task of making manifest something that is concealed or covered over. Under-pinned or at least burdened by the whole history of psychoanalytic theory, Campbell's use of the term participates in a depth hermeneutics that posits an irreducible essence inhabiting the subject and a tropology of the psyche that writes presence as consciousness, self-presence conceived within the opposition of consciousness to unconsciousness.[18] Out of this tropology comes Campbell's notion of audience and her understanding of the overriding exigence that the rhetoric of women's liberation must address. The discourse must, as she puts it, "violate the reality structure," "transcend alienation to create 'sisterhood,'" "indeed must produce "a radical form of consubstantiality" that transcends "differences in age, education, income, etc."[19] Here "consciousness raising" marks the deliberate attempt to recover the potential originary space *before* the sign "woman"; in staging the specifically feminist project in recuperative terms, rhetoric is understood, once again, as a purposive act that shuttles between consummate, sovereign, though perhaps estranged, identities.

Of course, Campbell is right to insist that women's access to subjectivity is indispensable to a political program that seeks, above all else, the empowerment of women. However, following the cues of both Jacques Lacan (who has taught us to be more than a bit skeptical of "the talking cure") and feminists working between the post-Freudian and materialist perspectives (who have warned us of the perils of sifting women's problems through pathologizing filters[20]), I must admit that I find less than satisfactory the conceptualization of history and social change implied in Campbell's reformulation of female subjectivity, a conceptualization wherein the ideology of individualism and the old patriarchal alignments are reinscribed. In Campbell's work, the possibility for social change is thought to be more or less a function of each individual woman's capacity to throw off the mantle of her own self-perpetuated oppression, to recognize her *real* self-interests (interests that are her own *as* a woman and, thus, are shared by all women) and to intervene on behalf of those interests. No doubt, Campbell's promotion of a kind of self-help program plays straight into the hands of the old order that has consistently sought to deflect critical attention away from those structures of oppression larger than individual consciousness and will. In Campbell's formulation, positivity lines up with activity, while passivity and with it femininity are identified as negative.

If feminists working in the history of Rhetoric could deconstruct the all-too-easy bipolarization of the active and the passive, we would go a long way toward dismantling the ideology of individualism that monumentalizes some acts and trivializes others. Not only would we realize that any active intervention is constituted by the so-called passive but, also, that the passive is inhabited by an active potential, since it *is*, to borrow and turn a phrase from Kenneth Burke, the substance of the active. Thus if, as feminists, we want to produce something more than the story of a battle over the right to individualism between men and women, we might begin by taking seriously post-structuralist objections to the model of human subjectivity that has served as the cognitive starting point of our practices and our histories. Indeed, following Campbell's initial impulse to reexamine and expand "the presumptions underlying symbolic approaches to human behavior,"[21] I want to argue that the post-structuralist interrogation of the subject and its concomitant call for the *radical* contextualization of all rhetorical acts can enable us to forge a new storying of our tradition that circumvents the veiled cultural supremacy operative in mainstream histories of Rhetoric. More specifically, I want to suggest that the strategic appropriation of post-structuralism on the part of feminists sets up the conditions for a "new" definition of *techne* that considerably alters our way of reading and writing history by displacing the active/passive opposition altogether.

A Reencounter with Post-Structuralism

As R. Radhakrishnan has recently argued, what is singular about post-structuralism is its interrogation of identity.[22] Unlike structuralism, Marxism, or Freudian psychoanalysis, post-structuralism attacks identity as such and not just particular and isolated forms or versions of identity. For example, in several of his works, Derrida challenges explicitly the presumed integrity of the phenomenological subject, the subject of the humanistic tradition that, as I hinted above and have argued elsewhere, underwrites most contemporary rhetorical analysis, feminist or otherwise.[23] Derrida launches a deconstruction of the subject by taking seriously the possibility that the human being, like writing and speech, is constituted by *différance*, as "starting from/in relation to time as difference, differing and deferral."[24] By way of an elaborate argument that I will not attempt to represent here, Derrida shows us how the identity of any subject, like the value of any element in a given system, is structured by and is the effect of its place in an economy of differences. In short, against an irreducible humanist essence of subjectivity, Derrida advances a subjectivity which, structured by *différance* and thus always differing from itself, is forever in process, indefinite, controvertible.

To claim that a movement outside the prisonhouse of the essentialist subject is necessary for writing a new history of Rhetoric is not to say that there are no subjects. As Gayatri Chakravorty Spivak has pointed out on more than one occasion, it is possible to read in Derridean deconstruction quite another story about the subject. Put succinctly, it runs as follows: "The subject is always centered. The critic is obliged to notice persistently that this centering is an 'effect,' shored up within indeterminate boundaries that can only be understood as determining."[25] By this reckoning, the presence of an "I" (that is not, however, identical to an "I"'s self-presence—and this is why we must not forget the previous story) records something like the provisional stabilization of a temporality and a spacing that always and already exceeds it. Thus, subjectivity in the general sense is to be deciphered as an historical articulation, and particular real-lived identities are to be deciphered as constituted and reconstituted in and by an infinitely pluralized weave of interanimating discourses and events.

I have drawn attention to Derrida's doubled morphology of the subject because I believe it can enable us to begin to write a quite different history of Rhetoric. Were we to follow the trajectory of Derrida's interrogation of the subject, keeping one foot firmly anchored in the former account (the subject is never coincident with or identical to itself and, thus, is open to change) and the other foot in the latter account (the subject is always centered, but that centering can only be understood as an effect of its place in a larger economy of discourses), it becomes possible to forge a storying that shifts the focus of historical inquiry from the question "who is speaking," a question that confuses the subjects of history with the agents for history, to the question "what play of forces made it possible for a particular speaking subject to emerge?" Nonetheless, by claiming Derridean deconstruction for a new history of Rhetoric that begins by thinking the subject as "historical through and through," I am not suggesting that we can find in Derrida's work anything like a general theory of history or a coherent set of directives for writing one. In fact, if such a project is not to be given up, if we are to broach the question that Derrida enables us to ask—"what play of forces made it possible for a particular speaking subject to emerge?"—we might find it useful to slip from Derridean deconstruction to Foucaultian archaeology. Perhaps it is worth remarking that this turn to Foucault seeks, as did the prior discussion of Derrida, to identify only a few aspects of his work that may help us to write a feminist history of Rhetoric that averts the shortcomings of the affirmative action approach.

In a certain sense, the definitive characteristic of Foucault's middle project, *The Archaeology of Knowledge*, is its insistence upon relating the radical reconceptualization of the subject, characteristic of post-Sartrean French thought, to forms of social organization that he calls "discursive formations." But what are these "discursive formations"? And what is the subject's relation to them? To be sure, Foucault mobilizes the concept-metaphor "discursive formation" in order to work against the widespread tendency amongst social theorists to presume that the socius is operated by a coherent logic that can account for all relations and practices.[26] Indeed, in the chapter on discursive formations, Foucault emphasizes time and again that the socius is a discontinuous space constituted by heterogeneous fields of objects operated by a "body of anonymous historical rules,"[27] a nonstatic arena woven of dispersed "I-slots."

Now it is important to note that while these "I-slots," most often referred to as subject-positions, are neither essential nor constant, they do, at the same time, assure a certain kind of being-in-the-world by "determining what position[s] can and must be occupied by any individual if he is to be a subject" at all. Here Foucault emphasizes the discursivity of the "I" since the condition for its making sense is a function of its positioning in the "stated." Thus for Foucault, identity is defined by way of one's relation to or place in a network of social, political, cultural, and economic practices that are provisional (in the sense of historical and not essential), discontinuous (in the sense of nontotalizable), and normative (in the sense of rule governed and governing).

Like Derrida, Foucault conceives subjectivity and identity as made available by, rather than existing outside of or prior to, language and representation. Of the subject and its relation to structure, Foucault writes:

> So the subject of the statement should not be regarded as identical with the author of the formulation. . . . He is not in fact the cause, origin or starting-point of the phenomenon of the written or spoken articulation of a sentence; nor is it that meaningful intention which, silently anticipating words, orders them like the visible body of its intuition; it is not the constant, motionless, unchanging focus of a series of operations that are manifested, in turn, on the surface of discourse through the statements. It is a particular, vacant place that may in fact be filled by different individuals. . . . If a proposition, a sentence, a group of signs can be called a "statement," it is not therefore because, one day, someone happened to speak them or put them into some concrete form of writing; it is because the position of the subject can be assigned.[28]

If both Foucault and Derrida redefine the speaking subject as a locus of effects,[29] what distinguishes Foucault's thinking on the subject from Derrida's is the former's refusal to decipher subjectivity and identity as infinitely or indefinitely pluralized: "The individual is not to be conceived as a sort of elementary nucleus, a primitive atom, a multiple and inert material on which power comes to fasten or against which it happens to strike. . . . In fact, it is already one of the prime effects of power that certain bodies, certain gestures, certain discourses, certain desires, come to be identified and constituted as individuals."[30] Where Derrida would speak of the ever-shifting limits that persistently thwart our desire to make the subject cohere in any final sense, Foucault would chart the localized rules and mechanisms of disciplinary power that insure the production and reproduction of differentially situated subjects in a nonstatic but hierarchically organized space. Indeed, Foucault himself seems interested in marking this constitutive difference between his own work and Derrida's. At the end of the second edition of *Madness and Civilization*, he writes:

> Today Derrida is the most decisive representative of a system in its final glory; the reduction of discursive practice to textual traces; the elision of the events that are produced there in order to retain nothing but marks for a reading; the invention of voices behind texts in order not to have to analyse the modes of implication of the subject in discourse; assigning the spoken and the unspoken in the text to an originary place in order not to have to reinstate the discursive practices in the field of transformations where they are effectuated. . . . it is not at all necessary to search elsewhere, for exactly here, to be sure not in the words, but in the words as erasures, in their *grill*, "the meaning of being" speaks itself.[31]

Though Foucault himself may be written both too much and too little by Derrida,[32] suffice it to say here that Foucault's commitment to demonstrating how specific practices not only constitute distinct forms of selfhood but normalize them into being is what lends his work its distinctive ethos.

Feminist and non-feminist historians alike have claimed that Foucault's decisive contribution to our understanding of social economies and their conditions of existence and emergence, is encapsulated in his theory of subject positions, a theory that resolutely challenges the assumption that ideology can be demystified since "individuals are not only the inert or consenting target of ideology and power but are always also the elements of their articulation."[33] But if individuals emerge always and already as particular lived-expressions of the limits and possibilities of a discursive formation, if, that is to say, subject positions are not a matter of choice but of assignation, is there then no possibility for human agency, rhetorical intervention, social change? To be sure, it is on the issue of human agency that Foucault's work has seemed to prove less than palatable to many critics. Nancy Hartstock's commentary may be taken as somewhat paradigmatic of a generalizable disappointment: "Foucault's is a world in which things move, rather than people, a world in which subjects become obliterated or, rather, recreated as passive objects, a world in which passivity or refusal represent the only possible choices."[34] If, as Foucault suggests, "power is everywhere," then it seems only reasonable to conclude that there is nowhere out of which anything like an insurrection may gain its foothold.[35] Set over and against the ubiquitous and hegemonizing effects of power, the very notion of resistance seems nothing more than a fragile proposition.

It would be difficult to object to this gloss on Foucault's project; it is quite true, as Frances Bartkowski has convincingly argued, that "even though he acknowledges quite clearly that 'you can't have one without the other,' Foucault never gives us as committed a look at resistance as we most certainly get at power."[36] Having said this much, however, it seems unwise to suggest, as Hardstock does, that the pressing demand for real social change obliges us to rule Foucault, indeed all post-structuralist theory, out of court or to presume, as Blair and Cooper do, that we can simply cover over the problem of human agency by refashioning Foucault into a humanist.[37] To preserve one's own emancipatory projects or salvage one's own disciplinary identity by ignoring Foucault's work altogether or repressing those aspects of it that make us uneasy with ourselves is myopic and politically naive.

Even though Foucault does not write at great length about resistance, there is one thing he makes abundantly clear: we must hold against the temptation to construe resistance as a structure that stands over and against power, as an event subsequent to the establishment of power. Resistance is always and already a structure of possibility within power and, it should be added, power is always and already a structure of possibility within resistance. Power and resistance are two sides of the same coin and, thus, emerge in tandem. But from where? Out of what? In a phrase, Foucault responds, "of something other than itself."[38]

The implicit challenge to fill out or specify the "other" that is the reserve of power and resistance has already been taken up by a handful of theorists and critics who, in contrast to Hardstock and Blair and Cooper, have attempted to articulate a theory of resistance based on Foucault's "anti-humanism." These critics productively regraft Foucault's notion of subject-positions along the lines of a conflict of interpretations schemata. Given that subjects emerge at the heterogeneous intersection of *multiple* and, presumably incompatible, interpellations—race, gender, and class—they cannot be made to cohere as Subjects. Hence, by reading the subject itself as a site of multiple and contestatory inscriptions, one can, they argue, locate a reservoir of revolutionary potential in the gaps, fissures and slippages of the nonidentical "I".[39]

Though I am more than sympathetic to the claim that lived-experience is a trying, oftentimes exasperating, oftentimes failed, exercise in self-negotiation, I do not think such experience can be exploited as the basis for a theory of change. Hence, my objection to the attempt is not that such experience fails to ring true but, rather, that "the theory of pluralized 'subject effects' gives an illusion of undermining subjective sovereignty while . . . providing a cover for this subject of knowledge."[40] Indeed, it seems to me that such a formula can make sense only if the human being is presumed, however unwittingly, to be motivated by an a priori drive for symmetry, a presumption fearfully analogous to Freud's pleasure principle: at the moment wherein the subject's knowledges become out of sync, at the point upon which the wear and tear of unsynchronized knowing congeals into intolerable epistemic violence, the subject's will-to-coherence manifests itself as a precarious sublation whose name is resistance. As Paul Smith put it in a recent book that cogently argues for this view, "the colligation of subject-positions, far from entailing a fixed or cerned 'subject,' is effected precisely by the principle which stands against unification—negativity, the forgotten fourth term of Hegel's dialectics."[41] In short, resistance is taken to be the real-lived outcome of a subject who, knowing that she does not know, is moved by an always and already unfulfilled drive to "get it together." But must the possibilities for resistance and social change be secured by scrupulously resurrecting an ontological guarantee under the guise of an epistemo-logical imperative? I think not. In fact, were we to allow certain aspects of Derrida's doubled morphology of the subject to interrupt Foucault's thinking on individuals-in-power, a more promising direction for theorizing resistance could be developed.[42] That is to say, because I believe Foucault's take on the subject-in-power is both instructive (in arguing that identity is manufactured and sustained through specifiable discursive means) and limited (in failing to adequately theorize the resources of and possibilities for social change), 1 want to press the issue of resistance to a further limit within the Foucaultian frame, once again using Derridean deconstruction as my lever.

Retooling *Techne*

Earlier in the essay I argued that what lends Foucault's work its particular ethos is his commitment to demonstrating how specific practices not only constitute distinct forms of selfhood but normalize them into being. What I should like to emphasize here is that the Foucaultian analyses of the operations of power circulate almost exclusively within, indeed are orchestrated by, a metaphorics of space. In Foucault's work, space is everything. With the precision of the cartographer, Foucault takes his reader from the leprosariums of the High Middle Ages to the Saint-Luke Hospital founded in 1751, from the radical reorganization of the *Maison de Force* to Bentham's Panopticon, from the Victorian bedroom to the analyst's couch. With him, we trace the proliferation of disciplines and the internal necessities that open up the frontiers of knowledge and chart the progressive interiorization of madness and sexuality. Indeed, in Foucault's hands, the history of the West is brilliantly divided, anatomized, and mapped as a landscape whose configuration is deciphered almost exclusively in terms of the constellation of objects: walls, irons, windows, mirrors, icons, bodies.

But what would happen if the Foucaultian project was deliberately made to incorporate rather than neglect one of Derrida's pivotal insights—namely, that the subject that is always centered is nonetheless outstripped by a *temporality and a spacing* that always already exceeds it? I have implied it repeatedly: were this excess that never appears as such figured into the Foucaultian calculation, it would become possible for us to recognize the formidable role structure plays in the (re)constitution of subjectivities and the capacity—albeit non-intentional in the strictest sense of the term—of those subjectivities to disrupt the structure within which and through which they are differently inscribed. Indeed, the exorbitant *play of spacing* is, I would argue, the "other" that is the reserve of power and resistance; *spacing* as such "speaks the articulation of space and time, the becoming-space of time and the becoming-time of space."[43] That such a notion cannot be recognized within Foucaultian archaeology should come as no surprise since it is that very thing that cannot be reduced to the form of *presence.*

Spacing as the name of that which inaugurates the constitution of time and space, subject and object, self and other, can be related to the central problematics of this essay—power and resistance. Most important, what must be noticed is that Derrida's particular notion of spacing as an excess that is never thoroughly absorbed by and into the present cannot be thought to be an inherent property of the subject, a pure reserve or ideologically uncontaminated pocket, which assures the subversion of power. In fact, a careful reading of Derrida's work will show that the very possibility of resistance is to be found in the articulation of an act and not in the negativity of the actor. That is to say, Derrida's thinking on spacing shifts the site of resistance from the subject proper to the exorbitant possibilities of the act since spacing in this special sense is precisely that which "suspends the accomplishment or fulfillment of 'desire' or 'will'."[44] In the end, then, such a shift enables us to work within the Foucaultian framework: subjects are effects of their sociopolitical, historical, economic, and cultural contexts. It also, however, makes it possible for us to push the limits of that framework: in claiming with Foucault that individuals are manufactured and sustained through specifiable discursive means, we need not presuppose that their practices are nothing but reflections of such contexts or that their practices are thoroughly disciplined by them.

But already a finer distinction needs to be made. For if what we are trying to indicate is a certain structure of reserve that breaks open a pathway within the hegemonizing effects of power by means of an act whose effluence eludes the mastery of the acting subject, then the word *practice* simply will not do. Indeed, at least since Aristotle, who seems to have been the first to use it as a technical term, "practice" designates a purposeful doing: "I accomplish (e.g., a journey)," "I manage (e.g., state affairs)," "I do or fare (e.g., well or ill)," and, in general, "I act, I perform some activity."[45] Still, today practice is the name for an intended doing, a deliberate—often theoretically informed—activity targeted to some end: practical criticism, practical argument and reasoning, the practice of rhetoric. Thus what I am seeking to point to is not practice per se but, instead, a force or structure of breaching in practice that establishes a cleft or fissure out of which an unforeseen and undesigned transgression may ensue.

Might we not then settle upon the word *techne* as the sign for an exorbitant doing that depends upon practice but which does not obey the imperatives of practice? Here I shall state my claim directly and unequivocally: by scrupulously working within and against the grain of the the word's historically constituted semantic field, *techne* can be used to refer to a kind of "getting through" or ad hoc "making do" by a subject whose resources are necessarily located in and circumscribed by the field within which she operates, but whose enunciation, in always and already exceeding and falling short of its intending subject, harbors within it the possibility of disrupting, fragmenting, and altering the horizon of human action out of which it emerges. Now without belaboring the obvious, it should be noted that to use *techne* as a word signifying a way or means by which something gets done is not new in the proper sense of the word. As I noted above, Aristotle, and even Plato before him, had said this much. What is "new" however, is the attempt to use *techne* differently by bracketing out the ethical/moral sedimentations that have, through the history of its uses, been attributed to the word and thereby making it possible for us to refuse to grasp the agent of history as identical with her intentions.

I should perhaps emphasize that it is precisely in refusing to conflate the always already intending subject with the potentially heterogeneous and counter-hegemonic effects of action that my use of the concept-metaphor *techne* differs from the way in which Michel de Certeau mobilizes the word. In *The Practice of Everyday Life*, de Certeau makes the important distinction between *techne* as "tactic" and *techne* as "strategy." While de Certeau distinguishes these two modalities of human action "according to whether they bet on place or on time," both are taken to be interventions whose implications can be calculated in advance.[46] Like Levi-Strauss's *bricoleur,* de Certeau's practician tinkers with the rules and tools of the established order and in so doing "establishes a degree of plurality and creativity" within "the place where he has no choice but to live."[47] These deliberate modes of use or re-use are simultaneously, for de Certeau, the modes of historical change. He writes, for example,

> ... even when they were subjected, indeed even when they accepted their subjection, the Indians often used the laws, practices, and representations that were imposed on them by force or by fascination to ends other than those of their conquerors; they made something else out of them; they subverted them from within—not by rejecting them or by transforming them (though that occurred as well), but by many different ways of using them in the service of rules, customs or convictions foreign to the colonization which they could not escape. They metaphorized the dominant order: they made it function in another register. They remained other within the system which they assimilated and which assimilated them externally. They diverted it without leaving it.[48]

Contrary to de Certeau, then, my own use of *techne* seeks to mark out a structure of possibility in action that never entered the space and temporality of the intending consciousness upon which its own legibility depends. Contrary to de Certeau, I am suggesting that if we use *techne* as a word signifying a way, manner or means whereby something is gained, without any sense of art or cunning,[49] then *techne* signifies a bringing-about in the doing-of on the part of an agent that does not necessarily take herself to be anything like a subject of historical or, as in the above instance, cultural change. Used in this way, *techne* displaces the active/passive binary that dominates even de Certeau's thinking on power and resistance. *Techne* points to a heterogeneous history of practices performed in the interstices between intention and subjection, choice and necessity, activity and passivity. It is, as Derrida would put, the trace of "the not-seen that opens and limits visibility."[50]

Back to History

As I see it, this essay could be summarized as a call for a gender-sensitive history of Rhetoric that, in working against the ideology of individualism by displacing the active/passive opposition, radically contextualizes speech acts. And although the historiographical approach advocated here does not deny that over time distinguishable and distinguished speaking subjects emerge, it does suggest that the conditions of possibility for their emergence must be located elsewhere. Thus, for the feminist historiographer interested in rewriting the history of Rhetoric, the plurality of practices that together constitute the everyday must be conceptualized as a key site of social transformation and, hence, of rhetorical analysis. To be sure, this is no easy task. Were the critic to take up such a project, not only would she be obliged to confront the limits of her own disciplinary expertise (deciphering "great speeches" would not be enough), she would also be forced to come to the sobering realization that little assistance is to be gained from even the most benevolent enclaves of the academy. It is not only the discipline of Rhetoric that is written by the ideology of individualism. History, History and Philosophy of Science, Philosophy, Literary Studies, Foreign Language and Literature programs, and even the more recent Women's Studies and Cultural Studies programs share that history and, thus, its burden with us. History and Philosophy of Science may be the most telling example. While scientific practice is routinely collective, historians of those practices tend to write figural histories that celebrate, indeed monumentalize, individuals.[51]

More important, perhaps, the critic taking up the project of rewriting the history of Rhetoric would be required to come to terms with rather than efface the formidable differences between and amongst women and, thus, address the real fact that different women, due to their various positions in the social structure, have available to them different rhetorical possibilities and, similarly, are constrained by different rhetorical limits. Indeed, the argument I have put forward presses for a feminist intervention into the history of Rhetoric that persistently critiques its own practices of inclusion and exclusion by relativizing rather than universalizing what Aristotle identified as "the available means of persuasion." It obliges the feminist historiographer interested in rewriting the history of Rhetoric to take on the full burden of the notion of unequal or non-synchronous development—obliges her to write the story not only of the differences between women's and men's subject (re)formation but, also, to write into that account the story of the differences between women as well. Put simply, not only would one have to declare "man cannot speak for her," one would also have to admit that no individual woman or set of women, however extraordinary, can speak for all women.

Does all of this mean, then, that we must abandon our canon, forfeit our masterpieces, renounce our tradition? Absolutely not. Even though the canon and the histories that have propped it up do not represent the way "things really were," we can learn to read them differently and, thus, teach ourselves something about who we are now or, more precisely, how we have become that which we now understand ourselves to be. Likewise, must the feminist project of retrieving texts spoken and written by women be stopped dead in its tracks? Again, I think not. For what is beginning to emerge there under the guise of information retrieval is the cathected story of what it is that we wish to become. For the academic feminist, however, that story may prove to be the most difficult of all to decipher. For in that story, we must begin to read ourselves as part and parcel of the history we so desperately seek to disown.

Rhetoric Department
The University of Iowa

Notes

1 What follows is a revised and extended version of a paper I first delivered at the 1989 Speech Communication Association meeting held in San Franscisco. I wish to thank the International Society for the History of Rhetoric and its then vice-president, Takis Poulakos, for having provided a forum for a discussion that signified, to borrow and turn Protagoras's phrase just a bit, a deliberate and collective attempt to reorder our own house. I should also like to thank Michael Calvin McGee, Bruce Gronbeck, and the director and staff at University House at the

University of Iowa for providing me with an occasion to rethink the notion of *techne* advanced here. Special thanks go to Alan Scult for having responded so carefully to my work during the summer workshop.

Finally, I wish to acknowledge formally my indebtedness to and profound respect for my teacher and friend Gayatri Chakravorty Spivak. This essay is dedicated to her.

 2 There is a steadily growing body of work dealing with the historiography of Rhetoric. Although a complete bibliography cannot be presented here, it may be useful to identify a few particularly recent and noteworthy contributions. See, for example, a special volume of *Pre/Text: A Journal of Rhetorical Theory* [8 (1987)] titled "Historiography and the Histories of Rhetorics I: Revisionary Histories." See also a special section in the *Western Journal of Speech Communication* [54 (1990)] on Rhetoric and Historiography.

 3 Gerard Hauser, *Introduction to Rhetorical Theory* (New York: Harper and Row, 1986), 20.

 4 Karlyn Kohrs Campbell, *Man Cannot Speak for Her. A Critical Study of Early Feminist Rhetoric*, Vol. I (New York: Greenwood Press, 1989), 1–13.

 5 Carole Spitzack and Kathryn Carter, "Women in Communication Studies: A Typology for Revision," *The Quarterly Journal of Speech* 73 (1987): 401–23.

 6 Karen A. Foss and Sonja K. Foss, "The Status of Research on Women and Communication," *Communication Quarterly* 31 (1983): 195–204.

 7 Adrienne Rich, *Ms.* 8. (September 1979): 43.

 8 Spitzack and Carter, 405.

 9 Dale Spender, "Women and Literary History," *The Feminist Reader. Essays in Gender and the Politics of Literary Criticism*, ed. Catherine Belsey and Jane Moore (New York: Basil Blackwell, 1989), 32.

10 Teresa de Laurentis, "The Essence of the Triangle or, Taking the Risk of Essentialism Seriously: Feminist Theory in Italy, the U.S., and Britain," *differences: A Journal of Feminist Cultural Studies* 1 (1989): 15.

11 For this very interesting connection, I am indebted to the work of Gayatri Chakravorty Spivak. See her "On Behalf of Cultural Studies," *Social Text* (forthcoming).

12 Gayatri Chakravorty Spivak, "On Behalf of Cultural Studies." For an earlier elaboration of this issue see: E.D. Hirsch Jr., Gayatri Spivak, Roger Shattuck, Jon Pareles and John Kaliski, "Who Needs the Great Works: A Debate on the Canon, Core Curricula, and Culture," *Harper's* (September 1989): 43–53.

13 Campbell, *Man Cannot Speak for Her*, 189.

14 Campbell, *Man Cannot Speak for Her*, 15.

15 Karlyn Kohrs Campbell, "The Rhetoric of Women's Liberation: An Oxymoron," *The Quarterly Journal of Speech* 59 (1973): 74–86.

16 Campbell, "The Rhetoric of Women's Liberation: An Oxymoron," 78.

17 Campbell, "The Rhetoric of Women's Liberation: An Oxymoron," 82.

18 I borrow the deconstruction of the Freudian tropology of the subject from Jacques Derrida, "Freud and the Scene of Writing," *Writing and Difference*, trails. Alan Bass (Chicago: The U of Chicago P, 1978), 196–231.

19 Campbell, "The Rhetoric of Women's Liberation: An Oxymoron," 79. What cannot go unnoticed here is that Campbell writes out the real-lived differences between women in order to establish a hegemonic feminism upon which she can then build her case. Rendering material differences as immaterial does enable her to construct what at least appears to be an elegant argument that explains a whole history of heterogeneous rhetorical practices in one fell swoop and to continue working within a traditional aesthetic axiology against which the value of particular discourses can be judged as worthy or not of canonization. This point will be taken up later in the essay.

20 Harriet Goldhor Lerner, "Problems for Profit?" *The Women's Review of Books* 8 (April 1990): 16.

21 Karlyn Kohrs Campbell, "Ontological Foundations of Rhetorical Theory," *Philosophy and Rhetoric* 3 (1970): 106.

22 R. Radhakrishnan, "Feminist historiography and post-structuralist thought: Intersections and departures," *The Difference Within: Feminism and Critical Theory*, ed. Elizabeth Meese and Alice Parker (Amsterdam/Philadelphia: John Benjamins Publishing Company, 1989), 189–206.

23 Barbara Biesecker, "Rethinking the Rhetorical Situation from Within the Thematic of Différance," *Philosophy and Rhetoric* 22 (1989): 110–30.

24 Cited in Jonathan Culler, *On Deconstruction: Theory and Criticism after Structualism* (Ithaca NY: Cornell U P, 1982), 95.

25 Gayatri Chakravorty Spivak, "Political Commitment and the Postmodern Critic," *The New Historicism*, ed. H. Aram Veeser (New York: Routledge, 1989), 279.

26 For a thorough and astute discussion of Foucault's work and its relation to social theory see Mark Cousins and Athar Hussain, *Michel Foucault* (New York: St. Martin's Press, 1984).

27 Michel Foucault, *The Archaeology of Knowledge and the Discourse on Language,* trans. A.M. Sheridan Smith (New York: Pantheon Books, 1972), 117.

28 Foucault, *Archaeology*, 95.

29 See also Michel Foucault, *The History of Sexuality, vol. 1: An Introduction,* trans. Robert Burley (New York: Pantheon, 1978), 142–43.

30 Michel Foucault, *Power/Knowledge: Selected Interviews and Other Writings,* ed. Colin Gordon, trans. Colin Gordon, Leo Marshall, John Mepham, Kate Soper (New York: Pantheon, 1980), 98.

31 Quoted in Gayatri Chakravorty Spivak, "Translator's Introduction," *of Grammatology* (Baltimore MD: The Johns Hopkins U P, 1976), lxi–lxii.

32 The point here is not to resurrect influence studies in the old way, but rather to note the uncanny play of *différance* within Foucault's own work.

33 Foucault, *Power/Knowledge,* 98.

34 Nancy Hartstock, "Foucault on Power: A Theory for Women?" *Feminism/Postmodernism,* ed. Linda J. Nicholson (New York and London: Routledge, 1990), 167.

35 As A. Belden Fields has pointed out in his article titled "In Defense of Political Economy and Systemic Analysis: A Critique of Prevailing Theoretical Approaches to the New Social Movements," even Foucault leaves us with very little to hold onto. He tells us that "power is amorphous, a machine in which everyone is caught up. And he finds that 'against these usurpations by the disciplinary mechanisms ... we find that there is no solid recourse avaliable to us today'." In *Marxism and the Interpretation of Culture,* ed. Cary Nelson and Lawrence Grossberg (Champaign IL: U of Illinois P, 1988), 144–45.

36 Frances Bartkowski, "Epistemic Drift in Foucault," *Feminism and Foucault: Reflections on Resistance,* ed. Irene Diamond and Lee Quinby (Boston: Northeastern U P, 1988), 44.

37 Carole Blair and Martha Cooper, "The Humanist Turn in Foucault's Rhetoric of Inquiry," *The Quarterly Journal of Speech* 73 (1987): 151–71. Indeed, in counter-distinction to Blair and Cooper, I do not think it necessary to dress Foucault up in the old humanist drag in order to make him useful for Rhetoric. For if rhetorical interventions are articulations of their socio-historical contexts, it does not follow that they are nothing but reflections of such contexts. This point will be taken up more fully in the following portion of the essay.

38 Michel Foucault, "The Question of Power," *Foucault Live.* trans. John Johnston, ed. Sylvere Lotinger (New York: Semiotext(e), 1989), 186.

39 See, for example, the essays collected in *Feminism and Foucault: Reflections on Resistance,* ed. Irene Diamond and Lee Quinby (Boston: Northeastern U P, 1988); Isaac D. Balbus, "Disciplining Women: Michel Foucault and the Power of Feminist Discourse," *Feminism as Critique: On the Politics of Gender,* ed. Seyla Benhabib and Drucilla Cornell (Minneapolis MN: U of Minnesota P, 1987), 11027; Judith Butler, *Gender Trouble: Feminism and the Subversion of Identity* (New York: Routledge, 1990).

40 Gayatri Chakravorty Spivak, "Can the Subaltern Speak?" *Marxism and the Interpretation of Culture,* ed. Cary Nelson and Lawrence Grossberg (Champaign IL: U of Illinois P, 1988), 271. In this essay, Spivak brings the critique of Foucault's and Deleuze's theories of pluralized "subject-effects" to bear upon the Western Intellectuals' role within contemporary relations of power.

41 Paul Smith, *Discerning the Subject* (Minneapolis MN: U of Minnesota P, 1988), 156. Smith's book may be summarized as a prolegomenon to theorizing resistance. In the book, he examines a multitude of contemporary perspectives (Derridean, Althusserian, Marxian, psychoanalytic, feminist, semiotic, anthropological) on the issue and identifies their latent deficiencies. It is interesting that Smith never offers a sustained analysis of Foucault's thinking on power and

resistance. It would not be far from the truth, however, to identify Foucault as the shadow figure that constitutes the margin of this text.

42 For a discussion of the productive notion of interruption as a cut of sorts that allows something to function, see Gayatri Chakravorty Spivak, "Practical Politics of The Open End," *The Post-Colonial Critic: Interviews, Strategies, Dialogues,* ed. Sarah Harasym (New York: Routledge, 1990), 110–11.

43 Jacques Derrida, *of Grammatology,* trans. Gayatri Chakravorty Spivak (Baltimore MD: The Johns Hopkins U P, 1976), 68.

44 Jacques Derrida, "Différance," *Margins* of *Philosophy,* trans. Alan Bass (Chicago: U of Chicago P. 1992), 8.

45 Nicholas Lobkowicz, *Theory and Practice: History of a Concept from Aristotle to Marx* (Notre Dame and London: U of Notre Dame P: 1967), 9.

46 Michel de Certeau, *The Practice of Everyday Life,* trans. Steven Rendall (Berkeley CA: U of California P, 1984), 39.

47 Michel de Certeau, *The Practice of Everyday Life,* 30.

48 Michel de Certeau, *The Practice of Everyday Life,* 31–32. 49.

49 *Oxford English Dictionary,* 1785.

50 Jacques Derrida, *of Grammatology,* 163.

51 For a critique of these histories, see, for example, Sandra Harding and Jean F. O'Barr, eds., *Sex and Scientific Inquiry* (Chicago: U of Chicago P), 1987.

4.
sex, lies, and manuscript:
REFIGURING ASPASIA IN
THE HISTORY OF RHETORIC
Cheryl Glenn

Editors' Note: *In many ways, this Braddock Award-winning essay addresses Biesecker's concerns at the same time that it mounts a spirited challenge to the dominant stories told about Western rhetoric. This essay goes a long way toward allowing us to hear Aspasia's voice coming down to us through the centuries while simultaneously striking at the foundations of masculinist rhetoric, history, and theory. In addition, this essay helped spawn a new wave of feminist investigations by scholars who responded to the author's call "to look backwards at all the unquestioned scholarship that has come before" in order to "write a more inclusive history of rhetoric."*

A fellow rhetorician recently gave me a nineteenth-century print entitled "Alcibiades and Aspasia." In beautiful detail, French artist J. L. Gerome (best-known for transfusing his journeys to the East with an exotic and erotic charm) presents Aspasia reclining seductively on Alcibiades, her hand cupping his breast, her head suspiciously near his stomach and wide-spread legs, while Alcibiades looks away from her and reaches out to grasp Socrates' hand. Thus Aspasia comes down to us as an odalisque, while Alcibiades, the object of her attention, comes to us wreathed in laurel.[1]

For the past 2500 years in Western culture, the ideal woman has been disciplined by cultural codes that require a closed mouth (silence), a closed body (chastity), and an enclosed life (domestic confinement).[2] Little wonder, then, that women have been closed out of the rhetorical tradition, a tradition of vocal, virile, public—and therefore privileged—men. Women's enclosed bodies provide lacunae in the patriarchal territory of rhetorical practices and displays, a gendered landscape, with no female rhetoricians clearly in sight. But just as recent feminist scholarship has begun to recover and recuperate women's contributions in the broad history of culture-making—in philosophy, literature, language, writing, societal structure, Christianity, history, education, reading, psychology, and gender—so too have feminist historians of rhetoric begun to re-map rhetorical history.[3] In her "Opportunities for Feminist Research in the History of Rhetoric," Patricia Bizzell accounts for various disruptions that could realign and

Cheryl Glenn, "sex, lies, and manuscript: Refiguring Aspasia in the History of Rhetoric." *College Composition and Communication* 45 (May 1994): 180–99.

regender the rhetorical terrain and anticipates the consequences of refiguring the role of women on that terrain.[4] And in "Coming to Terms with Recent Attempts to Write Women into the History of Rhetoric," Barbara Biesecker works to "forge a new storying of our tradition that circumvents the veiled cultural supremacy operative in main-stream histories of Rhetoric" (147). Such challenges not only restore women to rhetorical history and rhetorical history to women, but the restoration itself revitalizes theory by shaking the conceptual foundations of rhetorical study.[5] More than theory is, of course, at stake here. For in challenging the dominant stories of the West, feminist scholars are challenging the contemporary academic and cultural scene as well.

Aspasia of Miletus

As part of the feminist challenge to the history of rhetoric, I want to reconstruct and refigure a woman whose texts, life, and manuscripts have been annexed by men: Aspasia of Miletus. In fifth-century BC, Miletus was a Far-Eastern Greek subject-ally, a culti-vated city (in what is now Turkey) renowned for its literacy and philosophies of moral thought and nature.[6] A non-Athenian, citizen-class Greek, Aspasia arrived in Athens brilliantly educated by means that have never been fully explained.[7] Whether she was educated within a literate Milesian family or within a school for *hetaerae* (upper-class courtesans), she was exceptionally fortunate, for "there is no evidence at all that in the classical period girls attended schools, and it is entirely consistent with what we know about the seclusion of women in Athens that Athenian girls did not do so (some other cities may have been less benighted in this respect)" (Harris 96).[8] Married at an early age, Athenian women neither attended schools nor participated in the *polis*.[9] Yet the system of the *polis*, which implied both civic consciousness and "the extraordinary preeminence of speech over all other instruments of power" (Vernant, *Origins* 49), tripped the mecha-nism that powered the active diffusion and acquisition of literacy among Greek males (proper citizens). And we must assume that at least a few Athenian or Athenian-colony women of the citizen class, even those defined by good families and cultural constraints, became literate—and became conscious of civic rights and responsibilities (Cole 222–23; Harris 103, 107).[10] Aspasia of Miletus was one of those women.

As a free woman brought up in the transitional society of Asia Minor, Aspasia was freed from the rigidity of traditional marriage and from the identity that arose from that fixed role. And upon emigrating from Miletus, Aspasia emerged in Athens linked with the great statesman Pericles (fl. 442 BC), the aristocratic democrat who placed Athenian democratic power "in the hands not of a minority but of the whole people," with everyone equal before the law (Thucydides 2.37.1). Thus this non-Athenian, or "stranger-woman," was subject to Athenian law but did not have citizen rights. Nor was she accountable to the severe strictures of aristocratic Athenian women, whose activity, movement, education, marriage, and rights as citizens and property-holders were extremely circumscribed by male relatives. Aspasia could ignore—even rupture—the traditional enclosure of the female body. She could subvert Pericles' advice for ideal womanhood: "Your greatest glory is not to be inferior to what God has made you" (Thucydides 5.46.2). She could—and she did.

We know about Aspasia much the same way we know about Socrates: from secondary sources, for neither of their work exists in primary sources. Although the historical tradition has readily accepted secondary accounts of Socrates' influence, teaching, and beliefs, the same cannot be said about any female counterpart, especially a woman described so briefly and in so few accounts. But the fact that Aspasia is even mentioned by her male contemporaries is remarkable, for rare is the mention of any intellectual woman. Surviving fragments and references in the work of male authors provide tantalizing indications that the intellectual efforts of Aspasia were, at least occasionally, committed to writing—and to architecture. Aspasia is memorialized in a fresco over the portal of the University of Athens, in the company of Phidias, Pericles (on whom she leans), Sophocles, Antisthenes, Anaxagoras, Alcibiades, and Socrates.

When other women were systematically relegated to the domestic sphere, Aspasia seems to have been the only woman in classical Greece to have distinguished herself in the public domain. Her reputation as both a rhetorician and philosopher was memorialized by Plato (437–328 BC), Xenophon (fl. 450 BC), Cicero (100–43 BC), Athenaeus (fl. AD 200), and Plutarch (AD 46–c.120)—as was, of course, her enduring romantic attachment to Pericles. For those authors, Aspasia clearly represented the intelligentsia of Periclean Athens. Therefore, I want to consider seriously this historical woman who merited such documentation, for the story of her intellectual contributions to rhetoric may suggest the existence of an unrecognized subculture within that community, and the artistic and literary uses of Aspasia of Miletus may configure an emblem of Woman in rhetorical history.

The best-known source of information about Aspasia is Plutarch's *Lives of the Noble Grecians and Romans* (AD 100), an account written several hundred years after her existence. Nevertheless, all earlier mentions of Aspasia confirm this

> inquiry about the woman, what art or charming facility she had that enabled her to captivate, as she did, the greatest statesmen, and to give the philosophers occasions to speak so much about her, and that, too, not to her disparagement. That she was a Milesian by birth, the daughter of Axiochus, is a thing acknowledged. And they say it was in emulation of Thargelia, a courtesan of the old Ionian times, that she made her addresses to men of great power. Thargelia, was a great beauty, extremely charming, and at the same time sagacious; she had numerous suitors among the Greeks. . . . Aspasia, some say, was courted and caressed by Pericles upon account of her knowledge and skill in politics. Socrates himself would sometimes go to visit her, and some of his acquaintances with him; and those who frequented her company would carry their wives with them to listen to her. Her occupation was anything but creditable, her house being a home for young courtesans. . . . [I]n Plato's *Menexenus*, though we do not take the introduction as quite serious, still thus much seems to be historical, that she had the repute of being resorted to by many of the Athenians for instruction in the art of speaking. Pericles's inclination for her seems, however, to have rather proceeded from the passion of love. He had a wife that was near of kin to him, who had been married first to Hipponicus, by whom she had Callias, surnamed the Rich; and also she brought Pericles, while she lived with him, two sons, Xanthippus and Paralus. Afterwards, when they did not well agree, nor like to live together, he parted with her, with her own consent, to another man, and himself took Aspasia, and loved her with wonderful

affection; every day, both as he went out and as he came in from the market-place, he saluted and kissed her.

(200–01)

By every historical account, Aspasia ventured out into the common land, distinguishing herself by her rhetorical accomplishments, her sexual attachment to Pericles, and her public participation in political affairs. Her alleged connection with the courtesan life is only important so far as it explains her intellectual prowess and social attainments— and the surprise of an Athenian citizenry unaccustomed to (or perhaps jealous or suspicious of) a public woman.[11] As Marie Delcourt wrote in her study of Pericles:

> No one would have thought the less of Pericles for making love to young boys . . . but they were shocked by his treating [*Aspasia*] like a human being—by the fact that he *lived* with her instead of relegating her to the *gynaikeion* [women's quarters], and included his friends' wives when he issued invitations to dinner. It was all too amazing to be proper; and Aspasia was so brilliant she could not possibly be respectable.
>
> (77)

Aspasia opened an academy for young women of good families (or a school for *hetaerae*, according to some sources) that soon became a popular salon for the most influential men of the day: Socrates, Plato, Anaxagoras, Sophocles, Phidias, and Pericles.[12] Aspasia's appearance was unprecedented at a time when the construction of gender ensured that women would be praised only for such attributes as their inherent modesty, for their inborn reluctance to join males (even kinsmen) for society or dining, and for their absolute incapacity to participate as educated beings within the *polis*; at a time when a woman's only political contribution was serving as a nameless channel for the transmission of citizenship from her father to her son (Keuls 90); and at a time when Pericles pronounced that "the greatest glory of a woman is to be least talked about by men, whether they are praising . . . or criticizing" (Thucydides 5.46.2).[13] It is difficult to overemphasize how extraordinary the foreign-born Aspasia—a public woman, philosopher, political influence, and rhetorician—would have been in fifth-century BC Athenian society.

Fifth-Century BC Athens

In the burgeoning democracy of Periclean Athens, men were consciously forming human character in accordance with the new cultural ideals of military strength and justice (*diké*) tempered by the traditional concepts of *areté* (excellence of virtue, usually associated with the well-born and wealthy citizen-class).[14] Only aristocratic male citizens, equal in their *homonoia* (being of one mind), argued for civic and political *areté*, the essential principle of government by the elite—a democratic oligarchy. Yet the Platonic Socrates called for *areté* according to social role, be it male or female, free or slave (*Republic* 353b), and later Aristotle would write that both the rulers and the ruled, males and females alike, "must possess virtue" and that "all must partake of [moral virtues] . . . in such measure as is proper to each in relation to his own function" (*Politics*

1260a5; 1260a7). Thus was manifested the complex tension between the elitist *areté* and a more democratic *homonoia*.

In *The Origins of Greek Thought*, Jean-Pierre Vernant tells us that "Greek political life aimed to become the subject of public debate, in the broad daylight of the agora, between citizens who were defined as equals and for whom the state was the common undertaking" (11). Such public oratory fed the spirit of panhellenism, a doctrine sorely needed to unify the Greek city-states, just as it satiated the male appetite for public display. Vernant describes the *polis* as a system implying "the extraordinary preeminence of speech over all other instruments of power, [speech becoming] the political tool par excellence, the key to authority in the state, the means of commanding and dominating others" (49). In what would be an inestimable contribution to a democratic oratory possessed by aristocratic characteristics, former logographer (speech writer) Isocrates practiced rhetoric as a literary form, one imbued with civic, patriotic, and moral purpose. Confident in the power of words, he practiced and taught a morally influenced and rhetorically based system of general culture that propounded individual responsibility as well as political and social action. No longer were men deferring to their sovereign or the gods, who could reinforce *nomos* (beliefs, customs, laws, as enforced by universal opinion) with *physis* (nature, reality). "With this denial of the absolute status of law and moral things, the stage [was] set for a controversy between the two ... [and for drawing] different practical conclusions from it" (Gutherie III: 60). Individuals would be responsible for their own actions and collectively responsible for the actions of the democratic state, the *polis*.

The Athenian *polis* was founded upon the exclusion of women, just as, in other respects, it was founded upon the exclusion of foreigners and slaves (Vidal-Naquet 145). Although females born of Athenian-citizen parents were citizen-class and subjects within the *polis*, they were not actual citizens in any sense. Nor could foreign-born women or men hope for citizenship, regardless of their political influence, civic contributions, or intellectual ties with those in power. Therefore, noncitizens such as Protagoras, Gorgias, Prodicus, Thrasymachus, Anaxagoras, and Aspasia functioned within the *polis*, yet outside its restraints.

If we think of gender as a cultural role, a social rank, "a social category imposed on a sexed body" (Scott 32), or as "a primary way of signifying relations of power" (Laqueur 12), then we can more easily trace Aspasia's movement across gendered boundaries of appropriate roles for women and men in fifth-century BC Athens. She seems to have profited by her excursion into the male domain of politics and intellect, even at the expense of her respectability, reputation, and authority. Named among the rather short "list of Athenian citizen [class] women" known to us from literature (Schaps 323), the assertively intelligent Aspasia has been interpreted as self-indulgent, licentious, immoral. Historical records have successfully effaced the voice of the ideal Greek woman, rendering silent her enclosed body. And those same historical records have defaced any subversion of that ideal woman, rendering her unconfined body invalid.

Thus, even though her contributions to rhetoric are firmly situated and fully realized within the rhetorical tradition, those contributions have been directed through a powerful gendered lens to both refract toward and reflect Socrates and Pericles.

Ironically, then, Aspasia's accomplishments and influence have been enumerated by men, and most often attributed to men—or installed in the apocryphal, the safest place for wise (and therefore fictitious) women. And as for Aspasia's popular salon, it's often accredited to Pericles instead of to his female companion.

Aspasia, Pericles, and the Funeral Oration

Pericles, perhaps the most socially responsible, powerful, and influential of Athenians, was indeed surrounded with the greatest thinkers of his age—with Sophists, philosophers, architects, scientists, and rhetoricians. In his *Mass and Elite in Democratic Athens*, Josiah Ober refers to Pericles' intellectual circle as the "'educated elite' of late fifth-century Athens" and "a brain trust," describes the Sophists as "experts in political manipulation who were flocking to Athens from other Greek poleis," and places the "educated courtesan Aspasia ... among Pericles' closest associates," calling her "the power behind the throne" (89–90).[15] For forty years, the Athenians applauded Pericles' eloquence, often invoking his wise and excellent companions, including rhetorician Aspasia and philosopher Anaxagoras. In the *Phaedrus*, the Platonic Socrates calls Pericles "the most perfect orator in existence" and attributes Pericles' eloquence to the successful combination of his natural talents with the high-mindedness he learned from Anaxagoras, who "filled him with high thoughts and taught him the nature of mind ... and from these speculations [Pericles] drew and applied to the art of speaking what is of use to it" (269e4 ff.). Cicero later concurred that Pericles' teacher was indeed Anaxagoras, "a man distinguished for his knowledge of the highest sciences; and consequently Pericles was eminent in learning, wisdom and eloquence, and for forty years was supreme at Athens both in politics and at the same time in the conduct of war" (*De Oratore* III.xxxiv.138–39).

Yet several centuries later, Philostratus (fl. AD 250) wrote in his *Epistle* 73 that "Aspasia of Miletus is said to have sharpened the tongue of Pericles in imitation of Gorgias," with "the digressions and transitions of Gorgias' speeches [becoming] the fashion" (qtd. in Sprague 41–42). Philostratus echoes Plato, the earliest writer to mention Aspasia. In the *Menexenus*, the Platonic Socrates reveals Aspasia to be the author of Pericles' Funeral Oration (*Epitaphios*), an assertion I explore below. Aspasia becomes implicated even more in Pericles' education if we consider the "familiar knowledge at Athens that Aspasia had sat at the feet of Anaxagoras in natural philosophy" (Courtney 491). And several hundred years later, when Quintilian (AD 100) examined Pericles' written works, he concluded that some other pen had composed them: "I have been unable to discover anything in the least worthy of [Pericles'] great reputation for eloquence, and am consequently the less surprised that there should be some who hold that he never committed anything to writing, and that the writings circulating under his name are the works of others" (*Institutio Oratoria* 3.1.12). The rhetorician most closely associated with Pericles would no doubt have served as his logographer, as logography (the written composition of speech) was commonly the province of rhetoricians. Hence, Aspasia surely must have influenced Pericles in the composition of those speeches that both established him as a persuasive speaker and informed him as the most respected citizen-orator of the age.

Although Plutarch credits Aspasia with contributing greatly to intellectual life, specifically to philosophy, politics, and rhetoric, many scholars have since discredited her. In the aforementioned "Life of Pericles," Plutarch draws on a now-incomplete work of Aeschines (450 BC) to describe Aspasia, but neither his nor Aspasia's case has been strengthened by the fragments of Aeschines that survived. Those fragments present a controversial statement on gender equality: "the goodness of a woman is the same as that of a man," an assertion Aeschines illustrates with the political abilities of Aspasia (qtd. in Taylor 278).[16] Both Xenophon and Cicero (and later, medieval abbess Heloise, perhaps best-known for her attachment to Abelard), however, tap that same complete text, giving credence to the text—as well as to the existence of a historical Aspasia.[17]

According to several ancient authors, all of whom knitted together secondary sources to shape a reliable Socrates, Socrates deeply respected Aspasia's thinking and admired her rhetorical prowess, disregarding, it seems, her status as a woman and a *hetaera*. In Xenophon's *Memorabilia*, for instance, Socrates explains to Critobulus the "art of catching friends" and of using an intermediary:

> I can quote Aspasia. . . . She once told me that good matchmakers are successful only when the good reports they carry to and fro are true; false reports she would not recommend for the victims of deceptions hate one another and the matchmaker too. I am convinced that this is sound, so I think it is not open to me to say anything in your praise that I cannot say truthfully.
>
> (ii.36)

In Xenophon's *Oeconomicus*, Socrates ascribes to Aspasia the marital advice he gives to Critobulus: "There's nothing like investigation. I will introduce Aspasia to you, and she will explain the whole matter [of good wives] to you with more knowledge than I possess" (III.15) Plutarch writes that "Socrates sometimes came to see her [Aspasia] with her disciples, and his intimate friends brought their wives to her to hear her discourse . . . as a teacher of rhetoric" (200); Athenaeus calls Aspasia "clever . . . Socrates' teacher in rhetoric" (V.29) and goes on to account for the extent of Aspasia's influence over Socrates:

> [I]n the verses which are extant under her name and which are quoted by Herodicus . . . [she says]: "Socrates, I have not failed to notice that thy heart is smitten with desire for [Alcibiades]. . . . But hearken, if thou wouldst prosper in thy suit. Disregard not my message, and it will be much better for thee. For so soon as I heard, my body was suffused with the glow of joy, and tears not unwelcome fell from my eyelids. Restrain thyself, filling thy soul with the conquering Muse; and with her aid thou shalt win him; pour her into the ears of his desire. For she is the true beginning of love in both; through her thou shalt master him, by offering to his ears gifts for the unveiling of his soul."
>
> So, then, the noble Socrates goes a-hunting, employing the woman of Miletus as his preceptor in love, instead of being hunted himself, as Plato has said, [Socrates] being caught [as he was] in Alcibiades' net.
>
> (V.219)

Furthermore, in the *Menexenus*, the Platonic Socrates agrees that were the Council Chamber to elect him to make the recitation over the dead (the *Epitaphios*) he "should be able to make the speech . . . for she [Aspasia] who is my instructor is by no means weak in the art of rhetoric; on the contrary, she has turned out many fine orators, and amongst them one who surpassed all other Greeks, Pericles" (235–36). But it was Pericles—not Aspasia—who delivered that speech.

The *Menexenus* contains Plato's version of Socrates' version of Aspasia's version of Pericles' Funeral Oration, further recognition of Aspasia's reputation as rhetorician, philosopher, and as influential colleague in the Sophistic movement, a movement devoted to the analysis and creation of rhetoric—and of truth. Moreover, the Funeral Oration itself held political, philosophical, and rhetorical significance: by its delivery alone, the Funeral Oration played out "rhetoric's important role in shaping community" (Mackin 251). In *The Invention of Athens: The Funeral Oration in the Classical City*, Nicole Loraux clarifies the funeral oration as an "*institution*—an institution of speech in which the symbolic constantly encroached upon the functional, since in each oration the codified praise of the dead spilled over into generalized praise of Athens" (2). Besides conflating praise of the Athenians with praise of Athens, this institutionalized and specialized epideictic was useful for developing "consubstantiality *[homonoia]*" and creating a "similar rhetorical experience" for everyone present, be they citizens, foreigners, or women related to the dead."[18] The shared experience of this rhetorical ritual linked everyone present even as it connected them "with other audiences in the past" (Mackin 251). As "one of the authorized mouthpieces of classical Athens," the funeral oration translated into "Greek patriotism," for it was "Athenian eloquence" "adapted to the needs of patriotism," for it was "Athenian doquence". . . . a given historical situation" (Loraux 5). As such, the issues of translation and adaptation easily connect the *Epitaphios* with Sophistic philosophy.

In *Rereading the Sophists*, Susan Jarratt reminds us that "for the Sophists, human perception and discourse were the only measure of truths, all of which are contingent" (64); therefore, they focused on "the ability to create accounts of communal possibilities through persuasive speech" (98). And Loraux tells us that in every epitaphios, "a certain idea that the city wishes to have of itself emerges, beyond the needs of the present" (14). Thus the beliefs and practices of Sophists overlapped beautifully with one basic requirement of an epitaphios: "the personality of the orator has to yield to the impersonality of the genre . . . as an institution and as a literary form" (11). Aspasia's Sophistic training, political capacity, and powerful influence on Pericles' persuasive oratory easily translated into Socrates' pronouncement to Menexenus that she composed the famous funeral oration delivered by Pericles:

> I was listening only yesterday to Aspasia going through a funeral speech for [the Athenians] . . . [S]he rehearsed to me the speech in the form it should take, extemporizing in part, while other parts of it she had previously prepared, ... at the time when she was composing the funeral oration which Pericles delivered.
>
> (236b)

That Aspasia may well have composed Pericles' speech makes sense, since after all, being honored by the opportunity to deliver the *Epitaphios*, he would have prepared well, seeking and following the advice of his colleagues, including Aspasia, on points of style and substance. That she wrote it becomes more convincing when we consider Loraux's assurance that "the political orator must have the ascendant over the logographer" (11) and that the Sophist would preserve the "essential features of the civic representations" (107). For reasons of Aspasia's proximity to Pericles and her intellectual training, Quintilian was right, then, to doubt the originality of Pericles' work.

Before demonstrating her expertise at composing moving, patriotic epideictic oratory, Aspasia reminds Socrates of the efficacy of rhetoric. In the *Menexenus*, the Platonic Aspasia explains that "it is by means of speech finely spoken that deeds nobly done gain for their doers from the hearers the meed of memory and renown" (236e)—an accurate description of contingent truth. Jarratt explains the sophistic rhetorical technique and its social-constructionist underpinning with her definition of *nomos* as a "self-conscious arrangement of discourse to create politically and socially significant knowledge . . . thus it is always a social construct with ethical dimensions" (60).

Hence, the author of the *Epitaphios*—whether viewed as Aspasia or Pericles—makes clear the power of oratory to influence the public's belief that its history was other than it was. Loraux explains that "a Sophist and a rhetor [would have] used the official oration in order to write a fictitious logos; within the corpus, then, the 'false' follows hard upon the 'true'" (9). Accordingly, the most aggressive exploits of Attic imperialism are represented as "[bringing] freedom [to] all the dwellers of this continent" (*Menexenus* 240e), as "fighting in defence of the liberties of the Boeotians" (242b), as "fighting for the freedom of Leontini" (243a), as "setting free . . . friends" (243c), and as "saving their walls from ruin" (244c). In offering this version of Pericles' Funeral Oration, an exaggerated encomium abounding with historical misstatements and anachronisms, Plato makes explicit his own feelings about the use of rhetoric—just as Thucydides uses his own version of the *Epitaphios* to make explicit his belief in the necessary subjection of individual citizenship to the polis: "A man who takes no interest in politics is a man . . . who has no business here at all" (II.40).

Thinly disguised in the *Menexenus* is Plato's cynicism. In his opinion, the development of oratory had negative consequences for Athens, the most glaring defect of current oratory being its indifference to truth. A rhetorician such as Aspasia was, indeed, interested more in believability than in truth, more interested in constructing than delivering truth, more interested in *nomos* than *physis*—interests leading to Thucydides' claims that such "prose chroniclers . . . are less interested in telling the truth than in catching the attention of their public" (I.21). In the opening dialogue of the *Menexenus*, the Platonic Socrates disparages the orators in much the same way he does in the *Symposium*, saying that "in speeches long beforehand . . . they praise in such splendid fashion, that . . . they bewitch our souls. . . . [E]very time I listen fascinated [by their praise of me] I am exalted and imagine myself to have become all at once taller and nobler and more handsome . . . owing to the persuasive eloquence of the speaker" (235b). Thus Plato recoils from the touch of rhetoric.

Aspasia's Influence

Aspasia was an active member of the most famous intellectual circle in Athens, her influence reaching such well-known thinkers as Socrates and such exemplary orators as Pericles. Most importantly, her influence extended to Plato, coloring his concept of rhetoric as well. Like Aspasia, Plato taught that belief and truth are not necessarily the same, a sentiment he makes evident in his *Gorgias* when Gorgias admits that rhetoric produces "[mere] belief without knowledge" (454). Plato also agrees with Aspasia that rhetoric, which is the daughter of truth-disclosing philosophy, does not always carry on the family tradition; rhetoric can be used to obscure the truth, to control and deceive believers into belief. In the *Gorgias*, his Socrates says, "[R]hetoric seems not to be an artistic pursuit at all, but that of a shrewd, courageous spirit which is naturally clever at dealing with men; and I call the chief part of it flattery" (463). And in the *Phaedrus*, Plato writes that "in the courts, they say, nobody cares for truth about these matters [things which are just or good], but for that which is convincing; and that is probability" (272e).

Like Aspasia, Plato approved of a rhetoric of persuasion; he too sees the political potential of public rhetoric. But his rhetoric is foremost a search for the truth; only truth—not fictive effect over accuracy—should constitute persuasive rhetoric. His perfect orator of the *Phaedrus* "must know the truth about all the particular things of which he speaks and writes . . . [and] must understand the nature of the soul" (277c), for the ideal rhetorician speaks "in a manner pleasing to the gods" (273e). What Plato could have learned, then, from Aspasia was the potentially harmful uses of rhetoric as a branch of philosophy—as well as the as-yet uncalibrated potential of rhetoric to create belief.

In addition to influencing Socrates and Plato, Aspasia also influenced Xenophon and his wife, specifically in the art of inductive argument. In *De Inventione*, Cicero uses her lesson in induction as the centerpiece for his argumentation chapter. Like others before him, Cicero too acknowledges Aspasia's influence on Socrates as well as the existence of the Aeschines text:

> [I]n a dialogue by Aeschines Socraticus[,] Socrates reveals that Aspasia reasoned thus with Xenophon's wife and with Xenophon himself: "Please tell me, madam, if your neighbour had a better gold ornament than you have, would you prefer that one or your own?" "That one," she replied. "Now, if she had dresses and other feminine finery more expensive than you have, would you prefer yours or hers?" "Hers, of course," she replied. "Well, now, if she had a better husband than you have, would you prefer your husband or hers?" At this the woman blushed. But Aspasia then began to speak to Xenophon. "I wish you would tell me, Xenophon," she said, "if your neighbour had a better horse than yours, would you prefer your horse or his?" "His," was the answer. "And if he had a better farm than you have, which farm would you prefer to have?" "The better farm, naturally," he said. "Now if he had a better wife than you have, would you prefer yours or his?" And at this Xenophon, too, himself was silent. Then Aspasia: "Since both of you have failed to tell me the only thing I wished to hear, I myself will tell you what you both are thinking. That is you, madam, wish to have the best husband, and you, Xenophon, desire above all things to have the finest

wife. Therefore, unless you can contrive that there be no better man or finer woman on earth you will certainly always be in dire want of what you consider best, namely, that you be the husband of the very best of wives, and that she be wedded to the very best of men." To this instance, because assent has been given to undisputed statements, the result is that the point which would appear doubtful if asked by itself is through analogy conceded as certain, and this is due to the method employed in putting the question. Socrates used this conversation method a good deal, because he wished to present no arguments himself, but preferred to get a result from the material which the interlocutor had given him—a result which the interlocutor was bound to approve as following necessarily from what he had already granted.

(I.xxxi.51–53)

Few women participated in the intellectual life of ancient Greece. Aspasia was a striking exception.

Although Aspasia was a powerful force in Periclean Athens and seems to have affected the thinking of Plato and Socrates, few Greek thinkers accepted women as mental equals. Aristotle makes no provision for the intellectual woman, except for his nod to Sappho: "Everyone honours the wise. . . . [T]he Mytilenaeans [honour] Sappho, though she was a woman" (*Rhetoric* 1389b.12). Otherwise, Aristotle denied any philosophical or rhetorical contributions of women. He quotes Sophocles when he writes, "'Silence gives grace to woman'—though that is not the case likewise with a man" (*Politics* I.v.9). Reasoning from Aristotle's basic premise, Aspasia could not have become a teacher, much less a rhetorician. By the principle of *entelechy* (the vital force urging one toward fulfilling one's actual essence), she would have naturally followed her predetermined life course, her progress distinctly marked off and limited to a degree of perfection less than that for a man. The power politics of gender, the social category imposed on each sexed body, both gives rise to and then maintains the social creation of ideas about appropriate roles for women and men. Denied the *telos* of perfect maleness, Athenian women were denied a passport into the male intellectual battleground of politics, philosophy, rhetoric. But Aspasia had approached the border— and trespassed into masculine territory.

For the most part, Aristotle's accounts of woman, buttressed by the defective scientific understanding of reproduction and biological processes, belie woman's participation in the making of culture, leaving her daughters without access to any knowledge of a female tradition or intellectual underpinning. For Aristotle, men and women differed only in outward form but the inequality is permanent. Unlike Plato, he could not see beyond the contemporary and seemingly permanent inferior status of Greek women. In the *Politics*, Aristotle writes "between the sexes, the male is by nature superior and the female inferior, the male ruler and the female subject" (I.ii.12); in the *Poetics*, he pronounces goodness as possible "even in a woman . . . though [she] is perhaps an inferior . . . but it is not appropriate in a female Character to be manly, or clever" (15.1454a.20–24); and in the *Rhetoric*, he writes that "one quality or action is nobler than another if it is that of a naturally finer being: thus a man's will be nobler than a woman's" (I.9.15).

And those naturally finer beings (men) were awarded a public voice, which enabled them to participate as speakers, thinkers, and writers in the *polis*, in the "good" of public life. A public voice was the right and privilege of those who were declared to possess reason and goodness to its fullest extent—men only. In the *polis*—the public sphere of action, the realm of highest justice, the world of men—women and slaves should be invisible and aphonic. "Naturally" then, women and slaves—inferior beings in every way—were condemned to silence as their appointed sphere and condition. And most women spoke no memorable alternative—that is, except for Aspasia. But even Aspasia's voice is muted, for she speaks only through men.

Aspasia's Challenge to the History of Rhetoric

Aspasia colonized the patriarchal territory, but her colony was quickly appropriated by males. Although she herself escaped enclosure, although she publicly articulated her intelligence and her heterosexual love, she did not escape those who defined her. Her influence has been enclosed within the gendered rhetorical terrain— and neutralized. "And the trouble is," Myra Jehlen writes, "that the map of an enclosed space describes only the territory inside the enclosure. Without knowing the surrounding geography, how are we to evaluate this woman's estate . . ." (80). Few of us have ever heard of Aspasia of Miletus, teacher of rhetoric. But if we locate her colony within "its larger context" and "examine the borders along which [she] defined herself" (81)—the writings of the men she influenced, Plato, Socrates, and Pericles—we can better map out how Aspasia was perceived by those men and, perhaps, how she might have perceived her estate within the surrounding geography.

But even now, Aspasia's intellectual estate seems to be "off-limits," except in that her story serves as a morality tale for women who insist on entering the rhetorical arena: such a woman will be used, misappropriated, and eventually forgotten. Or worse, perhaps, they will be disfigured in artistic renderings such as Gerome's, inscribed with masculine fantasy and curiosity. Gerome's idyllic rendition of Aspasia and Alcibiades is both inaccurate and unfair: Our Mother of Rhetoric, life-long companion of Pericles and influential colleagues of famous men, is the harem girl to the arrogant, dissolute, untrustworthy, love-object of Socrates, Alcibiades. Thus the example of Gerome's print brings to the fore the whole notion of women's place in rhetoric. Where on that landscape we call rhetorical history should we begin to look for women? How many women remain hidden in the shadows of monumental rhetoricians? How many others remain misidentified as holes and bulges on out-of-the-way territories? And how much of rhetorical history is itself, as Carole Blair describes, "rhetorical iterations, saturated with the impure representations, intrinsic interestedness, and general obstreperousness of any discourse" (417)?

By acknowledging that rhetorical history is not neutral territory, the refiguring of Aspasia's role in the history of rhetoric has ramifications on past study as well as implications for future study. The most powerful ramification is an awareness of women's place on the rhetorical terrain. Until most recently, we had not even thought of looking for a woman in rhetoric. It had already been assumed, *a priori*, that no woman participated in the rhetorical tradition. We had been willing to believe the tautology that no women have been involved in rhetorical history because not a single rhetorical treatise by a woman appears in lists of primary works (we resolutely ignore Lucia Olbrechts-Tyteca) and because not a single woman appears in the indices of the most comprehensive histories of Western rhetoric. But upon examination, the fault line of gender reveals that women have indeed participated in and contributed to the rhetorical tradition, and that fault line reverberates down the corridors of past scholarship to the foundations of the Greek intellectual tradition.

Our first obligation, then, as rhetorical scholars is to look backwards at all the unquestioned scholarship that has come before; then, we must begin to re-map our notion of rhetorical history. By simply choosing which men and women to show and how to represent them, we subtly shape the perceptions of our profession, enabling the profession to recognize and remember—or to forget—the obvious and not-so-obvious women on our intellectual landscape. But looking backwards will not be enough; we must attend to the current professional scene as well. For example, the early and influential work of Ann Berthoff, Janet Emig, Janice Lauer, and Mina Shaughnessy could easily fade out of our professional consciousness if we don't keep these foremothers of composition studies in our professional narratives, if we don't know or remember the scholarship on which we're building our own work. Perhaps the most important consequence of refiguring rhetorical history, however, is the effect on our students, for we also shape the perceptions of them. By writing a more inclusive history of rhetoric, we can more easily enable and encourage both our female and male students to participate in a literature, in a history, in a profession, or in communities of discourse from which they may feel excluded or detached.

Fortunately, rhetorical scholars—females and males alike—around the country are involved in various feminist historiographic projects.[19] And their archeological findings are serving to challenge the history of rhetoric to recognize the full range of its texts, its lies, its manuscripts, its practices, and its theories. In fact, it's the "theoretical understanding of rhetorics of the past [that] underwrites our capacity for further theorizing" (Blair 404). And Aspasia's contribution to rhetoric is just one of many stories that disrupt, refigure, and then enrich what has long been held as patriarchal territory. Until recently, we didn't seem to realize that the rhetorical map had flattened out the truth, leaving scarcely a ridge on the surface that could suggest all the women, and the otherwise disenfranchised, that are buried beneath the surface. The significance of Aspasia's challenge lies in recharting the plains, valleys, and borders of rhetoric, and accounting for all the pockets of as-yet-unaccounted-for activity. Having passed through the familiar and patriarchal territory of exclusionary rhetoric, we are moving into a frontier—the rhetorics of the future that await our exploration, our settlements, and our mapping.

Cheryl Glenn is an assistant professor at Oregon State University. She has co-authored (with Robert Connors) The St. Martin's Guide to Teaching Writing *and has published articles on rhetorical theory, popular literacy, and medieval literature. "sex, lies, and manuscript" is part of her current book-length project,* Rhetoric Retold: Regendering the Tradition from Antiquity through the Renaissance *(forthcoming from Southern Illinois UP)*.

Notes

1 I am grateful to Robert Connors for the print, to Cynthia Selfe for sharing her work on Aspasia, and to Jon Olson for his careful readings of this essay.

2 Bodily definition maps out class as well as gender: "Silence, the closed mouth, is made a sign of chastity. And silence and chastity are, in turn, homologous to women's enclosure within the house" (Stallybrass 127).

3 In general, feminist scholarship has helped create a space for reconceiving and thereby transforming the rhetorical tradition (Ballif, Biesecker, Bizzell and Herzberg, Blair and Kaul, Glenn, Jarratt and Ong, Lunsford, Peaden, Selfe, Swearingen). Edward P.J. Corbett anticipated women's rhetorical contributions: "Rhetoric is one of the most patriarchal of all the academic disciplines. But because of the active feminist movement, we may be on the verge of recovering the names of women who could lay claim to being rhetors" (577). Patricia Bizzell and Bruce Herzberg include for consideration the rhetorical discourse of a number of Renaissance and post-Renaissance women. Andrea Lunsford is editing a forthcoming collection of women's rhetorical endeavors, *Reclaiming Rhetorica*.

4 A regendered history does not reproduce traditional gendered categories of the "empowered" and "other," nor does it reduce them, but rather imagines gender as an inclusive and nonhierarchical category. In *Rhetoric Retold* I locate women's contributions to and participation within the rhetorical tradition and write them into an expanded, inclusive tradition.

5 Joan Kelly tells us that "women's history has a dual goal: to restore women to history and to restore our history to women. . . . In seeking to add women to the fund of historical knowledge, women's history has revitalized theory, for it has shaken the conceptual foundations of historical study" ("Social Relation" 1). Carole Blair contests the histories of rhetoric both when she interrogates the politics of preservation as well as when, together with Mary L. Kahl, she argues for revising the history of rhetorical theory. And Barbara Herrnstein Smith's "Contingencies of Value" eloquently demonstrates how such inclusions do and must problematize genres.

6 Miletus had relatively large numbers of literate citizens, among them the philosophers Anaximander, Anaximenes, and Thales (Harris 63; Vernant, *Origins* 127, *Myth and Thought* 343 ff.; Kirk and Raven 73 ff.). In *Myth and Society in Ancient Greece*, Jean-Pierre Vernant writes that alongside moral thought, "a philosophy of nature starts to develop . . . in the Greek cities of Asia Minor. The theories of these first 'physicists' of Ionia have been hailed as the beginning of rational thought as it is understood in the West" (96).

7 Most scholars (Bloedow, Flaceliére, Halperin, Just, Keuls, Licht, Ober, for instance) have labeled Aspasia a courtesan, schooled in intellectual and social arts. But both Eva Cantarella and William Courtney argue that the Athenian suspicion and misunderstanding of such a powerful, political, non-Athenian, unmarriageable woman living with their controversial leader, Pericles, led automatically to the sexualized and undeserved label of *hetaera*; Nicole Loraux refers to Aspasia as a foreigner and as a nonpolitician; Mary Ellen Waithe calls her "a rhetorician and a member of the Periclean Philosophic Circle" (*History* 75); and Susan Cole writes only of Aspasia's intellectual influence and measure of literacy (225).

8 Cantarella clearly describes the *hetaera* as "more than a casual companion," "more educated than a woman destined for marriage, and intended 'professionally' to accompany men where wives and concubines could not go [namely social activities and discussions]" (30). "This relationship was meant to be somehow gratifying for the man, even on the intellectual level, and was thus completely different from men's relationships with either wives or prostitutes" (31). Robert Flaceliére agrees that "in practice, if not in law, they [*hetaerae*] enjoyed considerable freedom" (130). He goes on to quote Athenaeus' *Deipnosophists* (XIII) that the *hetaerae* "applied themselves to study and the knowledge of the sciences" (131).

9 H. D. F. Kitto places Athenian women in Oriental seclusion: "In this pre-eminently masculine society women moved in so restricted a sphere that we may reasonably regard them as a 'depressed area'" (222). He accepts such restrictions as sensible.

10 Keuls suggests that a female educational underground might have been the source of male anxiety, for the philosopher Democritus wrote, "Let a woman not develop her reason, for that would be a terrible thing" (Fr. 110, qtd. in Keuls 104). And a character in a lost play by Menander pronounced that "he who teaches letters to his wife is ill-advised: He's giving additional poison to a horrible snake" (Fr. 702 K, ibid.).

11 Roger Just reminds us that "Aspasia's notoriety and the popular resentment her supposed influence aroused should . . . be remembered—a resentment transmuted into mockery by comedy" (21). In the *Acharnians*, Aristophanes writes that the Megarians "abducted *two* whores from Aspasia's stable in Athens" (523); Plutarch writes that Cratinus, "in downright terms, calls her a harlot": "To find him a Juno the goddess of lust/Bore that harlot past shame,/Aspasia by name" (201). Flaceliére assures us that "the Athenian comic poets never tired of repeating that Aspasia led a life of debauchery, though apparently she was as well behaved as she was well informed, and even a scholar" (131). And Cantarella writes, "It is not surprising that many Athenians hated Aspasia. She was not like other women; she was an intellectual" (54–55).

12 Pomeroy, *Goddesses* 89; Just 144. But Hans Licht (a pseudonym for Paul Brandt) explains that "the preference for Aspasia shown by Pericles afforded a welcome excuse for his opponents to attack him; people would not hear of a woman having anything to say in political life, especially one who was not an Athenian but was brought from abroad, and even from Ionia . . . , which was notorious for the immorality of its women. . . . Hence she was severely criticized by the comic poets. . . . [A]ccording to a statement in Athenaeus . . . she was said to have maintained a regular brothel. . . . When she was accused of *asebeia* (impiety) and procuring, Pericles defended her and secured her acquittal" (352–53).

13 Pierre Vidal-Naquet writes that "the sole civic function of women was to give birth to citizens. The conditions imposed upon them by Pericles' law of 451 was to be the daughter of a citizen and a citizen's daughter" (145). Women of low reputation could be spoken of publicly and freely; for some, Aspasia fit such a category. For others, Aspasia's intellectual and political gifts earned her a measure of public distinction. David Schaps asserts that there were three categories of women whose "names could be mentioned freely: disreputable women, opposing women, and dead women" (329).

14 *Areté* is variously referred to as various manifestations of human excellence: as virtue (the prerequisite of a good human life; cf. Democritus' "On *Areté* or Manly Virtue"), as a combination of self-control, courage, and justice, as moral nobility, or as valor. See Gutherie III: 253 ff.

15 The tautology of Jean Bethke Elshtain's argument rightly encompasses Aspasia: "I am not impressed with the claims made for powerful women who influenced men through their private activities—in Athenian society this claim is frequently made for the *hetaera*. . . . Were such 'women-behind-the-men' to have attempted to enter the public arena to speak with their own voices, they would have been roundly jeered, satirized, and condemned" (14–15 n. 11).

16 Taylor quotes from the fragments of the *Aspasia* collated in H. Dittmar's *Aeschines von Sphettos*.

17 In her epistolary arguments with Abelard, Heloise relies on ancient authorities. In one particular case, her crown *auctoritas* is Aspasia. Quoting from the now-missing text of Aeschines, Heloise argues for the excellence of a good wife and a good husband (Montcrieff 58). In her reading of Heloise's letters, Andrea Nye challenges the philosophical community to be "informed by Heloise's and Aspasia's wisdom, their subtle, sensitive, mobile, flexible women's tongues." She also wants us to admit that "a woman can be the teacher of a man" (17).

18 Thucydides writes, "Everyone who wishes to, both citizens and foreigners, can join in the procession, and the women who are related to the dead are there to make their laments at the tomb" (II.34).

19 For example, recent issues of both *CCC* (October 1992) and *Rhetoric Society Quarterly* (Winter 1992) center on feminist readings of rhetoric and composition, theories and practices. Also see notes 3, 4, 5.

Works Cited

Aristophanes. *The Archarnians*. Trans. Douglass Parker. *Four Comedies*. Ed. William Arrowsmith. Ann Arbor: U of Michigan P, 1969. 99–112.

Aristotle. *Politics*. Trans. H. Rackman. Cambridge: Loeb-Harvard UP, 1977.

———. *The Rhetoric and Poetics of Aristotle*. Trans. W. Rhys Roberts and Ingram Bywater. New York: Modern Library, 1984.

Athenaeus. *The Deipnosophists*. Trans. Charles Burton Gulick. Cambridge: Harvard UP, 1967.

Ballif, Michelle. "Re/Dressing Histories; Or, On Re/Covering Figures Who Have Been Laid Bare by Our Gaze." *Rhetoric Society Quarterly* 22 (1992): 91–98.

Biesecker, Barbara. "Coming to Terms with Recent Attempts to Write Women into the History of Rhetoric." *Philosophy and Rhetoric* 25 (1992): 140–61.

Bizzell, Patricia. "Opportunities for Feminist Research in the History of Rhetoric." *Rhetoric Review* 11 (1992): 50–58.

———. *"The Praise of Folly*, The Woman Rhetor, and Post-Modem Skepticism." *Rhetoric Society Quarterly* 22 (1992): 7–17.

Bizzell, Patricia, and Bruce Herzberg. *The Rhetorical Tradition: Readings from Classical Times to the Present*. Boston: Bedford-St. Martin's, 1990.

Blair, Carole. "Contested Histories of Rhetoric: The Politics of Preservation, Progress, and Change." *Quarterly Journal of Speech* 78 (1992): 403–28.

——— and Mary L. Kahl. "Introduction: Revising the History of Rhetorical Theory." *Western Journal of Speech Communication* 54 (1990): 148–59.

Bloedow, Edmund F. "Aspasia and the 'Mystery' of the Menexenus." *Wiener Studien (Zeitschrift fur Klassiche Philologie and Patristic)* Neu Folge 9 (1975): 32–48.

Cantarella, Eva. *Pandora's Daughters*. 1981. Baltimore: Johns Hopkins UP, 1987.

Cicero. *De Inventione, De Optimo Genere, Oratorum, Topica*. Trans. H. M. Hubbell. Cambridge: Harvard UP, 1976. 1–348.

———. *De Oratore*. 2 vols. Trans. E. W. Sutton. Cambridge: Harvard UP, 1979.

Cole, Susan Guettel. "Could Greek Women Read and Write?" Foley 219–45.

Corbett, Edward P. J. *Classical Rhetoric for the Modern Student*. 3rd ed. New York: Oxford UP, 1990.

Courtney, William. "Sappho and Aspasia." *Fortnightly Review* 97 (1912): 488–95.

Delcourt, Marie. Pericles. N.p.: Gallemard, 1939.

Elshtain, Jean Bethke. *Public Man, Private Woman*. Princeton: Princeton UP, 1987.

Ferguson, Margaret W., Maureen Quilligan, and Nancy J. Vickers, eds. *Rewriting the Renaissance*. Chicago: U of Chicago P, 1986.

Flaceliére, Robert. *Love in Ancient Greece*. 1960. Trans. James Cleugh. London: Frederick Muller, 1962.

Foley, Helene P. *Reflections of Women in Antiquity*. New York: Gordon, 1981.

Glenn, Cheryl. "Author, Audience, and Autobiography: Rhetorical Technique in *The Book of Margery Kempe*." *College English* 53 (1992): 540–53.

———. *Rhetoric Retold: Regendering the Tradition from Antiquity through the Renaissance*. Carbondale: Southern Illinois UP, forthcoming.

Gutherie, W. K. C. *A History of Greek Philosophy*. 6 vols. Cambridge: Cambridge UP, 1969.

Halperin, David M. *One Hundred Years of Homosexuality*. New York: Routledge, 1990.

Harris, William V. *Ancient Literacy*. Cambridge: Harvard UP, 1989.

Jarratt, Susan C. "The First Sophists and Feminism: Discourses of the 'Other.'" *Hypatia* 5 (1990): 27–41.

———. "Performing Feminisms, Histories, Rhetorics." *Rhetoric Society Quarterly* 22 (1992): 1–6.

———. *Rereading the Sophists: Classical Rhetoric Refigured.* Carbondale: Southern Illinois UP 1991.

Jarratt, Susan L., and Rory Ong. "Aspasia: Rhetoric, Gender, and Colonial Ideology." Lunsford, *Reclaiming Rhetorica*, in press.

Jehlen, Myra. "Archimedes and the Paradox of Feminist Criticism." Warhol and Herndl. 75–96.

Just, Roger. *Women in Athenian Law and Life.* London: Routledge, 1989.

Kelly, Joan. "The Social Relation of the Sexes." Kelly 1–18.

———. *Women, History, and Theory: The Essays of Joan Kelly.* Chicago: U of Chicago P, 1984.

Keuls, Eva C. *The Reign of the Phallus.* New York: Harper, 1985.

Kirk, G. S., and J. E. Raven. *The Presocratic Philosophers.* Cambridge: Cambridge UP, 1962.

Kitto, H. D. F. *The Greeks.* Middlesex: Penguin, 1951.

Kneupper, Charles, ed. *Rhetoric and Ideology: Compositions and Criticisms of Power.* Arlington: Rhetoric Society of America, 1989.

Laqueur, Thomas. *Making Sex.* Cambridge: Harvard UP 1990.

Licht, Hans [Paul Brandt]. *Sexual Life in Ancient Greece.* London: Abbey Library, 1932.

Loraux, Nicole. *The Invention of Athens.* Trans. Alan Sheridan. Cambridge: Harvard UP, 1986.

Lunsford, Andrea A., ed. *Reclaiming Rhetorica.* Pittsburgh: U of Pittsburgh P, in press.

Mackin, James A., Jr. "Schismogenesis and Community: Pericles' Funeral Oration." *Quarterly Journal of Speech* 77 (1991): 251–62.

Moncrieff, C. K. *The Letters of Abelard and Heloise.* New York: Knopf, 1942.

Nye, Andrea. "A Woman's Thought or a Man's Discipline? The Letters of Abelard and Heloise." *Hypatia* 7 (1992): 1–22.

Ober, Josiah. *Mass and Elite in Democratic Athens.* Princeton: Princeton UP, 1989.

Peaden, Catherine. "Feminist Theories, Historiographies, and Histories of Rhetoric: The Role of Feminism in Historical Studies." Kneupper, 116–26.

Plato. *Euthyphro, Apology, Crito, Phaedo, Phaedrus.* Trans. H. N. Fowler. Cambridge: Harvard UP, 1977. 405–579.

———. *Gorgias.* Trans. W. C. Helmbold. Indianapolis: Bobbs-Merrill, 1952.

———. *Republic.* Trans. Paul Shorey. 2 vols. Cambridge: Harvard UP, 1982.

———. *Timaeus, Critias, Cleitophon, Menexenus, Epistles.* Trans. R. G. Bury. 1929. London: Heinemann-Loeb, 1981.

Plutarch. *The Lives of the Noble Grecians and Romans.* Trans. John Dryden. Rev. Arthur Hugh Clough. New York: Modern Library, 1932.

Pomeroy, Sarah. *Goddesses, Whores, Wives, and Slaves.* New York: Schocken, 1975.

———. *Women's History and Ancient History.* Chapel Hill: U of North Carolina P, 1991.

Quintilian. *Institutio Oratoria.* Trans. H. E. Butler. 1920 4 vols. London: Heinemann, 1969.

Schaps, David M. "The Woman Least Mentioned: Etiquette and Women's Names." *Classical Quarterly* 27 (1977): 323–31.

Scott, Joan Wallach. *Gender and the Politics of History.* New York: Columbia UP, 1988.

Selfe, Cynthia. "Aspasia: The First Woman Rhetorician." Unpublished essay.

Smith, Barbara Herrnstein. "Contingencies of Value." *Contingencies of Value.* Cambridge: Harvard UP, 1988. 30–53.

Sprague, Rosamond Kent, ed. *The Older Sophists.* Columbia: U of South Carolina P, 1972.

Stallybrass, Peter. "Patriarchal Territories: The Body Enclosed." Ferguson et al. 123–44.

Swearingen, C. Jan. *Rhetoric and Irony*. New York: Oxford UP, 1991.

Taylor, A. E. *Plato, the Man and his Work*. 7th ed. London: Methuen, 1960.

Thucydides. *History of the Peloponnesian War*. Trans. Rex Warner. London: Penguin, 1954.

Vemant, Jean-Pierre. *Myth and Society in Ancient Greece*. 1974. New York: Zone, 1980.

——. *Myth and Thought Among the Greeks*. 1965. London: Routledge, 1983.

——. *The Origins of Greek Thought*. 1962. Ithaca: Cornell UP, 1982.

Vidal-Naquet, Pierre. *The Black Hunter*. Trans. Andrew Szegedy-Maszak. Baltimore: Johns Hopkins UP, 1986.

Waithe, Mary Ellen, ed. *A History of Women Philosophers, Vol. 1/600 BC–500 AD*. Dordrecht: Martinus Nijhoff, 1987. 4 vols.

Warhol, Robyn R., and Diane Price Herndl. *Feminisms*. New Brunswick: Rutgers UP, 1991.

Xenophon. *Memorabilia and Oeconomicus*. Trans. E. C. Marchant. Cambridge: Harvard UP, 1988.

5.
BLACK WOMEN ON THE SPEAKER'S PLATFORM (1832–1899)
Shirley Wilson Logan

Editors' Note: *Rounding out the section on recovery and recuperation, this essay responds to Glenn's call of three years earlier by demonstrating the rhetorical prowess of such brilliant speakers as Maria Stewart, Mary Ann Shadd Cary, Frances Ellen Watkins Harper, Mary Church Terrell, Sharah Parker Remond, Maria Miller, Isabella Baumfree (Sojourner Truth), Lucy Wilmot Smith, Ida B. Wells, Victoria Earle Matthews, Fannier Barrier Williams, Anna Julia Cooper, Lucy Laney, and others about whom the rhetorical community knew almost nothing. This author has led the way in introducing the powerful rhetorical displays of Black women during the nineteenth century.*

To speak of the rhetorical activities of African American women in the nineteenth century is to speak of their advocacy for change. The term *rhetorical activities* in this discussion includes those occasions when black women delivered persuasive public speeches. Such a discussion could develop around the oratorical careers of the most vocal and prominent women rhetors of the century, beginning in 1832 with Maria Stewart in Boston and ending at the close of the century with the speeches of Nannie Helen Burroughs or Victoria Matthews. It could also focus on varying tactics of delivery, arrangement, invention, and style, from the strongly religious and self-referencing appeals of Sojourner Truth or Stewart to the factual, disengaged approach of Ida Wells and the traditional grand style of Frances Ellen Watkins Harper or Anna Julia Haywood Cooper. Literary societies, such as the Bethel Literary and Historical Association, founded in 1881 by Washington, D.C.'s black elite, provided opportunities for black women to develop skills in oratory.

But perhaps one can acquire a better sense of the extent of black women's public involvement in nineteenth-century political life by considering their rhetorical responses to the panoply of issues challenging peoples of African descent throughout America at the time. In addition to the oppressive defining issue of slavery, these concerns included employment, civil rights, woman's rights, emigration, and self-improvement. After the Civil War mob violence, racial uplift, and support for the southern black woman were added to the list of concerns demanding articulation.

Shirley Wilson Logan, "Black Women on the Speaker's Platform (1832–1899)" in *Listening to Their Voices: The Rhetorical Activities of Historical Women*. Ed. Molly Meijer Wertheimer. Columbia: U of South Carolina P, 1997. 150–73.

Nineteenth-century black women articulated them all. They spoke out at church con-ferences, political gatherings, woman's rights conventions, and antislavery meetings. Not limiting themselves to mere participation in public forums, black women also created, organized, and publicized a large number of them. Maria Stewart, the first American-born woman to speak publicly to a mixed group of women and men, was African American. She delivered her first address in 1832, six years before Angelina Grimké's appearance at Pennsylvania Hall, and her speeches were published in William Lloyd Garrison's *Liberator.* Mary Ann Shadd Cary, after considerable discus-sion, was reluctantly seated at the 1855 Colored National Convention in Philadelphia, becoming the first woman to address that body by a vote of 38 yeas and 23 nays (*Minutes* 1855, 10). An article in the 26 October 1855 edition of *Frederick Douglass' Paper* describes that performance: "She at first had ten minutes granted her as had the other members. At their expiration, ten more were granted, and by this time came the hour of adjournment; but so interested was the House, that it granted additional time to her to finish, at the commencement of the afternoon session; and the House was crowded and breathless in its attention to her masterly exposition of our present condi-tion, and the advantages open to colored men of enterprise" (Sterling 1984, 171).

Frances Harper was employed as a lecturer for the Maine Anti-Slavery Society in 1854, becoming possibly the first black woman to earn a living as a traveling lecturer. She was certainly the most prolific. The black women's club movement also sparked extensive issue-oriented public discussion, as any edition of the *Woman's Era* demon-strates. The pages of this periodical, published by the Woman's Era Club of Boston from 1894 to 1897, were filled with reports from the various black women's clubs around the country relating their very public presence in current affairs. For example, the April 1895 issue carried an article by Mary Church Terrell, editor of the Washington, D.C., column, in which she condemned T. Thomas Fortune, editor of the *New York Age,* for criticizing "the race with which he is identified for whining." In the same issue, the column from Georgia, edited by Alice Woodby McKane, reported on the club's interest in the emigration of two hundred blacks to Liberia. In the 1 June 1894 issue Ednah Cheney commended the *Woman's Era* for its involvement in opening the medical pro-fession to women. Later issues teemed with support for a national gathering of women, which did occur in 1895. This conference of black women held in Boston was an occasion for black women publicly to address urgent race concerns. These intersecting concerns and occasions have been classified here for discussion into the following necessarily overlapping categories: the abolition of slavery, women's rights, lynching, and racial uplift. They represent some of the interwoven consequences of African existence in America.

Abolition of Slavery

It should be clear that the abolition of slavery dominated discourse among black women during the first half of the century. Of the 750,000 blacks living in the United States at the time of the census of 1790, approximately 92 percent, or 691,000, were enslaved, and most lived in the South Atlantic states. In 1808 legislation finally made the African slave trade illegal, although it continued underground for many years. In the 1790 census Boston was the only city that listed no slaves, with approximately 27,000 free blacks living in the North and 32,000 free blacks in the South (Franklin and Moss 1988, 80–81).

This discussion of black women's abolitionist rhetoric centers on the public discourse of three speakers who migrated to new locales, delivering their antislavery messages to audiences in England, Canada, and across the United States. Sarah Parker Remond, a member of a prominent abolitionist family in Massachusetts, lectured in England and Scotland. Mary Ann Shadd Cary, whose father was a leader in the Underground Railroad movement in Delaware, fled with her family to Canada to avoid the consequences of the Fugitive Slave Act of 1850 and developed into an outspoken presence in the antislavery movement there. Frances Harper, whose uncle William Watkins was active in the abolitionist movement, left Baltimore in about 1850, also in response to the Fugitive Slave Act, eventually traveling across the country with her antislavery message.

Although slavery was abolished in the British Empire in 1833, antislavery activities against its American version continued throughout the first half of the century, at which time a number of black abolitionists traveled to the British Isles to generate support for their cause. Some were freeborn blacks, like Charles Lenox Remond, and others were, like Frederick Douglass and William Wells Brown, formerly enslaved. Sarah Remond (1815–1894) was one of eight children born to Nancy and John Remond, a native of Curaçao. Her family was part of the abolitionist society of Salem, Massachusetts. In 1856 she was appointed agent for the American Anti-Slavery Society and, as an associate of Garrison, became one of the first black women to lecture regularly before antislavery audiences. Initially a reluctant speaker, Remond toured throughout New England, New York, and Ohio between 1856 and 1858 and developed into an accomplished orator. She traveled to England in 1859 to deliver a series of lectures. From 1859 to 1861 she delivered more than forty-five lectures in eighteen cities in England, three cities in Scotland, and four cities in Ireland (Wesley 1994, 974). She was received enthusiastically wherever she spoke. In 1866 she returned to the United States and applied her oratorical skills to the task of racial uplift, in the manner of her brother Charles Remond and of Douglass. In 1867 she returned to England and subsequently settled in Florence, Italy, to practice medicine. It was said that she spoke in a "well-toned" and "pleasing style" and "demonstrated an unerring sensitivity to the political and social concerns of her listeners—particularly women reform activists" (Ripley 1985, 441).

Although most male lecturers were reluctant to speak about the exploitation of enslaved black women, Sarah Parker Remond, probably the most prominent woman abolitionist to travel and speak in the British Isles, was not. In a one-and-a-quarter-hour lecture delivered to an overflowing crowd at the Music Hall in Warrington, England, on 24 January 1859, Remond relentlessly detailed the treatment of the enslaved black woman, using as a case in point the story of Kentucky slave mother Margaret Garner. Garner, who "had suffered in her own person the degradation that a woman could not mention," escaped with her children to Cincinnati. Rather than allow her to be recaptured, Garner killed her three-year-old daughter, but she was prevented from killing her other children. Remond stated that "above all sufferers in America, American women who were slaves lived in the most pitiable condition. They could not protect themselves from the licentiousness which met them on every hand—they could not protect their honour from the tyrant" (Remond [1859] 1985a, 437). She also criticized the Dred Scott Decision of 1857, denying blacks the right to citizenship, and the heinous Fugitive Slave Act, which sent many blacks fleeing to northern states, Canada, and the British Isles.

Remond drew support for her arguments from contemporary events. She chronicled current and widely publicized incidents with significant impact on American slavery, showing how such events—for example, the trial of Margaret Garner and the Dred Scott Decision—mirrored the sad conditions of a slave society. Stressing the hypocrisy of the Christian church, in this same speech Remond cited the shooting of a black man for insubordination by a clergyman in Louisiana and the dismissal of a minister in Philadelphia after he preached an antislavery sermon. From her English audiences she wanted public outcry. In a 14 September 1859 speech delivered at the Athenaeum in Manchester, England, she asked them to exert their influence to abolish slavery in America: "Give us the power of your public opinion, it has great weight in America. Words spoken here are read there as no words written in America are read. . . . I ask you, raise the moral public opinion until its voice reaches the American shores. Aid us thus until the shackles of the American slave melt like dew before the morning sun" (Remond [1859] 1985b, 459).

Mary Ann Shadd Cary (1823–1893), the first black female newspaper editor, published the *Provincial Freeman,* a weekly Canadian newspaper for fugitive slaves and others who had fled to Canada in the wake of the Fugitive Slave Act during the 1850s. From 1852 to 1853 she was the only black missionary in the field for the American Missionary Association (AMA), the largest abolitionist organization in America (DeBoer 1994, xi). Cary taught fugitive slaves recently arrived who, in her view, lacked motivation and self-discipline. She, along with Samuel Ward and Alexander McArthur, established the *Provincial Freeman* in March 1853, after the AMA informed her that it would no longer support her school. The *Freeman* soon became Cary's vehicle for promoting industry among former slaves and exposing the misconduct of unscrupulous antislavery agents. In 1863 Cary returned to the United States, eventually settling in Washington, D.C., where she taught and ultimately practiced law.

In her historic 1855 address to the Colored National Convention, she advocated for the emigration of blacks from America to Canada and for their total integration into Canadian society. Cary's intense speaking style left its impression, as noted by the eyewitness quoted here: "Miss Shadd's eyes are small and penetrating and fairly flush when she is speaking. Her ideas seem to flow so fast that she, at times, hesitates for words; yet she overcomes any apparent imperfections in her speaking by the earnestness of her manner and the quality of her thoughts. She is a superior woman; and it is useless to deny it; however much we may differ with her on the subject of emigration" (Sterling 1984, 170–71).

All accounts of the works and days of the strong-willed Cary suggest that she rarely held her tongue or backed down from a position. She opposed the growing popularity of evangelical, better-life-in-the-afterworld preachers who neglected contemporary issues, with "their gross ignorance and insolent bearing, together with their sanctimonious garb," and who hung "tenaciously to exploded customs," giving some the impression that "money, and not the good of the people" motivated them (Cary 1986a, 32–33). One biographer describes her style as follows: "By nineteenth-century norms, Cary's caustic, jolting language seemed ill-suited to a woman. She used phrases such as 'gall and wormwood,' 'moral pest,' 'petty despot,' 'superannuated minister,' 'nest of unclean birds,' 'moral monsters,' and 'priest-ridden people,' in order to keep her ideas before the public" (Calloway-Thomas 1994, 225).

Most of Cary's extant writings are letters and scathing editorials from the *Provincial Freeman* railing against intemperance, "addled brained young people," and any number of other displeasing states of affairs. Texts of her speeches are scarce, but the following excerpt, reprinted with limited editorial intervention, comes from a sermon "apparently delivered before a Chatham [Canada West] audience on 6 April 1858" (Ripley 1986, 388) and suggests the fervor of her biblically based and feminist antislavery rhetoric: "We cannot successfully Evade duty because the Suffering fellow . . . is only a woman! She too is a neighbor. The good Samaritan of this generation must not take for their Exemplars the priest and the Levite when a fellow woman is among thieves—neither will they find excuse in the custom as barbarous and anti-Christian as any promulgated by pious Brahmin that . . . they may be only females. The spirit of true philanthropy knows no sex" (Cary 1986b, 389).

As William Still's history of the Underground Railroad documents, Frances Ellen Watkins Harper (1825–1911) joined the abolitionist movement largely because of an incident that occurred in the slave state of Maryland, her home state. In 1853 a law was passed prohibiting free blacks from entering Maryland. When a man unintentionally violated that law, he was arrested and sent to Georgia as a slave. He escaped but was recaptured and soon died. Hearing of this sequence of events, Harper remarked, "Upon that grave I pledge myself to the Anti-Slavery cause" (Still 1872, 786). In 1854 Harper gave up teaching to become a lecturer for the Maine Anti-Slavery Society.

Harper delivered what was probably her first antislavery speech at a meeting in New Bedford, Massachusetts, in 1854; it was possibly titled "Education and Elevation of the Colored Race" (Still 1872). She continued to speak out against slavery and its consequences, traveling throughout the New England area, southern Canada, and west to Michigan and Ohio. During one six-week period in 1854 she gave at least thirty-three lectures in twenty-one New England towns (Foster 1990). Because of her articulate and reserved manner, many who heard her found it difficult to believe that she was of African descent. Grace Greenwood, a journalist, labeled her "the bronze muse" and bemoaned the fact that a woman of such stature could possibly have been a slave, as if to suggest that slavery was more acceptable for some human beings than for others. For such observers she was considered a fascinating aberration, as this account by a Maine abolitionist suggests: "Miss W. is slightly tinged with African blood, but the color only serves to add a charm to the occasion which nothing else could give, while at the same time it disarms the fastidious of that so common prejudice which denies to white ladies the right to give public lectures" (Sterling 1984, 161). This commentary also highlights the perception that white women were different and that, while they were yet denied the right to give public lectures, black women were not always frowned upon in this role.

Harper frequently focused on the economic aspects of slavery and the irony of owning "property that can walk." In a lecture titled "Could We Trace the Record," delivered during the 1857 meeting of the New York City Anti-Slavery Society, she argued that slavery's financial benefits would make its abolishment more difficult: "A hundred thousand newborn babes are annually added to the victims of slavery; twenty thousand lives are annually sacrificed on the plantations of the South. Such a sight should send a thrill of horror, through the nerves of civilization and impel the heart of humanity to lofty deeds. So it might, if men had not found a fearful alchemy by which this blood can be transformed into gold. Instead of listening to the cry of agony, they listen to the ring of dollars and stoop down to pick up the coin" (Harper 1990a, 101).

Her commitment to the abolition of slavery led her to do more than lecture. Harper was active in the Philadelphia Underground Railroad, giving time, money, and talents to its efforts. She never refused an opportunity to engage in activities designed to promote emancipation. Without exception, those who reviewed Harper's lectures commented as much on her platform presence and her ethos as upon the content of her speeches. Such phrases as "splendid articulation," "pure language," "pleasant voice," "thought flowed in eloquent and poetic expression," "never assuming, never theatrical," "spoke feelingly and eloquently," and "a nature most femininely sensitive" characterize the lasting impression she left on her audiences. Even her contemporary Mary Ann Shadd Cary acknowledged Harper's superiority as an orator. In an 1858 letter to her husband Cary wrote, "She is the greatest female speaker ever was here, so wisdom obliges me to keep out of the way as with her prepared lectures there would just be no chance of a favorable comparison" (Sterling 1984, 174). These reactions add credence to the claim that a speaker's personality may be her most persuasive appeal.

Harper's magnetic personality should not, however, overshadow the powerful substance of her antislavery messages. One of her strongest messages, "Our Greatest Want," appeared in an 1859 issue of the *Anglo-African Magazine*, addressed not to whites but to northern blacks, in response to a growing interest in material wealth: "The respect that is bought by gold is not worth much. It is no honor to shake hands politically with men who whip women and steal babies. If this government has no call for our services, no aim for your children, we have the greater need of them to build up a true manhood and womanhood for ourselves" (Harper [1859] 1990b, 103).

Women's Rights

Prominent black women abolitionists such as Remond and Cary, as well as Maria W. Stewart and Sojourner Truth, frequently combined antislavery discussions with dis-cussions of feminist issues, framing their antislavery arguments in feminist terms. By the same token, white free antislavery feminists, as Jean Fagan Yellin puts it, conflated the oppression of enslaved and free women by equating the literal enslavement of black women to their own figurative enslavement. Yellin goes on to point out, however, that the speeches of black women testify to no confusion between the two experiences. "Nor," she writes, "did they confuse the free women's struggle for self-liberation from a metaphorical slavery with their own struggle for self-liberation from slavery. For them, the discourse of antislavery feminism became not liberating but confining when it colored the self-liberated Woman and Sister white and reassigned the role of the passive victim, which the patriarchy traditionally had reserved for white women, to women who were black" (Yellin 1989, 78–79).

Remond often cited the abuses of enslaved black women to bolster her abolitionist appeals. In her 1859 speech in Manchester she made a special appeal to the women of England, pointing out that "women are the worst victims of the slave power." Cary, in addition to her abolitionist activities in Canada, addressed groups on behalf of woman's rights, assigning the emancipation of slaves and the liberation of women equal importance. In her 1858 Chatham sermon, quoted from above, she makes appeals for "the Slave mother as well as the Slave father" and places in the same "pit" the "colored people of this country" and "the women of the land," invoking Christ as the supreme example of one who implied "an Equal inheritance" for the sexes. When in 1869 Cary, under pressure from black women delegates, was allowed to address the National Colored Labor Union, she spoke on woman's rights and suffrage. As a result, the union voted to include women workers in its organizations (Giddings 1984).

Black women had been defending their rights well before these and other more organized events occurred. A religious abolitionist who justified social activism with biblical scriptures, Maria W. Stewart (1803–1879) addressed the Afric-American Female Intelligence Society of Boston in 1832, exhorting the women to exert their influence: "O woman, woman! Your example is powerful, your influence great; it extends over your husbands and your children, and throughout the circle of your acquaintance" (Stewart [1832] 1995a, 16). In a speech at Franklin Hall she commented on the lack of employment opportunities for young black women in Boston as a consequence of "the powerful force of prejudice," a force which prevented them from becoming more than domestic workers (Stewart [1832] 1995b, 6).

Born in Connecticut, Maria Miller moved to Boston and married James W. Stewart, a ship's outfitter, in 1826. They were members of Boston's black middle class and friends of David Walker, the fiery, outspoken abolitionist and author of *Walker's Appeal, in Four Articles, Together With a Preamble, to The Coloured Citizens of the World, But in Particular And Very Expressly, To Those of the United States of America* in 1829. In this pamphlet Walker urged the slaves to revolt, slay their masters, if necessary, and escape to freedom. Incorporating much of Walker's style, Stewart delivered her Franklin Hall address in 1832, shortly after her husband's death. Stewart spoke on several other occasions between 1832 and 1833, but because of strong criticism she retired from public speaking, delivering her farewell address on 21 September 1833. In her 1833 "Farewell Address" Stewart lamented the fact that she was not well received as a public speaker, declaring, "I am about to leave you, perhaps never more to return. For I find it is no use for me as an individual to try to make myself useful among my color in this city. It was contempt for my moral and religious opinions in private that drove me thus before a public. Had experience more plainly shown me that it was the nature of man to crush his fellow, I should not have thought it so hard" (Stewart [1833] 1987, 70). Marilyn Richardson points out the irony that, although Stewart's speeches called for the liberation of all men and women, when published in William Lloyd Garrison's abolitionist newspaper, the *Liberator,* they were "for the sake of editorial propriety" relegated to the "Ladies' Department" (1987, 11).

After leaving slavery Isabella Baumfree (1797–1883) moved to New York City, became a domestic worker, and joined a religious commune. In 1843, at that time about forty-six years old, Baumfree declared herself to be Sojourner Truth, called by God to travel and preach. In this manner she began her career as a lecturer. She told her story across Long Island and entered Connecticut and then Massachusetts, where she joined the Northampton Association of Education and Industry. While in Massachusetts she met some of the leading abolitionists, including William Lloyd Garrison, Frederick Douglass, David Ruggles, Parker Pillsbury, and Wendell Phillips. It was during her affiliation with the association that she sharpened her speaking skills.

At the Akron, Ohio, Woman's Rights Convention in 1851, Sojourner Truth publicly validated all women when she contradicted previous speakers who had claimed women weak and helpless. Truth, after observing convention proceedings for one day, asked for permission to speak. Permission was granted even though many of the women feared that Truth's appearance would damage their cause by association with the slavery issue. It was on this occasion that she delivered her well-known "Ain't I a Woman" speech. Interestingly, the speech, quite popular among women activists today, received little attention at the time it was delivered. No mention of it was made in the conference proceedings. In this speech she pointed to contradictions exemplified in her ability to perform physical tasks as well as any man and reminded her audience that Jesus was the product of God and a woman, without the help of a man. Several years later, at the 9 May 1867 meeting of the American Equal Rights Association (AERA), Truth entered the debate over the proposed Fifteenth Amendment to grant black men but not women the right to vote. There she estimated the consequence of such a change on black women in particular: "There is a great stir about colored men getting their rights, but not a word about the colored woman; and if colored men get their rights, and not colored women get theirs, you see the colored men will be masters over the women, and it will be just as bad as it was before. . . . I want women to have their rights. In the courts women have no right, no voice; nobody speaks for them. I wish woman to have her voice there among the pettifoggers. If it is not a fit place for women, it is unfit for me to be there" (Truth [1867] 1995, 28). A former slave, Truth, perhaps more than any of the other black women activists discussed in this chapter, embodied the arguments she made in support of women and abolition. She spoke not of weakness but of power, "the lack of power that men ascribe to womankind and the presence of her own power and the power of all women" (Yellin 1989, 80).

After emancipation black women speakers concentrated on the newly freed women in the South, who needed training and protection. They addressed women's rights conventions and church conferences, and they organized their own gatherings to defend their honor and claim their place in public life. Frances Harper continued to lecture on convergence in the plights of black and white women. In her 1866 address to the Eleventh National Woman's Right's Convention, "We Are All Bound up Together," she described her shabby treatment by the state of Ohio two years earlier upon the death of her husband Fenton Harper. She acknowledged that "justice is not fulfilled so long as woman is unequal before the law." Later in that same speech, however, she expressed doubt that all white women could be counted on to look out for the best interests of black women: "I do not believe that white women are dewdrops just exhaled from the skies. I think that like men they may be divided into three classes, the good, the bad, and the indifferent. The good would vote according to their convictions and principles; the bad, as dictated by prejudice or malice; and the indifferent will vote on the strongest side of the question, with the winning party" (Harper [1866] 1990c, 217–18). Harper's words here indicate black women's awareness that although there were common interests among black and white women, there were also major differences.

The black church provided a number of rhetorical opportunities for black preaching women and black women advocates of such secular causes as woman's rights and abolitionism. As C. Eric Lincoln and Lawrence H. Mamiya point out, "many of these community service and political activities stemmed from a moral concern to uplift the race that was deeply rooted in religious motivation" (1990, 281). In fact, nearly all the women discussed in this essay were active members of black churches. It is not surprising, then, that much of the discourse on women's rights emerged from church women such as those associated with the Black Baptist Convention.

Lucy Wilmot Smith (1861–1890) spoke of black women's needs to a largely male audience at the 1886 meeting of the American National Baptist Convention. At the time of her address she was historian of the association and, along with two other Baptist churchwomen, Mary Cook and Virginia Broughton, led the challenge against this predominantly male organization (Higginbotham 1993). Smith opened her address, "The Future Colored Girl," by decrying the lack of adequate professional training for all women through the ages, and she closed by describing in particular the black woman's condition. She cataloged employment options for black women, among them raising poultry, small fruit or flowers; bee farming; dairying; lecturing; newspaper work; photography; medicine; teaching; and practicing elocution. Her point was that black women needed to explore a range of work opportunities in order to move beyond domestic labor toward some independence: "It is one of the evils of the day that from babyhood girls are taught to look forward to the time when they will be supported by a father, a brother or somebody's [sic] else brother. In teaching her that in whatever field of labor she enters she will abandon after a few years is teaching her to despise the true dignity of labor. The boy is taught to fill this life with as many hard strokes as possible. The girl should receive the same lesson" (Smith 1887, 74). She spoke uncompromisingly of the lack of training and employment opportunities for black women. A close friend and colleague, Mary Cook, eulogized her as follows: "She was connected with all the leading interest of her race and denomination. Her pen and voice always designated her position so clearly that no one need mistake her motive" (Higginbotham 1993, 126). Cook, in an essay prepared for an 1890 work titled *The Negro Baptist Pulpit: A Collection of Sermons and Papers,* encouraged the church to give women more responsibilities for "the salvation of the world" and to enlist them "to labor by the side of the men" so that "it will not be many years before a revolution will be felt all over this broad land, and the heathen will no longer walk in darkness, but will praise God, the light of their salvation" (Brawley [1890] 1971, 285).

In the 1890s black women organized themselves nationally, in part as a result of the powerful rhetorical activities of Ida B. Wells. In 1895 Josephine St. Pierre Ruffin, a Boston woman's activist, issued a call for a conference of black women. One concern was an open letter from John W. Jacks, president of the Missouri Press Association. The letter attacked Wells's character and by implication the morality of all black women in an attempt to rebut Ida Wells's accounts of southern lynching. As a result of Ruffin's call, the First Congress of Colored Women convened on 29 July 1895 in Boston. On the program at the 1895 conference were the names of several prominent black women who spoke on issues affecting all black women.

One of the most provocative addresses, "The Value of Race Literature," was delivered by Victoria Earle Matthews (1861–1907). Matthews, born in Fort Valley, Georgia, moved to New York in 1873. She became a journalist and helped to organize the Women's Loyal Union of New York and Brooklyn. In the speech Matthews paraded before her elite audience the range of stereotypical black characters portrayed in literature by whites, and she called for those present to take the lead in creating more literature of their own. But the speech more specifically focused on women's rights was "The Awakening of the Afro-American Woman," delivered in 1897 at the San Francisco meeting of the Society of Christian Endeavor. A former slave, Matthews recalled slavery's past horrors: "As I stand here to-day clothed in the garments of Christian womanhood, the horrible days of slavery, out of which I came, seem as a dream that is told, some horror incredible. Indeed, could they have been, and are not?" (Matthews [1897] 1995, 150). Matthews also protested the laws forbidding mixed marriages, laws which, she claimed, disgraced black women most: "As long as the affections are controlled by legislation in defiance of Christian law, making infamous the union of black and white, we shall have unions without the sanction of the law, and children without legal parentage, to the degradation of black womanhood and the disgrace of white manhood" (154).

At the World's Congress of Representative Women race activists addressed white women about black women. The congress, part of the Columbian Exposition, was held 15–22 May 1893 in Chicago. The women's exhibit was to illuminate the accomplishments of American women, but only after much political maneuvering were a few prominent black women invited to participate. Fannie Williams, well-known in Chicago women's circles, presented one of the major addresses, "The Intellectual Progress of the Colored Women of the United States since the Emancipation Proclamation."

Fannie Barrier Williams (1855–1944) was born to a prominent New York family and attended the Collegiate Institute of Brockport, the New England Conservatory of

Music, and the School of Fine Arts in Washington, D.C., where she taught for almost ten years. Williams eventually settled in Chicago and gained a solid reputation as a speaker. In her speech to the Congress Williams spoke of common womanhood shared by all those present. Given the constraints under which she spoke, Williams wisely emphasized similarities rather than differences. She argued that many black women were rapidly becoming social and intellectual equals to white women and that those who were not needed their support. Such support, she claimed, would be in the best interest of all women: "The fixed policy of persecutions and injustice against a class of women who are weak and defenseless will be necessarily hurtful to the cause of all women. Colored women are becoming more and more a part of the social forces that must help to determine the questions that so concern women generally. . . . If it be the high purpose of these deliberations to lessen the resistance to woman's progress, you can not fail to be interested in our struggles against the many oppositions that harass us" (Williams [1893] 1995, 118).

Anna Julia Cooper (1858–1964), present at both the National Conference of Colored Women and the Congress of Representative Women, delivered her most challenging defense of black women at the 1886 Convocation of Colored Clergy in Washington, D.C. She criticized the clergy and the Episcopalian Church for discriminating against women. Cooper taught at Wilberforce College in Xenia, Ohio, from 1884 to 1885, then returned to St. Augustine's College in Raleigh, North Carolina, where she began her education, and remained there until 1887. Cooper then moved to Washington, D.C., where she held several teaching positions. She was also in the vanguard of the black women's club movement, helping to organize the Washington Colored Women's League.

In her speech "Womanhood A Vital Element in the Regeneration and Progress of a Race," she rehearsed the history of women in general and the future prospects for the southern black woman in particular. Like Frances Harper twenty years earlier, Cooper employed the "same but different" argument directed to audiences throughout the century. Appealing, on the one hand, to a common womanhood, Cooper highlighted, on the other, those differences resulting from slavery and color prejudice: "With all the wrongs and neglects of her past, with all the weakness, the debasement, the moral thralldom of her present, the black woman of to-day stands mute and wondering at the Herculean task devolving upon her. But the cycles wait for her. No other hand can move the lever. She must be loosed from her bands and set to work" (Cooper [1892] 1995, 63).

Lynching

That the entry "antilynching movement" in *Black Women in America: An Historical Encyclopedia* (1994) is essentially an article about Ida Wells indicates clearly the extent of her campaign against mob violence. Although most of the speakers discussed in this chapter spoke out against lynching, none did it more effectively and more consistently than Ida B. Wells. This discussion of antilynching discourse also centers on this forceful speaker.

In manner of speaking and reputation, Wells can be compared to Cary. Both were bold, straightforward, and hard-hitting. Wells also attended the 1893 World's Congress of Representative Women, but unlike her contemporaries Frances Harper and Fannie Barrier Williams, Wells had no official slot on the program of speakers. Instead, she positioned herself near the Haitian Pavilion, where Frederick Douglass was presiding, and distributed copies of an eighty-one page protest pamphlet, *The Reason Why the Colored American Is Not in the World's Columbian Exposition.* The pamphlet contained pieces by Douglass; Ferdinand Barnett, a prominent Chicago attorney who later married Wells; I. Garland Penn, a newspaperman; and Wells herself. Over ten thousand copies were circulated during the fair. But this was only one of many causes Wells espoused. Wells the social activist spoke out over a period of almost forty years, until her death in 1931, against the denial of women's rights, against racism generally, and, of course, against the practice of lynching.

Ida B. Wells (1862–1931), born in Holly Springs, Mississippi, was the child of former slaves. Both parents died of yellow fever in 1878, leaving Wells, at sixteen the oldest, in charge of five siblings. Taking two sisters with her, she eventually moved to Memphis to teach. However, she soon discovered that she did not adapt well to the profession's constraints, and she confesses in her autobiography, "I never cared for teaching" (Wells 1970, 31). In 1889 Wells became editor and part owner of the *Memphis Free Speech and Headlight.* Her editorials protested racial injustice in education, voting rights, and public transportation. Eager to get her newspaper into the homes of those who could not read, Wells printed several editions on easily identified pink paper. Not until 1892, after three of her friends had been lynched in Memphis and her newspaper office had been burned down by an angry mob, did Wells launch a verbal war against lynching that continued into the twentieth century. In response to the events in Memphis, a group of prominent black women from New York and Brooklyn organized a testimonial in her honor at Lyric Hall on 5 October 1892. On this occasion Wells delivered her first public speech, "Southern Horrors: Lynch Law in All Its Phases," in which she proposed corrective action against lynching: "Nothing is more definitely settled than [that] he must act for himself. I have shown how he may employ the boycott, emigration, and the press, and I feel that by a combination of all these agencies can be effectually stamped out lynch law, that last relic of barbarism and slavery" (Wells [1892]1989, 419). Many prominent blacks, including Wells, had convinced themselves that those being lynched were indeed guilty and deserved to die. But after incidents such as the one in Memphis, they began to recognize lynching as an attempt to suppress black progress. Wells stressed this point in her first public speech.

Not limiting herself to this country, she took her antilynching campaign to Europe and found favor there, in the face of disparagement by the southern press in the United States. Wells traveled to England and Scotland in April 1893 to deliver a series of antilynching lectures. She returned to England for a six-month stay in 1894, serving as paid correspondent for the *Chicago Inter-Ocean.* On 13 February 1893, before leaving for her first tour of England, Wells addressed the Boston Monday Lectureship. In this speech, "Lynch Law in All Its Phases," Wells rehearsed in detail the Memphis incident and appealed to her audience with gruesome details of a lynching in Paris, Texas, only two weeks earlier. She appealed to this predominantly white audience for public outcry, advancing her belief that their failure to act was a result of ignorance rather than apathy and drawing on their concern for America's reputation:

> I am before the American people to-day ... because of a deep-seated conviction that the country at large does not know the extent to which lynch law prevails in parts of the Republic, nor the conditions which force into exile those who speak the truth. I cannot believe that the apathy and indifference which so largely obtains regarding mob rule is other than the result of ignorance of the true situation. ... Repeated attacks on the life, liberty and happiness of any citizen or class of citizens are attacks on distinctive American institutions; such attacks imperiling as they do the foundation of government, law and order, merit the thoughtful consideration of far-sighted Americans; not from a standpoint of sentiment, not even so much from a standpoint of justice to a weak race, as from a desire to preserve our institutions.
>
> (Wells [1893] 1995, 80)

Racial Uplift

In the midst of the struggle for freedom and equality, black women pressed their people toward self-help, self-improvement, and racial uplift. Racial uplift was emphasized from two perspectives: encouraging those who were in need to take initiative; and challenging those who had accomplished to "lift" those who had not. Although public address focused specifically on improving the working and living conditions of black women is considered above in the section called "Women's Rights," the speeches of three activist educators who argued for general assistance to southern blacks after the Civil War are considered under the heading of "Racial Uplift." Frances Harper made a point of addressing directly those in need of social and emotional uplift in the post-Civil War South. Edmonia G. Highgate spent her brief life teaching the newly freed in the South and lecturing for financial support in the North. Lucy Craft Laney in 1893 organized a day and boarding school in Augusta, Georgia; developed the city's first kindergarten; and stressed in her speeches to educated blacks their crucial role in the work of racial advancement.

Frances Harper, who spoke on all the issues discussed in this essay, adopted the first perspective—encouraging self-help. She availed herself of every opportunity to speak directly to the people for whom she fought, traveling throughout the Midwest before the war and in the deep South after the war. In a biographical sketch William Still writes, "For the best part of several years, since the war, she has traveled very extensively through the Southern States, going on the plantations and amongst the lowly, as well as to the cities and towns, addressing schools, Churches, meetings in Court Houses, Legislative Halls, &c., and, sometimes, under the most trying and hazardous circumstances" (1872, 767). According to one story, during an appearance in Darlington, South Carolina, instead of standing in the pulpit of the church in which she spoke, she stood near the door where those outside as well as those inside could hear her.

In a 21 September 1860 letter to Jane E. Hitchcock Jones, a Quaker abolitionist from Ohio, she expresses her view that such lectures among free and formerly enslaved blacks help to lift morale and develop self-esteem:

> There are a number of colored settlements in the West, where a few words of advice and encouragement among our people might act as a stimulant and charm; and if they would change the public opinion of the country, they should not find it, I hope, a useless work to strive to elevate the character of the colored people, not merely by influencing the public *around* them but *among* them; for after all, this prejudice of which such complaint has been made, if I understand it aright, is simply a great protest of human minds rising up against slavery, and so hating it for themselves that they learn not only to despise it, but the people that submit to it, and those identified with them by race.
>
> (Harper 1992, 82)

Harper must have recognized the opportunity for instruction that public speaking afforded to those who did not read and did not subscribe to newspapers. She also wrote of giving lectures privately to women at no charge. Her speeches to such audiences were usually impromptu, and generally journalists were not present; consequently, no extant texts of these spontaneous orations remain.

Born to former slaves in Syracuse, New York, Edmonia Highgate (1844–1870) lived for only twenty-six years, but during those years she did all she could for racial uplift, alternately teaching the newly freed in the South and lecturing for their support in the North. At the age of twenty Highgate was sent to Norfolk, Virginia, by the American Missionary Association to teach. After three months of intense work, she had a mental breakdown and returned to Syracuse. Shortly after her return Highgate addressed the 1864 National Convention of Colored Men, held in Syracuse. Highgate and Frances Harper were the only women to address the exclusively male organization. When Frederick Douglass introduced her he said, "You have your Anna Dickinsons; and we have ours. We wish to meet you at every point" (*Minutes* 1969, 14). Douglass was referring here to the orator Anna Dickinson, who had achieved fame after her 1861 Philadelphia address on "The Rights and Wrongs of Women" at the age of nineteen. Although the convention minutes do not include the text of Highgate's speech, a summary in the 26 October 1864 *New Orleans Tribune* demonstrates the tenor of her political activism and astuteness: "Miss Highgate said she would not be quite in her place, perhaps, if a girl as she is, she should tell the Convention what they ought to do; but she had, with others *thought* about what had been proposed and those thoughts she would tell them. Miss Highgate was evidently a strong *Lincoln* Man; so much so, that she felt that Gen. Fremont ought not to be a candidate.... Miss Highgate urged the Convention to press on, to not abate hope until the glorious time spoken of to-night, shall come" (Sterling 1984, 296).

While back in New York, Highgate lectured to raise funds for freedmen's relief. She returned to the South in 1865, teaching for a while in Maryland, Louisiana, and Mississippi. After four years she resumed lecturing in New York, New England, and Canada. In February 1879 she spoke at the Thirty-sixth Annual Meeting of the Massachusetts AntiSlavery Society. Following a lengthy address by John M. Langston, a prominent black activist from Ohio, Highgate warned against hasty optimism. A paraphrase in the *National Anti-Slavery Standard* stated the following:

> Miss Highgate said that, after laboring five years as a teacher in the South, it was perhaps appropriate for her to give a report on the state of things there. In her opinion, even if the Fifteenth Amendment should now be ratified, it would be only a paper ratification. Even in the instruction given to the ignorant there lacks some of the main essentials of right instruction. The teachers sent out by the evangelical organizations do very little to remove caste-prejudice, the twin sister of slavery ... President Lincoln was accustomed to take credit to himself for moving forward no faster than the people demanded. The Republicans in the South do no better. We need *Anti-Slavery* teachers there; teachers who will show that it is safe to do right. The Anti-Slavery Society must not disband, because its work in the South is not yet half done; and if not now thoroughly done, it will have to be done over again.
>
> (*National Anti-Slavery Standard* 1870)

In a June 1870 letter to the abolitionists Gerrit and Ann Smith, Highgate mentions the advice of Theodore Tilton, famous speaker and friend, who, impressed with her speaking skills, urged her "to write a lecture to interest the general public, deliver it as other lecturers do and you will then be on your way to secure the funds necessary to aid the cause to which you are so devoted" (Sterling 1984, 301). Highgate implied in the letter that she might like to visit the Smiths to gain the privacy needed to write such a lecture. But she never did so. A month later she requested instead that the AMA send her south again to Jackson, Mississippi, for another teaching tour. She never returned to the South, however. Edmonia Highgate died in Syracuse in October 1870.

As the title of Lucy Laney's 1899 speech, "The Burden of the Educated Colored Woman," indicates, the lecture centered on racial uplift. During the post-Reconstruction period, those who had acquired education and prosperity felt a duty to educate those less fortunate. This education extended to morality and economy as well as reading and writing, for as Paula Giddings, at one point quoting Laney, writes, "Whatever their views about social sanctions, one reason for the emphasis on morality was that lack of it could be impoverishing. ... a good part of the philosophy of racial uplift had to do with lifting the burdens of 'ignorance and immorality' with 'true culture and character, linked with—cash'" (1984, 102). Although Laney called this challenge a "burden," she was not resentful but despairing that the times had created this triple burden of "shame and crime and prejudice." The "shame" Laney saw as a consequence of nonlegalized slave marriages, poor parenting skills, and ignorance of hygiene. The large numbers of young men and women incarcerated provided evidence of the "crime." The "prejudice" came from those in power, who made it difficult to overcome the other two burdens. This speech was delivered in 1899 at the third Hampton Negro Conference on the Virginia campus of Hampton University, one of the black schools formed after the Civil War. At these annual conferences Hampton graduates and other prominent race leaders discussed strategies toward racial improvement. As was the case at many such conferences, the men and women met separately, under the unfortunate assumption that women operated in a separate sphere and had no need to address issues that were, in fact, of collective importance.

Lucy Craft Laney (1854–1933) was born in Macon, Georgia, to free, literate parents. Her father, an ordained Presbyterian minister, earned enough money while enslaved to purchase freedom for himself and his wife. Laney was graduated from Atlanta University in 1873, a member of the first graduating class. After teaching for ten years, Laney established a school in Augusta, Georgia, which eventually became the Haines Normal and Industrial Institute. Near the end of the century Laney, one of several black women who founded their own schools, offered a curriculum in liberal arts as well as vocational training and was especially interested in the education of girls. By the time she spoke to the Hampton Negro Conference in 1899, Laney's school was on its way to becoming an established success. In "The Burden of the Educated Colored Woman" she called specifically on "the educated Negro woman" not only to teach but to speak. Laney argued that "as a public lecturer she may give advice, helpful suggestions, and important knowledge that will change a whole community and start its people on the upward way." She cited the example of Frances Harper (as well as four other women). She closed her speech with a story about a group of male laborers who successfully lifted "a heavy piece of timber to the top of a building" only when they asked the women to help them, reinforcing her message that women as well as men were needed to ensure successful racial uplift: "Today not only the men on top call, but a needy race—the whole world, calls loudly to the cultured Negro women to come to the rescue. Do they hear? Are they coming? Will they push?" (Laney [1899] 1992, 174).

Summary

The rhetorical activities of numerous other nineteenth-century black women speakers have not been mentioned here. These women spoke their minds from platform and pulpit and went to work correcting the wrongs they saw before them. They left no records, wrote no books, organized no conferences; but they helped to establish a tradition of political activism among black women. The activities of the women discussed merely illustrate the ranges of issues brought to public attention by women using oratory to effect change. The general response of white audiences to the very presence of intelligent, articulate black women was often much stronger than their response to anything the women had to say. These speakers were the embodiment of their messages—whether the message was antislavery, feminist, or an appeal for racial dignity. They authenticated their arguments; the messengers were their messages. African American women of the nineteenth century participated in history largely through their rhetorical activities. The pages of the *Woman's Era* provide ample evidence of their participation in the political discourse of their time. On the front page of its 24 March 1894 inaugural edition can be found a photograph and tribute to Lucy Stone, pioneer women's rights advocate and anti-slavery lecturer, known for her moving oratory. The Women's Era Club members chose as their motto a phrase from her last message, "Make the world better" (*The Women's Era*, Vol. 1, No. 1, 24 March 1894, p. 1).

References

Brawley, Edward M. [1890] 1971. *The Negro Baptist Pulpit: A Collection of Sermons and Papers.* Freeport, N.Y.: Books for Libraries Press.

Calloway-Thomas, Carolyn. 1994. "Cory, Mary Ann Shadd." In *Black Women in America: An Historical Encyclopedia, Vol. 2,* edited by Darlene Clark Hine et al., 224–26. Bloomington: Indiana University Press.

Cary, Mary Ann Shadd. 1986a. "Mary Ann Shadd Cary to Frederick Douglass, 25 January 1849." In *The Black Abolitionist Papers, Vol. 4: The United States 1847–1858,* edited by C. Peter Ripley, 31–34. Chapel Hill: University of North Carolina Press.

———. 1986b. "Sermon" [6 April 1858]. In *The Black Abolitionist Papers, Vol. 2: Canada, 1830–1865,* edited by C. Peter Ripley, 388–91. Chapel Hill: University of North Carolina Press.

Cooper, Anna Julia. [1892] 1995. "Womanhood a Vital Element in the Regeneration and Progress of a Race." In *With Pen and Voice: A Critical Anthology of Nineteenth-Century African-American Women,* edited by Shirley Wilson Logan, 53–74. Carbondale: Southern Illinois University Press.

DeBoer, Clara Merritt. 1994. *Be Jubilant My Feet: African American Abolitionists in the American Missionary Association 1839–1861.* New York: Garland.

Foster, Frances Smith, ed. 1990. *A Brighter Coming Day: A Frances Ellen Watkins Harper Reader.* New York: Feminist Press.

Franklin, John Hope, and Alfred Moss. 1988. *From Slavery to Freedom: A History of Negro Americans.* New York: McGraw-Hill.

Giddings, Paula. 1984. *When and Where I Enter: The Impact of Black Women on Race and Sex in America.* New York: William Morrow.

Harper, Frances E. W. 1990a. "Could We Trace the Record of Every Human Heart." In *A Brighter Coming Day: A Frances Ellen Watkins Harper Reader,* edited by Frances Smith Foster, 100–102. New York: Feminist Press.

———. [1859] 1990b. "Our Greatest Want." In *A Brighter Coming Day: A Frances Ellen Watkins Harper Reader,* edited by Frances Smith Foster, 102–4. New York: Feminist Press.

———. [1866] 1990c. "We Are All Bound up Together." In *A Brighter Coming Day: A Frances Ellen Watkins Harper Reader,* edited by Frances Smith Foster, 217–19. New York: Feminist Press.

———. 1992. "Letter to Jane E. Hitchcock Jones, 21 September 1860." In *The Black Abolitionist Papers, Vol. 5: The United States, 1859–1865,* edited by C. Peter Ripley, 81–83. Chapel Hill: University of North Carolina Press.

Higginbotham, Evelyn Brooks. 1993. *Righteous Discontent: The Women's Movement in the Black Baptist Church, 1880–1920.* Cambridge: Harvard University Press.

Laney, Lucy. [1899] 1992. "The Burden of the Educated Colored Woman." In *The Rhetoric of Struggle: Public Address by African American Women,* edited by Robbie Walker, 167–74. New York: Garland Publishing.

Lincoln, C. Eric, and Lawrence H. Mamiya. 1990. *The Black Church in the African American Experience.* Durham: Duke University Press.

Matthews, Victoria Earle. [1897] 1995. "The Awakening of the Afro-American Woman." In *With Pen and Voice: A Critical Anthology of Nineteenth-Century African-American Women,* edited by Shirley Wilson Logan, 149–55. Carbondale: Southern Illinois University Press.

Minutes of the Proceedings of the National Negro Conventions 1830–184. 1969. Ed. Howard Holman Bell. New York: Arno Press.

National Anti-Slavery Standard. 1870 (5 February).

Remond, Sarah Parker. [1859] 1985a. "Speech at the Music Hall." In *The Black Abolitionist Papers, Vol. 1: The British Isles 1830–1865,* edited by C. Peter Ripley, 435–44. Chapel Hill: University of North Carolina Press.

———. [1859] 1985b. "Speech at the Athenauem." In *The Black Abolitionist Papers, Vol. 1: The British Isles, 1830–1865,* edited by C. Peter Ripley, 457–61. Chapel Hill: University of North Carolina Press.

Richardson, Marilyn, ed. 1987. *Maria W. Stewart, America's First Black Woman Political Writer: Essays and Speeches.* Bloomington: Indiana University Press.

Ripley, C. Peter, ed. 1985. *The Black Abolitionist Papers. Vol. 1: The British Isles 1830–1865.* Chapel Hill: University of North Carolina Press.

———. 1986. *The Black Abolitionist Papers. Vol. 2: Canada, 1830–1865.* Chapel Hill: University of North Carolina Press.

Smith, Lucy Wilmot. 1887. "The Future Colored Girl." In *Minutes and Addresses of the American National Baptist Convention,* Saint Louis, Mo., 25–29 August 1886, 68–74. Jackson, Miss.: J. J. Spelman.

Sterling, Dorothy, ed. 1984. *We Are Your Sisters: Black Women in the Nineteenth Century.* New York: Norton.

Stewart, Maria W. [1833] 1987. "Mrs. Stewart's Farewell Address to her Friends in the City of Boston." In *Maria W. Stewart, America's First Black Woman Political Writer: Essays and Speeches,* edited by Marilyn Richardson, 65–74. Bloomington: Indiana University Press.

———. [1832] 1995a. An Address Delivered before the Afric-American Female Intelligence Society of Boston." In *With Pen and Voice: A Critical Anthology of Nineteenth-Century African-American Women,* edited by Shirley Wilson Logan, 11–16. Carbondale: Southern Illinois University Press.

———. [1832] 1995b. "Lecture Delivered at the Franklin Hall." In *With Pen and Voice: A Critical Anthology of Nineteenth-Century African-American Women,* edited by Shirley Wilson Logan, 6–10. Carbondale: Southern Illinois University Press.

Still, William. 1872. *The Underground Rail Road.* Philadelphia: Porter & Coates.

Truth, Sojourner. [1867] 1995. "Speech Delivered to the First Annual Meeting of the American Equal Rights Association." In *With Pen and Voice: A Critical Anthology of Nineteenth-Century African-American Women,* edited by Shirley Wilson Logan, 28–29. Carbondale: Southern Illinois University Press.

Wells, Ida B. 1970. *Crusade for Justice: The Autobiography of Ida B. Wells.* Chicago: University of Chicago Press.

———. [1892] 1989. "Southern Horrors: Lynch Law in All Its Phases." In *Man Cannot Speak for Her, Vol. 2: Key Texts of the Earliest Feminists,* edited by Karlyn Kohrs Campbell, 385–419. Westport, Conn.: Greenwood Press.

———. [1893] 1995. "Lynch Law in All Its Phases." In *With Pen and Voice: A Critical Anthology of Nineteenth-Century African-American Women,* edited by Shirley Wilson Logan, 80–99. Carbondale: Southern Illinois University Press.

Wesley, Dorothy Porter. 1994. "Remond, Sarah Parker." In *Black Women in America: An Historical Encyclopedia, Vol. 2,* edited by Darlene Clark Hine et al., 972–74. Bloomington: Indiana University Press.

Williams, Fannie Barrier. [1893] 1995. "The Intellectual Progress of the Colored Women of the United States since the Emancipation Proclamation." In *With Pen and Voice: A Critical Anthology of Nineteenth-Century African-American Women,* edited by Shirley Wilson Logan, 106–19. Carbondale: Southern Illinois University Press.

The Woman's Era (Boston, Mass.). 24 March 1894, 1 June 1894, April 1895.

Yellin, Jean Fagan. 1989. *Women & Sisters: The Antislavery Feminists in American Culture.* New Haven: Yale University Press.

SECTION 3

METHODS AND METHODOLOGIES

6.
SPEAKING TO THE PAST: FEMINIST HISTORIOGRAPHY IN RHETORIC
Susan C. Jarratt

Editors' Note: *This essay opens by challenging the goal of history-writing: is it discovery, narration, objectivity, or reportage? The author argues that as a reflective, social practice history-writing (or historiography) aims not only to provide as much accuracy as possible (by writing women into the traditional history of rhetoric) but to "create histories aimed at a more just future" (by producing gendered readings of male-authored texts). Therefore, the author proposes to embody a "normative ethics," that is an "ethical way of acting, to be argued about, refuted, or taken up by other members of my social group." As feminist rhetorical methods, the author develops positionality, standpoint theory, gendered readings, and pedagogy.*

> The past is made of meanings, actions, and events far more eclectic and various than any hegemonic culture would be eager to tolerate were the past to become present, or, and this is the real worry, were it to become actively a source of inspiration for the future. Thus for its own protection, such a culture is impelled to create out of its variegated history a much narrower but also differently varying "significant" past, by selecting only certain meanings and events for emphasis and celebration; isolating others for the purposes of revilement and stigmatization; neglecting or excluding others; and diluting or converting the rest into non-threatening forms.
>
> —Joan Cocks, *The Oppositional Imagination*

> If, in one respect, the function of history expresses the position of one generation in relation to preceding ones by stating, "I can't be that," it always affects the statement of a no less dangerous complement, forcing a society to confess, "I am other than what I would wish to be, and I am determined by what I deny." It attests to an autonomy and a dependence whose proportions vary according to the social settings and political situations in which they are elaborated.
>
> —Michel de Certeau, *The Writing of History*

Long ago, this issue of *PRE/TEXT* was proposed to engage a question about ethics and historiography. At that time, I was troubled by the prospect that the revitalized project of historicizing rhetoric might take shape as a scientific or positivistic "research" practice. Some of us were arguing over whether an historical account should strive

Susan C. Jarratt, "Speaking to the Past: Feminist Historiography in Rhetoric." *Pre/Text* 11 (1990): 189–209. *Pre/Text* 11 (1990): 189–209. Note: This essay has been condensed.

for objectivity, could discover the unknown and make it known; or, on the other hand, whether history-writing had more to do with making than finding, with selection and narration than report.[1] De Certeau voices this concern as an absence of theory: "in history as in other fields, one day or another a practice without theory will necessarily drift into the dogmatism of 'eternal values' or into an apology for a 'timelessness'" (57). I believe those of us who work in the history of rhetoric—a growing number— have come some distance in the last few years from a relatively unreflective historical practice to a reflective one. The conference on Writing Histories of Rhetoric held in October 1989 in Arlington, Texas (proceedings of which will be published at some point) and Stephen North's description of historical practice as a series of confrontations between alternative narratives (78–90) are signs of wider and wider agreement that history-writing is an interpretive act and has to do with the construction of a narrative by a writer located in time, place, institution.

My concern now is quite different. I am writing here "as a woman," describing history-writing as a social practice that contributes to a radical critique of dominant discourses on gender.[2] The question here is how feminists writing histories of rhetoric can take up the challenge posed in the two epigraphs: to create histories aimed at a more just future. Certainly a gendering of history requires the kind of historiographical revision currently under way in rhetoric; turning away from an "Edmund Hillary" approach to history—one encounters it because it's there—a feminist historiography points the way to a different set of subjects for historical inquiry and questions the narrative logic operative in traditional histories. But acknowledging that histories are socially constructed narratives is no guarantee of a particular ideological valence or of an ethical practice. It only prevents a certain kind of scientistic blindness to the ways choices get made within institutions. How can feminist practices in the history of rhetoric become an active source of inspiration for the future, as Cocks proposes? How can they best elicit the recognition of which de Certeau writes: "'I am other than what I would wish to be'"? The mode of discourse I use for exploring these questions might be termed "normative ethics": i.e., I am proposing an ethical way of acting, to be argued about, refuted, or taken up by other members of my social group. I am not engaging in a metaethical discourse, establishing a definition of "ethics" or carrying out a philosophical exploration about ethics as a category of thought. Ethical decisions are understood in anthropological or sociological terms to express communal values—what the sophists called *nomoi*— always susceptible to reformulation. Such reformulation is central to feminism, a transformative social practice contested from outside and from within. Those internal contestations, so consuming at this historical moment, will later become the focus of this discussion.

Having some time in the past proposed a practice of history-writing based on the rhetoric of the first sophists, I have enjoyed very much hearing ideas from colleagues about how that work connects with other historiography, both feminist and other.[3] I found in the two works cited above, as well as in my readings of feminist utopian novels, a way of seeing history that looks backward *and* forward. Joan Cocks speaks of a forward-looking history-writing and describes the way hegemonic histories work ideologically to narrow and control historical understanding.[4] De Certeau outlines the simultaneous working of determination and agency; I like the element of danger in his account. Histories are powerful; much is at stake in their writing, and in writing about their writing. The point of a feminist excursion into ethics and historiography will be to speculate about how current differences within feminist theory might direct heterogeneous practices of history-writing in rhetoric toward the aims suggested by the opening epigraphs. The inquiry begins with some reflections on two kinds of historical work: histories about women who spoke and wrote in the past and histories that concern themselves not solely or even at all with women but with the category of gender.

Feminist Histories of Rhetoric: Women's History/Gendered Historiography

Though Elizabeth Flynn is right in pointing out that feminism and composition/ rhetoric have been slow to align themselves within English departments, feminist work in the history of rhetoric has gained an exciting momentum in the few years since it first appeared. In two of the last three College Composition and Communication Conference conventions, seven out of 36 history panels were devoted to women in the history of rhetoric. In 1988, three and one-third out of 20 panels on history of rhetoric/ history of writing instruction concerned women; in 1989, there were four women's panels out of 16 history sessions.[5]

As I began listening to conference presentations about women in rhetoric, I listened both with excitement and enthusiasm but also with sense of hesitation. Would feminist work in the history of rhetoric be limited to women's history? Feminist historians like Joan Scott and Joan Kelly, as well as women working on curriculum transformation, are wary of developing a separate women's canon, or of simply adding a few titles to a list constructed within a masculinist system of knowledge and value. At the Writing Histories of Rhetoric conference (October 1989), I used Joan Scott's key article on gender in history to argue that in rhetoric as well as in other disciplines we needed not only women's history but gendered readings of male-authored texts. Gendered analysis, unlike "women's history," applies feminist perspectives in periods of history when women's issues or gender had not been taken up in texts authored by women. I'd like to present that case as I made it then and afterwards offer a critique of it.

The Case for Gendered Histories of Rhetoric over "Women's History"

Joan Wallach Scott's essay, "Gender as a Useful Category for Analysis in History," first appeared in *American Historical Review* (December 1986) and has since been reprinted in *Gender and the Politics of History*. I draw on Scott's essay as a way of marking a point in the development of feminist histories of rhetoric paralleling a development in feminist literary studies and other feminist histories. In rhetoric, we are recapitulating the movement from a discovery of women's history—i.e., women in history—to a diversification of projects focused not only on the presence of biological women but on gender as a discursive and social category. In numerous commentaries on the recent history of American and French feminisms, a similar taxonomy has been employed, contrasting an empirically oriented American practice with a theoretically self-conscious French tradition. Toril Moi's controversial *Sexual/Textual Politics*, for example, diminishes the achievements of the first American feminist literary critics, because of their privileging of unmediated women's experience, in favor of French feminism's engagement with the ways discourse operates to shape understandings of experience, self, and history. Among efforts to negotiate this supposed difference are works like Betsy Draine's review article, "Refusing the Wisdom of Solomon," which evaluates work by American feminists seeking a "cautious engagement" with European critical issues (148–49).

Because feminist work in rhetoric has come rather lately into the conversation, we might be able to use these commentaries to avoid some of the conflicts of the American/French division. Rather than proceeding solely under the banner of "women's history," I suggest a shift in emphasis, or an expansion of the feminist project in rhetoric, to include gendered analysis as well. We should learn from feminist historians in literary studies that the relations of feminist history to "history" should not be only additive. Writing women into history "implies not only a new history of women, but also a new history" (Scott 82). Scott points out the need for theoretical synthesis of descriptive case studies. Without such theorizing, marginalization seems almost inevitable: history of rhetoric here, *women's* history of rhetoric over there. In Joan Kelly's terms, "compensatory history" is not enough (2). Gender as a category— i.e., as constitutive of social relations and as a way of signifying power—allows for more than addition: it shakes up dominant disciplinary concepts. Gender is relational: a history conceived in terms of gender as an analytic differs from "women's history" in that it investigates the ways social categories are constituted around or in the absence of each other. With Scott, I feel we should be asking not only "Who are the neglected women rhetoricians?" but also "How does gender give meaning to the organization and perception of historical knowledge?" (83). A feminist history sees woman's place in human social life not only as a product of things she does but in terms of the meaning her activities acquire through concrete social interaction (Scott 91). Thus, even in the work of men within a patriarchal tradition, the category of gender is operative because of the meanings ascribed to all by gender differences. Shakespearean scholar Phyllis Rackin imagines the operation of gender visually:

> In androcentric culture, the female principle is negative, like the blank space that defines a positive pictorial image or like the concept of feminine gender that allows the male to define itself as masculine; it is also supplementary, like the artistic imitation that represents natural life.
>
> (34)

Drawing on the work of Michel Foucault, literary critics like Nancy Armstrong and Susan Morgan chart the gendering of a literary age or genre across the lines of biological sex of authors and characters. Morgan argues for the feminization of heroic virtue in some examples of nineteenth-century fiction, culminating her study with a vision of Henry James's character Lambert Strether as the embodiment of this new "feminine" heroism. Historians of rhetoric might likewise investigate the relationships between gender and genre in particular historical periods. Is rhetoric a feminine supplement to philosophy in some ages and a masculine master discipline in others? Have certain figures (male or female) feminized rhetoric in their times? These are broadly stated questions awaiting more refined answers available through the practice of a gendered historiography.

In supporting a feminist history built on gender as a category my intention is not to correct women's history of rhetoric but rather to connect with it. Along with Mary Jacobus (and against a post-feminist position), I would argue for the preservation of gender-specific terms to describe historical texts. Jacobus argues,

> we need the term "women's writing" if only to remind us of the social conditions under which women wrote and still write—to remind us that the conditions of their (re) production are the economic and educational disadvantages, the sexual and material organizations of society, which, rather than biology, form the crucial determinants of women's writing.
>
> (*Reading Woman: Essays in Feminist Criticism* quoted in Draine 63)

Though the phrase "women's writing" calls up the specter of biological essentialism for historians committed to poststructuralist theories of textuality, feminists such as Gayatri Chakravorty Spivak have managed to position their concern for the lives and suffering of "real women" within the terms of poststructuralism (see "Displacement"). Gender as the constitution of social relations locates dominant forms of discourse—for rhetoric, politics, law, and performance—within the fuller context of what they excluded, thus providing a ground for examining discursive energies deflected into the drawing room, the nursery, the personal letter, the "literary" text.

I am still convinced of the importance of Scott's historiography and find in the 1990 4Cs program confirmation that feminist historical work in composition and rhetoric has moved in the direction she indicates. Panels were distributed between women's history and gender issues, including some feminist analysis of male-authored texts in rhetoric. But I now have some reservations about sharply dividing the two practices. Any division risks separation and hierarchization—a sort of ranking like that created by the typologies of American feminism of the first two decades on which I was drawing. While works like Alison Jagger's *Feminist Politics and Human Nature,* Linda Alcoff's "Identity Crisis in Feminism," and Jean Bethke Elshtain's *Public Man, Private Woman* respond to an urgent need to keep a running account of the rapid changes and proliferating arguments in feminist theory, like all typologies they have had undesirable effects. The categories offered in those accounts and elsewhere narrate an early feminism called cultural/radical, acknowledge a middle-stage liberal feminism seeking equal rights, and culminate in poststructural feminism, which seems to out-shine its dowdy sisters in sophistication and analytic power. Though my description is over-simplified, and none of the authors mentioned above advocates simply a renunciation of earlier feminisms in favor of poststructuralism, the narrative power of these stages creates such an effect. Despite their differences, all these pieces and many more do taxonomize feminisms.

　　With some distance from that original talk, I have come to see that dividing histories of rhetoric carries the same risks as categorizing feminisms. In one sense, this sequence simply reports how feminist historiography has developed in the field and for individual scholars: first comes a question about women, then a perspective on gender itself as a determining factor in all historical accounts. But emphasizing the theoretical differences between these two kinds of feminist historiography can lead to the binarism that always puts one above another. Though deconstruction might be called in here as a therapeutic reading practice, a masculinist deconstruction (as many feminists have argued) creates particular problems for the feminist reader. There is, then, a need for ways to articulate multiple feminist historical practices without taxonomizing. The issue here concerns women's identification as women with each other and with a reconstructed history without the construction of a "woman's voice" in history out of nostalgia for lost origins. How to do a history informed by poststructural analysis of the way difference constructs language—i.e., a gendered analysis—but responsive to women's desire to "find" themselves in history? My current thinking on the problem takes in two issues—a politics of location and the question of representation—which I will pursue in the rest of this essay, ending with some notes on teaching history.

Location as an Ethical Orientation for Feminist Historiography

When "gender" totally eclipses "women" as the focus for feminist research, there is a sense of loss—loss of a common place. But searching for "identity" raises the specter of essentialism. I've found that the theoretical discourses formulating this association in terms of space, place, or location cross the lines of damaging taxonomies without erasing differences. The themes of location have been important from the beginning of second wave feminism, as women have described their relation to patriarchy in terms of location. They found themselves positioned at the margins, "elsewhere," in the "space off" the centers of power (de Lauretis). While for some feminists, moving into the center has been an important agenda, others seek to explore the implications of being located at the margins. Adrienne Rich's "Notes toward a Politics of Location" speaks eloquently of the "need to understand how a place on the map is also a place in history within which as a woman, a Jew, a lesbian, a feminist I am created and trying to create" (212). For Rich, this sense of location is a way of taking up "the long struggle against lofty and privileged abstraction": an old, familiar difference between rhetoric and the philosophy that tries to deny not only place, but time, and specific embodiment. Location means starting with the material, but it never stays simply or unreflectively in a single experience or history. In this long passage, Rich captures in a striking but sympathetic way my hesitation about feminist historiography settling simply into "women's history":

　　　I've been thinking a lot about the obsession with origins. It seems a way of stopping time
　　in its tracks. The sacred Neolithic triangles, the Minoan vases with staring eyes and breasts,

the female figurines of Anatolia—weren't they concrete evidence of a kind, like Sappho's fragments, for earlier woman-affirming cultures, cultures that enjoyed centuries of peace? But haven't they also served as arresting images, which kept us attached and immobilized? Human activity didn't stop in Crete or Çatal Hüyük. We can't build a society free from domination by fixing our sights backward on some long-ago tribe or city.

The continuing spiritual power of an image lives in the interplay between what it reminds us of—what it *brings to mind*—and our own continuing actions in the present. When the labrys becomes a badge for a cult of Minoan goddesses, when the wearer of the labrys has ceased to ask herself what she is doing on this earth, where her love of women is taking her, the labrys, too, becomes abstraction—lifted away from the heat and friction of human activity. The Jewish star on my neck must serve me both for reminder and as a goad to continuing and changing responsibility.

(227, emphasis in original)

The way labrys becomes abstraction is the way "woman" can become an abstraction. We—i.e., those who wish to write feminist histories of rhetoric—can avoid that, I believe, by moving in two directions: moving earthward in the gesture of locating oneself as a person writing in a particular context and moving outward from women's experience to an analysis of how women are represented within a gendered system— never upward in a transcendence, attempting to supersede, for where's the history in that? This locatedness might be called Antaean, from the Greek wrestler Antaeus whose strength came from contact with the earth. Only this coinage would recast the "he" who struggles alone into the "s/he" who thinks, talks, and acts with others.

The aim of the first move is to correct the illusion of universality created by occupying the space at the center of power. Of course women have not historically occupied that space. But as academics, we are trained to masquerade as those who have, a cross-dressing more difficult and complex when color, class, and sexual orientation increase the distance from the model.[6] From my safe, now tenured position in a well-funded state university filled with well-fed, white, middle-class students, it is easy to sink back into the white privilege (McIntosh) and arrogant perception (Lugones) characteristic of many North Americans, in the academy and out, feminist or not. By naming these locations, I engage an always partial effort to discover where they blind me. They may help explain the appeal of the roots of Western civilization in classical antiquity, while reminding me to ask questions about color and class that often seem to interrupt a line of thinking or research. Stated simply, feminists have helped us to see how all discourses are located, but that some fail to locate themselves, assuming an omnipresence. In the writing of history, this failure of location expresses itself through the oracular voice proclaiming the (single) truth of the past. For women's history, that voice can become the mother's voice of truth and right. Embodying and specifying voices requires locating them in time and space.

I see connections between Rich's politics of location and two more recent feminist uses of the metaphor of space. Alcoff's essay offers "positionality" as a way to describe a desirable relationship among contradictory theoretical foundations in contemporary feminisms. Positionality offers subjectivity through historicized experience (431). Describing the subject as a complex of concrete habits, practices, and discourses, Alcoff then names gender as a position from which to act politically. She is not essentializing women in this move and rejects a universal, ahistorical definition of gender. Gendered identities are constructed by a position in an existing cultural and social network:

> [A woman] herself is part of the historicized, fluid movement, and she therefore actively contributes to the context within which her position can be delineated . . . the identity of a woman is the product of her own interpretation and reconstruction of her history, as mediated through the cultural discursive context to which she has access.
>
> (434)

Alcoff argues for a concept of positionality as "a place from which values are interpreted and constructed rather than as a locus of an already determined set of values" (434). Women's lived experience becomes part (not all) of their equipment for theorizing and historicizing. Louise Wetherbee Phelps asserts this in her Preface to *Composition as a Human Science* when she calls theory autobiography. Gayatri Chakravorty Spivak offers a characteristically elegant and cautiously circumscribed version of herself as critic in "Can the Subaltern Speak?" Questioning the role of the Western intellectual in contemporary relations of power, she uses situations of British colonialism in India to demonstrate the problem of representation from within oppressive economies (namely, world-wide capitalism) and from dominant ideology:

> First, a few disclaimers: In the United States the third-worldism currently afloat in human-istic disciplines is often openly ethnic. I was born in India and received my primary, second-ary, and university education there, including two years of graduate work. My Indian example could thus be seen as a nostalgic investigation of the lost roots of my own identity. Yet even as I know that one cannot freely enter the thickets of "motivations," I would main-tain that my chief project is to point out the positivist-idealist variety of such nostalgia. I turn to Indian material because, in the absence of advanced disciplinary training, that accident of birth and education has provided me with a sense of the historical canvas, a hold on some of the pertinent languages that are useful tools for a *bricoleur* especially when armed with the Marxist skepticism of concrete experience as the final arbiter and a critique of disciplinary formations. Yet the Indian case cannot be taken as representative of all coun-tries, nations, cultures, and the like that may be invoked as the Other of Europe as Self.
>
> ("Subaltern" 281, emphasis in original)

I quote this long passage because in it Spivak locates herself so carefully without engag-ing a discourse of "identity" or privileging personal experience outside of discursive analysis.

Spivak's evocation of Marxism provides a transition to another form of feminism using the metaphor of place: the socialist feminist conception of standpoint. Standpoint theory finds its roots in Marx's recognition that different practices create different ways of knowing. Georg Lukacs, in his elaboration of Marx's theory, locates epistemological standpoints in group experience, groups being defined as economic classes within capitalism. Following this line of argument, Nancy Hartsock has identified general characteristics of the standpoint of the proletariat and then applied these to women's labor, claiming that women have an understanding of oppression "from beneath" the dominant ideology, enabling them to see the "perverse inversions" practiced by patriarchal, capitalist institutions (Hartsock 284–85). Because of the special forms of exploitation and oppression experienced by women under capitalism today, their standpoint, Hartsock argues, "carries a historically liberatory role" (285). According to Alison Jaggar, standpoint is "a position in society from which certain features of reality come into prominence and from which others are obscured" (382). Feminist standpoint theory draws on the variety of women's experiences and considers the "epistemological consequences" of differences (Jaggar 386); experience and difference are key terms in standpoint theory, which identifies "not simply an interested position (interpreted as bias) but interested in the sense of being engaged" (Hartsock 285). No one can "see" all perspectives, but by foregrounding specific epistemological and political claims, a standpoint can offer "engaged vision" (Hartsock 285). This spatial politics creates an ethics of experience but avoids a naive privileging of any single person's "experience" thought to be transmitted unmediated through transparent language.

Standpoint theory provides a more specific emphasis on economy and ideology than positionality, but as it has been theorized thus far, it has some drawbacks. Hartsock has been criticized for identifying reproduction as the defining feature of women's experience and for ignoring the complex ways women are positioned in power relations other than gender. I would reject Hartsock's view that women's experiences can be brought together under the wing of "reproduction" but do support a more basic Marxist position that sees "conceptual frameworks as shaped and limited by their social origins" (Jaggar 369–70). On the second objection, Jane Flax has noted that standpoint theory disturbingly assumes "that women, unlike men, can be free from participating in relations of domination" such as those rooted in race and class differences (642). While I agree that Hartsock's concept of "perversion" effects only a binary reversal of power relations, I wouldn't go so far as Flax in rejecting totally the epistemological claims of standpoint theory. The approach seems to me to offer new possibilities for thought and action to *all* marginalized groups. Fredric Jameson here describes such an extension:

> Standpoint analysis specifically demands a differentiation between the various negative experiences of constraint, between the exploitation suffered by workers and the oppression suffered by women and continuing on through the distinct structural forms of exclusion and alienation characteristic of other kinds of group experience.
>
> (70)

Though I would not argue for the necessary epistemological priority of *women's* experience in particular (or that every woman, by virtue of biology, will necessarily see the world in the same way), I endorse feminist standpoint theory because it creates a "capacity for . . . seeing features and dimensions of the world and of history masked to other social actors" (Jameson 70). Feminist standpoint theory does not produce the Truth, but rather makes possible a "principled relativism," under which epistemological claims may be "inspected (and respected) for their . . . respective 'moments of truth'"

(Jameson 65). When the "subject" is understood as the locus of a multiplicity of subject positions on axes of class, race, gender, and so on, then standpoint theory can be used to call into play multiple, sometimes overlapping, sometimes contradictory epistemological perspectives. Here the connection with classical rhetoric, specifically sophistic rhetoric, suggests itself. The sophists trained their students to work with *dissoi logoi*, contradictory propositions available for every position; this heuristic opens up ideological tension and lays out courses of possible action.

Standpoint theory cannot be a sufficient means of accounting for the calls one heeds amid the cacophony of voices in late capitalism; it doesn't, for example, speak of the unconscious. Jaggar acknowledges that

> Although a standpoint makes certain features of reality visible, however, it does not necessarily reveal them clearly nor in their essential interconnections with each other. . . . [T]he standpoint of women is not expressed directly in women's naive and unreflective world view.
>
> (382, 371)

Like Jaggar, I see the relevance of discourses such as psychoanalysis and sociology of science in dialogue with standpoint theory for the project of developing more complex conceptualizations of reality. Despite reservations about some forms of standpoint theory, I find that collectively these ideas of place, position, and standpoint in contemporary feminisms offer to feminist historiography a way of maintaining connection with a collective identity and purpose without falling into abstraction.

Historical Practice: From Identification to Representation

The most obvious extension [of] these processes of positioning for feminist history is that women writing history in a male-centered tradition and academy seek female sources. In locating themselves as female within a male tradition, they look for the same in history. But given the now-common understanding of history as constructed, the problem of representation arises. To reformulate the original dilemma, how does one acknowledge that women seek an identity in history—i.e., the same—while also arguing for history as a process of constructing the "other"? Or again, how does a located feminist historian create the "other" of history, when that "other" is a woman? The terms of "otherness" I use here come both from earlier work of my own (Introduction and chapter 3 in *Rereading the Sophists*) and from the work of Michel de Certeau, who defines history-writing as "intelligibility established through a relation with the other" (3). For Certeau, "the other is the phantasm of historiography, the object that it seeks, honors, and buries" (2). His fascination with identity and difference in the practice of historiography make[s] him a compelling source for feminist ruminations, though he does not concern himself directly with gender issues. He offers a scenario for history-writing much like the positioning I've described above when he sees the fundamental situation of historiography expressed in the relationship of a history to its preface, in which the historian speaks of his own labor:

"two uneven but symbolic halves, join[ing] to the history of the past the itinerary of a procedure" (38).

Certeau frames his theoretical speculations within the notion of place as well. Finding history on the boundary that both joins and separates a society from its past, he figures the constant movement along that margin through a modernist visual metaphor:

> [History] takes place along these lines which trace the figure of a current time by dividing it from its other, but which the return of the past is continually modifying or blurring. As in the paintings of Miró, the artist's line, which draws differences with contours and makes a writing possible (a discourse and a "historicization"), is crisscrossed by a movement running contrary to it. It is the vibration of limits. The relation that organizes history is a changing rapport, of which neither of its two terms can be the stable point of reference.
>
> (37–38)

How provocative to apply this shifting, sliding, vibrating image of history to women! If history eludes us, fixing itself on a margin at the limits of reason or of the possible (43), this marginalized space sounds much like the space of "woman" as a figure of difference from many versions of "man" in Western history: man as rational animal, man as self-created by thought, man as polis animal or citizen, creating in negative woman as irrational, woman as uncreated, woman as outside the boundaries of the polis. If history is a construction of an "other"—i.e., the past as other—how does a woman author such a text? As a disguised man? Another "other"? Would that make her the "same"?

The theory of representation Spivak lays out in "Can the Subaltern Speak?" offers not a model but guidance in this problem. The essay begins as a critique of intellectual invisibility in a conversation between Michel Foucault and Gilles Deleuze. Spivak observes that these two European academicians recreate a Western subjectivity through their failure to locate themselves in relation to the others about whom they speak: "Maoists," "workers," or "the Third World" ("Subaltern" 272). She insists that theories of economy and ideology are necessary to expose the "surreptitious subject of power and desire marked by the transparency of the intellectual," such a subject belonging to "the exploiters' side of the international division of labor" (280). In a double move, Spivak wants to go beyond the constitution of the colonial subject (the "subaltern") as Other to ask about the sexed subaltern: can a subject removed from dominant discourse in the West by two kinds of imperialism—national and sexual—speak?

While I would not collapse the task of the (white, middle-class) North American academic seeking women's histories of rhetoric with that of an Asian intellectual of a certain class, training, and history investigating the representation of the subaltern woman, I do hear Spivak speaking to feminist critics in the West. Her warning is, simply put, that in writing history we do not "represent" in the sense of advocating the women of the past but rather always "re-present" in the sense of imaging our own desire, while in the process recording as well as recommitting epistemic violence. To retell in every woman's history a "herstory" of suppression and silencing might be to miss a more subtle operation of what Spivak calls a "vast two-handed engine" ("Subaltern" 281): the mechanism by which a normative narrative is constituted in the context of others. While Spivak is concerned with comprehensive and agentless theories of "power and desire" advanced by Foucault and Deleuze, the issue to which I apply her critique is the adequacy of a women's history of rhetoric that remains within the mainstream American feminist goal of attaining equal rights as an individual—a project often characterized as finding a "voice." Aware of what the work cannot say, the historian must keep before her the ways her own consciousness urges her to create an object which recreates her own struggle. The trouble comes in "the slippage from rendering visible the mechanism to rendering vocal the individual" ("Subaltern" 285). The whole issue of colonialism, primary to Spivak's argument, is variable for the large area I take in under "history of rhetoric." To my knowledge, no one is yet working on a specifically rhetorical project in non-Western, female discourse. But the issue of constructing a consciousness in the object of history is relevant, and a focus on representation opens up the problem more fully, I now believe, than a discussion of categories. Essentialism, liberalism, post-feminism: none of these terms serves to describe adequately the painfully necessary work Spivak performs on Hindu widow sacrifice, a work free from the sentimentality some find tiresome in the language of the "pragmatic radical" but washed over inevitably with the pain of association. The following passage brings together for me processes of positioning and representation in a most helpful way:

> In seeking to learn to *speak to* (rather than listen to or speak for) the historically muted subject of the subaltern woman, the postcolonial intellectual *systematically* "unlearns" female privilege.
>
> (295, first emphasis added)

Spivak leads us to see how the practice of writing history is not so much about finding the voice of the past but about moving toward a finer understanding of the ways temporal discourses shape our own desires and sketch out futures both determined and open.

A Case in Point: Gendering Rhetoric in Classical Antiquity

As a way of suggesting directions for historiographical practice under the auspices of location and representation, I will review some recent work in classics that clears a space for feminist inquiry in history of rhetoric. Gerda Lerner describes the condition of women in ancient cultures in terms of their exclusion from the world of the symbolic, as language was created and religious narratives were codified. Women appear most often as *objects* of symbolic activity (both discursive and visual) from prehistory forward. Though we might desire women with agency, sketching woman as a *subject*— i.e., as a producer of symbols—particularly in antiquity is, of course, much more difficult than observing her as an object. For centuries, we have very few fragments of text unmediated by male re-presentation. [. . .]

As a practice through which a public space for political deliberation was defined from Homer forward, rhetoric has traditionally been defined by gender to the extent that access to and uses of that space are accorded differently to men and women. Using rhetorical tools such as topoi, forms of argument, and *ethos,* however, we can chart women's discourse along a continuum from the public sphere in to realms of private, sometimes non-rational performances. If norms for public speech are in some sense defined by the gender of the Greek citizen, then a gendered analysis may reveal what is reflected, adjusted, distorted, or completely absent from that discourse. Froma Zeitlin's analysis of Aristophanes's *Thesmophoriazousae,* for example, establishes a parallel between gender and genre in the late fifth century B.C. The elaborate transvestism of actor and playwright in this comedy signal for Zeitlin a link between the feminine and mimesis. She reads in the presence of Helen in the play

> the ambivalence which Greek thought will manifest with increasing articulation toward the mimetic powers of the verbal and visual arts to persuade with the truths of their fictions. This ambivalence is not incongruent, at some level, with the increasing ambivalence with which the city's male ideology view[s] its other gender, an attitude which serves to connect the feminine still more closely with art and artifice.
>
> (206)

Another kind of "feminization" is presented in Page duBois's reading of Plato's Socrates in the *Phaedrus.* Noting Socrates' frequent use of metaphors drawn from female reproduction, duBois finds early fourth-century B.C. philosophy appropriating and neutralizing the feminine:

> In the *Phaedrus,* there is, I will argue, as there is in the *Theaetetus* and the *Symposium,* a *mimesis* of the female, so that in the homoerotic movement of the dialogue, the female is perhaps more present than she is in later texts of the tradition where the less absolute social oppression of women leaves space for philosophy to be more radically phallocentric.
>
> (*Sowing,* 171)

Both critics read the literary text against the social text, assessing the figuration of the feminine in relation to the status of women in society. Zeitlin finds in Aristophanic comedy that the anxiety and frustration over the Peloponnesian War at the end of the fifth century B.C. are compensated for by "a shift [in attention] away from masculine values of politics to the private sphere—to the domestic milieu at home, to the internal workings of the psyche, and to a new validation of *eros,* all of which the feminine as a cultural category best exemplifies" (211).

These gendered readings speak suggestively to rhetorical issues, and the modes of analysis employed by Zeitlin and duBois offer rich possibilities for approaching other texts with questions relevant to rhetoric. We need to investigate Plato's use of Aspasia to recast the ideological function of the funeral oration in *Menexenus* and of Diotima to give voice to Socratic eros in the multivocality of the *Symposium.* Studies of drama-tists Aristophanes and Euripides could yield gendered analyses of the sophisticated rhetorical persuasions by women in *Lysistrata* and *Trojan Women*. While the question of whether real women ever existed to whom such performances could be attributed has dominated some discussions (Waithe), readings of these "literary" sources in terms of gender as constitutive of social relations may open a new interpretive space for rhetoric in the classical period. Another strategy would force the historian outside the boundaries of public assembly and court, toward the frenzied cries of the maenadic celebrants of Dionysus, the profanity uttered in fall fertility festival of Thesmophoria, and ritual laments for Adonis and Kore. These forms of women's speech, performed during the religious festivals which provided the only acceptable form of public activity for women in Greek antiquity, stand as a radical alternative to the "rational" discourses of rhetoric and philosophy taking shape in the fifth century. Again, the category of gender provides a theoretical ground for analyzing the construction of difference between these modes of expression. Gendered readings would seek the interplay of these various forms of women's speech with conventional rhetoric in ancient Greece. Beyond speech itself gender, according to Scott, constitutes women as cultural symbols and generates the normative interpretations cultures adopt for them. Conceptual languages of many types employ differentiation to establish meaning, and I would argue that a feminist history of rhetoric would take in the investigation of such languages.

Teaching Feminist History

How might feminist histories and historiography affect courses in the history of rhetoric? This question struck with some urgency as I confronted my most recent graduate seminar in classical rhetoric. With only one semester of exposure to the field, would my students wish to "sacrifice" big names in the tradition in order to venture into more complex encounter with a historiography "of that which is not immediately visible" (Leydesdorff 19)? We achieved a resolution (a local and temporary practice) by clustering canonical and non-canonical texts around the figure of Helen in Greek antiquity. We read Gorgias's *Encomium of Helen* and Socrates' "correction" of Gorgias against duBois's analysis of the figure of Helen in Sappho's Fragment 16 ("Sappho and Helen"). This gendering of the two male rhetoric texts by the woman's poem raised questions of subjectivity and agency, of causation and desire, of genealogy and ideology. While Aristotle and Plato remained in our canon, undisplaced by an alternative women's history of classical rhetoric, we were able in some cases to apply gendered readings to the definitions and categories, inclusions and exclusions, visions and blindnesses of the central figures in the male-authored tradition. French feminists assist in the gendering of classical texts. Cixous's rereading of Achilles and Penthesileia in *The Newly Born Women* (112–122) speaks of the desire to recast Homer; Irigaray kaleidoscopically constructs a case against Plato the feminist by shaking fragments of his own texts into the figure of woman (152–59).

Beyond the manipulation of reading lists, I think the concepts of positioning and representation can be brought fruitfully into the classroom. We should ask our students (as well as ourselves) to write their multiple selves—gendered, racial, classed—into history, creating narratives not in a unique voice but in polylog with past and future selves and others, singular accounts intertextualized with histories recent and distant. As we resist the curricular impetus toward coherence in favor of an eclectic and variegated historical practice, we complicate a unified narrative of the past with our own desires for the present and future.

Notes

1 These issues were taken up in a colloquium called "Politics of Historiography" (published in *Rhetoric Review* 7, 1988: 5–49) and in a *PRE/TEXT* volume devoted to historiography (8, 1987).

2 By writing "as a woman" I mean to place myself neither from within a permanent, natural state of female sexuality nor in a post-gendered condition of gender irrelevance, but rather within a fluctuating identity always in the historical process of being shaped and reshaped. Because this essay concerns the terms under which a collectivity labeled "women" become both objects and agents of history, I will postpone any further discussion of the label, other than to cite Denise Riley's assertion that "both a concentration and a refusal of the identity of 'women' are essential to feminism" (1).

3 See the Introduction and chapter 1 of my *Rereading the Sophists*.

4 Though my use of the word "ideology" here sounds pejorative, I understand the term to mean pervasive and inevitable systems of power and knowledge, but not a system of total subjection. I agree with Paul Smith that there is a place for agency within the workings of ideology and seek to describe an historical practice that works to reveal (always partially) the workings of ideology in the past and to act on the ideologies of the present. [. . .]

5 For complete information about these panels, see *Program, 1988 CCCC Convention, St. Louis, Missouri. Language, Self and Society*, (61, 79, 87, 125) and *Program, 1989 CCCC, Seattle, Washington. Empowering Students and Ourselves in an Interdependent World* (33, 70, 101, 110). For comparison, the 1989 "Topic Index to Concurrent Sessions" (2–13) listed 25 entries under "Women and Writing," whereas the 1988 index did not include any category containing the words "women" or "feminist." There were no panels or papers on women in history in 1987 and one paper in 1986 (26). Prior to the excellent offerings in feminist history in the Rhetoric Society proceedings of 1989, no such titles appeared in the 1987 or 1985 collections. Based on this brief survey, it could be said that a woman-oriented history of rhetoric has only begun to develop in the late 1980s. [. . .]

6 Patricia Bizzell, in her essay on Erasmus's *Praise of Folly* and the status of the woman speaker, proposes that women foreground their ambivalent relationship to the position of authority created by public discourse by overtly playing the fool. [. . .]

Works Cited

Alcoff, Linda. "Cultural Feminism Versus Post-Structuralism: The Identity Crisis in Feminist Theory." *Signs* 13 (1988): 405–36.

Armstrong, Nancy. *Desire and Domestic Fiction. A Political History of the Novel.* New York: Oxford, 1987.

Bizzell, Patricia. "The Praise of Folly, the Woman Rhetor, and Postmodern Skepticism." Forthcoming in *Rhetoric Society Quarterly.*

Cixous, Hélène, and Catherine Clement. *The Newly Born Woman.* Trans. Betsy Wing. Minneapolis: U of Minnesota P, 1986.

de Certeau, Michel. *The Writing of History.* Trans. Tom Conley. New York: Columbia UP, 1988.

de Lauretis, Teresa. *Technologies of Gender: Essays on Theory, Film, and Fiction.* Bloomington: Indiana UP, 1987.

Draine, Betsy. "Refusing the Wisdom of Solomon: Some Recent Feminist Literary Theory." *Signs* 15 (1989): 144–70.

duBois, Page. "Sappho and Helen." *Women in the Ancient World: The Arethusa Papers*. Albany: SUNY, 1984: 95–105.

———. *Sowing the Body: Psychoanalysis and Ancient Representations of Women*. Chicago: U of Chicago P, 1988.

Elshtain, Jean Bethke. *Public Man, Private Woman*. Princeton: Princeton UP, 1981.

Flax, Jane. "Postmodernism and Gender Relations in Feminist Theory." *Signs* 12:4 (1987): 621–43.

Flynn, Elizabeth. "Composing as a Woman." *College Composition and Communication* 39 (1988): 423–435.

Foley, Helene P., ed. *Reflections of Women in Antiquity*. New York: Gordon and Breach Science Publishers, 1981.

Fuss, Diane. *Essentially Speaking: Feminism, Nature and Difference*. New York: Routledge, 1989.

Hartsock, Nancy C. M. "The Feminist Standpoint: Developing the Ground for a Specifically Feminist Historical Materialism." In *Discovering Reality*. Eds. Sandra Harding and Merrill B. Hintikka. Boston: D. Reidel, 1983. 283–310.

Irigaray, Luce. "On the Index of Plato's Works: Woman." *Speculum of the Other Woman*. Trans. Gillian C. Gill. New York. Cornell UP, 1985.

Jaggar, Alison M. *Feminist Politics and Human Nature*. Totowa, NJ: Rowman and Littlefield, 1983.

Jameson, Fredric. "History and Class Consciousness as an Unfinished Project." *Rethinking Marxism* 1 (1988): 49–72.

Jarratt, Susan C. *Rereading the Sophists. Classical Rhetoric Refigured*. Carbondale: Southern Illinois UP, 1991.

Kelly, Joan. *Women, History and Theory*. Chicago: U of Chicago P, 1984.

Lerner, Gerda. *The Creation of Patriarchy*. New York: Oxford UP, 1986.

Leydesdorff, Selma. "Politics, Identification and the Writing of Women's History." Trans. Lonette Wiemans. *Current Issues in Women's History:* 9–20.

Lugones, Maria. "Playfulness, 'World'-Travelling, and Loving Perception." *Making Face, Making Soul, Haciendo Caras*. Ed. Gloria Anzaldúa. San Francisco: Aunt Lute Foundation Books, 1990.

McIntosh, Peggy. "White Privilege, Male Privilege." Unpublished ms.

Moi, Toril. *Sexual/Textual Politics. Feminist Literary Theory*. London: Methuen, 1985.

———. "Feminism, Postmodernism, and Style" *Cultural Critique* (Spring 1988): 3–22.

Morgan, Susan. *Sister in Time: Imagining Gender in Nineteenth-Century British Fiction*. New York: Oxford, 1989.

North, Stephen. *The Making of Knowledge in Composition: Portrait of an Emerging Field*. Upper Montclair, NJ: Boynton/Cook, 1987.

Perradotto, John, and J. P. Sullivan, eds. *Women in the Ancient World: The Arethusa Papers*. Albany: SUNY, 1984.

Phelps, Louise Wetherbee. *Composition as a Human Science: Contributions to the Self-Understanding of a Discipline*. New York: Oxford, 1988.

Rackin, Phyllis. "Androgyny, Mimesis, and the Marriage of the Boy Heroine on the English Renaissance Stage." *PMLA* 102 (1987): 29–41.

Rich, Adrienne. "Notes toward a Politics of Location." *Blood, Bread, and Poetry: Selected Prose 1979–1985*. New York: Norton and Co., 1986.

Riley, Denise. *"Am I That Name?" Feminism and the Category of "Women" in History.* Minneapolis: U of Minnesota P, 1988.

Scott, Joan Wallach. *Gender and the Politics of History.* New York: Columbia, 1988.

Smith, Paul. *Discerning the Subject.* Minneapolis: U of Minnesota P, 1988.

Snyder, Jane McIntosh. *The Woman and the Lyre: Women Writers in Classical Greece and Rome.* Carbondale: Southern Illinois UP, 1989.

Spivak, Gayatri Chakravorty. "Displacement and the Discourse of Woman." *Displacement: Derrida and After.* Ed. Mark Krupnick. Bloomington: Indiana UP, 1983: 169–95.

——. "Can the Subaltern Speak?" *Marxism and the Interpretation of Culture.* Ed. Cary Nelson and Lawrence Grossberg. Urbana: U of Illinois P, 1988.

Waithe, Mary Ellen, ed. *A History of Women Philosophers, Vol. I, 600 B.C.–500 A.D.* Dordrecht: Martinus Nijhoff, 1987.

Weedon, Chris. *Poststructuralist Theory and Feminist Practice.* Oxford: Basil Blackwell, 1987.

Zeitlin, Froma I. "Travesties of Gender and Genre in Aristophanes' *Thesmorphoriazousae.*" In Foley, ed.

7.
WHEN THE FIRST VOICE YOU HEAR
IS NOT YOUR OWN
Jacqueline Jones Royster

Editors' Note: *Using three scenes drawn from the author's own experience, this essay examines the "cross-cultural misconduct" rife in the United States today. Such misconduct grows out of a myopia that fails to recognize and value the experiences of those who come from disparate communities and reveals a lack of "home-training" that would produce cross-cultural good manners of honor, respect, and generous codes of conduct toward others. A new paradigm of good behaviors would allow voices to speak and to be heard and respected and would allow for better practices in cross-boundary discourse—in teaching, research, writing, and talking with others.*

This essay emerged from my desire to examine closely moments of personal challenge that seem to have import for cross-boundary discourse. These types of moments have constituted an ongoing source of curiosity for me in terms of my own need to understand human difference as a complex reality, a reality that I have found most intriguing within the context of the academic world. From a collectivity of such moments over the years, I have concluded that the most salient point to acknowledge is that "subject" position really is everything.

Using subject position as a terministic screen in cross-boundary discourse permits analysis to operate kaleidoscopically, thereby permitting interpretation to be richly informed by the converging of dialectical perspectives. Subjectivity as a defining value pays attention dynamically to context, ways of knowing, language abilities, and experience, and by doing so it has a consequent potential to deepen, broaden, and enrich our interpretive views in dynamic ways as well. Analytical lenses include the process, results, and impact of negotiating identity, establishing authority, developing strategies for action, carrying forth intent with a particular type of agency, and being compelled by external factors and internal sensibilities to adjust belief and action (or not). In a fundamental way, this enterprise supports the sense of rhetoric, composition, and literacy studies as a field of study that embraces the imperative to understand truths and consequences of language use more fully. This enterprise supports also the imperative to reconsider the beliefs and values which inevitably permit our attitudes and actions in discourse communities (including colleges, universities, and classrooms) to be systematic, even systemic.

Jacqueline Jones Royster, "When the First Voice You Hear Is Not Your Own." *College Composition and Communication* 47 (1996): 29–40.

Adopting subjectivity as a defining value, therefore, is instructive. However, the multidimensionality of the instruction also reveals the need for a shift in paradigms, a need that I find especially evident with regard to the notion of "voice," as a central manifestation of subjectivity. My task in this essay, therefore, is threefold. First, I present three scenes which serve as my personal testimony as "subject." These scenes are singular in terms of their being my own stories, but I believe that they are also plural, constituting experiential data that I share with many. My sense of things is that individual stories placed one against another against another build credibility and offer, as in this case, a litany of evidence from which a call for transformation in theory and practice might rightfully begin. My intent is to suggest that my stories in the company of others demand thoughtful response.

Second, I draw from these scenes a specific direction for transformation, suggesting dimensions of the nature of voicing that remain problematic. My intent is to demonstrate that our critical approaches to voice, again as a central manifestation of subjectivity, are currently skewed toward voice as a spoken or written phenomenon. This intent merges the second task with the third in that I proceed to suggest that theories and practices should be transformed. The call for action in cross-boundary exchange is to refine theory and practice so that they include voicing as a phenomenon that is constructed and expressed visually and orally, *and* as a phenomenon that has import also in being a *thing* heard, perceived, and reconstructed.

Scene One

I have been compelled on too many occasions to count to sit as a well-mannered Other, silently, in a state of tolerance that requires me to be as expressionless as I can manage, while colleagues who occupy a place of entitlement different from my own talk about the history and achievements of people from my ethnic group, or even about their perceptions of our struggles. I have been compelled to listen as they have comfortably claimed the authority to engage in the construction of knowledge and meaning about me and mine, without paying even a passing nod to the fact that sometimes a substantive version of that knowledge might already exist, or to how it might have already been constructed, or to the meanings that might have already been assigned that might make me quite impatient with gaps in their understanding of my community, or to the fact that I, or somebody within my ethnic group, might have an opinion about what they are doing. I have been compelled to listen to speakers, well-meaning though they may think they are, who signal to me rather clearly that subject position is everything. I have come to recognize, however, that when the subject matter is me and the voice is not mine, my sense of order and rightness is disrupted. In metaphoric fashion, these "authorities" let me know, once again, that Columbus has discovered America and claims it now, claims it still for a European crown.

Such scenes bring me to the very edge of a principle that I value deeply as a teacher and a scholar, the principle of the right to inquiry and discovery. When the discovering hits so close to home, however, my response is visceral, not just intellectual, and I am made to look over a precipice. I have found it extremely difficult to allow the voices and experiences of people that I care about deeply to be taken and handled so carelessly and without accountability by strangers.

At the extreme, the African American community, as my personal example, has seen and continues to see its contributions and achievements called into question in grossly negative ways, as in the case of *The Bell Curve*. Such interpretations of who we are as a people open to general interrogation, once again, the innate capacities of "the race" as a whole. As has been the case throughout our history in this country, we are put in jeopardy and on trial in a way that should not exist but does. We are compelled to respond to a rendering of our potential that demands, not that we account for attitudes, actions, and conditions, but that we defend ourselves as human beings. Such interpretations of human potential create a type of discourse that serves as a distraction, as noise that drains off energy and sabotages the work of identifying substantive problems within and across cultural boundaries and the work also of finding solutions that have import, not simply for "a race," but for human beings whose living conditions, values, and preferences vary.

All such close encounters, the extraordinarily insidious ones and the ordinary ones, are definable through the lens of subjectivity, particularly in terms of the power and authority to speak and to make meaning. An analysis of subject position reveals that these interpretations by those outside of the community are not random acts of unkindness. Instead, they embody ways of seeing, knowing, being, and acting that probably suggest as much about the speaker and the context as they do about the targeted subject matter. The advantage with this type of analysis, of course, is that we see the obvious need to contextualize the stranger's perspective among other interpretations and to recognize that an interpretive view is just that—interpretive. A second advantage is that we also see that in our nation's practices these types of interpretations, regardless of how superficial or libelous they may actually be within the context of a more comprehensive view, tend to have considerable consequence in the lives of the targeted group, people in this case whose own voices and perspectives remain still largely under considered and uncredited.

Essentially, though, having a mechanism to see the under considered helps us see the extent to which we add continually to the pile of evidence in this country of cross-cultural misconduct. These types of close encounters that disregard dialectical views are a type of free touching of the power-less by the power-full. This analytical perspective encourages us to acknowledge that marginalized communities are not in a good position to ward off the intrusion of those authorized in mainstream communities to engage in willful action. Historically, such actions have included everything from the displacement of native people from their homelands, to the use of unknowing human subjects in dangerous experiments, to the appropriation and misappropriation of cultural artifacts—art, literature, music, and so on. An insight using the lens of subjectivity, however, is a recognition of the ways in which these moments are indeed moments of violation, perhaps even ultimate violation.

This record of misconduct means that for people like me, on an instinctive level, all outsiders are rightly perceived as suspect. I suspect the genuineness of their interest, the altruism of their actions, and the probability that whatever is being said or done is not to the ultimate benefit and understanding of the people who are subject matter but not subjects. People in the neighborhood where I grew up would say, "Where is their home training?" Imbedded in the question is the idea that when you visit other people's "home places," especially when you have not been invited, you simply can not go tramping around the house like you own the place, no matter how smart you are, or how much imagination you can muster, or how much authority and entitlement outside that home you may be privileged to hold. And you certainly can not go around name calling, saying things like, "You people are intellectually inferior and have a limited capacity to achieve," without taking into account who the family is, what its living has been like, and what its history and achievement have been about.

The concept of "home training" underscores the reality that point of view matters and that we must be trained to respect points of view other than our own. It acknowledges that when we are away from home, we need to know that what we think we see in places that we do not really know very well may not actually be what is there at all. So often, it really is a matter of time, place, resources, and our ability to perceive. Coming to judgment too quickly, drawing on information too narrowly, and saying hurtful, discrediting, dehumanizing things without undisputed proof are not appropriate. Such behavior is not good manners. What comes to mind for me is another saying that I heard constantly when I was growing up, "Do unto others as you would have them do unto you." In this case, we would be implored to draw conclusions about others with care and, when we do draw conclusions, to use the same type of sense and sensibility that we would ideally like for others to use in drawing conclusions about us.

This scene convinces me that what we need in a pressing way in this country and in our very own field is to articulate codes of behavior that can sustain more concretely notions of honor, respect, and good manners across boundaries, with cultural boundaries embodying the need most vividly. Turning the light back onto myself, though, at the same time that my sense of violation may indeed be real, there is the compelling reality that many communities in our nation need to be taken seriously. We all deserve to be taken seriously, which means that critical inquiry and discovery are absolutely necessary. Those of us who love our own communities, we think, most deeply, most uncompromisingly, without reservation for what they are and also are not, must set aside our misgivings about strangers in the interest of the possibility of deeper understanding (and for the more idealistic among us, the possibility of global peace). Those of us who hold these communities close to our hearts, protect them, and embrace them; those who want to preserve the goodness of the minds and souls in them; those who want to preserve consciously, critically, and also lovingly the record of good work within them must take high risk and give over the exclusivity of our rights to know.

It seems to me that the agreement for inquiry and discovery needs to be deliberately reciprocal. All of us, strangers and community members, need to find ways to sustain productivity in what Pratt calls contact zones (199), areas of engagement that in all likelihood will remain contentious. We need to get over our tendencies to be too possessive and to resist locking ourselves into the tunnels of our own visions and direct experience. As community members, we must learn to have new faith in the advantage of sharing. As strangers, we must learn to treat the loved people and places of Others with care and to understand that, when we do not act respectfully and responsibly, we leave ourselves rightly open to wrath. The challenge is not to work with a fear of abuse or a fear of retaliation, however. The challenge is to teach, to engage in research, to write, and to speak with Others with the determination to operate not only with professional and personal integrity, but also with the specific knowledge that communities and their ancestors are watching. If we can set aside our rights to exclusivity in our own home cultures, if we can set aside the tendencies that we all have to think too narrowly, we actually leave open an important possibility. In our nation, we have little idea of the potential that a variety of subjectivities—operating with honor, respect, and reasonable codes of conduct—can bring to critical inquiry or critical problems. What might happen if we treated differences in subject position as critical pieces of the whole, vital to thorough understanding, and central to both problem-finding and problem-solving? This society has not, as yet, really allowed that privilege in a substantial way.

Scene Two

As indicated in Scene One, I tend to be enraged at what Tillie Olsen has called the "trespass vision," a vision that comes from intellect and imagination (62), but typically not from lived experience, and sometimes not from the serious study of the subject matter. However, like W. E. B. Du Bois, I've chosen not to be distracted or consumed by my rage at voyeurs, tourists, and trespassers, but to look at what I can do. I see the critical importance of the role of negotiator, someone who can cross boundaries and serve as guide and translator for Others.

In 1903, Du Bois demonstrated this role in *The Souls of Black Folk*. In the "Forethought" of that book, he says: "Leaving, then, the world of the white man, I have stepped within the Veil, raising it that you may view faintly its deeper recesses—the meaning of its religion, the passion of its human sorrow, and the struggle of its greater souls" (1). He sets his rhetorical purpose to be to cross, or at least to straddle boundaries with the intent of shedding light, a light that has the potential of being useful to people on both sides of the veil. Like Du Bois, I've accepted the idea that what I call my "home place" is a cultural community that exists still quite significantly beyond the confines of a well-insulated community that we call the "mainstream," and that between this world and the one that I call home, systems of insulation impede the vision and narrow the ability to recognize human potential and to understand human history both microscopically and telescopically.

Like Du Bois, I've dedicated myself to raising this veil, to overriding these systems of insulation by raising another voice, my voice in the interest of clarity and accuracy. What I have found too often, however, is that, unlike those who have been entitled to talk about me and mine, when I talk about my own, I face what I call the power and function of deep disbelief, and what Du Bois described as, "the sense of always looking at one's self through the eyes of others, of measuring one's soul by the tape of a world that looks on in amused contempt and pity" (5).

An example comes to mind. When I talk about African-American women, especially those who were writing non-fiction prose in the nineteenth century, I can expect, even today after so much contemporary scholarship on such writers, to see people who are quite flabbergasted by anything that I share. Reflected on their faces and in their questions and comments, if anyone can manage to speak back to me, is a depth of surprise that is always discomforting. I sense that the surprise, or the silence, if there is little response, does not come from the simple ignorance of unfortunate souls who just happen not to know what I have spent years coming to know. What I suspect is that this type of surprise rather "naturally" emerges in a society that so obviously has the habit of expecting nothing of value, nothing of consequence, nothing of importance, nothing at all positive from its Others, so that anything is a surprise; everything is an exception; and nothing of substance can really be claimed as a result.

In identifying this phenomenon, Chandra Talpade Mohanty speaks powerfully about the ways in which this culture coopts, dissipates, and displaces voices. As demonstrated by my example, one method of absorption that has worked quite well has been essentially rhetorical. In discussing nineteenth century African American women's work, I bring tales of difference and adventure. I bring cultural proofs and instructive examples, all of which invariably must serve as rites of passage to credibility. I also bring the power of storytelling. These tales of adventure in odd places are the transitions by which to historicize and theorize anew with these writers re-inscribed in a rightful place. Such a process respects long-standing practices in African-based cultures of theorizing in narrative form. As Barbara Christian says, we theorize "in the stories we create, in riddles and proverbs, in the play with language, since dynamic rather than fixed ideas seem more to our liking" (336).

The problem is that in order to construct new histories and theories such stories must be perceived not just as "simple stories" to delight and entertain, but as vital layers of a transformative process. A reference point is Langston Hughes and his Simple stories, stories that are a model example of how apparent simplicity has the capacity to unmask truths in ways that are remarkably accessible—through metaphor, analogy, parable, and symbol. However, the problem of articulating new paradigms through stories becomes intractable, if those who are empowered to define impact and consequence decide that the stories are simply stories and that the record of achievement is perceived, as Audre Lorde has said, as "the random droppings of birds" (Foreword xi).

If I take my cue from the life of Ida Wells, and I am bold enough and defiant enough to go beyond the presentation of my stories as juicy tidbits for the delectation of audiences, to actually shift or even subvert a paradigm, I'm much more likely to receive a wide-eyed stare and to have the value and validity of my conceptual position held at a distance, in doubt, and wonderfully absorbed in the silence of appreciation. Through the systems of deep disbelief I become a storyteller, a performer. With such absorptive ability in the systems of interpretation, I have greater difficulty being perceived as a person who theorizes without the mediating voices of those from the inner sanctum, or as a person who might name myself a philosopher, a theorist, a historian who creates paradigms that allow the experiences and the insights of people like me to belong.

What I am compelled to ask when veils seem more like walls is who has the privilege of speaking first? How do we negotiate the privilege of interpretation? When I have tried to fulfill my role as negotiator, I have often walked away knowing that I have spoken, but also knowing, as Anna Julia Cooper knew in 1892, that my voice, like her voice, is still a muted one. I speak, but I can not be heard. Worse, I am heard but I am not believed. Worse yet, I speak but I am not deemed believable. These moments of deep disbelief have helped me to understand much more clearly the wisdom of Audre Lorde when she said: "I have come to believe over and over again that what is most important to me must be spoken, made verbal and shared, even at the risk of having it bruised or misunderstood" (*Sister* 40). Lorde teaches me that, despite whatever frustration and vulnerability I might feel, despite my fear that no one is listening to me or is curious enough to try to understand my voice, it is still better to speak (*Black* 31). I set aside the distractions and permeating noise outside of myself, and I listen, as Howard Thurman recommended, to the sound of the genuine within. I go to a place inside myself and, as Opal Palmer Adisa explains, I listen and learn to "speak without clenching my teeth" (56).

Scene Three

There have been occasions when I have indeed been heard and positively received. Even at these times, however, I sometimes can not escape responses that make me most weary. One case in point occurred after a presentation in which I had glossed a scene in a novel that required cultural understanding. When the characters spoke in the scene, I rendered their voices, speaking and explaining, speaking and explaining, trying to translate the experience, to share the sounds of my historical place and to connect those sounds with systems of belief so that deeper understanding of the scene might emerge, and so that those outside of the immediacy of my home culture, the one represented in the novel, might see and understand more and be able to make more useful connections to their own worlds and experiences.

One, very well-intentioned response to what I did that day was, "How wonderful it was that you were willing to share with us your 'authentic' voice!" I said, "My 'authentic' voice?" She said, "Oh yes! I've never heard you talk like that, you know, so relaxed. I mean, you're usually great, but this was really great! You weren't so formal. You didn't have to speak in an appropriated academic language. You sounded 'natural.' It was nice to hear you be yourself." I said, "Oh, I see. Yes, I do have a range of voices, and I take quite a bit of pleasure actually in being able to use any of them at will." Not understanding the point that I was trying to make gently, she said, "But this time, it was really you. Thank you."

The conversation continued, but I stopped paying attention. What I didn't feel like saying in a more direct way, a response that my friend surely would have perceived as angry, was that all my voices are authentic, and like bell hooks, I find it "a necessary aspect of self-affirmation not to feel compelled to choose one voice over another, not to claim one as more authentic, but rather to construct social realities that celebrate, acknowledge, and affirm differences, variety" (12). Like hooks, I claim all my voices as my own very much authentic voices, even when it's difficult for others to imagine a person like me having the capacity to do that.

From moments of challenge like this one, I realize that we do not have a paradigm that really allows for what scholars in cultural and postcolonial studies (Anzuldua, Spivak, Mohanty, Bhaba) have called hybrid people—people who either have the capacity by right of history and development, or who might have created the capacity by right of history and development, to move with dexterity across cultural boundaries, to make themselves comfortable, and to make sense amid the chaos of difference.

As Cornel West points out, most African Americans, for example, dream in English, not in Yoruba, or Hausa, or Wolof. Hybrid people, as demonstrated by the history of Africans in the Western hemisphere, manage a fusion process that allows for survival, certainly. However, it also allows for the development of a peculiar expertise that extends one's range of abilities well beyond ordinary limits, and it supports the opportunity for the development of new and remarkable creative expression, like spirituals, jazz, blues, and what I suspect is happening also with the essay as genre in the hands of African American women. West notes that somebody gave Charlie Parker a saxophone, Miles Davis a trumpet, Hubert Laws a flute, and Les McCann a piano. I suggest that somebody also gave Maria Stewart, Gertrude Mossell, Frances Harper, Alice Walker, Audre Lorde, Toni Morrison, Patricia Williams, June Jordan, bell hooks, Angela Davis and a cadre of other African American women a pencil, a pen, a computer keyboard. In both instances, genius emerges from hybridity, from Africans who, over the course of time and circumstance, have come to dream in English, and I venture to say that all of their voices are authentic.

In sharing these three scenes, I emphasize that there is a pressing need to construct paradigms that permit us to engage in better practices in cross-boundary discourse, whether we are teaching, researching, writing, or talking with Others, whoever those Others happen to be. I would like to emphasize, again, that we look again at "voice" and situate it within a world of symbols, sound, and sense, recognizing that this world operates symphonically. Although the systems of voice production are indeed highly integrated and appear to have singularity in the ways that we come to sound, voicing actually sets in motion multiple systems, prominent among them are systems for speaking but present also are the systems for hearing. We speak within systems that we know significantly through our abilities to negotiate noise and to construct within that noise sense and sensibility.

Several questions come to mind. How can we teach, engage in research, write about, and talk across boundaries *with* others, instead of for, about, and around them? My experiences tell me that we need to do more than just talk and talk back. I believe that in this model we miss a critical moment. We need to talk, yes, and to talk back, yes, but when do we listen? How do we listen? How do we demonstrate that we honor and respect the person talking and what that person is saying, or what the person might say if we valued someone other than ourselves having a turn to speak? How do we translate listening into language and action, into the creation of an appropriate response? How do we really "talk back" rather than talk also? The goal is not, "You talk, I talk." The goal is better practices so that we can exchange perspectives, negotiate meaning, and create understanding with the intent of being in a good position to cooperate, when, like now, cooperation is absolutely necessary.

When I think about this goal, what stands out most is that these questions apply in so much of academic life right now. They certainly apply as we go into classrooms and insist that our students trust us and what we contend is in their best interest. In light of a record in classrooms that seriously questions the range of our abilities to recognize potential, or to appreciate students as non-generic human beings, or to appreciate that they bring with them, always, knowledge, we ask a lot when we ask them to trust. Too often, still, institutionalized equations for placement, positive matriculation, progress, and achievement name, categorize, rank, and file, while our true-to-life students fall between the cracks. I look again to Opal Palmer Adisa for an instructive example. She says:

> Presently, many academics advocate theories which, rather than illuminating the works under scrutiny, obfuscate and problematize these works so that students are rendered speechless. Consequently, the students constantly question what they know, and often, unfortunately, they conclude that they know nothing.
>
> (54)

Students may find what we do to be alienating and disheartening. Even when our intentions are quite honorable, silence can descend. Their experiences are not seen, and their voices are not heard. We can find ourselves participating, sometimes consciously, sometimes not, in what Patricia Williams calls "spirit murder" (55). I am reminded in a disconcerting way of a troubling scene from Alex Haley's *Roots*. We engage in practices that say quite insistently to a variety of students in a variety of ways, "Your name is Toby." Why wouldn't students wonder: Who can I trust here? Under what kinds of conditions? When? Why?

In addition to better practices in our classrooms, however, we can also question our ability to talk convincingly with deans, presidents, legislators, and the general public about what we do, how we do it, and why. We have not been conscientious about keeping lines of communication open, and we are now experiencing the consequences of talking primarily to ourselves as we watch funds being cut, programs being eliminated, and national agencies that are vital to our interests being bandied about as if they are post-it notes, randomly stuck on by some ill-informed spendthrift. We must learn to raise a politically active voice with a socially responsible mandate to make a rightful place for education in a country that seems always ready to place the needs of quality education on a sideboard instead of on the table. Seemingly, we have been forever content to let voices other than our own speak authoritatively about our areas of expertise and about us. It is time to speak for ourselves, in our own interests, in the interest of our work, and in the interest of our students.

Better practices are not limited, though, even to these concerns. Of more immediate concern to me this year, given my role as Chair of CCCC, is how to talk across boundaries within our own organization as teachers of English among other teachers of English and Language Arts from kindergarten through university with interests as varied as those implied by the sections, conferences, and committees of our parent organization, the National Council of Teachers of English (NCTE). Each of the groups within NCTE has its own set of needs, expectations, and concerns, multiplied across the amazing variety of institutional sites across which we work. In times of limited resources and a full slate of critical problems, we must find reasonable ways to negotiate so that we can all thrive reasonably well in the same place.

In our own case, for years now, CCCC has recognized changes in our relationships with NCTE. Since the mid-1980s we have grown exponentially. The field of rhetoric and composition has blossomed and diversified. The climate for higher education has increasingly degenerated, and we have struggled in the midst of change to forge a more satisfying identity and a more positive and productive working relationship with others in NCTE who are facing crises of their own. After 50 years in NCTE, we have grown up, and we have to figure out a new way of being and doing in making sure that we can face our challenges well. We are now in the second year of a concerted effort to engage in a multi-leveled conversation that we hope will leave CCCC well-positioned to face a new century and ongoing challenges. Much, however, depends on the ways in which we talk and listen and talk again in crossing boundaries and creating, or not, the common ground of engagement.

As I look at the lay of this land, I endorse Henry David Thoreau's statement when he said, "Only that day dawns to which we are awake" (267). So my appeal is to urge us all to be awake, awake and listening, awake and operating deliberately on codes of better conduct in the interest of keeping our boundaries fluid, our discourse invigorated with multiple perspectives, and our policies and practices well-tuned toward a clearer respect for human potential and achievement from whatever their source and a clearer understanding that voicing at its best is not just well-spoken but also well-heard.

Jacqueline Jones Royster, an associate professor of English at The Ohio State University and 1995 Chair of CCCC, defines her primary area of research as the history and uses of literacy among African American women. Her publications include a co-edited anthology, Double-Stitch: Black Women Write about Mothers and Daughters *(1991); a language arts textbook series,* Writer's Choice, Grades 6–8 *(1994); an edited volume,* Southern Horrors and Other Writings: The Anti-Lynching Campaign of Ida B. Wells-Barnett, 1892–1900 *(1996); and various articles in women's studies and literacy studies. This essay is a revised version of her chair's address to the 1995 CCCC meeting in Washington, DC.*

Works Cited

Adisa, Opal Palmer. "I Must Write What I Know So I'll Know That I've Known It All Along." *Sage: A Scholarly Journal on Black Women* 9.2 (1995): 54–57.

Anzuldua, Gloria. *Borderlands/La Frontera*. San Francisco: Aunt Lute, 1987.

Bhabha, Homi K. *The Location of Culture*. London: Routledge, 1994.

Christian, Barbara. "The Race for Theory." *Cultural Critique* 6 (1987): 335–45.

Cooper, Anna Julia. *A Voice from the South*. New York: Oxford UP, 1988.

Du Bois, W. E. B. *The Souls of Black Folk*. New York: Grammercy, 1994.

Haley, Alex. *Roots*. Garden City: Doubleday, 1976.

Hernstein, Richard J., and Charles Murray. *The Bell Curve: Intelligence and Class Structure in American Life*. New York: Free, 1994.

hooks, bell. *Talking Back: Thinking Feminist, Thinking Black*. Boston: South End, 1989.

Lorde, Audre. *The Black Unicorn*. New York: Norton, 1978.

——. Foreword. *Wild Women in the Whirlwind*. Ed. Joanne M. Braxton and Andree Nicola McLaughlin. New Brunswick: Rutgers UP, 1990. xi–xiii.

——. *Sister Outsider*. Freedom: The Crossing Press, 1984.

Mohanty, Chandra Talpade. "On Race and Voice: Challenges for Liberal Education in the 1990s." *Cultural Critique* 14 (Winter 1989–90):179–208.

——. "Decolonizing Education: Feminisms and the Politics of Multiculturalism in the 'New' World Order." Ohio State University. Columbus, April 1994.

Olsen, Tillie. *Silences*. New York: Delta, 1978.

Pratt, Mary Louise. "Arts of the Contact Zone." *Profession* 91 (1991): 33–40.

Spivak, Gayatri Chakravorty. *In Other Worlds: Essays in Cultural Politics*. New York: Routledge, 1988.

Thoreau, Henry David. *Walden*. New York: Vintage, 1991.

Thurman, Howard. "The Sound of the Genuine." Spelman College, Atlanta, April 1981.

West, Cornel. "Race Matters." Ohio State U, Columbus, OH, February 1995.

Williams, Patricia. *The Alchemy of Race and Rights*. Cambridge: Harvard UP, 1991.

8.
FEMINIST METHODS OF RESEARCH IN THE HISTORY OF RHETORIC: WHAT DIFFERENCE DO THEY MAKE?
Patricia Bizzell

Editors' Note: *Feminist research in the history of rhetoric has used traditional research methods to recover women rhetoricians. Nevertheless, such work has been criticized for making tendentious arguments on behalf of women rhetors. These criticisms partially arise from not understanding that feminist researchers do not seek traditional objective truth. Rather, they look for truths relative to the interests of specific communities. Scholars who reject their findings may be motivated by distaste for emotional allegiances these communities invoke.*

Ten years of scholarship in the history of rhetoric had to be accounted for when Bruce Herzberg and I undertook to prepare the second edition of our anthology of readings in rhetorical theory, *The Rhetorical Tradition.* It was first published in 1990 and the second edition is now in press. The past decade has seen a tremendous outpouring of work in the history of rhetoric, as researchers in classics, history, philosophy and speech communication have been joined in unprecedented numbers by scholars from English studies and composition. Herzberg and I have, of course, attempted to reflect this new work in the changes we have made in our anthology. But in my opinion as co-editor, the most significant change in the second edition comprises the presence of women's rhetorics and rhetorics of color. I don't wish to suggest that I think the new book adequately represents these strands in Western rhetoric. But I wish to argue that their increased presence is significant for two reasons. I will explore these reasons primarily in terms of women's rhetorics here, although I believe that similar arguments could be made with respect to rhetorics of color, and as suggested below, there is considerable overlap. On the one hand, as Richard Enos contends in "Recovering the Lost Art of Researching the History of Rhetoric," feminist research in the history of rhetoric is perhaps the best current example of what humanistic scholarship in rhetoric can accomplish. On the other hand, feminist research in the history of rhetoric presents the most trenchant challenges to traditional scholarly practices, opening up exciting

Patricia Bizzell, "Feminist Methods of Research in the History of Rhetoric: What Difference Do They Make?" *Rhetoric Society Quarterly* 30.4 (Fall 2000): 5–17.

new paths not only in the material scholars can study, but also, and perhaps ultimately more significantly, in the methods whereby we can study it.

I

First, what has feminist research in the history of rhetoric produced? Preparing the second edition of the *Rhetorical Tradition* anthology puts me in a relatively good position to answer that question, because of my avowed agenda of representing women's rhetorics in that volume coupled with the anthologist's necessity of relying on already published scholarship. I felt that the state of scholarship in 1989, when the first edition of the book was sent to the printers, permitted me to include only the following: Christine de Pizan and Laura Cereta combined in a single unit, with two brief excerpts, within the Renaissance section; Margaret Fell and Sarah Grimké similarly combined, though with slightly longer excerpts, in what was then the Enlightenment section, covering the eighteenth and nineteenth centuries; and Julia Kristeva and Hélène Cixous also combined, with longer excerpts, in the twentieth-century section. This is not very many women. Furthermore, as many readers have pointed out, combining the women tends to imply a devaluation of their work, as if it were not important or substantial enough to stand on its own. And indeed, the only men presented in combination in the first edition are four nineteenth-century composition textbook authors, representing what is openly treated as a minor genre. The women are presented in combination because I felt the need to preface their work in every case with a rather lengthy headnote justifying their inclusion and providing hints for how to read these texts as rhetorical theory, since they usually do not resemble the kinds of theoretical texts written by men and familiar in the canonical tradition.

The explosion of feminist scholarship in the history of rhetoric over the last ten years has enabled the table of contents of the second edition of the anthology to look very different: first, no women are presented in combination. Second, every section of the book now contains at least one woman: Aspasia in the classical section; Christine de Pizan, with more excerpts, in the medieval section (where she really seems to belong); Madeleine de Scudéry, Margaret Fell, and Sor Juana Inès de la Cruz in the Renaissance section; Mary Astell in the eighteenth-century section; Maria Stewart, Sarah Grimké, Phoebe Palmer, and Frances Willard in the nineteenth-century section; and Virginia Woolf, Hélène Cixous, and Gloria Anzaldúa in the twentieth-century section. Adrienne Rich would have been included here as well if she had given us permission to reprint her work. From six women, we have gone up to thirteen, and moreover, what was the Enlightenment section in the first edition has been split into separate eighteenth- and nineteenth-century sections in large part because my co-editor and I felt that the advent of people of color and white women on the speaker's platform in the nineteenth century constituted a sufficiently significant change in the possibilities for rhetoric that the century—which in traditional histories is usually thought of as advancing little over the theoretical developments of the previous century—demanded its own section. Furthermore, this list is by no means exhaustive. It represents only those women on whom my co-editor and I felt sufficient research had been done to enable us to include them without tendentiousness.

The importance of this research is addressed by Enos. He is concerned to mount a defense of what he calls "the humanistic study of rhetoric" (8). He wishes to argue ultimately for improved graduate training in primary research methods, to correct a situation which, he says, "encourages students to passively respond to research rather than to actively produce it" (13). Lest anyone think that this line of argument identifies Enos as some sort of conservative old fogey in rhetoric scholarship, I want to point out that his position was anticipated, to some extent, by a more recent in-comer to the field of historical research, Linda Ferreira-Buckley, in her essay entitled "Rescuing the Archives from Foucault," which appeared as part of a discussion in a May 1999 *College English* forum, "Archivists with an Attitude." Moreover, and most radically given the state of scholarship only ten years ago, Enos concludes his essay by holding up as models of the kind of historical research he is calling for, feminist scholars Lisa Ede, Cheryl Glenn, Andrea Lunsford, and other contributors to Lunsford's collection *Reclaiming Rhetorica.* Interestingly, Ferreira-Buckley ends up in almost the same place, featuring among her approved examples the feminist work of Elizabeth McHenry, Jacqueline Jones Royster, and Susan Jarratt.

I mean to imply that feminist research in the history of rhetoric has indeed had a tremendous impact, if we find it cited as exemplary in two essays with ultimately rather different argumentative agendas—Enos calling for a sort of return to traditio-nal research while Ferreira-Buckley openly advocates revisionist history while pointing out that "revisionist historians depend upon traditional archival practices" (581). If we think of the tasks of traditional research as discovering neglected authors, providing basic research on their lives and theories, and bringing out critical editions of their work, my survey of current work undertaken for the new edition of the *Rhetorical Tradition* anthology suggests that few, if any, other areas of research in the history of rhetoric have produced such rich results of this kind as feminist research.

II

Enos, however, misses an important implication of this new work in feminist research. As the "Archivists with an Attitude" forum shows us, historical research now, though relying on some traditional methods, must also raise new methodological questions. The problems that arise when the new wine is poured into old bottles can be seen in another *College English* exchange, that in the January 2000 issue between Xin Liu Gale and Cheryl Glenn and Susan Jarratt.

In "Historical Studies and Postmodernism: Rereading Aspasia of Miletus," Gale evaluates three scholarly works on the ancient Greek rhetorician Aspasia, comparing Glenn's and Jarratt's accounts, the latter co-authored with Rory Ong, with Madeleine Henry's book-length treatment. Gale favors Henry's work because, she says, Henry gives us "meticulous treatment of historical sources," "rather than eschewing the tradi-tional historical method or twisting the male texts to suit her feminist needs" (379).

Again and again, Gale uses the term "traditional" to characterize what she likes about Henry's approach. From these terms of praise, we may anticipate the terms of reproach used against Glenn, Jarratt and Ong. They are continually accused of distortions and contradictions.

Gale's critique helpfully reminds us of the importance of traditional historical research methods in feminist scholarship. But Gale does not appreciate the extent to which Glenn, Jarratt and Ong employ the traditional research methods she favors. As a glance at their bibliographies will reveal, their arguments are based in detailed scholarship every bit as "meticulous" and textually oriented as that which Gale praises in Henry, although Henry has the advantage of being more exhaustive because she gives Aspasia book-length treatment, as opposed to the limits of an essay or book chapter. Glenn, Jarratt, and Ong have all read the classical sources and secondary scholarship carefully. Indeed, their grasp on traditional methods may be seen in their replies to Gale, in which their defense takes the fundamentally traditional tack of accusing Gale of not reading their work carefully and not quoting from it responsibly. This exchange actually testifies to the importance of the position taken by Enos and Ferreira-Buckley that I described above, namely that people who are going to do research in the history of rhetoric do need training in traditional humanistic scholarly methods, even in this postmodern day and age.

At the same time, I think that none of the participants in this exchange adequately address the role of postmodern theory in feminist research methods. They do not adequately bring out just how revolutionary it has been. Gale acknowledges that all of the scholars she analyzes attest to the influence of postmodern theory on their work, but then she forgets about it in Henry's case in order to re-cast her as a more "traditional" researcher, and she forgets about it in the cases of Glenn and Jarratt and Ong in order to damn them for trying to do something that they explicitly said they were not trying to do, namely, to set up a new master narrative—what Glenn calls in her response a "mater narrative" (388)—to establish traditional sorts of truth claims against the truth claims of traditional rhetorical histories that leave Aspasia out. Hence for Gale, there is a deep "contradiction" in the work she attacks:

> on the one hand, we are asked to accept the post-modern belief that we are never able to obtain objective truth in history; on the other hand, we are asked to consider the reconceived story of Aspasia as a "truer" reality of women in history, a rediscovery of the obliterated "truth" independent of the existing historical discourse of men.
>
> (366)

But I would argue that this is a contradiction only if there is only one kind of truth, what Gale calls here the "objective" kind, which might be taken as the object of historical research. That is not the kind of truth that the scholars she attacks are seeking. Here, for example, is how Glenn characterizes her project in her reply:

> Writing women (or any other traditionally disenfranchised group) into the history of rhetoric ... interrogates the availability, practice, and preservation (or destruction) of

historical evidence, [and] simultaneously exposes relations of exploitation, domination, censorship, and erasure.

(389)

Similarly, Jarratt makes no bones about using what she calls an "intertextual interpretive method" that allows her to "take 'Aspasia' both as a rhetorical construct in Plato's text and as a real person" and to make a "speculative leap," as she says Henry does (I believe correctly), "that [allows] scholars to imagine women in relation to the practices of rhetoric, philosophy, and literary production so long considered almost completely the domain of men" (391).

Yet Gale does seem to be aware of this theoretical orientation in her opponents. In spite of accusing them of a contradiction involving objective truth, Gale does know that Glenn, Jarratt and Ong are not after objective truth. In the same paragraph in which she identifies the contradiction, as quoted above, she notes that Glenn is working from a "postmodern conception of truth as relative and contingent" (366), and she similarly acknowledges Jarratt's and Ong's research premises. I guess that what Gale would say is that the contradiction is not in her argument, but in theirs. In other words, she contends that in spite of claiming that they are not after objective truth, they argue as if they were. But it is not clear exactly what they are doing to draw this attack from Gale. Yes, they argue as if they wished to persuade readers of the merits of their positions. But it seems to me we must allow any scholar to attempt to be persuasive, without thereby accusing him or her of closet foundationalism. Indeed, Glenn, Jarratt and Ong might be expected to make more strenuous efforts to be persuasive than scholars who believe in objective truth would do, because their postmodern view of truths-plural-with-a-small-t suggests that only through persuasion do arguments get accepted as normative. They must be persuasive because they cannot count on their audience being moved simply by clearly perceiving the Truth-unitary-with-a-capital-T in their arguments.

I believe that this tangle arises from Gale's not naming accurately what it is that bothers her in the work of Glenn, Jarratt and Ong. I am moving here into the realm of speculation, and I want to be cautious about seeming to put words in Gale's mouth or to appropriate her arguments. But I am trying to tease out a subtle problem in feminist historiography. I suspect that what really bothers Gale is not that Glenn, Jarratt and Ong neglect traditional methods of historical research, because they in fact share these methods with Henry, whom Gale approves. I don't think it really is that they are making unsupportable claims for new objective truths in their scholarship, because as Gale shows that she knows, they are not in fact making any objective truth claims—that is not the kind of truth they are interested in. What, then, is the problem? I believe that it has to do with the role of emotion in feminist historiography.

Gale begins to get at this problem in her complaints about the ways that Glenn and Jarratt define feminist communities. As I have noted, Gale is aware that the scholars she attacks are working from what she calls a "community-relative view of truth" (370). Jarratt describes this view of truth as follows (mixing, as

I have already suggested, what might be called traditional along with postmodern criteria):

> Does this history instruct, delight, and move the reader? Is the historical data probable? Does it fit with other accounts or provide a convincing alternative? Is it taken up by the community and used? Or is it refuted, dismissed, and forgotten?
>
> (391)

But, says Gale in discussing Glenn's work, "all women do not belong to the same community, all women are not feminists, all feminists are not women, and even all feminists do not belong to the same community" (371). Gale makes a similar point when discussing Jarratt's work in her book *Rereading the Sophists:*

> If Jarratt has to attribute all the feminist characteristics to the First Sophists to include them in her feminist system, does she risk making the mistake of essentializing women? . . . [This move] may well raise questions such as how the resemblance between the Sophists and women would empower women and whether her feminist sophistic would create new exclusions, such as the exclusion of men.
>
> (377)

It seems that Gale is concerned about exclusions in the communities that Glenn, Jarratt and Ong define as normative—indeed, a very legitimate concern.

The problem here, though, cannot exactly be that Glenn's, Ong's or Jarratt's view of feminism is not inclusive enough. In her reply, for example, Jarratt states that Gale's "warning that my approach in this section of the book could have the effect of erasing differences among women is well taken" (392). Jarratt questions "the specter of a feminism that is One," and she praises the multiplicity of debate in feminist work and calls it to Gale's attention (392). This would appear to agree with Gale's own call "to invite other perspectives to correct our own partiality" (372). But Gale, it appears, wants closure never to be achieved, persuasion never to be accomplished, because she is afraid that the influence of any community values must be oppressive. She quotes Barry Brummett's caution in this regard, "'*Whose* community?'", as if this were a question that was unanswerable (371; emphasis in original). I would argue, on the contrary, that it is answerable by a process of debate and discussion, provisionally but persuasively—though indeed, the process may require the avowal of values and may not rely on supposedly value-neutral logical demonstration. I do not believe that humanistic knowledge can ever be established above debate. That is perhaps the ultimate epistemological question on which Gale and I disagree.

Therefore, I would redefine Gale's problem with the scholars she attacks as being one that arises when persuasion does not work. Glenn, Jarratt and Ong have not drawn Gale in. I am wondering whether an important reason for her resistance is that she feels excluded not so much from their discourse or their arguments as from their emotions. Gale hears in this work expressions of feelings of solidarity that trouble her, as noted in her commentary on feminist communities above. Perhaps, she feels herself to be excluded from these feelings for reasons she does not discuss. It is notable to me that Gale is very sensitive to the emotions animating work she doesn't like. More than once, she calls Glenn's treatment of Aspasia "passionate" (365), a "personal 'truth'" (366), too "assertive" (366 *et passim*). Jarratt is also too emotional, it seems, "intent on writing women into the history of rhetoric for the purpose of exposing male oppression and exclusion in order to liberate and empower women" (375). In contrast, Henry's emotional valence as described by Gale is cool: she is "meticulous," "painstakingly" "sifting, ordering, and evaluating evidence" (379), and arriving at a conclusion that "may not be as exciting as Glenn's or Jarratt's and Ong's" but that "commands respect" (381).

I think Jarratt is right on the money in her reply when she suggests that Gale harbors "aversions to both rhetoric and feminism" (392). But of course, Gale is under no compulsion to value either. My point would be, however, that Gale should clarify the grounds for her attack. It really isn't that the scholars she censures have vitiated traditional research methods. They have extended them in the service of feminist values and relied in part on rhetorical ethos to promote their positions. What Gale really objects to, I suspect, are these values, and she is not moved by the ethos. Let her be clear about that. And this brings me to the methodological point that I do believe is raised by this debate, namely the function of emotions in scholarly work. We perhaps need more discussion of the part played in the setting of scholarly research agendas and the constructing of scholarly arguments by our emotions about our research topics—or subjects—and our imagined readers. Think, for example, about the unexamined role of emotion in the famous debate between Barbara Biesecker and Karlyn Kohrs Campbell over historical research that focuses on individual figures. I believe we need a more thoroughly rhetorical discussion of these complications of research. Fortunately, that discussion has already begun, and I will conclude by pointing to a few examples.

III

We can now find feminist researchers in rhetoric openly discussing their feelings, both positive and negative, about their subjects of study. For example, in her essay "Women in the History of Rhetoric: The Past and the Future," Christine Mason Sutherland has provided us with a nuanced discussion of the difficulties a twentieth-century believer in feminism and democracy encounters in studying Mary Astell, an important eighteenth-century thinker on political and religious questions and on women's rhetoric who was opposed to democratic forms of government and to many of the liberal tenets of the contemporary women's movement. Sutherland walks us through the ways the researcher must negotiate her feelings about a woman whom she can admire but not entirely agree with. A different example can be found in one of Vicki Tolar Collins's first essays on women in Methodism, in which she tells how she was mysteriously drawn to the work of Hester Rogers, first acquiring her journal from Collins's elderly relative who thought Hester might be part of the family, and then having a dream shortly after she began doctoral studies that compelled her in the middle of the night to dig the book out of boxes as yet unpacked from a move, read until dawn, and discover a research subject. Interestingly, Collins chose to omit this moving story from the longer essay on women and Methodism that she published later in Molly Meijer Wertheimer's collection *Listening to Their Voices:* did she fear that, being too personal, it might taint her scholarship in traditional eyes? And one more short example: in her essay on Ida B. Wells published in *Reclaiming Rhetorica,* Jacqueline Jones Royster repeatedly expresses her admiration for Wells, rather than simply recounting the facts of her life and analyzing her rhetorical practices. Royster observes that Wells practiced the rhetorical arts "with flair and style" (169), that she worked for a world "in which we, African American included, could all flourish" (173), and, in short, that "Ida B. Wells was a wonder, personally and rhetorically" (181).

I believe it is to Royster that we owe our most thorough theorizing of the role of emotions in feminist research to date. In her study of African American women's rhetoric and social action, entitled *Traces of a Stream,* Royster concludes with a chapter that addresses in detail the methodological questions I have raised here. She articulates an approach that frankly begins in her identification—she takes the term from Kenneth Burke—with the subjects of her inquiries (see 252, 272). On the one hand, this is a deeply personal identification, springing from a mutual African American heritage. As Roster says, "theory begins with a story" (255), and she shares her story of community allegiances and multiple experiences with extant archives on African American women, with colleagues on the scholarly journal *SAGE,* and with her students at Spelman College. At the same time, Royster pointedly rejects an essentialized notion of identity. She notes:

> There is a constancy in the need for negotiation, beginning with the uncomfortable question of how much I actually do share identities with the women I study and how much I do not. (271) . . . identity is not natural. It is constructed. I have indeed identified multiple connections between these women and myself, despite our not being perfectly matched. (272) . . . However, as full-fledged members of humanity, this work is not by necessity ours alone. Others can also have interests and investments in it that can be envisioned from their own standpoints, from their own locations. What becomes critical to good practice, however, is that these researchers—who are indeed outsiders in the communities they study—have special obligations that begin with a need to articulate carefully what their viewpoints actually are, rather than letting the researchers' relationships to the work go unarticulated, as is often the case with practices of disregard.
>
> (277)

What becomes critical, in other words, is the acknowledgment of the multiple functions of emotions and experiences in defining one's relationship to one's research, a departure from traditional methods that Royster calls "practices of disregard," which might be the practices that produce the emotional coolness I saw Gale preferring in Henry.

It follows from this acknowledgment of personal connection in Royster's theory that the scholar will care for the subjects being researched. Here is where emotional attachments come most clearly into the open. Royster notes that for students who learned about the history of African American women's rhetoric and social action, "the most frequent types of responses . . . were affective" (266), relating not only to how they felt about the women they studied but also to how they felt about their own lives as intellectuals. Royster observes that over the years of doing archival research herself, "I was developing a habit of caring as a rhetorician" (258)—note how this formulation links caring with disciplinary activity—"caring *as a rhetorician*" (emphasis added). Particularly for African American women engaged in such research, Royster argues, what she calls an "afrafeminist" methodology should "acknowledge a role for caring, for passionate attachments" (276)—there again is that passion that Gale detected, it seems somewhat disapprovingly, in the work of Glenn, Jarratt and Ong.

Lest this kind of attachment lead to what Gale regards as merely "personal truth," however, Royster repeatedly emphasizes the necessity for feminist researchers to ground their work in the collective wisdom of their scholarly community and, importantly, in the community that they are studying. As Royster puts it:

> I recognize as valuable the perspectives of the scholarly fields in which I operate; simultaneously I respect the wisdom of the community with which I identify. I seek to position myself in academic writing, therefore, in a way that merges membership in two communities: the one I am studying and the ones in which I have gained specialized knowledge.
>
> (254)

> . . . [Afrafeminist scholars] speak and interpret *with* the community [of African American women], not just *for* the community, or about the community.
>
> (275; emphasis in original)

Royster makes explicit the discursive consequences of this orientation to multiple communities. Traditional academic discourse will not serve to express her research, but rather she must devise a kind of "academic writing" that mixes the cognitive and linguistic styles of her academic and African American communities—what I have called a "hybrid" form of academic discourse. Royster describes it this way:

> Critical to such methodological practices, therefore, is the idea that, whatever the knowledge accrued, it would be both presented and represented with this community [that is, the community being studied], and at least its potential for participation and response, in mind. This view of subjects as both audiences and agents contrasts with a presentation and representation of knowledge in a more traditional fashion. Typically, subjects [in traditional discourse] are likely to be perceived in a more disembodied way.
>
> (274)

Clearly, this is an attempt to embody in discourse an answer to the question Gale rightly indicates as crucial for all postmodern historiography, namely, *whose* community is normative? Royster gives us more, and more specific, information on how she answers this question than any other researcher I have encountered. She does not rely on any unitary category of "women" to define her communities. Moreover, Royster is at pains to specify that even the values and perspectives of communities she holds dear cannot be allowed to hold uninterrogated sway over critical discourse. She continually stresses the need for cross-questioning among communities, not only, as noted above, between the academic community and the African American women's community (two which obviously overlap, in the person, for example, of Royster herself), but also between these communities and representatives of other standpoints who may be drawn to research in this area. As Royster says:

> the need for negotiation is, therefore, not arbitrary. It is part and parcel of the consubstantial process. The need for negotiation is yoked to the need for a well-balanced analytical view that takes into account shifting conditions, values, and circumstances between human beings.
>
> (272)

Royster concludes her discussion by articulating a four-part "afrafeminist ideology" or what I would call "methodology," that organizes these insights. It is notable that the first element Royster mentions is "careful analysis" (279 ff), by which she appears to mean the traditional "basic skills" of research for which Enos and Ferreira-Buckley call and which, I contend, Glenn, Jarratt, and Ong, as well as Henry, employ. To them, Royster adds three elements that bespeak the emotions and value commitments I have outlined in her theory above: "acknowledgment of passionate attachment" (280) to the subjects of one's research; "attention to ethical action" (280) in one's scholarship, which requires one to be rigorous in the traditional sense and at the same time "accountable to our various publics" (281); and "commitment to social responsibility" (281), which indicates the need not only to think about the social consequences of the knowledge we generate but also to use it ourselves for the greater common good.

In conclusion, I want to stress why Royster needs the new methodology that she theorizes so thoroughly in this book. She articulates the challenges that face her at the outset:

> The first and most consistent challenges have come hand in hand with the very choosing of the work itself, that is, with identifying myself as a researcher who focuses on a multiply marginalized group; whose interests in this group center on topics not typically associated with the group, such as nonfiction and public discourse rather than imaginative literature and literary criticism; and who is called upon by the material conditions of the group itself to recognize the necessity of employing a broader, sometimes different range of techniques in garnering evidence and in analyzing and interpreting that evidence.
>
> (251)

Later on, she explains how these challenges impacted her research methods:

> The project required that I learn something about history, economics, politics, and the social context of women's lives. For the first time, I had to spend more time considering context than text. I had to take into account insights and inquiry patterns from disciplines other than those in which I was trained. I had to take into account the specific impact of

race, class, gender and culture on the ability to be creative and to achieve—not in some generic sense, but in terms of a particular group of human beings who chose deliberately to write and to speak, often in public.

(257)

As Royster notes, her techniques are "quite recognizably interdisciplinary and feminist" (257); she also characterizes them as a sort of ethnographic research in which she was unable to interview her subjects, because most of them were already dead (see 282). These techniques enabled her, as she says, to explore how "knowledge, experience, and language merge" in the lives of her research subjects (259). The point I wish to emphasize is that she thus generates scholarly knowledge that clearly could be developed no other way.

Have Royster, and other feminist scholars for whom she has now more completely articulated methodologies already in practice, departed radically from the rhetorical tradition? Yes, and no. No, because their work relies upon many of the traditional tools of research in the history of rhetoric. No, because the rhetors they have added to our picture of the history of Western rhetoric seem to me to be working within this tradition and enriching it, rather than constituting utterly separate or parallel rhetorical traditions. But yes, because in order to get at the activities of these new rhetors, researchers have had to adopt radically new methods as well, methods which violate some of the most cherished conventions of academic research, most particularly in bringing the person of the researcher, her body, her emotions, and dare one say, her soul, into the work. From my perspective as editor of an anthology called *The Rhetorical Tradition,* contemplating the major changes in scholarship over the last ten years, these new methods have made all the difference.

Department of English
The College of the Holy Cross

Works Cited

Biesecker, Barbara. "Coming to Terms with Recent Attempts to Write Women into the History of Rhetoric." *Philosophy and Rhetoric* 25(1992): 140–161.

Bizzell, Patricia. "Hybrid Academic Discourses: What, Why, How." *Composition Studies* 27 (Fall 1999): 7–21.

—— and Bruce Herzberg. *The Rhetorical Tradition: Readings from Classical Times to the Present.* Boston: Bedford Books, 1990 (second edition expected, 2001).

Campbell, Karlyn Kohrs. "Biesecker Cannot Speak for Her Either." *Philosophy and Rhetoric* 26 (1993): 153–159.

Collins, Vicki Tolar. "Walking in Light, Walking in Darkness: The Story of Women's Changing Rhetorical Space in Early Methodism." *Rhetoric Review* 14 (Spring 1996): 336–354.

——. "Women's Voices and Women's Silence in the Tradition of Early Methodism." In *Listening to Their Voices: The Rhetorical Activities of Historical Women.* Molly Meijer Wertheimer, ed. Columbia: University of South Carolina Press, 1997.

Enos, Richard. "Recovering the Lost Art of Researching the History of Rhetoric." *Rhetoric Society Quarterly* 29 (Fall 1999): 7–20.

Ferreira-Buckley, Linda. "Rescuing the Archives from Foucault " *College English* 61 (May 1999): 577–583.

Gale, Xin Liu. "Historical Studies and Postmodernism: Rereading Aspasia of Miletus." *College English* 62 (January 2000): 361–386.

Glenn, Cheryl. "Comment: Truth, Lies, and Method: Revisiting Feminist Historiography." *College English* 62 (January 2000): 387–389.

Jarratt, Susan. "Comment: Rhetoric and Feminism: Together Again." *College English* 62 (January 2000): 390–393.

——. *Rereading the Sophists: Classical Rhetoric Refigured.* Carbondale: Southern Illinois University Press, 1991.

Lunsford, Andrea, ed. *Reclaiming Rhetorica: Women in the Rhetorical Tradition.* Pittsburgh: University of Pittsburgh Press, 1995.

Royster, Jacqueline Jones. "To Call a Thing by Its True Name: The Rhetoric of Ida B. Wells." In *Reclaiming Rhetorica: Women in the Rhetorical Tradition.* Andrea Lunsford, ed. Pittsburgh: University of Pittsburgh Press, 1995.

——. *Traces of a Stream: Literacy and Social Change among African-American Women.* Pittsburgh: University of Pittsburgh Press, 2000.

Sutherland, Christine Mason. "Women in the History of Rhetoric: The Past and the Future." In *The Changing Tradition: Women in the History of Rhetoric.* Christine Mason Sutherland and Rebecca Sutcliffe, eds. Calgary: University of Calgary Press, 1999.

SECTION 4

PRACTICES AND PERFORMANCES

9.
THE TRANSFORMATION OF SILENCE
INTO LANGUAGE AND ACTION*
Audre Lorde

Editors' Note: *A clarion call to women everywhere, and especially to Black women, to "break the silence," this essay admonishes women to find and share their voices and thus to move from silence to language and action. This movement can help to bridge the debilitating differences among women.*

I have come to believe over and over again that what is most important to me must be spoken, made verbal and shared, even at the risk of having it bruised or misunderstood. That the speaking profits me, beyond any other effect. I am standing here as a Black lesbian poet, and the meaning of all that waits upon the fact that I am still alive, and might not have been. Less than two months ago I was told by two doctors, one female and one male, that I would have to have breast surgery, and that there was a 60 to 80 percent chance that the tumor was malignant. Between that telling and the actual surgery, there was a three-week period of the agony of an involuntary reorganization of my entire life. The surgery was completed, and the growth was benign.

But within those three weeks, I was forced to look upon myself and my living with a harsh and urgent clarity that has left me still shaken but much stronger. This is a situation faced by many women, by some of you here today. Some of what I experienced during that time has helped elucidate for me much of what I feel concerning the transformation of silence into language and action.

In becoming forcibly and essentially aware of my mortality, and of what I wished and wanted for my life, however short it might be, priorities and omissions became strongly etched in a merciless light, and what I most regretted were my silences. Of what had I *ever* been afraid? To question or to speak as I believed could have meant pain, or death. But we all hurt in so many different ways, all the time, and pain will either change or end. Death, on the other hand, is the final silence. And that might be coming quickly, now, without regard for whether I had ever spoken what needed to be said, or had only betrayed myself into small silences, while I planned someday to speak, or waited for someone else's words. And I began to recognize a source of power within myself that comes from the knowledge that while it is most desirable not to be afraid, learning to put fear into a perspective gave me great strength.

I was going to die, if not sooner then later, whether or not I had ever spoken myself. My silences had not protected me. Your silence will not protect you. But for every

Audre Lorde, "The Transformation of Silence into Language and Action." *Sinister Wisdom* 6 (1978): 11–15.

real word spoken, for every attempt I had ever made to speak those truths for which I am still seeking, I had made contact with other women while we examined the words to fit a world in which we all believed, bridging our differences. And it was the concern and caring of all those women which gave me strength and enabled me to scrutinize the essentials of my living.

The women who sustained me through that period were Black and white, old and young, lesbian, bisexual, and heterosexual, and we all shared a war against the tyrannies of silence. They all gave me a strength and concern without which I could not have survived intact. Within those weeks of acute fear came the knowledge—within the war we are all waging with the forces of death, subtle and otherwise, conscious or not—I am not only a casualty, I am also a warrior.

What are the words you do not yet have? What do you need to say? What are the tyrannies you swallow day by day and attempt to make your own, until you will sicken and die of them, still in silence? Perhaps for some of you here today, I am the face of one of your fears. Because I am woman, because I am Black, because I am lesbian, because I am myself—a Black woman warrior poet doing my work—come to ask you, are you doing yours?

And of course I am afraid, because the transformation of silence into language and action is an act of self-revelation, and that always seems fraught with danger. But my daughter, when I told her of our topic and my difficulty with it, said, "Tell them about how you're never really a whole person if you remain silent, because there's always that one little piece inside you that wants to be spoken out, and if you keep ignoring it, it gets madder and madder and hotter and hotter, and if you don't speak it out one day it will just up and punch you in the mouth from the inside."

In the cause of silence, each of us draws the face of her own fear—fear of contempt, of censure, or some judgment, or recognition, of challenge, of annihilation. But most of all, I think, we fear the visibility without which we cannot truly live. Within this country where racial difference creates a constant, if unspoken, distortion of vision, Black women have on one hand always been highly visible, and so, on the other hand, have been rendered invisible through the depersonalization of racism. Even within the women's movement, we have had to fight, and still do, for that very visibility which also renders us most vulnerable, our Blackness. For to survive in the mouth of this dragon we call America, we have had to learn this first and most vital lesson—that we were never meant to survive. Not as human beings. And neither were most of you here today, Black or not. And that visibility which makes us most vulnerable is that which also is the source of our greatest strength. Because the machine will try to grind you into dust anyway, whether or not we speak. We can sit in our corners mute forever while our sisters and our selves are wasted, while our children are distorted and destroyed, while our earth is poisoned; we can sit in our safe corners mute as bottles, and we will still be no less afraid.

In my house this year we are celebrating the feast of Kwanza, the African-american festival of harvest which begins the day after Christmas and lasts for seven days. There are seven principles of Kwanza, one for each day. The first principle is Umoja, which means unity, the decision to strive for and maintain unity in self and community.

The principle for yesterday, the second day, was Kujichagulia—self-determination—the decision to define ourselves, name ourselves, and speak for ourselves, instead of being defined and spoken for by others. Today is the third day of Kwanza, and the principle for today is Ujima—collective work and responsibility—the decision to build and maintain ourselves and our communities together and to recognize and solve our problems together.

Each of us is here now because in one way or another we share a commitment to language and to the power of language, and to the reclaiming of that language which has been made to work against us. In the transformation of silence into language and action, it is vitally necessary for each one of us to establish or examine her function in that transformation and to recognize her role as vital within that transformation.

For those of us who write, it is necessary to scrutinize not only the truth of what we speak, but the truth of that language by which we speak it. For others, it is to share and spread also those words that are meaningful to us. But primarily for us all, it is necessary to teach by living and speaking those truths which we believe and know beyond understanding. Because in this way alone we can survive, by taking part in a process of life that is creative and continuing, that is growth.

And it is never without fear—of visibility, of the harsh light of scrutiny and perhaps judgment, of pain, of death. But we have lived through all of those already, in silence, except death. And I remind myself all the time now that if I were to have been born mute, or had maintained an oath of silence my whole life long for safety, I would still have suffered, and I would still die. It is very good for establishing perspective.

And where the words of women are crying to be heard, we must each of us recognize our responsibility to seek those words out, to read them and share them and examine them in their pertinence to our lives. That we not hide behind the mockeries of separations that have been imposed upon us and which so often we accept as our own. For instance, "I can't possibly teach Black women's writing—their experience is so different from mine." Yet how many years have you spent teaching Plato and Shakespeare and Proust? Or another, "She's a white woman and what could she possibly have to say to me?" Or, "She's a lesbian, what would my husband say, or my chairman?" Or again, "This woman writes of her sons and I have no children." And all the other endless ways in which we rob ourselves of ourselves and each other.

We can learn to work and speak when we are afraid in the same way we have learned to work and speak when we are tired. For we have been socialized to respect fear more than our own needs for language and definition, and while we wait in silence for that final luxury of fearlessness, the weight of that silence will choke us.

The fact that we are here and that I speak these words is an attempt to break that silence and bridge some of those differences between us, for it is not difference which immobilizes us, but silence. And there are so many silences to be broken.

Note

* Paper delivered at the Modern Language Association's "Lesbian and Literature Panel," Chicago, Illinois, December 28, 1977. First published in *Sinister Wisdom* 6 (1978) and *The Cancer Journals* (Spinsters, Ink, San Francisco, 1980).

10.
HOW TO TAME A WILD TONGUE
Gloria Anzaldúa

Editors' Note: *A dentist's comment about a "wild" tongue opens a meditation on the relationship between language and identity and an exploration of the complexities of the languages of the author's self(ves). These languages arise from many sources, including everyday talk, literature, movies, and music, though these forms can also be the sources of internalized conflict and (self-) rejection. The history of forms of Spanish in the United States is one of deep discrimination, in spite of ongoing efforts to include such forms in educational and public settings. Thus the struggle for voice and for identity continues, calling on the abiding patience of los Chicanos.*

"We're going to have to control your tongue," the dentist says, pulling out all the metal from my mouth. Silver bits plop and tinkle into the basin. My mouth is a motherlode.

The dentist is cleaning out my roots. I get a whiff of the stench when I gasp. "I can't cap that tooth yet, you're still draining," he says.

"We're going to have to do something about your tongue," I hear the anger rising in his voice. My tongue keeps pushing out the wads of cotton, pushing back the drills, the long thin needles. "I've never seen anything as strong or as stubborn," he says. And I think, how do you tame a wild tongue, train it to be quiet, how do you bridle and saddle it? How do you make it lie down?

> "Who is to say that robbing a people of
> its language is less violent than war?"
>
> —Ray Gwyn Smith[1]

I remember being caught speaking Spanish at recess—that was good for three licks on the knuckles with a sharp ruler. I remember being sent to the corner of the classroom for "talking back" to the Anglo teacher when all I was trying to do was tell her how to pronounce my name. "If you want to be American, speak 'American.' If you don't like it, go back to Mexico where you belong."

"I want you to speak English. *Pa' hallar buen trabajo tienes que saber hablar el inglés bien. Qué vale toda tu educación si todavía hablas inglés con un* 'accent,'" my mother would say, mortified that I spoke English like a Mexican. At Pan American University,

Gloria Anzaldúa, "How to Tame a Wild Tongue." In *Borderlands/La Frontera*. 2e. 1987. San Francisco: Aunt Lute Books, 1999. 75–86.

I, and all Chicano students were required to take two speech classes. Their purpose: to get rid of our accents.

Attacks on one's form of expression with the intent to censor are a violation of the First Amendment. *El Anglo con cara de inocente nos arrancó la lengua.* Wild tongues can't be tamed, they can only be cut out.

Overcoming the Tradition of Silence

> *Ahogadas, escupimos el oscuro.*
> *Peleando con nuestra propia sombra*
> *el silencio nos sepulta.*

En boca cerrada no entran moscas. "Flies don't enter a closed mouth" is a saying I kept hearing when I was a child. *Ser habladora* was to be a gossip and a liar, to talk too much. *Muchachitas bien criadas,* well-bred girls don't answer back. *Es una falta de respeto* to talk back to one's mother or father. I remember one of the sins I'd recite to the priest in the confession box the few times I went to confession: talking back to my mother, *hablar pa''trás, repelar. Hocicona, repelona, chismosa,* having a big mouth, questioning, carrying tales are all signs of being *mal criada.* In my culture they are all words that are derogatory if applied to women—I've never heard them applied to men.

The first time I heard two women, a Puerto Rican and a Cuban, say the word "*nosotras,*" I was shocked. I had not known the word existed. Chicanas use *nosotros* whether we're male or female. We are robbed of our female being by the masculine plural. Language is a male discourse.

> And our tongues have become
>
> dry   the wilderness has
>
> dried out our tongues   and
>
> we have forgotten speech.
>
> —Irena Klepfisz[2]

Even our own people, other Spanish speakers *nos quieren poner candados en la boca.* They would hold us back with their bag of *reglas de academia.*

Oyé como ladra; el lenguaje de la frontera

> *Quien tiene boca se equivoca.*
>
> —Mexican saying

"*Pocho,* cultural traitor, you're speaking the oppressor's language by speaking English, you're ruining the Spanish language," I have been accused by various Latinos and Latinas. Chicano Spanish is considered by the purist and by most Latinos deficient, a mutilation of Spanish.

But Chicano Spanish is a border tongue which developed naturally. Change, *evolución, enriquecimiento de palabras nuevas por invención o adopción* have created variants of Chicano Spanish, *un nuevo lenguaje. Un lenguaje que corresponde a un modo de vivir.* Chicano Spanish is not incorrect, it is a living language.

For a people who are neither Spanish nor live in a country in which Spanish is the first language; for a people who live in a country in which English is the reigning tongue but who are not Anglo; for a people who cannot entirely identify with either standard (formal, Castillian) Spanish nor standard English, what recourse is left to them but to create their own language? A language which they can connect their identity to, one capable of communicating the realities and values true to themselves— a language with terms that are neither *español ni inglés,* but both. We speak a patois, a forked tongue, a variation of two languages.

Chicano Spanish sprang out of the Chicanos' need to identify ourselves as a distinct people. We needed a language with which we could communicate with ourselves, a secret language. For some of us, language is a homeland closer than the Southwest—for many Chicanos today live in the Midwest and the East. And because we are a complex, heterogeneous people, we speak many languages. Some of the languages we speak are:

1 Standard English
2 Working class and slang English
3 Standard Spanish
4 Standard Mexican Spanish
5 North Mexican Spanish dialect
6 Chicano Spanish (Texas, New Mexico, Arizona and California have regional variations)
7 Tex-Mex
8 *Pachuco* (called *caló*)

My "home" tongues are the languages I speak with my sister and brothers, with my friends. They are the last five listed, with 6 and 7 being closest to my heart. From school, the media and job situations, I've picked up standard and working class English. From Mamagrande Locha and from reading Spanish and Mexican literature, I've picked up Standard Spanish and Standard Mexican Spanish. From *los recién llegados,* Mexican immigrants, and *braceros,* I learned the North Mexican dialect. With Mexicans I'll try to speak either Standard Mexican Spanish or the North Mexican dialect. From my parents and Chicanos living in the Valley, I picked up Chicano Texas Spanish, and I speak it with my mom, younger brother (who married a Mexican and who rarely mixes Spanish with English), aunts and older relatives.

With Chicanas from *Nuevo México* or *Arizona* I will speak Chicano Spanish a little, but often they don't understand what I'm saying. With most California Chicanas I speak entirely in English (unless I forget). When I first moved to San Francisco, I'd rattle off something in Spanish, unintentionally embarrassing them. Often it is only with another Chicana *tejana* that I can talk freely.

Words distorted by English are known as anglicisms or *pochismos*. The *pocho* is an anglicized Mexican or American of Mexican origin who speaks Spanish with an accent characteristic of North Americans and who distorts and reconstructs the language according to the influence of English.[3] Tex-Mex, or Spanglish, comes most naturally to me. I may switch back and forth from English to Spanish in the same sentence or in the same word. With my sister and my brother Nune and with Chicano *tejano* contemporaries I speak in Tex-Mex.

From kids and people my own age I picked up *Pachuco. Pachuco* (the language of the zoot suiters) is a language of rebellion, both against Standard Spanish and Standard English. It is a secret language. Adults of the culture and outsiders cannot understand it. It is made up of slang words from both English and Spanish. *Ruca* means girl or woman, *vato* means guy or dude, *chale* means no, *simón* means yes, *churro* is sure, talk is *periquiar, pigionear* means petting, *que gacho* means how nerdy, *ponte águila* means watch out, death is called *la pelona*. Through lack of practice and not having others who can speak it, I've lost most of the *Pachuco* tongue.

Chicano Spanish

Chicanos, after 250 years of Spanish/Anglo colonization have developed significant differences in the Spanish we speak. We collapse two adjacent vowels into a single syllable and sometimes shift the stress in certain words such as *maíz/maiz, cohete/cuete*. We leave out certain consonants when they appear between vowels: *lado/lao, mojado/mojao*. Chicanos from South Texas pronounce *f* as *j* as in *jue (fue)*. Chicanos use "archaisms," words that are no longer in the Spanish language, words that have been evolved out. We say *semos, truje, haiga, ansina*, and *naiden*. We retain the "archaic" *j*, as in *jalar*, that derives from an earlier *h* (the French *halar* or the Germanic *halon* which was lost to standard Spanish in the 16th century), but which is still found in several regional dialects such as the one spoken in South Texas. (Due to geography, Chicanos from the Valley of South Texas were cut off linguistically from other Spanish speakers. We tend to use words that the Spaniards brought over from Medieval Spain. The majority of the Spanish colonizers in Mexico and the Southwest came from Extremadura—Hernán Cortés was one of them—and Andalucía. Andalucians pronounce *ll* like a *y*, and their *d*'s tend to be absorbed by adjacent vowels: *tirado* becomes *tirao*. They brought *el lenguaje popular, dialectos y regionalismos*.[4])

Chicanos and other Spanish speakers also shift *ll* to *y* and *z* to *s*.[5] We leave out initial syllables, saying *tar* for *estar, toy* for *estoy, hora* for *ahora* (*cubanos* and *puertorriqueños* also leave out initial letters of some words). We also leave out the final syllable such as *pa* for *para*. The intervocalic *y*, the *ll* as in *tortilla, ella, botella*, gets replaced by *tortia* or *tortiya, ea, botea*. We add an additional syllable at the beginning of certain words: *atocar* for *tocar, agastar* for *gastar*. Sometimes we'll say *lavaste las vacijas*, other times *lavates* (substituting the *ates* verb endings for the *aste*).

We use anglicisms, words borrowed from English: *bola* from ball, *carpeta* from carpet, *máchina de lavar* (instead of *lavadora*) from washing machine. Tex-Mex argot, created by adding a Spanish sound at the beginning or end of an English word such as *cookiar* for cook, *watchar* for watch, *parkiar* for park, and *rapiar* for rape, is the result of the pressures on Spanish speakers to adapt to English.

We don't use the word *vosotros/as* or its accompanying verb form. We don't say *claro* (to mean yes), *imagínate,* or *me emociona,* unless we picked up Spanish from Latinas, out of a book, or in a classroom. Other Spanish-speaking groups are through the same, or similar, development in their Spanish.

Linguistic Terrorism

> *Deslenguadas. Somos los del español deficiente.* We are your linguistic nightmare, your linguistic aberration, your linguistic *mestizaje,* the subject of your *burla.* Because we speak with tongues of fire we are culturally crucified. Racially, culturally and linguistically *somos huérfanos*—we speak an orphan tongue.

Chicanas who grew up speaking Chicano Spanish have internalized the belief that we speak poor Spanish. It is illegitimate, a bastard language. And because we internalize how our language has been used against us by the dominant culture, we use our language differences against each other.

Chicana feminists often skirt around each other with suspicion and hesitation. For the longest time I couldn't figure it out. Then it dawned on me. To be close to another Chicana is like looking into the mirror. We are afraid of what we'll see there. *Pena.* Shame. Low estimation of self. In childhood we are told that our language is wrong. Repeated attacks on our native tongue diminish our sense of self. The attacks continue throughout our lives.

Chicanas feel uncomfortable talking in Spanish to Latinas, afraid of their censure. Their language was not outlawed in their countries. They had a whole lifetime of being immersed in their native tongue; generations, centuries in which Spanish was a first language, taught in school, heard on radio and TV, and read in the newspaper.

If a person, Chicana or Latina, has a low estimation of my native tongue, she also has a low estimation of me. Often with *mexicanas y latinas* we'll speak English as a neutral language. Even among Chicanas we tend to speak English at parties or conferences. Yet, at the same time, we're afraid the other will think we're *agringadas* because we don't speak Chicano Spanish. We oppress each other trying to out-Chicano each other, vying to be the "real" Chicanas, to speak like Chicanos. There is no one Chicano language just as there is no one Chicano experience. A monolingual Chicana whose first language is English or Spanish is just as much a Chicana as one who speaks several variants of Spanish. A Chicana from Michigan or Chicago or Detroit is just as much a Chicana as one from the Southwest. Chicano Spanish is as diverse linguistically as it is regionally.

By the end of this century, Spanish speakers will comprise the biggest minority group in the U.S., a country where students in high schools and colleges are encouraged to take French classes because French is considered more "cultured." But for a language to remain alive it must be used.[6] By the end of this century English, and not Spanish, will be the mother tongue of most Chicanos and Latinos.

So, if you want to really hurt me, talk badly about my language. Ethnic identity is twin skin to linguistic identity—I am my language. Until I can take pride in my language, I cannot take pride in myself. Until I can accept as legitimate Chicano Texas Spanish, Tex-Mex and all the other languages I speak, I cannot accept the legitimacy of myself. Until I am free to write bilingually and to switch codes without having always to translate, while I still have to speak English or Spanish when I would rather speak Spanglish, and as long as I have to accommodate the English speakers rather than having them accommodate me, my tongue will be illegitimate.

I will no longer be made to feel ashamed of existing. I will have my voice: Indian, Spanish, white. I will have my serpent's tongue—my woman's voice, my sexual voice, my poet's voice. I will overcome the tradition of silence.

> My fingers
> move sly against your palm
> Like women everywhere, we speak in code. . . .
>
> —Melanie Kaye/Kantrowitz[7]

"Vistas," corridos, y comida: My Native Tongue

In the 1960s, I read my first Chicano novel. It was *City of Night* by John Rechy, a gay Texan, son of a Scottish father and a Mexican mother. For days I walked around in stunned amazement that a Chicano could write and could get published. When I read *I Am Joaquín*[8] I was surprised to see a bilingual book by a Chicano in print. When I saw poetry written in Tex-Mex for the first time, a feeling of pure joy flashed through me. I felt like we really existed as a people. In 1971, when I started teaching High School English to Chicano students, I tried to supplement the required texts with works by Chicanos, only to be reprimanded and forbidden to do so by the principal. He claimed that I was supposed to teach "American" and English literature. At the risk of being fired, I swore my students to secrecy and slipped in Chicano short stories, poems, a play. In graduate school, while working toward a Ph.D., I had to "argue" with one advisor after the other, semester after semester, before I was allowed to make Chicano literature an area of focus.

Even before I read books by Chicanos or Mexicans, it was the Mexican movies I saw at the drive-in—the Thursday night special of $1.00 a carload—that gave me a sense of belonging. "*Vámonos a las vistas,*" my mother would call out and we'd all— grandmother, brothers, sister and cousins—squeeze into the car. We'd wolf down cheese and bologna white bread sandwiches while watching Pedro Infante in melo-dramatic tearjerkers like *Nosotros los pobres,* the first "real" Mexican movie (that was not an imitation of European movies). I remember seeing *Cuando los hijos se van* and surmising that all Mexican movies played up the love a mother has for her children and what ungrateful sons and daughters suffer when they are not devoted to their mothers. I remember the singing-type "westerns" of Jorge Negrete and Miquel Aceves Mejía. When watching Mexican movies, I felt a sense of homecoming as well as alien-ation. People who were to amount to something didn't go to Mexican movies, or *bailes* or tune their radios to *bolero, rancherita,* and *corrido* music.

The whole time I was growing up, there was *norteño* music sometimes called North Mexican border music, or Tex-Mex music, or Chicano music, or *cantina* (bar) music. I grew up listening to *conjuntos,* three- or four-piece bands made up of folk musicians playing guitar, *bajo sexto,* drums and button accordion, which Chicanos had borrowed from the German immigrants who had come to Central Texas and Mexico to farm and build breweries. In the Rio Grande Valley, Steve Jordan and Little Joe Hernández were popular, and Flaco Jiménez was the accordion king. The rhythms of Tex-Mex music are those of the polka, also adapted from the Germans, who in turn had borrowed the polka from the Czechs and Bohemians.

I remember the hot, sultry evenings when *corridos*—songs of love and death on the Texas-Mexican borderlands—reverberated out of cheap amplifiers from the local *cantinas* and wafted in through my bedroom window.

Corridos first became widely used along the South Texas/Mexican border during the early conflict between Chicanos and Anglos. The *corridos* are usually about Mexican heroes who do valiant deeds against the Anglo oppressors. Pancho Villa's song, "*La cucaracha,*" is the most famous one. *Corridos* of John F. Kennedy and his death are still very popular in the Valley. Older Chicanos remember Lydia Mendoza, one of the great border *corrido* singers who was called *la Gloria de Tejas.* Her "*El tango negro,*" sung during the Great Depression, made her a singer of the people. The everpresent *corridos* narrated one hundred years of border history, bringing news of events as well as entertaining. These folk musicians and folk songs are our chief cultural myth-makers, and they made our hard lives seem bearable.

I grew up feeling ambivalent about our music. Country-western and rock-and-roll had more status. In the 50s and 60s, for the slightly educated and *agringado* Chicanos, there existed a sense of shame at being caught listening to our music. Yet I couldn't stop my feet from thumping to the music, could not stop humming the words, nor hide from myself the exhilaration I felt when I heard it.

There are more subtle ways that we internalize identification, especially in the forms of images and emotions. For me food and certain smells are tied to my identity, to my homeland. Woodsmoke curling up to an immense blue sky; woodsmoke perfuming my grandmother's clothes, her skin. The stench of cow manure and the yellow patches on the ground; the crack of a .22 rifle and the reek of cordite. Homemade white cheese sizzling in a pan, melting inside a folded *tortilla.* My sister Hilda's hot, spicy *menudo, chile colorado* making it deep red, pieces of *panza* and hominy floating on top. My brother Carito barbequing *fajitas* in the backyard. Even now and 3,000 miles away, I can see my mother spicing the ground beef, pork and venison with *chile.* My mouth salivates at the thought of the hot steaming *tamales* I would be eating if I were home.

Si le preguntas a mi mama, "¿Que eres?"

> "Identity is the essential core of who
> we are as individuals, the conscious
> experience of the self inside."

—Kaufman[9]

Nosotros los Chicanos straddle the borderlands. On one side of us, we are constantly exposed to the Spanish of the Mexicans, on the other side we hear the Anglos' incessant clamoring so that we forget our language. Among ourselves we don't say *nosotros los americanos, o nosotros los españoles, o nosotros los hispanos.* We say *nosotros los mexicanos* (by *mexicanos* we do not mean citizens of Mexico; we do not mean a national identity, but a racial one). We distinguish between *mexicanos del otro lado* and *mexicanos de este lado.* Deep in our hearts we believe that being Mexican has nothing to do with which country one lives in. Being Mexican is a state of soul—not one of mind, not one of citizenship. Neither eagle nor serpent, but both. And like the ocean, neither animal respects borders.

> *Dime con quien andas y te diré quien eres.*
> (Tell me who your friends are and I'll tell you who
> you are.)
>
> —Mexican saying

Si le preguntas a mi mamá. "¿Qué eres?" te dirá, "Soy mexicana." My brothers and sister say the same. I sometimes will answer *"soy mexicana"* and at others will say *"soy Chicana" o "soy tejana"*. But I identified as *"Raza"* before I ever identified as *"mexicana"* or *"Chicana."*

As a culture, we call ourselves Spanish when referring to ourselves as a linguistic group and when copping out. It is then that we forget our predominant Indian genes. We are 70–80% Indian.[10] We call ourselves Hispanic[11] or Spanish-American or Latin American or Latin when linking ourselves to other Spanish-speaking peoples of the Western hemisphere and when copping out. We call ourselves Mexican-American[12] to signify we are neither Mexican nor American, but more the noun "American" than the adjective "Mexican" (and when copping out).

Chicanos and other people of color suffer economically for not acculturating. This voluntary (yet forced) alienation makes for psychological conflict, a kind of dual identity—we don't identify with the Anglo-American cultural values and we don't totally identify with the Mexican cultural values. We are a synergy of two cultures with various degrees of Mexicanness or Angloness. I have so internalized the borderland conflict that sometimes I feel like one cancels out the other and we are zero, nothing, no one. *A veces no soy nada ni nadie. Pero hasta cuando no lo soy, lo soy.*

When not copping out, when we know we are more than nothing, we call ourselves Mexican, referring to race and ancestry; *mestizo* when affirming both our Indian and Spanish (but we hardly ever own our Black ancestry); Chicano when referring to a politically aware people born and/or raised in the U.S.; *Raza* when referring to Chicanos; *tejanos* when we are Chicanos from Texas.

Chicanos did not know we were a people until 1965 when Ceasar Chavez and the farmworkers united and *I Am Joaquín* was published and *la Raza Unida* party was formed in Texas. With that recognition, we became a distinct people. Something momentous happened to the Chicano soul—we became aware of our reality and acquired a name and a language (Chicano Spanish) that reflected that reality. Now that we had a name, some of the fragmented pieces began to fall together—who we were, what we were, how we had evolved. We began to get glimpses of what we might eventually become.

Yet the struggle of identities continues, the struggle of borders is our reality still. One day the inner struggle *will* cease and a true integration take place. In the meantime, *tenemos que hacer la lucha. ¿Quién está protegiendo los ranchos de mi gente? ¿Quién está tratando de cerrar la fisura entre la india y el blanco en nuestra sangre? El Chicano, sí, el Chicano que anda como un ladrón en su propia casa.*

Los Chicanos, how patient we seem, how very patient. There is the quiet of the Indian about us.[13] We know how to survive. When other races have given up their tongue, we've kept ours. We know what it is to live under the hammer blow of the dominant *norteamericano* culture. But more than we count the blows, we count the days the weeks the years the centuries the eons until the white laws and commerce and customs will rot in the deserts they've created, lie bleached. *Humildes* yet proud, *quietos* yet wild, *nosotros los mexicanos-Chicanos* will walk by the crumbling ashes as we go about our business. Stubborn, persevering, impenetrable as stone, yet possessing a malleability that renders us unbreakable, we, the *mestizas* and *mestizos*, will remain.

Notes

1 Ray Gwyn Smith, "*Moorland is Cold Country.*" Unpublished book.
2 Irena Klepfisz, "Di rayze aheym / The Journey Home," in *The Tribe of Dina: A Jewish Women's Anthology*, Melanie Kaye/Kantrowitz and Irena Klepfisz, eds. (Montpelier, VT: Sinister Wisdom Books, 1986), 49.
3 R. C. Orgeta, *Dialectologia Del Barrio*, trans. Hortencia S. Alwan (Los Angeles, CA: R. C. Ortega Publisher & Bookseller, 1977), 132.
4 Eduardo Hernandez-Chavez, Andrew D. Cohen, and Anthony F. Beltramo, *El Lenguaje de los Chicanos: Regional and Social Characteristics of Language Used by Mexican Americans* (Arlington, VA: Center for Applied Linguistics, 1975), 39.
5 Hernandez-Chavez, xvii.
6 Irena Klepfisz, "Secular Jewish Identity: Yidishkayt in America," in *The Tribe of Dina*, Kay/Kantrowitz and Klepfisz, eds., 43.
7 Melanie Kay/Kantrowitz, "Sign," in *We Speak in Code: Poems and Other Writings* (Pittsburgh, PA: Motherroot Publications, Inc. 1980), 85.
8 Rodolfo Gonzales, *I Am Joaquín / Yo Soy Joaquín* (New York, NY: Bantam books, 1972). It was first published in 1967.
9 Kaufman, 68.
10 Chavez, 88–90.
11 "Hispanic" is derived from Hispanis (Espana, a name given to the Iberian Peninsula in ancient times when it was a part of the Roman Empire) and is a term designated by the U.S. government to make it easier to handle us on paper.
12 The Treaty of Guadalupe Hidalgo created the Mexican-American in 1848.
13 Anglos, in order to alleviate their guilt for dispossessing the Chicano, stressed the Spanish part of us and perpetrated the myth of the Spanish Southwest. We have accepted the fiction that we are Hispanic, that is Spanish, in order to accommodate ourselves to the dominant culture and its abhorrence of Indians. Chavez, 88–91.

11.
ON RECLAIMING RHETORICA
Andrea A. Lunsford

Editors' Note: *This introduction details the development of this very early volume in the field of rhetoric and writing studies devoted to "reclaiming" women and including them in the history of western rhetoric. The essays included, on Aspasia, Diotima, Margery Kempe, Christine de Pisan, Mary Astell, Mary Wollstonecraft, Margaret Fuller, Ida B. Wells, Sojourner Truth, Laura Riding Jackson, Suzanne Langer, Louise Rosenblatt, Julia Kristeva, and others, collectively listen to the voices of long-ignored women rhetors and do so using non-traditional and often controversial methods.*

The story of *Reclaiming Rhetorica is* a long one, full of the gaps and silences and erasures that also characterize its subject, the history of women in rhetoric. I entered this story late in 1990, when I received a cryptic request from a university press to review a manuscript they had received. Its title was *Reclaiming Rhetorica*; I did not receive the names of its authors.

Fresh from directing a dissertation on women in the history of rhetoric from classical times to the Renaissance, I read through the manuscript eagerly and soon after wrote to the press, saying, "This volume proves to be the first of its kind" and thus "extremely important." I urged that the authors revise with an eye to more inclusiveness and that the press publish the result as soon as possible. Consequently, I expected to hear that such a volume was forthcoming sometime fairly soon. How surprised I was, then, to receive a letter many months later, from two contributors to the volume saying they had not found a publisher and asking if I would consider joining the project.

I jumped at the chance to work with this exciting material, and I was delighted to find that, indeed, I already knew some of the contributors to the original collection in manuscript. I thus set about augmenting that collection, soliciting additional contributions (on Aspasia, Diotima, Margery Kempe, Mary Astell, Mary Wollstonecraft, Ida B. Wells, and Julia Kristeva) which attempted to reach back to classical and medieval times as well as to add some additional American and contemporary women's voices to the collection. Eventually the new submissions arrived; contributors read one another's essays, the entire volume, and then revised accordingly; and we traded seemingly endless memos and E-mail and fax messages to compose the afterword to this volume. As a result, some two years later we had a new manuscript ready to submit for publication.

Andrea A. Lunsford, "On Reclaiming Rhetorica." *Reclaiming Rhetorica.* Carbondale: Southern Illinois UP, 1995: 3–8.

As these remarks suggest, I was a latecomer to *Rhetorica,* for the story of this volume actually began in 1986–1987, when Annette Kolodny, then professor of literature in the Department of Languages, Literature, and Communication at Rensselaer Polytechnic Institute, was approached by a group of students who wanted to study the history of women as rhetoricians and theorists of rhetoric. Annette writes:

> The students' approaches were marked by hesitation and frustration: hesitation because they were uncertain as to whether much material really existed; and frustration because none of their courses in rhetoric had introduced them to women or even hinted at women's contributions. . . . Increasingly, I was coming to share my students' frustration at the absence of women in these materials. And, no less important, I was seeing interesting parallels and coincidences between discussions of contemporary rhetorical theory and the ongoing debates over literary critical theories and methods.
>
> (Letter to author)

During the 1987–1988 year, Annette taught a two-semester graduate seminar on "Women Rhetoricians," a seminar whose members included the original contributors to this volume. (Only one of those seminarians, Colleen O'Toole, has been unable to participate in this project.) They spent the year doing difficult archival research, sharing the results of that research, defining and refining their views on the positioning of particular women in rhetoric, and drafting essays. Annette describes it this way:

> Perhaps the most exciting outcomes of our year together were these: a powerful bonding based on friendship and mutual respect which included everyone. And an excited sense that we had uncovered a rich and unexplored field that would sustain us for years to come. I do not recall any one of us ever getting bored with our projects. On the contrary, we felt we were at the beginning of a much larger enterprise. And we knew that the history of women as rhetors and rhetoricians needed to be written.

By the end if their year together, Annette and her students were convinced that they had the core of a potentially important book. When Annette left Rensselaer Polytechnic Institute in the summer of 1988 to become dean of the faculty of humanities at the University of Arizona, however, the process of editing a final manuscript necessarily slowed. Still, the students persisted, Annette remained in contact with them, and gradually the conception of the book outgrew the confines of the original seminar. It was at this point that I was enlisted as a potential editor and contributor. As Annette remembers it, "The students in the seminar knew better than I did how important this book could be. And they were determined to see the project through to completion."

Why were the contributors to this volume so impassioned, so persistent in their pursuit of publication? Although the reasons vary widely, one stands out as paramount: if ever woman's place in the rhetorical tradition were to be reconfigured, if ever a new rhetoric full of such influences were to arise, the work of this volume had to be done.

Of course, many have called for or invoked "new" rhetorics before, most notably George Campbell in his 1776 work, *A Philosophy of Rhetoric,* and Daniel Fogarty in his

1959 volume, *Roots for a New Rhetoric*. In that work, Fogarty identifies what he calls the "old model" of "current-traditional rhetoric," against which he posits his own version of a "new" rhetoric. To illustrate the roots of this new rhetoric, Fogarty turns to the work of I. A. Richards, Kenneth Burke, and Alfred Korzybski, arguing that their views can form the basis of an art and science of communication that provides an "understanding of the basic presuppositions underlying the functions of discourse, makes use of the findings of literature and science, and teaches the individual how to talk, listen and read" (Fogarty 134).

In spite of its contributions, however, Fogarty's "new rhetoric" is limited—as was Campbell's—by both training and tradition to an exclusively masculinist reading of rhetoric, one that in many ways continues to echo Locke's earlier and decidedly not "new" views on the subject:

> 'Tis evident how much Men love to deceive, and be deceived, since Rhetoric, that powerful instrument of Error and Deceit, has its established Professors, is publicly taught, and has always been had in great Reputation. And, I doubt not, but it will always be thought great boldness, if not brutality in me, to have said thus much against it. Eloquence, like the fair sex, has too prevailing beauties in it, to suffer it self ever to be spoken against. And 'tis in vain to find fault with those Arts of Deceiving, wherein Men find pleasure to be deceived.
>
> (Locke 106)

The essays in *Reclaiming Rhetorica* attempt to move beyond such limited—and limiting—understandings. In doing so, however, they do not attempt to redefine a "new" rhetoric but rather to interrupt the seamless narrative usually told about the rhetorical tradition and to open up possibilities for multiple rhetorics, rhetorics that would not name and valorize one traditional, competitive, agonistic, and linear mode of rhetorical discourse but would rather incorporate other, often dangerous moves: breaking the silence; naming in personal terms; employing dialogics; recognizing and using the power of conversation; moving centripetally towards connections; and valuing—indeed insisting upon—collaboration. The characteristic tropes for a reclaimed Rhetorica include, therefore, not only definition, division, and synecdoche, but also metonymy, metaphor, and consubstantiality; its characteristic and principal aim is not deception or conquest—as Locke and much of the familiar rhetorical tradition would have it—but understanding, exploration, connection, and conversation. Taken together, the essays in *Reclaiming Rhetorica* suggest that the realm of rhetoric has been almost exclusively male not because women were not practicing rhetoric—the arts of language are after all at the source of human communication—but because the tradition has never recognized the forms, strategies, and goals used by many women as "rhetorical."

The authors of *Reclaiming Rhetorica* hope, then, to add to recent work—particularly in books by Karlyn Kohrs Campbell, Patricia Bizzell and Bruce Herzberg, Miriam Brody, and Sonja Foss, and in articles by scholars such as Catherine Peaden, Nan Johnson, Anne Ruggles Gere, Susan Miller, Karyn Hollis, Sue Ellen Holbrook, and others, who are currently carrying on the archaeological investigations necessary to the success of this project. More particularly, the essays in this volume aim to contribute to that work first of all by *listening*—and listening hard—to and for the voices of women in the history of rhetoric; by becoming, as Cheryl Glenn suggests, the audience who can at last give voice to women lost to us; by examining in close detail their speech and writing; and by aknowledging and exploring the ways in which they have been too often dismissed and silenced.

For the women whose voices animate the pages of *Reclaiming Rhetorica* are a widely diverse group. Some deliberately learned and used the conventions of scholarly rhetoric to make a place for women among the voices of men. Others, self-taught and working within the context of strong religious and political communities, spoke and wrote with deep conviction shaped through conscious rhetorical technique. Still others created comprehensive theories or approaches to language in the tradition of academic scholarship. Some were recognized as prominent rhetoricians in their own time and have since been forgotten, while others made contributions to language that are only now being recognized as vitally rhetorical.

Like the women whose work this volume seeks to reclaim, the contributors to this volume hold widely varying views about their subjects and take widely varying approaches to them. Some, comfortable with more traditional definitions of rhetorical aims and taxonomies, work to illuminate the dark corners of the discipline to which women have often been banished. Others, dismissing not only the traditional male canon but also the rhetorical theorists and practitioners of that tradition, develop new definitions that encompass the set of excellences demonstrated by the women they study. The underlying principle of this volume is not unity, therefore, but diversity and inclusivity; we seek most of all to embody here widely varying and contrasting approaches, methodologies, scholarly styles, and individual voices.

But such diversity should not suggest iconoclasm or disengagement from one another. Rather, a rich and intense collaboration—beginning with the original graduate seminar and expanding to include all contributors—has been indispensable as both the technique and the spirit of the writing of this book. Through group critiques and the reading and rereading of all the essays gathered here, the contributors have developed ideas in a far more communal and supportive environment than is usually possible in the academic setting or in a collection of this kind. While each essay in this book is separate, then, it owes much to the common ground so laboriously marked out in years of conversation and correspondence. If this book holds the echoes of the women it studies, its individual pages also echo the voices of all of its authors who, together, persist in reclaiming Rhetorica—in all her shapes, forms, and voices.

References

Bizzell, Patricia, and Bruce Herzberg, eds. *The Rhetorical Tradition: Readings from Classical Times to the Present.* Boston: Bedford, 1990.

Brody, Miriam. *Manly Writing: Gender, Rhetoric, and the Rise of Composition.* Carbondale: Southern Illinois UP, 1993.

Campbell, George. *The Philosophy of Rhetoric.* 1776. Ed. Lloyd Bitzer. Carbondale: Southern Illinois UP, 1963.

Campbell, Karyln Kohrs. *Man Cannot Speak for Her.* New York: 1989.

Fogarty, Daniel John. *Roots for a New Rhetoric.* 1959. New York: Russell, 1986.

Foss, Karen A., and Sonya K. Foss. *Women Speak: The Eloquence of Women's Lives.* Prospect Heights: Waveland Press, 1991.

Gere, Anne Ruggles. "Kitchen Tables and Rented Rooms: The Extracurriculum of Composition." *College Composition and Communication* 45.1 (1994): 75–92.

Holbrook, Sue Ellen. "Women's Work: The Feminizing of Composition." *Rhetoric Review* 9.2 (1992): 201–29.

Hollis, Karen. "Liberating Voices: Autobiographical Writing at the Bryn Mawr Summer School for Women Workers, 1921–1938." *College Composition and Communication* 45.1 (1994): 31–60.

——. *Liberating Voices: Writing at the Bryn Mawr Summer School for Women Workers, 1921–1938.* New York: Prentice, Writing and Culture Series, 1995 (forthcoming).

Johnson, Nan. *Rhetorical Performance and the Construction of Culture* (work in progress).

Kolodny, Annette. Letter to author.

Locke, John. *An Essay Concerning Human Understanding.* Vol. 2. New York: Dutton, 1961.

Miller, Susan. "Things Inanimate May Move: A Different History of Writing and Class." *College Composition and Communication* 45.1 (1994): 102–07.

Peaden, Catherine Hobbs. "Jane Addams and the Social Rhetoric of Democracy." *Oratorical Culture in Nineteenth Century America: Transformations in the Theory and Practice of Rhetoric.* Ed. Gregory Clark and S. Michael Halloran. Carbondale: Southern Illinois UP, 1993.

——. ed. *Nineteenth-Century Women Learn to Write: Past Cultures and Practices of Literacy.* Charlottesville: U of Virginia P (in press).

Rhetoric Society Quarterly 22.1 (1992). Special Issue on "Feminist Rereadings in the History of Rhetoric."

SECTION 5

PEDAGOGICAL APPLICATIONS AND IMPLICATIONS

12.
COMPOSING AS A WOMAN
Elizabeth A. Flynn

Editors' Note: *Composition studies has been shaped by women who, among other things, moved beyond the study of written products to focus on the processes of individual writers. While feminist inquiry and composition studies share commonalities, the fields have not engaged productively. Given the efforts of feminist sociologists and psychologists to describe differences between men and women's self-conceptions and modes of interaction, composition scholars must attend to gendered differences in writing and reading. A study of four first-year student essays reveals patterns of difference between male and female writers reflective of those patterns identified by earlier researchers and calls for further study of such distinctions.*

> It is not easy to think like a woman in a man's world, in the world of the professions; yet the capacity to do that is a strength which we can try to help our students develop. To think like a woman in a man's world means thinking critically, refusing to accept the givens, making connections between facts and ideas which men have left unconnected. It means remembering that every mind resides in a body; remaining accountable to the female bodies in which we live; constantly retesting given hypotheses against lived experience. It means a constant critique of language, for as Wittgenstein (no feminist) observed, "The limits of my language are the limits of my world." And it means that most difficult thing of all: listening and watching in art and literature, in the social sciences, in all the descriptions we are given of the world, for silences, the absences, the nameless, the unspoken, the encoded—for there we will find the true knowledge of women. And in breaking those silences, naming ourselves, uncovering the hidden, making ourselves present, we begin to define a reality which resonates to *us*, which affirms *our* being, which allows the woman teacher and the woman student alike to take ourselves, and each other, seriously: meaning, to begin taking charge of our lives.
>
> —Adrienne Rich, "Taking Women Students Seriously"

The emerging field of composition studies could be described as a feminization of our previous conceptions of how writers write and how writing should be taught.[1] In exploring the nature of the writing process, composition specialists expose the limitations of previous product-oriented approaches by demystifying the product and in so doing empowering developing writers and readers. Rather than enshrining the text in its final form, they demonstrate that the works produced by established

---

Elizabeth A. Flynn, "Composing as a Woman." *College Composition and Communication* 39 (Dec. 1988): 423–35.

authors are often the result of an extended, frequently enormously frustrating process and that creativity is an activity that results from experience and hard work rather than a mysterious gift reserved for a select few. In a sense, composition specialists replace the figure of the authoritative father with an image of a nurturing mother. Powerfully present in the work of composition researchers and theorists is the ideal of a committed teacher concerned about the growth and maturity of her students who provides feedback on ungraded drafts, reads journals, and attempts to tease out meaning from the seeming incoherence of student language. The field's foremothers come to mind— Janet Emig, Mina Shaughnessy, Ann Berthoff, Win Horner, Maxine Hairston, Shirley Heath, Nancy Martin, Linda Flower, Andrea Lunsford, Sondra Perl, Nancy Sommers, Marion Crowhurst, Lisa Ede. I'll admit the term foremother seems inappropriate as some of these women are still in their thirties and forties—we are speaking here of a very young field. Still, invoking their names suggests that we are also dealing with a field that, from the beginning, has welcomed contributions from women—indeed, has been shaped by women.

The work of male composition researchers and theorists has also contributed significantly to the process of feminization described above. James Britton, for instance, reverses traditional hierarchies by privileging private expression over public transaction, process over product. In arguing that writing for the self is the matrix out of which all forms of writing develop, he valorizes an activity and a mode of expression that have previously been undervalued or invisible, much as feminist literary critics have argued that women's letters and diaries are legitimate literary forms and should be studied and taught alongside more traditional genres. His work has had an enormous impact on the way writing is taught on the elementary and high school levels and in the university, not only in English courses but throughout the curriculum. Writing-Across-the-Curriculum Programs aim to transform pedagogical practices in all disciplines, even those where patriarchal attitudes toward authority are most deeply rooted.

Feminist Studies and Composition Studies

Feminist inquiry and composition studies have much in common. After all, feminist researchers and scholars and composition specialists are usually in the same department and sometimes teach the same courses. Not surprisingly, there have been wonderful moments when feminists have expressed their commitment to the teaching of writing. Florence Howe's essay, "Identity and Expression: A Writing Course for Women," for example, published in *College English* in 1971, describes her use of journals in a writing course designed to empower women. Adrienne Rich's essay, "'When We Dead Awaken': Writing as Re-Vision," politicizes and expands our conception of revision, emphasizing that taking another look at the texts we have generated necessitates revising our cultural assumptions as well.

There have also been wonderful moments when composition specialists have recognized that the marginality of the field of composition studies is linked in important ways to the political marginality of its constituents, many of whom are women who teach part-time. Maxine Hairston, in "Breaking Our Bonds and Reaffirming

Our Connections," a slightly revised version of her Chair's address at the 1985 convention of the Conference on College Composition and Communication, draws an analogy between the plight of composition specialists and the plight of many women. For both, their worst problems begin at home and hence are immediate and daily. Both, too, often have complex psychological bonds to the people who frequently are their adversaries (273).

For the most part, though, the fields of feminist studies and composition studies have not engaged each other in a serious or systematic way. The major journals in the field of composition studies do not often include articles addressing feminist issues, and panels on feminism are infrequent at the Conference on College Composition and Communication.[2] As a result, the parallels between feminist studies and composition studies have not been delineated, and the feminist critique that has enriched such diverse fields as linguistics, reading, literary criticism, psychology, sociology, anthropology, religion, and science has had little impact on our models of the composing process or on our understanding of how written language abilities are acquired. We have not examined our research methods or research samples to see if they are androcentric. Nor have we attempted to determine just what it means to compose as a woman.

Feminist research and theory emphasize that males and females differ in their developmental processes and in their interactions with others. They emphasize, as well, that these differences are a result of an imbalance in the social order, of the dominance of men over women. They argue that men have chronicled our historical narratives and defined our fields of inquiry. Women's perspectives have been suppressed, silenced, marginalized, written out of what counts as authoritative knowledge. Difference is erased in a desire to universalize. Men become the standard against which women are judged.

A feminist approach to composition studies would focus on questions of difference and dominance in written language. Do males and females compose differently? Do they acquire language in different ways? Do research methods and research samples in composition studies reflect a male bias? I do not intend to tackle all of these issues. My approach here is a relatively modest one. I will survey recent feminist research on gender differences in social and psychological development, and I will show how this research and theory may be used in examining student writing, thus suggesting directions that a feminist investigation of composition might take.

Gender Differences in Social and Psychological Development

Especially relevant to a feminist consideration of student writing are Nancy Chodorow's *The Reproduction of Mothering,* Carol Gilligan's *In a Different Voice,* and Mary Belenky, Blythe Clinchy, Nancy Goldberger, and Jill Tarule's *Women's Ways of Knowing.* All three books suggest that women and men have different conceptions of self and different modes of interaction with others as a result of their different experiences, especially their early relationship with their primary parent, their mother.

Chodorow's book, published in 1978, is an important examination of what she calls the "psychoanalysis and the sociology of gender," which in turn influenced

Gilligan's *In a Different Voice* and Belenky et al.'s *Women's Ways of Knowing*. Chodorow tells us in her preface that her book originated when a feminist group she was affiliated with "wondered what it meant that women parented women." She argues that girls and boys develop different relational capacities and senses of self as a result of growing up in a family in which women mother. Because all children identify first with their mother, a girl's gender and gender role identification processes are continuous with her earliest identifications whereas a boy's are not. The boy gives up, in addition to his oedipal and preoedipal attachment to his mother, his primary identification with her. The more general identification processes for both males and females also follow this pattern. Chodorow says,

> Girls' identification processes, then, are more continuously embedded in and mediated by their ongoing relationship with their mother. They develop through and stress particularistic and affective relationships to others. A boy's identification processes are not likely to be so embedded in or mediated by a real affective relation to his father. At the same time, he tends to deny identification with and relationship to his mother and reject what he takes to be the feminine world; masculinity is defined as much negatively as positively. Masculine identification processes stress differentiation from others, the denial of affective relation, and categorical universalistic components of the masculine role. Feminine identification processes are relational, whereas masculine identification processes tend to deny relationship.
>
> (176)

Carol Gilligan's *In a Different Voice*, published in 1982, builds on Chodorow's findings, focusing especially, though, on differences in the ways in which males and females speak about moral problems. According to Gilligan, women tend to define morality in terms of conflicting responsibilities rather than competing rights, requiring for their resolution a mode of thinking that is contextual and narrative rather than formal and abstract (19). Men, in contrast, equate morality and fairness and tie moral development to the understanding of rights and rules (19). Gilligan uses the metaphors of the web and the ladder to illustrate these distinctions. The web suggests interconnectedness as well as entrapment; the ladder suggests an achievement-orientation as well as individualistic and hierarchical thinking. Gilligan's study aims to correct the inadequacies of Lawrence Kohlberg's delineation of the stages of moral development. Kohlberg's study included only male subjects, and his categories reflect his decidedly male orientation. For him, the highest stages of moral development derive from a reflective understanding of human rights (19).

Belenky, Clinchy, Goldberger, and Tarule, in *Women's Ways of Knowing*, acknowledge their debt to Gilligan, though their main concern is intellectual rather than moral development. Like Gilligan, they recognize that male experience has served as the model in defining processes of intellectual maturation. The mental processes that are involved in considering the abstract and the impersonal have been labeled "thinking" and are attributed primarily to men, while those that deal with the personal and interpersonal fall under the rubric of "emotions" and are largely relegated to women. The particular study they chose to examine and revise is William Perry's *Forms of Intellectual and Ethical Development in the College Years* (1970). While Perry did include some women subjects in his study, only the interviews with men were used in illustrating and validating his scheme of intellectual and ethical development. When Perry assessed women's development on the basis of the categories he developed, the women were found to conform to the patterns he had observed in the male data. Thus, his work reveals what women have in common with men but was poorly designed to uncover those themes that might be more prominent among women. *Women's Ways of Knowing* focuses on "what else women might have to say about the development of their minds and on alternative routes that are sketchy or missing in Perry's version" (9).

Belenky et al. examined the transcripts of interviews with 135 women from a variety of backgrounds and of different ages and generated categories that are suited for describing the stages of women's intellectual development. They found that the quest for self and voice plays a central role in transformations of women's ways of knowing. Silent women have little awareness of their intellectual capacities. They live—selfless and voiceless—at the behest of those around them. External authorities know the truth and are all-powerful. At the positions of received knowledge and procedural knowledge, other voices and external truths prevail. Sense of self is embedded either in external definitions and roles or in identifications with institutions, disciplines, and methods. A sense of authority arises primarily through identification with the power of a group and its agreed-upon ways for knowing. Women at this stage of development have no sense of an authentic or unique voice, little awareness of a centered self. At the position of subjective knowledge, women turn away from others and any external authority. They have not yet acquired a public voice or public authority, though. Finally, women at the phase of constructed knowledge begin an effort to reclaim the self by attempting to integrate knowledge they feel intuitively with knowledge they have learned from others.

Student Writing

If women and men differ in their relational capacities and in their moral and intellectual development, we would expect to find manifestations of these differences in the student papers we encounter in our first-year composition courses. The student essays I will describe here are narrative descriptions of learning experiences produced in the first of a two-course sequence required of first-year students at Michigan Tech. I've selected the four because they invite commentary from the perspective of the material discussed above. The narratives of the female students are stories of interaction, of connection, or of frustrated connection. The narratives of the male students are stories of achievement, of separation, or of frustrated achievement.

Kim's essay describes a dreamlike experience in which she and her high school girlfriends connected with each other and with nature as a result of a balloon ride they decided to take one summer Sunday afternoon as a way of relieving boredom. From the start, Kim emphasizes communion and tranquility: "It was one of those Sunday afternoons when the sun shines brightly and a soft warm breeze blows gently. A perfect day for a long drive on a country road with my favorite friends." This mood is intensified as they ascend in the balloon: "Higher and higher we went, until the view was overpowering. What once was a warm breeze turned quickly into a cool crisp wind. A feeling of freedom and serenity overtook us as we drifted along slowly." The group felt as if they were "just suspended there on a string, with time non-existent." The experience made them contemplative, and as they drove quietly home, "each one of us collected our thoughts, and to this day we still reminisce about that Sunday afternoon." The experience solidified relationships and led to the formation of a close bond that was renewed every time the day was recollected.

The essay suggests what Chodorow calls relational identification processes. The members of the group are described as being in harmony with themselves and with the environment. There is no reference to competition or discord. The narrative also suggests a variation on what Belenky et al. call "connected knowing," a form of procedural knowledge that makes possible the most desirable form of knowing, constructed knowledge. Connected knowing is rooted in empathy for others and is intensely personal. Women who are connected knowers are able to detach themselves from the relationships and institutions to which they have been subordinated and begin to trust their own intuitions. The women in the narrative were connected doers rather than connected knowers. They went off on their own, left their families and teachers behind (it was summer vacation, after all), and gave themselves over to a powerful shared experience. The adventure was, for the most part, a silent one but did lead to satisfying talk.

Kathy also describes an adventure away from home, but hers was far less satisfying, no doubt because it involved considerably more risk. In her narrative she makes the point that "foreign countries can be frightening" by focusing on a situation in which she and three classmates, two females and a male, found themselves at a train station in Germany separated from the others because they had gotten off to get some refreshments and the train had left without them. She says,

> This left the four of us stranded in an unfamiliar station. Ed was the only person in our group that could speak German fluently, but he still didn't know what to do. Sue got hysterical and Laura tried to calm her down. I stood there stunned. We didn't know what to do.

What they did was turn to Ed, whom Kathy describes as "the smartest one in our group." He told them to get on a train that was on the same track as the original. Kathy realized, though, after talking to some passengers, that they were on the wrong train and urged her classmates to get off. She says,

> I almost panicked. When I convinced the other three we were on the wrong train we opened the doors. As we were getting off, one of the conductors started yelling at us in German. It didn't bother me too much because I couldn't understand what he was saying. One thing about trains in Europe is that they are always on schedule. I think we delayed that train about a minute or two.

In deciding which train to board after getting off the wrong one, they deferred to Ed's judgment once again, but this time they got on the right train. Kathy concludes, "When we got off the train everyone was waiting. It turned out we arrived thirty minutes later than our original train. I was very relieved to see everyone. It was a very frightening experience and I will never forget it."

In focusing on her fears of separation, Kathy reveals her strong need for connection, for affiliation. Her story, like Kim's, emphasizes the importance of relationships, though in a different way. She reveals that she had a strong need to feel part of a group and no desire to rebel, to prove her independence, to differentiate herself from others. This conception of self was a liability as well as a strength in the sense that she became overly dependent on the male authority figure in the group, whom she saw as smarter and more competent than herself. In Belenky et al.'s terms, Kathy acted as if other voices and external truths were more powerful than her own. She did finally speak and act, though, taking it on herself to find out if they were on the right train and ushering the others off when she discovered they were not. She was clearly moving toward the development of an authentic voice and a way of knowing that integrates intuition with authoritative knowledge. After all, she was the real hero of the incident.

The men's narratives stress individuation rather than connection. They are stories of individual achievement or frustrated achievement and conclude by emphasizing separation rather than integration or reintegration into a community. Jim wrote about his "Final Flight," the last cross-country flight required for his pilot's license. That day, everything seemed to go wrong. First, his flight plan had a mistake in it that took 1½ hours to correct. As a result, he left his hometown 2 hours behind schedule. Then the weather deteriorated, forcing him to fly as low as a person can safely fly, with the result that visibility was very poor. He landed safely at his first destination but flew past the second because he was enjoying the view too much. He says,

> Then I was off again south bound for Benton Harbor. On the way south along the coast of Lake Michigan the scenery was a beautiful sight. This relieved some of the pressures and made me look forward to the rest of the flight. It was really nice to see the ice flows break away from the shore. While enjoying the view of a power plant on the shore of Lake Michigan I discovered I had flown past the airport.

He finally landed and took off again, but shortly thereafter had to confront darkness, a result of his being behind schedule. He says,

> The sky turned totally black by the time I was half-way home. This meant flying in the dark which I had only done once before. Flying in the dark was also illegal for me to do at this time. One thing that made flying at night nice was that you could see lights that were over ninety miles away.

Jim does not emphasize his fear, despite the fact that his situation was more threatening than the one Kathy described, and his reference to his enjoyment of the scenery suggests that his anxiety was not paralyzing or debilitating. At times, his solitary flight was clearly as satisfying as Kim's communal one. When he focuses on the difficulties he encountered, he speaks only of his "problems" and "worries" and concludes that the day turned out to be "long and trying." He sums up his experience as follows: "That day I will long remember for both its significance in my goal in getting my pilot's license and all the problems or worries that it caused me during the long and problem-ridden flight." He emerges the somewhat shaken hero of his adventure; he has achieved his goal in the face of adversity. Significantly, he celebrates his return home by having a bite to eat at McDonald's by himself. His adventure does not end with a union or reunion with others.

Jim's story invites interpretation in the context of Chodorow's claims about male interactional patterns. Chodorow says that the male, in order to feel himself adequately masculine, must distinguish and differentiate himself from others. Jim's adventure was an entirely solitary one. It was also goal-directed—he wanted to obtain his pilot's license and, presumably, prove his competence to himself and others. His narrative calls into question, though, easy equations of abstract reasoning and impersonality with male modes of learning since Jim was clearly as capable as Kim of experiencing moments of exultation, of communion with nature.

Joe's narrative of achievement is actually a story of frustrated achievement, of conflicting attitudes toward an ethic of hard work and sacrifice to achieve a goal. When he was in high school, his father drove him twenty miles to swim practice and twenty miles home every Tuesday through Friday night between October and March so he could practice for the swim team. He hated this routine and hated the Saturday morning swim meets even more but continued because he thought his parents, especially his father, wanted him to. He says, "I guess it was all for them, the cold workouts, the evening practices, the weekend meets. I had to keep going for them even though I hated it." Once he realized he was going through his agony for his parents rather than for himself, though, he decided to quit and was surprised to find that his parents supported him. Ultimately, though, he regretted his decision. He says,

> As it turns out now, I wish I had stuck with it. I really had a chance to go somewhere with my talent. I see kids my age who stuck with something for a long time and I envy them for their determination. I wish I had met up to the challenge of sticking with my swimming, because I could have been very good if I would have had their determination.

Joe is motivated to pursue swimming because he thinks his father will be disappointed if he gives it up. His father's presumed hold on him is clearly tenuous, however, because once Joe realizes that he is doing it for him rather than for himself, he quits. Finally, though, it is his gender role identification, his socialization into a male role and a male value system, that allows him to look back on his decision with regret. In college, he has become a competitor, an achiever. He now sees value in the long and painful practices, in a single-minded determination to succeed. The narrative reminds us of Chodorow's point that masculine identification is predominantly a gender role identification rather than identification with a particular parent.

I am hardly claiming that the four narratives are neat illustrations of the feminist positions discussed above. For one thing, those positions are rich in contradiction and complexity and defy easy illustration. For another, the narratives themselves are as often characterized by inconsistency and contradiction as by a univocality of theme and tone. Kathy is at once dependent and assertive; Joe can't quite decide if he should have been rebellious or disciplined. Nor am I claiming that what I have found here are characteristic patterns of male and female student writing. I would need a considerably larger and more representative sample to make such a claim hold. I might note, though, that I had little difficulty identifying essays that revealed patterns of difference among the twenty-four papers I had to choose from, and I could easily have selected others. Sharon, for instance, described her class trip to Chicago, focusing especially on the relationship she and her classmates were able to establish with her advisor. Diane described "An Unwanted Job" that she seemed unable to quit despite unpleasant working conditions. Mike, like Diane, was dissatisfied with his job, but he expressed his dissatisfaction and was fired. The frightening experience Russ described resulted from his failed attempt to give his car a tune-up; the radiator hose burst, and he found himself in the hospital recovering from third-degree burns. These are stories of relatedness or entanglement; of separation or frustrated achievement.

The description of the student essays is not meant to demonstrate the validity of feminist scholarship but to suggest, instead, that questions raised by feminist researchers and theorists do have a bearing on composition studies and should be pursued. We ought not assume that males and females use language in identical ways or represent the world in a similar fashion. And if their writing strategies and patterns of representation do differ, then ignoring those differences almost certainly means a suppression of women's separate ways of thinking and writing. Our models of the composing process are quite possibly better suited to describing men's ways of composing than to describing women's.[3]

Pedagogical Strategies

The classroom provides an opportunity for exploring questions about gender differences in language use. Students, I have found, are avid inquirers into their own language processes. An approach I have had success with is to make the question of gender difference in behavior and language use the subject to be investigated in class. In one honors section of first-year English, for instance, course reading included selections from Mary Anne Ferguson's *Images of Women in Literature*, Gilligan's *In a Different Voice*, Alice Walker's *Meridian*, and James Joyce's *A Portrait of the Artist as a Young Man*. Students were also required to keep a reading journal and to submit two formal papers. The first was a description of people they know in order to arrive at generalizations about gender differences in behavior, the second a comparison of some aspect of the Walker and Joyce novels in the light of our class discussions.

During class meetings we shared journal entries, discussed the assigned literature, and self-consciously explored our own reading, writing, and speaking behaviors. In one session, for instance, we shared retellings of Irwin Shaw's "The Girls in Their

Summer Dresses," an especially appropriate story since it describes the interaction of a husband and wife as they attempt to deal with the husband's apparently chronic habit of girl-watching. Most of the women were sympathetic to the female protagonist, and several males clearly identified strongly with the male protagonist.

The students reacted favorably to the course. They found Gilligan's book to be challenging, and they enjoyed the heated class discussions. The final journal entry of one of the strongest students in the class, Dorothy, suggests the nature of her development over the ten-week period:

> As this is sort of the wrap-up of what I've learned or how I feel about the class, I'll try to relate this entry to my first one on gender differences.
>
> I'm not so sure that men and women are so similar anymore, as I said in the first entry. The reactions in class especially make me think this. The men were so hostile toward Gilligan's book! I took no offense at it, but then again I'm not a man. I must've even overlooked the parts where she offended the men!
>
> Another thing really bothered me. One day after class, I heard two of the men talking in the hall about how you just have to be really careful about what you say in HU 101H about women, etc. *Why* do they have to be careful?! What did these two *really* want to say? That was pretty disturbing.
>
> However, I do still believe that MTU (or most any college actually) does bring out more similarities than differences. But the differences are still there—I know that.

Dorothy has begun to suspect that males and females read differently, and she has begun to suspect that they talk among themselves differently than they do in mixed company. The reading, writing, and discussing in the course have clearly alerted her to the possibility that gender affects the way in which readers, writers, and speakers use language.

This approach works especially well with honors students. I use somewhat different reading and writing assignments with non-honors students. In one class, for instance, I replaced the Gilligan book with an essay by Dale Spender on conversational patterns in high school classrooms. Students wrote a paper defending or refuting the Spender piece on the basis of their experiences in their own high schools. I have also devised ways of addressing feminist issues in composition courses in which the focus is not explicitly on gender differences. In a course designed to introduce students to fundamentals of research, for instance, students read Marge Piercy's *Woman on the Edge of Time* and did research on questions stimulated by it. They then shared their findings with the entire class in oral presentations. The approach led to wonderful papers on and discussions of the treatment of women in mental institutions, discrimination against minority women, and the ways in which technology can liberate women from oppressive roles.

I return now to my title and to the epigraph that introduces my essay. First, what does it mean to "compose as a woman"? Although the title invokes Jonathan Culler's "Reading as a Woman," a chapter in *On Deconstruction,* I do not mean to suggest by it that I am committed fully to Culler's deconstructive position. Culler maintains that "to read as a woman is to avoid reading as a man, to identify the specific defenses and distortions of male readings and provide correctives" (54). He concludes,

> For a woman to read as a woman is not to repeat an identity or an experience that is given but to play a role she constructs with reference to her identity as a woman, which is also a construct, so that the series can continue: a woman reading as a woman reading as a woman. The noncoincidence reveals an interval, a division within woman or within any reading subject and the "experience" of that subject.
>
> (64)

Culler is certainly correct that women often read as men and that they have to be encouraged to defend against this form of alienation. The strategy he suggests is almost entirely reactive, though. To read as a woman is to avoid reading as a man, to be alerted to the pitfalls of men's ways of reading.[4] Rich, too, warns of the dangers of immasculation, of identifying against oneself and learning to think like a man, and she, too, emphasizes the importance of critical activity on the part of the woman student—refusing to accept the givens of our culture, making connections between facts and ideas which men have left unconnected. She is well aware that thinking as a woman involves active construction, the recreation of one's identity. But she also sees value in recovering women's lived experience. In fact, she suggests that women maintain a critical posture in order to get in touch with that experience—to name it, to uncover that which is hidden, to make present that which has been absent. Her approach is active rather than reactive. Women's experience is not entirely a distorted version of male reality, it is not entirely elusive, and it is worthy of recuperation. We must alert our women students to the dangers of immasculation and provide them with a critical perspective. But we must also encourage them to become self-consciously aware of what their experience in the world has been and how this experience is related to the politics of gender. Then we must encourage our women students to write from the power of that experience.

Elizabeth A. Flynn, Head of the Department of Humanities at Michigan Technological University, edits the journal, Reader. She is co-editor, with Patrocinio Schweickart, of Gender and Reading: Essays on Readers, Texts and Contexts (1986), and has published articles in College Composition and Communication, College English, The Writing Instructor, and elsewhere.

Notes

1 I received invaluable feedback on drafts of this essay from Carol Berkenkotter, Art Young, Marilyn Cooper, John Willinsky, Diane Shoos, John Flynn, Richard Gebhardt, and three anonymous CCC reviewers.

2 The 1988 Conference on College Composition and Communication was a notable exception. It had a record number of panels on feminist or gender-related issues and a number of sessions devoted to political concerns. I should add, too, that an exception to the generalization that feminist studies and composition studies have not confronted each other is Cynthia Caywood and Gillian Overing's very useful anthology, *Teaching Writing: Pedagogy, Gender, and Equity.* In their

introduction to the book, Caywood and Overing note the striking parallels between writing theory and feminist theory. They conclude, "[T]he process model, insofar as it facilitates and legitimizes the fullest expression of the individual voice, is compatible with the feminist re-visioning of hierarchy, if not essential to it" (xiv). Pamela Annas, in her essay, "Silences: Feminist Language Research and the Teaching of Writing," describes a course she teaches at the University of Massachusetts at Boston, entitled "Writing as Women." In the course, she focuses on the question of silence—"what kinds of silence there are; the voices inside you that tell you to be quiet, the voices outside you that drown you out or politely dismiss what you say or do not understand you, the silence inside you that avoids saying anything important even to yourself, internal and external forms of censorship, and the stress that it produces" (3–4). Carol A. Stanger in "The Sexual Politics of the One-to-One Tutorial Approach and Collaborative Learning" argues that the one-to-one tutorial is essentially hierarchical and hence a male mode of teaching whereas collaborative learning is female and relational rather than hierarchical. She uses Gilligan's images of the ladder and the web to illustrate her point. Elisabeth Daeumer and Sandra Runzo suggest that the teaching of writing is comparable to the activity of mothering in that it is a form of "women's work." Mothers socialize young children to insure that they become acceptable citizens, and teachers' work, like the work of mothers, is usually devalued (45–46).

3 It should be clear by now that my optimistic claim at the outset of the essay that the field of composition studies has feminized our conception of written communication needs qualification. I have already mentioned that the field has developed, for the most part, independent of feminist studies and as a result has not explored written communication in the context of women's special needs and problems. Also, feminist inquiry is beginning to reveal that work in cognate fields that have influenced the development of composition studies is androcentric. For an exploration of the androcentrism of theories of the reading process see Patrocinio P. Schweickart, "Reading Ourselves: Toward a Feminist Theory of Reading."

4 Elaine Showalter, in "Reading as a Woman: Jonathan Culler and the Deconstruction of Feminist Criticism," argues that "Culler's deconstructionist priorities lead him to overstate the essentialist dilemma of defining the *woman* reader, when in most cases what is intended and implied is a *feminist* reader" (126).

Works Cited

Annas, Pamela J. "Silences: Feminist Language Research and the Teaching of Writing." *Teaching Writing: Pedagogy, Gender, and Equity.* Ed. Cynthia L. Caywood and Gillian R. Overing. Albany: State U of New York P, 1987. 3–17.

Belenky, Mary Field, et al. *Women's Ways of Knowing: The Development of Self, Voice, and Mind.* New York: Basic Books, 1986.

Britton, James, et al. *The Development of Writing Abilities* (11–18). London: Macmillan Education, 1975.

Caywood, Cynthia L., and Gillian R. Overing. Introduction. *Teaching Writing: Pedagogy, Gender, and Equity.* Ed. Cynthia L. Caywood and Gillian R. Overing. Albany: State U of New York P, 1987. xi–xvi.

Chodorow, Nancy. *The Reproduction of Mothering: Psychoanalysis and the Sociology of Gender.* Berkeley: U of California P, 1978.

Culler, Jonathan. *On Deconstruction: Theory and Criticism after Structuralism.* Ithaca: Cornell UP, 1982.

Daeumer, Elisabeth, and Sandra Runzo. "Transforming the Composition Classroom." *Teaching Writing: Pedagogy, Gender, and Equity.* Ed. Cynthia L. Caywood and Gillian R. Overing. Albany: State U of New York P, 1987. 45–62.

Gilligan, Carol. *In a Different Voice: Psychological Theory and Women's Development.* Cambridge: Harvard UP, 1982.

Hairston, Maxine. "Breaking Our Bonds and Reaffirming Our Connections." *College Composition and Communication* 36 (October 1985): 272–82.

Howe, Florence. "Identity and Expression: A Writing Course for Women." *College English* 32 (May 1971): 863–71. Rpt. in Howe, *Myths of Coeducation: Selected Essays, 1964–1983*. Bloomington: Indiana UP, 1984. 28–37.

Kohlberg, Lawrence. "Moral Stages and Moralization: The Cognitive-Developmental Approach." *Moral Development and Behavior*. Ed. T. Lickona. New York: Holt, 1976. 31–53.

Perry, William G. *Forms of Intellectual and Ethical Development in the College Years.* New York: Holt, Rinehart & Winston, 1970.

Rich, Adrienne. "Taking Women Students Seriously." *On Lies, Secrets, and Silence: Selected Prose, 1966–1978*. New York: W.W. Norton, 1979. 237–45.

——. "'When We Dead Awaken': Writing as Re-Vision." *On Lies, Secrets, and Silence: Selected Prose, 1966–1978*. New York: W. W. Norton, 1979. 33–49.

Schweickart, Patrocinio P. "Reading Ourselves: Toward a Feminist Theory of Reading." *Gender and Reading: Essays on Readers, Texts and Contexts*. Ed. Elizabeth A. Flynn and Patrocinio P. Schweickart. Baltimore: Johns Hopkins UP, 1986. 31–62.

Showalter, Elaine. "Reading as a Woman: Jonathan Culler and the Deconstruction of Feminist Criticism." *Men and Feminism*. Ed. Alice Jardine and Paul Smith. New York: Methuen, 1987. 123–27.

Stanger, Carol A. "The Sexual Politics of the One-to-One Tutorial Approach and Collaborative Learning." *Teaching Writing: Pedagogy, Gender, and Equity*. Ed. Cynthia L. Caywood and Gillian R. Overing. Albany: State U of New York P, 1987. 31–44.

13.
THE OTHER "F" WORD: THE FEMINIST IN THE CLASSROOM
Dale M. Bauer

Editors' Note: *Student resistance to feminism in the classroom appears in student evaluations that reject any focus on feminist theory and methodology, on the grounds that classrooms should be "neutral." An adaptation of critical pedagogy yields a strategy that asks students not only to challenge preconceived notions but to build up positive alternatives. Negotiating the gap between student resistance and feminist experience calls for accepting authority in the classroom but using that authority in pursuit of Burkean identification. Teaching texts like Pat Barker's* Blow Your House Down *can lead students to question internalized values and to learn to "speak in the language of a voice within."*

Evaluating Feminist Teachers

The best of our writing is entangled in the messiness of our experience.

—Nina Auerbach

In just about half of a colleague's teaching evaluations (twelve of twenty-six evaluations) from two first-year composition and introduction to literature sections, she read objections to her feminist stance, especially her discussions of feminism and pedagogy. Most of the objections came from students who insisted that the classroom ought to be an ideologically neutral space free from the instructor's interests and concerns. The following samples, copied verbatim, suggest the drift of the students' complaints:

I feel this course was dominated and overpowered by feminist doctrines and ideals.
I feel the feminist movement is very interesting to look at, but I got extremely bored with it and it lost all its punch & meaning because it was so drilled into our brains.
I also think you shouldn't voice your "feminist" views because we don't need to know that—
It's something that should be left outside of class.
I found it very offensive that all of our readings focused on feminism.
Feminism is an important issue in society—but a very controversial one. It needs to be confronted on a personal basis, not in the classroom. I didn't appreciate feminist comments on papers or expressed about a work. This is not the only instructor—others in the English Dept. have difficulties leaving personal opinions out of their comments.

Dale M. Bauer, "The Other 'F' Word: The Feminist in the Classroom." *College English* 52.4 (April 1990): 385–96.

As one of those other instructors who have "difficulties" leaving that other "f" word, feminism, out of my classroom, I am troubled by the easy separation these students insist upon between the private or personal and the public space. Precisely because they insist on this separation, our first task should be to show how the personal is public. Perhaps the last quote is the most telling: feminism is a social issue; the classroom, however, is removed from society. Social issues are not to be publicized, either to know the issues, to engage them, or to challenge the issues in the process. Rather, established truth, as Paulo Freire has told us, is to be banked. The students fear more than anything a perceived intellectual bankruptcy in the classroom. For this student, the classroom is a place of absorption, but it should not be a social arena.

Another student articulates a fear of gendered subjectivity:

> My professor has one distinct and overburying [sic] problem. She is a feminist and she incorporates her ideas and philosophy into her grading scale. If you do not make women sound superior to men or if you make women sound inferior, despite the belief of the writer, she will grade lower. I think the University should investigate this class and compare the scores of the males in the class with the females. It is my belief that among males that we are getting lower grades because of our sex.

The instructor in a personal note to me glossed this evaluation as follows: "The closest I can come to 'mak[ing] women sound superior' is to require that all essays be written in inclusive language." This evaluation is striking for two reasons. First, the metaphor of detection and investigation, of eradicating gender difference in the classroom, indicates many students' beliefs about classroom neutrality. Second, and perhaps more important, it represents the fear of gender issues invading the public world of the classroom during an era in which it is necessary for most students to insist on rationalizing intellectual labor. For most feminists, there is no separation between the outer world and the inner word, let alone between politics and intellectual work.

This second issue concerns feminism as a topic of intellectual and academic value. In the students' complaints, I hear a suggestion, echoed by some of my colleagues, that feminism is not a discipline, that gender issues are based on perspectives unsuitable for the labor of the intellectual. Consider the following student comment: "I think works should be more well-rounded without a continual stress on feminism." "Well-rounded" and balanced are set off against "feminism"—that locus of imbalance, fanaticism, eccentricity. "Continual stress" comes out of the perception of aggravation. The irony in the student comments, however, arises from a cultivated distance from the authority in the classroom, here an authority identified with an alien, radical, and threatening political position. On this point, I am persuaded by Suzanne Clark's articulation of literary studies as part of the continuum of rhetorical studies: "Feminist writing ... breaks down the distances established by irony and provokes rhetorical responsiveness—the dialectic of resistance and identification that can then lead to critical thinking" (10; see Paine's definition of critical thinking 538–39).

How can a feminist rhetoric constitute this dialectic in the classroom? In the student comments I quoted above, there is an often overwhelming insistence on individualism and isolation; they also insist on the alienated work of the classroom, even if the professor holds forth the goal of collaborative learning in contrast to a traditional sense of knowledge as mechanized or routinized labor (see Paine 559). The students (responding here to feminism) labor at developing a critical distance to avoid participating in "the dialectic of resistance and identification" crucial not only to teaching and critical thinking, but also to political responsibility. Interrogating her students on the understanding of indoctrination, Gayatri Spivak addresses this problem in her recent book, *In Other Worlds.* She challenges her students' accept-ance of the split between "moral speculation" and decision making. Spivak sees this separation as rendering them "incapable of thinking collectively in any but the most inhumane way":

> Suppose an outsider, observing the uniformity of the moves you have all sketched in your papers, were to say that you had been indoctrinated? That you could no longer conceive of public decision-making except in the quantified areas of your economics and business classes, where you learn all about rational expectations theories? You *know* that decisions in the public sphere, such as tax decisions, legal decisions, foreign policy decisions, fiscal decisions, affect your *private* lives deeply. Yet in a speculative field such as the interpreta-tion of texts, you feel that there is something foolish and wrong and regimented about a public voice.
>
> (99)

What Spivak notes as the public—private split in the academy is fostered by the teaching of decision-making policy as a science, as corporate policy. Decision making in the realm of ethics and values (the stuff of the humanities classroom) is still conceived as intensely intimate, insular, isolated from what we see as the public voice of politics, business, and multinational capitalism.

Why this resistance to collective moral and ethical rhetoric? How do we move ourselves out of this political impasse and resistance in order to get our students to identify with the political agenda of feminism?

My response, like Ira Shor's and Freire's, is to foreground dialogics in the classroom. This strategy uses one kind of mastery, feminist and dialogic in practice, against another, monologic and authoritarian. I am working from the notion that the classroom is a place to explore resistances and identifications, a place also to explore the ambiguous and often ambivalent space of values and ethics. That is not to say that we return to the politics of the personal, a politics often mired in contradiction and confusion. The contradictions that the feminist encounters in the classroom—as outlined in *Gendered Subjects,* for instance, by the collaborators on "The Politics of Nurturance"—reveal the internalized patriarchal structures and our resistances to them (see Pheterson's definitions of internalized oppression and domination 141).

Consider the collective claim about ambivalence in "The Politics of Nurturance": "As a result of our successes in the system, we are more deeply and passionately ambivalent about the intellectual life than our students can be" (13). I focus on this sentence because I sense that our students are often more deeply ambivalent about commitment than we, their instructors, are—in part because we realize that commitment is the only survival tactic and in part because we have more experience in dealing with confusion about several, often contradictory allegiances. My students seem often quite unambiguously committed to "the system"; their ambivalence is buried deeply, already reconciled. In recognizing their unacknowledged ambivalence, feminists must teach a way not of reconciling this division but of fostering the critical urgency born out of it.

Fostering that ambivalence does not mean leaving students in a void or teaching critical thinking without a critical alternative to dominant social norms. In effect, we teach ethics as a kind of counter-indoctrination, a debriefing, to privatizing personal ethics. One of my own evaluations in a first-year composition course brought the lesson home: "[The teacher] consistently channels class discussions around feminism & does not spend time discussing the comments that oppose her beliefs. In fact, she usually twists them around to support her beliefs." In my defense, I would say, following Charles Paine (563), that we must accept our own roles as rhetoricians. On the student's behalf, I would argue that his or her recognition of the rhetorical agenda of the class—to foreground feminism as a classroom strategy—is sophisticated and aware. That is, the teacher is responsible for clarifying the agenda of the classroom, the student for challenging that agenda. Each agent—whether teacher or student—is responsible as citizen for ethical choices, although those choices often involve contradictory positions. Because agency involves a complex intersection of historically conditioned practices, discourses, and customs or habits, choice is never unambivalent or easy or unmediated. Students may ask, is it possible—or even desirable—to occupy an unambivalent position, to assume an identity without crisis? Gender complicates one's position, and this gendered mode of identifying is political: it rejects biological essence in favor of rhetorical choice. Gender identification, then, becomes a set of choices that signify the marking or signing of one's body in the world. The ambivalent space of this signing (a double participation in the imaginary and the symbolic) should not always be read negatively. Rather than opposing the public and private voices or opposing masculine and feminine, we need to see how to negotiate that opposition in order to speak a multiplicity of voices into the cultural dialogue.

With this in mind, I dispute the analysis of the feminist teacher's position the authors of "The Politics of Nurturance" offer. They suggest that the feminist teacher is nurturer, mother:

> Our students see us as something more, or certainly something other, than simply their teachers. We are, inescapably, also their mothers—necessary for comfort but reinforcing a feared and fearful dependency if such comfort is too easily accepted. But we are also, in part, their fathers—word-givers, truth-sayers—to the extent we incorporate what Dinnerstein calls the father's 'clean' authority in our female bodies.
>
> (14)

This distinction between mother and father roles, like the one between public and private invoked in the student evaluation comments, belies the positive ambivalence students feel about the confusion of familial roles and authoritative spaces which occurs in the feminist classroom. The Oedipal model doesn't hold up.

While the feminist classroom is not "the place where the cultural split between mother and father may be healed" (18), the authors' strategy to articulate the unconscious is nevertheless on target. For the feminist classroom is the place where the cultural split can be investigated for its effect in the conscious and unconscious processes which make ambivalence a part of radical pedagogy. This is why I find Gregory Jay's "The Subject of Pedagogy: Lessons in Psychoanalysis and Politics" useful in determining the unconscious processes of resistance (and, by implication, identification) in teaching: "There is a 'pedagogical unconscious' . . . informing the educational performance, and what we resist knowing is intricately tied to our constitution as social subjects" (789). Where there is no ambivalence, there is no dialogue (see Fine 165). Where there is no dialogue, there is no dialectic of resistance and identification.

One way to tap into this urgency is to offer something else in the place of the resistance that critical pedagogy offers. It is not enough to foster critical thinking; we need to suggest something in the place of what we tear down when we ask students to resist cultural hegemony (see Bizzell and Clark). Cultural optimism, what Henry Giroux criticizes as the pedagogy of "positive thinking" (123–25), is too broad; nonetheless, we need an antidote to cultural criticism's and critical pedagogy's negativity.

In short, I would argue that political commitment—especially feminist commitment—is a legitimate classroom strategy and rhetorical imperative. The feminist agenda offers a goal toward our students' conversions to emancipatory critical action (see Paine 564).

Private into Public Discourse: A Rhetoric of Conversion

> To refuse the task of building a critical language is to refuse to re-invent oneself collectively outside the atomized and privatized self and liberal (possessive) individualism of the dominant culture.
>
> —Peter McLaren and Michael Dantley

Nina Auerbach's "Engorging the Patriarchy" is one narrative of conversion or, rather, "unconversion" into feminist agency. This conversion emerges from a rejection of the authoritative word—the word of former Governor Reagan's mandate to the Cal State System where Auerbach first taught after graduate school—to be "drearily functional and nothing more" (233). Auerbach sees her first years as an assistant professor as a period in which she was "*unconverted*—into a loss of faith—forced to see (and sometimes to implement) the ways in which books betrayed experience" (233). Her realization is a matter of transforming the outer word—what she resists in the dominant culture, in Reagan's California—into an internally persuasive word which "converts" her into feminism. The process of turning the outer word (that is, received cultural and social opinion) into an inner speech (her political self-declaration) is even clearer in Auerbach's following claim: "I became a feminist critic at the University of Pennsylvania because my department assumed I already was one" (234). This may seem backward, but this is more often the case than not: we do not declare ourselves feminist critics and then change our critical orientation to the world. Rather by virtue of our ideologies, our words, we are marked and judged by the community around us as feminists. Similarly, we do not transform students and then change their critical orientation to the world. Rather, the process of self-identification is more complex and more fruitful than an easy declaration of their resistance to hegemony.

I use Auerbach's confession as a paradigm for the pedagogical model to break down resistances and offer identifications in the classroom (see Emerson 33). The question is, how do we make the word respond to our own intentions in a feminist pedagogy? How do we make our authority as feminist rhetors available to our students for their language and thus contravene their resistance? In asking our students to deconstruct dominant ideology, "we exercise authority over them in asking them to give up their foundational beliefs, and at the same time, we give them nothing to put in the place of these foundational beliefs because we deny the validity of all authority, including, presumably, our own" (Bizzell 14). So goes Pat Bizzell's argument for the current trend in critical studies. But a feminist—or identificatory—rhetoric is an appropriate form of classroom authority, a conception of authority designed to promote "collective participation in the rhetorical process" (Bizzell 16, 18). At the base of this is the conviction that all signs are social; all language, therefore, is ideologically charged and can unite us rather than divide us socially. Language has a material reality that goes beyond individual differences and is culturally shared, although every shared language means negotiation and commitment. We are in line, then, in the classroom to negotiate the gap of understanding between our students' experience and our own, a gap which often seems insurmountable (Emerson 36–37). Negotiating this stance is often the hardest for the feminist rhetor. But it's clear that there is no way not to accept this authority; anything less ends up being an expressivist model, one which reinforces, however inadvertently, the dominant patriarchal culture rather than challenges it.

My emphasis on feminist rhetoric relies on Kenneth Burke's formulation of education as persuasion. Advocates of radical pedagogy often use the term "identification" without understanding its rhetorical base or, more important, how to employ identification in the classroom. Burke's *Rhetoric of Motives* provides this compelling political (indeed, personal) identification with an ideological stance: "In accordance with the rhetorical principle of identification, whenever you find a doctrine of 'nonpolitical' esthetics affirmed with fervor, look for its politics" (28). Why not apply this claim to the pedagogical situation itself? Whenever we hear students or colleagues affirming the "'nonpolitical' esthetics" of the classroom, look for its political consequences. For Burke, education is persuasion, making a rhetorical identification possible with the position (even of difference and conflict) from which we speak. Burke distinguishes between realistic and idealistic identifications. In realistic identification, persuasion compels social action. The idealistic identification occurs when the powerful identify with someone less powerful. Feminists yearn for the latter—when we can hope for a change in patriarchal attitudes—but work within the former, a realistic identification with those oppressed. Like Burke, I hold out for the magic of the idealistic identification, but I work in the classroom and in criticism for the realistic identification.

In "Identification and Consubstantiality," Burke puts the case for an ethics of motives based on the rhetoric of identification:

> A is not identical with his colleague, B. But insofar as their interests are joined, A *is identified* with B. Or he may *identify himself* with B even when their interests are not joined, if he assumes that they are, or is persuaded to believe so.... Similarly, two persons may be identified in terms of some principle they share in common, an "identification" that does not deny their distinctness.
>
>   (20–21)

Burke rightly suggests that division is implied in identification since without it there would be no need for the rhetorician to work to achieve community. Again, Burke's *Rhetoric of Motives:* "But put identification and division ambiguously together, so that you cannot know for certain just where one ends and the other begins, and you have the characteristic invitation to rhetoric" (25). Burke goes on to label rhetoric as a *"body of identifications"*—a multiplicity of situations, stances, positions (26). It is up to the ideological critic, therefore, to show how these positions contradict each other and, in practical terms, demand a choice. "Belonging" is rhetorical (28). In this sense, we can think of feminism as a rhetorical criticism, an act by which we teach students how to belong, how to identify, as well as how to resist.

Finally, Burke writes about the relationship of identification as an awareness of contingent joining and separating with another. Thus, Burke implies that identification allows for another voice to be in sync but not to erase difference: "to begin with *identification* is ... , though roundabout, to confront the implications of *division*. ... If men were not apart from one another, there would be no need for the rhetorician to proclaim their unity" (22). The implications of this claim are at least twofold for feminist criticism: the feminist can work toward social change by suggesting identificatory readings rather than (or only) resisting ones (as I will discuss later). Opposition creates the necessity of rhetoric, of resistance and identification. Burke argues that political conditions call for a powerful identification with others, but those same conditions escalate "the range of human conflict, the incentives to division. It would require sustained rhetorical effort, backed by the imagery of a richly humane and spontaneous poetry, to make us fully sympathize with people in circumstances greatly different from our own" (34). Burke's humanism aside, his argument brings to the fore the divisiveness of a culture which we, as radical teachers of English, try to overcome.

When we ask our students to identify with a political position offered in class or to identify with us as the most immediate representative of that political stance, we are asking them to give allegiance to an affinity or coalition politics that often competes with or negates other allegiances they have already formed (see Alcoff 423, 431). We ask them to recognize identity—and politics—as social constructions. But without that critical tension between internally persuasive words and externally authoritative rhetoric, we have no hope, nor offer any, for radical social change. Thus, paradoxically,

I affirm the students voicing their concerns against feminism in their teaching evaluations; that voicing shows that their feminist teachers (who bravely offered their evaluations for my study) brought their students into some conflict with their previously held norms. In short, there is no natural or essential identification, but only one forged from rhetorical situations and political awareness. In that case, in the classroom, we are not presenting objective categories of political affiliation but a rhetorical context of modes or bodies of identifications.

In teaching identification and teaching feminism, I overcome a vehement, even automatic, insistence on pluralistic relativism or on individualism. I teach how signs can be manipulated, appropriated, and also liberated. Coming to consciousness of any kind is the recognition of the social signs we all internalize and inherit, inevitably against our will. As Auerbach explains, her coming to consciousness as a feminist meant for her becoming aware of the ideological signs she represented for others. Feminism, then, proved to be both social (her interaction with her colleagues "marking" and "de-signing" or, better yet, "resigning" her to her oppositional stance) and psychological, since her internally persuasive voice resulted in her rejection of another social category: the "good" mother and caretaker/teacher.

Auerbach uses her social de-signation as feminist in order to open up the question of cultural politics with her students. She works, then, from the notion that there is no individual stance that would be alien to her but that the classroom is thoroughly social, a locus of many voices, often conflicting, always in flux. In her words:

> No doubt all beginning teachers identify with their students rather than with their colleagues, and I did too. Trying to negotiate the den of vipers which the Cal State English Department looked like to me at that time, I saw myself in my students, and I saw myself for the first time.... Like my students, I tried to learn to be blandly affable and to keep my mind in the closet, my unorthodox scholarly writing a secret.... I was converted into subservience.
>
> (233)

The "answers" about feminism don't come from "within"; but, as Auerbach notes, we designate ourselves through our dialogue with others and with ourselves. In advancing the dialogue within herself, Auerbach hopes to affect the one with her students.

Whose signs we articulate as part of our internally persuasive speech make all the difference. As I see it, the dialogue in the feminist classroom helps clarify the contradictions between what we all have internalized as part of a patriarchal unconscious and a resistance to those assumptions. As feminist rhetors, we supply an authoritative word about potential sites of identification and of resistance to patriarchy.

Ultimately, we don't think "feminism" until we have the sign-system to do so. Our task, then, is to make this speech readily available and heard—sometimes over and against the social objections of others. As Pat Bizzell argues in "Orators and Philosophers in English Studies, or, The Rhetorical Turn Versus Schemes for Cultural Literacy," we need the oratorical perspective of feminism, what she aligns with the anti-foundationalist theoretical concerns of English studies. "We have nothing to study but the matter of persuasion, in other words ideologies, the kind of value orators have always dealt with" (6). I want to advocate feminism as a matter of persuasion, as a "rhetorical turn."

Narration and Social Change

So far, critical pedagogy has generally slighted the problem of identification; excellent studies like Giroux's, McLaren's, Weiler's, and Shor and Freire's are filled with narratives of students' resistance to hegemonic forms. There are few or no narratives about the identification students have with, say, antiracist, antisexist, or antihomophobic politics. The process comes down to articulating social change in the literature classroom so that it strikes a middle ground between optimism and pessimism. The feminist teacher must offer a language of resistance and identification: both are confessional forms—direct addresses—designed as rhetorical invitations to the reader. They invite participation in narratives, in the literature we teach (see Warhol).

How do we draw out and discuss those resistances to theory, to feminism? I do so by compelling students to work through them in literature by confronting fears and values mediated by the form of fiction. Let me explain how I use Pat Barker's *Blow Your House Down* (1984) as one example of breaking down cultural stereotypes. This novel about working-class British women, many of whom have turned to prostitution because of the 1974 coal strike and the failing British economy, is ostensibly a detective/murder mystery, but it eventually explodes our expectations about the genre as well as about violence against women. A prostitute-killer is loose, and the first three sections of the novel, each one from the perspective of a different woman, detail responses to arbitrary violence against women. In the first, Brenda explains how she became a prostitute when her first husband left her and how difficult it is to give up life on the streets: "It was hard to say really why you stuck with it. Money, friends, habit—and of course it was easy, if you were ever short, if you ever needed anything, it was always there" (63–64). Kath's section, the second, leads up to her murder, after Kath has lost her boys and daughter to the social welfare system. In the third part, Jean avenges that murder, along with the murder of Carol, her own lover.

Each section also raises questions about these women's relations to their clients, to the dole, to dominant cultural morality, to capitalism in general. The final section, Maggie's, begins with another act of random violence, this time against a "respectable" woman who works in a chicken factory rather than on the streets. Like Maggie, the students must come to terms with a violence against women which is random and senseless and which finally makes the victim more victimized by the neighbors and the police than by the assailant. She is suspected of "asking for it," if only because she takes a shortcut home from work on Friday night after her weekly drink with her colleagues: "you needed a drink, you needed something to swill the blood and guts away, and make you fit to face the world" (177). Another sort of victimization occurs in the novel: like the prostitutes, Maggie is "cut"—interrogated about the events of the attack and then shunned by her neighbors. Maggie comes to feel as though her neighbors were, in her terms, "enjoying it too": "They read the papers, they tried to read *between* the lines, and the same questions were there. *What does he do to them? How much did he do to her?* It was all very exciting, having a victim living in the same street" (193). The spectacle of violence perpetuates the rationalization of that violence.

This is a confusing novel for many students, in part because of the explicit economics of prostitution (there is no point of view from which the sexual encounters that occur appear anything other than economic and quotidian). But the students are willing enough to accept the violence against the prostitutes since part of their job, the students reason, is an acceptance of risk. What they are not prepared to accept is the violence against Maggie, the wife and mother, whose shortcut home endangers her life. Maggie has not "asked for it," nor is Maggie's profession morally suspect. Because of this rupture of generic and moral expectations, the students are led to question their assumptions about violence against women. There is no rationale or logic to violence; the only logic behind violence, they learn, is patriarchal power.

Barker historicizes that violence; her novel calls into question women's expectations of violence both in the home and outside of it. The women debate what to do about the recent prostitute killings going on:

> And there were all sorts of ideas flying around. "Always get out of the car." "Never get out of the car." "Take the numbers." "Work in pairs." "Don't bend down." "Don't turn your back." "Don't suck them off." Load of rubbish. I never did any of it. I did start carrying a knife and then I thought well, you dozy cow, you're just handing him the weapon. So after that I didn't bother.
>
> (17)

In rehearsing the contradictory advice about dealing with violence on the streets where she works, Maureen reveals the mystification of male violence, no less frightening because it is random and aleatory.

After her attack, Maggie's heterosexual marriage is no longer a safe place, nor is the master bedroom. She comes to expect violence from Bill in the same way that the prostitutes anticipate it on the streets. As Elaine says, "the way I look at it, if you're living with a bloke he's gunna hit you about something" (105). Maggie's experience of violence leads her to a rejection of the alienated work in the chicken factory and a moral confusion, one of the only positive effects of her encounter with what Barker terms the "abyss" of violence:

> Their own bedroom. She knew every mark on the wallpaper, every creak of the floorboards, every bump and sag in the mattress. It ought to've been completely safe, but it wasn't. She found herself listening for Bill's footsteps on the stairs.
>
> This was something she couldn't understand. As long as she could *see* Bill, as long as he was in the same room with her, she was alright. But if he was behind her, or in a different part of the house, she started to worry. It wasn't fear exactly, but she needed to know what he was doing. . . .
>
> But she was left with a feeling that the road back to "normal" might be longer than she had wanted to believe.
>
> (186)

Maggie also comes to understand that her middle-class notions about violence—that it happens only to women who provoke men, women who work on the streets—are illusory. Both Jean's and Maggie's sections suggest what happens when women cannot comprehend violence according to "rational" categories. Violence, in Barker's text, is not a masculine construction; rather, it is symbolic, available to both men and women and destructive to both. Barker provides a middle-class audience with an identificatory model in Maggie, a model to explore in class discussions of ethics.

Because this text raises so many questions about class and gender, it opens up as topics of discourse values and assumptions which have been naturalized in dominant culture. These classes, indeed perhaps feminist pedagogy and rhetoric in general, end ambivalently: these disrupted values or assumptions are not occasions for reconstituting consciousness into clear categories of good faith feminism and bad faith—or, worse, good and bad politics. Having access to a common language is only a first step; speaking languages of difference is another.

My final appeal is to Kenneth Burke's *Rhetoric of Motives* and the call for rhetorical criticism:

> Education ("indoctrination") exerts such pressure upon [the student] from without; [students complete] the process from within. If [they do] not somehow act to tell [themselves] what the various brands of rhetorician have told [them], [the] persuasion is not complete. Only those voices from without are effective which can speak in the language of a voice within.
>
> (39)

As feminist rhetors, our task is to make compelling the wider implications of the feminist dialogue in the classroom. Because my voice in the classroom is one in competition with other voices speaking for the students' allegiance, the most pernicious voice that reinforces the split between public and private, I would do well to be aware of the rhetorical situation of the classroom—of the necessity for a mastery that is not oppressive, of an authoritative voice that is not the only authority.

Dale M. Bauer *is an assistant professor of English and an affiliate in the Women's Studies Program at Miami University. Author of Feminist Dialogics, she is completing a book on the connections among reproductive technology, eugenics, and fascism.*

Works Cited

Alcoff, Linda. "Cultural Feminism versus Post-Structuralism: The Identity Crisis in Feminist Theory." *Signs* 13 (Spring 1988): 405–36.

Auerbach, Nina. "Engorging the Patriarchy." *Historical Studies and Literary Criticism.* Ed. Jerome J. McGann. Madison: U of Wisconsin P, 1985.

Barker, Pat. *Blow Your House Down.* New York: Ballantine, 1984.

Bizzell, Patricia. "Orators and Philosophers in English Studies, or, The Rhetorical Turn Versus Schemes for Cultural Literacy." Forthcoming in *College English.*

Burke, Kenneth. *A Rhetoric of Motives.* New York: Prentice, 1950.

Clark, Suzanne. "Feminism, Poststructuralism and Rhetoric: If We Change Language, Do We Also Change the World?". CCCC paper. March 16, 1989.

Culley, Margo, Arlyn Diamond, Lee Edwards, Sara Lennox, and Catherine Portuges. "The Politics of Nurturance." *Gendered Subjects.* Eds. Margo Culley and Catherine Portuges. Boston: Routledge & Kegan Paul, 1985: 11–20.

Emerson, Caryl. "The Outer Word and Inner Speech: Bakhtin, Vygotsky, and the Internalization of Language." *Bakhtin.* Ed. Gary Saul Morson. Chicago: U of Chicago P, 1986: 21–40.

Fine, Michelle. "Sexuality, Schooling, and Adolescent Females: The Missing Discourse of Desire." *Harvard Educational Review* 58 (February 1988): 29–53.

——. "Silencing in Public Schools." *Language Arts* 64 (February 1987): 157–74.

Giroux, Henry. *Schooling and the Struggle for Public Life.* Minneapolis: U Minnesota P, 1988.

Jay, Gregory S. "The Subject of Pedagogy: Lessons in Psychoanalysis and Politics." *College English* 49 (November 1987): 785–800.

McLaren, Peter, and Michael Dantley. "Leadership and a Critical Pedagogy of Race: Cornel West, Stuart Hall, and the Prophetic Tradition." *Journal of Negro Education,* forthcoming.

Paine, Charles. "Relativism, Radical Pedagogy, and the Ideology of Paralysis." *College English* 51 (October 1989): 557–70.

Pheterson, Gail. "Alliances between Women: Overcoming Internalized Oppression and Internalized Domination." *Reconstructing the Academy: Women's Education and Women's Studies.* Eds. Elizabeth Minnich, Jean O'Barr, and Rachel Rosenfeld. Chicago: U Chicago Press, 1988: 139–53.

Shor, Ira, and Paulo Freire. *A Pedagogy for Liberation: Dialogues on Transforming Education.* South Hadley, MA: Bergin & Garvey, 1987.

Spivak, Gayatri Chakravorty. *In Other Worlds.* New York: Methuen, 1988.

Warhol, Robyn R. *Gendered Interventions.* New Brunswick: Rutgers UP, 1989.

Weiler, Kathleen. *Women Teaching for Change: Gender, Class & Power.* South Hadley, MA: Bergin & Garvey, 1988.

14.
VOICE: THE SEARCH FOR A FEMINIST RHETORIC FOR EDUCATIONAL STUDIES(*)
Madeleine R. Grumet

Editors' Note: *Voice has been a key metaphor for feminists, especially those advocating autobiographical studies of educational experience and establishing the validity of women's voices. But women's voices have also been used to reaffirm male dominance, as in most film documentaries, where the male voice provides the dominant voiceover and any female voices are figured as marginal and private. Moving beyond marginalized voices or the nostalgia of the maternal voice to a plurality of voices, a choral and collaborative identity offers a strong alternative understanding of "voice."*

> It was her voice that made
> The sky acutest at its vanishing.
> She measured to the hour its solitude.
> She was the single artificer of the world
> In which she sang. And when she sang, the sea,
> Whatever self it had, became the self
> That was her song, for she was the maker. Then we,
> As we beheld her striding there alone,
> Knew there never was a world for her
> Except the one she sang and, singing made.[1]

The world she sang and singing made. Once this verse of Wallace Stevens's was sufficient to reassure me that expression and creation and order could coincide. This mellifluous image of rhetoric recapitulates the ancient conception of its efficacy. Then rhetoric was not considered to be mere social exhortation. Discourse that shaped the polls was thought to be the expression of both a divine order of the universe as well as the full realization of human possibility. As the song of Stevens's singer defines the boundaries of time, of space, and of meaning, it too appears to extend rhetoric's promise of coherence. Once I identified with the singer. Now I am not so sure. Then I was more comfortable with the voice of feminist theory and pedagogy than I am now. Then I was more comfortable with voice as a metaphor for feminist theory and pedagogy than I am now. Now I stand on the beach with the others watching her, striding there, on the boundary of the world that she sang, and singing made.

Madeleine R. Grumet, "Voice: The Search for a Feminist Rhetoric for Educational Studies." *Cambridge Journal of Education* 20 [or 30] (1990): 277–82.

In 1976 I gave the title "Another Voice" to the final chapter of *Toward a Poor Curriculum*, a book that William Pinar and I wrote to develop the rationale for autobiographical studies of educational experience.[2] This final chapter was an autobiographical account of a seminar for student teachers. The chapter received that title because it shifted the theoretical and discursive mood of the preceding chapters to narrative, where my identity as teacher of the seminar and writer of the chapter coincided.

This use of "voice" to denote a shift from the expected discourse reappeared in 1977 in Carol Gilligan's essay, "In a different voice: women's conceptions of self and morality", published in the *Harvard Educational Review*, and was echoed again when her book was published in 1982. Gilligan also used voice to mark the distinction between the research on the development of conceptions of morality derived from studies of male subjects from that drawn from studies of women subjects.

I can't speak for Gilligan, but I can say that my use of voice as a marker to differentiate my work from male work and my text from male text allowed me to express my ambivalence as I joined the procession of "educated men" in the late 1970s.[3] Voice promised presence, contact, and relations that would take place within range of another's hearing. And in that proximity the sound of the voice, the movement of breath, of teeth and tongue and lips carried the promise of speech. After all, consciousness raising was never a silent levitation but always grounded in talk, and in the relations of women who "opened up to each other" and through "disclosure". And so, in the 1970s voice carried with it the promise of cultural transformation, as it announced resistance to a distant, universalistic knowledge, and as it provided conversations that generated collective action.

But voice has carried only some of us only so far. For those of us whose daily labor is the welding of words in texts and lectures, discussions and analyses, voice has sounded in the new scholarship on women and in the critique of the methods of the disciplines. It has challenged the methods of social science, literary criticism and history, of scientific method by reminding us all that texts are generated by speakers hoping to be heard by imagined listeners. Drawn from the body and associated with gender, voice splinters the fiction of an androgynous speaker as we hear rhythms, relations, sounds, stories, and style that we identify as male or female.

I suspect that the metaphor of voice has been most persuasive when it has been used to challenge another speaker, thus discriminating that speaker from another. It may be most discernible against a background of other sounds, against which it discriminates itself. This figure/ground gestalt frames both the salience as well as the subordination of the feminist voice in the academy.

In *The Acoustic Mirror* Kaja Silverman studies the presence of women's voices in film.[4] She describes the interplay of male and female voices common to traditional films of the 1940s and 1950s, an acoustic politic that I hear echoed in the rhetoric of educational discourse. She points out that male voices often provide the totalizing narratives often heard in voice-overs. I remember those voices. We heard them at the beginning of historical films as they read the text of the yellowed parchment displayed on the screen, that for some reason would curl up in flames signalling the start of the action. The anonymity of those voices was their appeal.

To this day my husband is tracking the voice of Superman from his radio childhood. Most recently he heard its resonance in the voice of the announcer for Thompson's water seal, exulting less in the announcer's fall from glory than in his own ability to crack the code and determine identity and history in the sound designed to speak timeless and ubiquitous power and authority.

Silverman points out that women rarely speak the voice-over narratives. Instead the female voice is located in the interior of the film, often lodged in its recesses. Silverman argues that the female voice in films is often intertwined with images of the female body, emphasizing female sexuality. If the voice is the medium for the projection of meaning, then woman as a meaning maker is undermined by the visual emphasis on her body as an object of display and desire. The interaction of image and voice is, as I have argued elsewhere, implicated in pedagogy.[5] Positioned in the front of the room, receiving, if not demanding, the gaze of the student, the female teacher receives a gaze that the mise en scene of the classroom had originally directed toward the pastor whose position vis-a-vis his congregation is the blueprint for the theatre of the contemporary classroom. If he projected the gaze as accuser or interrogator, she receives it, and I suspect, uses speech to deflect it. Teacher talk is then a defensive move deployed to assert her subjectivity in the face of the objectifying gaze.

Pointing to films where the woman's voice provides much of the narrative, Silverman shows us that this speaking is often elicited by drugs or therapy, so that the narrative is seen as elicited by men who ultimately control it and the female speaker. Silverman also suggests that these female narratives are often confessions, exposing private and hidden histories to public reception. These exposures carry the connotation of sexual penetration, as if they have been drawn from the dark internal continent of female sexuality, and Silverman points to the screams and cries that punctuate female vocalization in pornographic and sexually sadistic films, as vocal ejaculations designed to present involuntary female expressions of agony or terror as sounds of sexual release and pleasure.

Once we are no longer satisfied with just being heard and address the politics of our utterances, we find that the rhetoric of discourse in education is not exempt from the politics that the more explicitly erotic medium of film displays. For decades the voice-over of educational research and discourse was dominated by quantitative measures of learning and schooling. Statistical analyses that obscure individual experience have given ground in the last decade to qualitative studies employing history, literature, anthropology, and journalism to convey a subject's sense of educational experience. The voices of these subjects are frequently drawn from the recesses of the school, pulled out from behind the classroom door, they too disclose what has been hidden from the normative discourse of the curriculum.

In contrast to the language of administration, curriculum, educational psychology, and research, these voices of schoolteachers and students are discernible because of their texture, their presence, their connection to the bodies that schools sequester in

gym lockers and teachers' lounges. And frequently those voices are elicited in interviews that recapitulate the "talking cures" of the films Silverman describes, leaving
ethnographers to apologize for the theft of another's subjectivity even as they subordinate the confession to the theory for which it is an example.

If the narrative or autobiographical voices in educational discourse echo the
female inferiority that Silverman hears in film, and if the male discourse of education
is located as an exterior, generalizing over-voice, then it is possible that all we have
established is an appeal for recognition that petitions phallocentric discourse but
does not challenge its control. The expressivity of the female voice may recapitulate
the hysteric's flashy subterfuge that constructs a facade of affect and expression to
conceal ambivalence and an avoidance of real contact or action.

There is another interpretation available to us, however. One that hears the
narrative voice not as a petitioning appeal or exhibitionistic gesture, but as a stream
of negativity, constantly challenging the generalizing, hegemonic discourse with the
inflections, images and sounds reminiscent of preoedipal or what Kristeva calls
"semiotic" discourse. In this version the female voice is an echo of the maternal voice,
the sonorous envelope within which we come to consciousness, from which we
differentiate as ego grows into identity. While this version of the female voice may seem
stronger than the masochistic speaker whom Silverman hears in dominant film, it is
not without its complexities.

> Listen again to the maternal voice:
> And when she sang, the sea,
> Whatever self if had, become the self
> That was her song, for she was the maker.

This portrayal of dissolving boundaries, as identity passes from the singer to the
sea. The situation just described is one where the object has as yet no externality, since
it is no sooner identified than it is assimilated by the child. Nor, since the subject
lacks boundaries, does it as yet have anything approximating an inferiority. However,
the foundations for what will later function as identity are marked out by these primitive encounters with the outer world, encounters which occur along the axis of the
mother's voice. Since the child's economy is organized around incorporation, and since
what is incorporated is the auditory field articulated by the maternal voice, the child
could be said to hear itself initially through that voice—to first "recognize" itself in the
vocal "mirror" supplied by the mother.[6]

Julia Kristeva's concept of the chora is a name for this amalgam of space and
sound and sense of existence.[7] She has argued that our sense of connection to
the maternal voice and to the world it sang us into never disappears, but lingers in
language, in culture and in fantasy as human possibility, always erupting to undermine
the grip of language, of paternal law and symbolic code. Nevertheless, in Lacan's
version of ego development, the mother's voice is, according to Silverman, a metaphor
for the child's appropriation of identity. Like her breast, once experienced as part of the
infant's self, voice is differentiated as belonging to her and not to the infant, and the

infant gives up not only that which belonged to another but some strata of its subjectivity as well. Lacan argues that this preoedipal separation castrates all who achieve ego identity by requiring them to amputate their earliest sense of world and self, a sense of connection and loss that lingers like a phantom limb.[8]

Silverman presents Rosolato's reminder that however powerful the chora and its semiotic echoes may seem to us as we imagine what we can barely remember, we know it from our place within the symbolic from which the maternal voice speaks to us of lost loves, lost selves, and lost worlds.

Thus burdened by nostalgia, the maternal voice in educational discourse is prey to sentimentality and to an audience that consigns its melodies to fantasy, no matter how compelling. And these are not necessarily comforting fantasies, as Odysseus can tell you. The sirens, whose sweet songs lured seamen to their death, were located between Circe's island and Scylla's rock, hardly refuges. Odysseus escapes their call by binding himself to the mast of his ship and by filling the ears of his crew with wax. Hear no evil.

Despite her criticism, Silverman recuperates the chora of Kristeva as a positive icon of female collectivity, as a "powerful image of women's unity and necessary separatism".[9] She chastises Kristeva for consigning the maternal voice to singing only, and argues appropriately that the mother is also the person who introduces the child to language, to objects, to self. In *Bitter Milk: women and teaching*[5] I discussed at some length the ways in which psychoanalytic theory projects connection and symbiosis on the mother, appropriating knowledge, ego and ultimately subjectivity for the father. How can we rescue voice from such an adoring, yet finally patronizing and trivializing score?

One escape is found in the chorus that is our own voice. As difficult as it may be for us to stretch our identities across multiple discourses we are both the writers and readers of our own stories, and we diminish our experience and our rhetoric if we limit ourselves to only one voice. We need not dissolve identity in order to acknowledge that identity is a choral and not a solo performance. Structures of this choral self are usually organized in three parts. Roy Schafer's *A New Language for Psychoanalysis* presented the trio of self as object, agent, and place. "The processes of reflection that yield self-as-object inform a creative and free will, self-as-agent, who then acts through self-as-place".[10] In *Beyond Feminist Aesthetics*, Rita Felski points to Gidden's tripartite model of the subject that distinguishes practical consciousness, discursive consciousness, and the unconscious.[11] A triad is also summoned by Habermas in *The Theory of Communicative Action*. He argues that in standard speech acts we take up a pragmatic relation—to something in the objective world (as the totality of entities about which true statements are possible); or—to something in the social world (as the totality of legitimately regulated interpersonal relations); or—to something in the subjective world (as the totality of experiences to which a speaker has privileged access and which he can express before a public): such that what the speech act refers to appears to the speaker as something objective, normative or subjective.[12]

Let me suggest a similar triad for the voices of educational theory. Let our songs have three parts, situation, narrative, and interpretation. The first, situation, acknowledges that we tell our story as a speech event that involves the social, cultural, and political relations in and to which we speak. Narrative, or narratives as I prefer, invites all the specificity, presence, and power that the symbolic and semiotic registers of our speaking can provide. And interpretation provides another voice, a reflexive and more distant one, the exterior voice-over in Silverman's acoustics. What is essential is that all three voices usher from one speaker and that each becomes a location through which the other is heard. None is privileged.

This trio may save us from the objectification of "identity politics"[13] by recognizing the dynamic process through which identity is grounded in history, and desire, subjected to description and reflection and constantly presented to and negotiated with other people. A dynamic, reflective, and finally collaborative version of voice is required if the projects of teacher empowerment and school-based management will generate new ways of teaching and schooling. The assertion of an individual history and passion is necessary if instruction is once again to be a valid sharing of a meaningful world. Reflection is necessary if that vision is to acknowledge its own partiality and assume the irony that challenges its own dogma and invites another view. Collaboration is the foundation for the transformation of the space, time, and politics of schooling and yet it must constantly be challenged by another voice, if collaboration is not to degenerate into a coerced consensus. There is no "single artificer of the world," nor will there be a world for us but for the one that we sing and singing make.

Correspondence: Madeleine R. Grumet, School of Education, Brooklyn College, City University of New York, Brooklyn, NY 11210, USA.

Notes

* Presented to the symposium, Studying Words at Work: Rhetorical Analysis of Educational Research, at the Annual Meeting of the American Educational Research Association, 19 April 1990, Boston, MA.
1 Wallace Stevens (1954) *The Collected Poems of Wallace Stevens. . . 'The Idea of Order at Key West',* pp. 129–130 (New York, Vintage).
2 Madeleine Grumet (1976) "Another Voice," in: *Toward a Poor Curriculum* (with William Pinar) (Dubuque, IA, Kendall/Hunt).
3 The phrase is Virginia Woolf's.
4 Kaja Silverman (1988) *The Acoustic Mirror: the female voice in psychoanalysis and cinema* (Bloomington, IN, University of Indiana Press).
5 See Madeleine Grumet (1988) *Bitter Milk: women and teaching* (Amherst, MA, University of Massachusetts Press); see "My face in shine eye, shine in mine appeares; the look in parenting and pedagogy".
6 Silverman, p. 80.
7 Julia Kristeva (1980) Desire in Language (ed. by Leon S. Roudiez; trans. by Thomas Gora, Alice Jardine & Leon S. Roudiez) (New York, Columbia University Press).
8 Silverman, p. 85.
9 See Silverman, p. 125.

10 See Madeleine Grumet (1976) Toward a poor curriculum, in: *Toward a Poor Curriculum* (with William Pinar, p. 69) (Dubuque, IA, Kendall/Hunt) for a discussion of Schafer's model on consciousness and the process of autobiography.
11 Rita Felski (1989) *Beyond Feminist Aesthetics*, p. 57 (Cambridge, MA, Harvard University Press).
12 Jurgen Habermas (1981) *The Theory of Comunicative Action*, Vol. II, p. 120 (Trans. by Thomas McCarthy) (Boston, MA, Beacon Press).
13 See Hank Bromley (1989) Identity politics and critical pedagogy, *Educational Theory*, 38, pp. 207–224

SECTION 6

NEW THEORIES AND HISTORIES

15.
THE WOMANIZATION OF RHETORIC
Sally Miller Gearhart

Editors' Note: *This author's powerful salvo that any act of persuasion is an "act of violence" jolted the long-held notion that successful persuasion equates with winning, even being right. The essay demonstrates the difference between self-determined changing and being the target of change, persuasion, or conversion; in other words, being the targets of violence or conquest. This essay set into motion a rethinking of the rhetorical transaction itself, of ways to move from a goal of "persuasion" to one of understanding, collaboration, and mutual respect—in other words, to a womanization of rhetoric.*

I

My indictment of our discipline of rhetoric springs from my belief that any intent to persuade is an act of violence. In this first section I'd like briefly to review our culpability as teachers of persuasion, explore the distinction between change and intent-to-change, and finally describe a culture-wide phenomenon, the conquest/conversion mentality, in which I find public discourse to be but one of many participants.

The patriarchs of rhetoric have never called into question their unspoken assumption that mankind (read "mankind") is here on earth to alter his (read "his") environment and to influence the social affairs of other men (read "men"). Without batting an eye the ancient rhetors, the men of the church, and scholars of argumentation from Bacon, Blair, and Whately to Toulmin, Perelman, and McLuhan, have taken as given that it is a proper and even necessary human function to attempt to change others. As modern critics and practitioners of public discourse we have been committed to the improvement in our students of the fine art of persuasion. In fact, our teaching, even if it were not the teaching of persuasion, is in itself an insidious form of violence. The "chicken soup" attitude or the "let me help you, let me enlighten you, let me show you the way" approach which is at the heart of most pedagogy is condescending and acutely expressive of the holier-than-thou mindset. Void of respect and openness, it makes even the informative lecture into an oppressive act.

Until the last few decades speech or rhetoric has been a discipline concerned almost exclusively with persuasion in both private and public discourse; it has spent whole eras examining and analyzing its eloquence, learning how to incite the passions, move the will. Over the centuries rhetoric has wearied itself in the ancient and honorable act

Sally Miller Gearhart, "The Womanization of Rhetoric." *Women's Studies International Quarterly* 2 (1979): 195–201.

of finding the available means of persuasion, the better to adapt a discourse to its end. Of all the human disciplines, it has gone about its task of educating others to violence with the most audacity. The fact that it has done so with language and metalanguage, with refined functions of the mind, instead of with whips or rifles does not excuse it from the mindset of the violent.

The indictment of the profession is not an attack on the tools of rhetoric; nor does it suggest that we, its practitioners, serve the world best by forsaking education or committing suicide. With our expertise in persuasion, rhetoricians and rhetorical theorists are in the best position to change our own use of our tools. The indictment is of our *intent* to change people and things, of our attempt to educate others in that skill. The indictment is of our participation in the conquest/conversion mindset that sends us now as a species pell-mell down the path to annihilation.

It is important to know that we can and do change each other daily. Our physical bodies respond to energy; even without our will they react in measurable ways to objects or people generating high energy. We are constantly being changed by each other. Further, we come closer each day to a recognition in our lives of the meaning of Einstein's reduction of matter to energy. It is only in density that the energy fields surrounding each of us differ from the solid energy that is our physical bodies; it is only in density that the energy we generate in our minds or our psyches differs from our auras. As Kurlian photography tracks down revolutionaries by the energy exuded from their very bodies and as Western medicine adopts techniques of visualization and fantasy in the curing of cancer, we realize that to thrust a sword into another person does not differ significantly from wishing them ill or from fantasizing a sword thrust into their heart. Our physical being, our movement, our thoughts, our metaphors: all are forms of energy in constant and infinitely varied exchange.

It is important that we recognize the communication that takes place between entities as well as between humans and entities that we do not count as human. Just as the lunacy of "talking to yourself" has now become a highly recommended technique of intrapersonal communication, even so has the lunacy of "talking to your plants" become recognized as an exchange of energy that revitalizes both communicators. (Here in the Bay Area of California you are thought taciturn if you do not talk to your plant and plants have been known to resent such neglect.) We have been human chauvinists too long, calling consciousness our own, cornering the market upon it, setting ourselves above everything nonhuman because of our "higher awareness." Chimpanzees and porpoises more and more frequently make mockery of the Crown of Creation we have thought ourselves to be.

To change other people or other entities is not in itself a violation. It is a fact of existence that we do so. The act of violence is in the *intention* to change another. The cultural manifestation of that intention makes up the pages of our history books. It is the *conquest* model of human interaction. More significantly, it is the *conversion* model of human interaction, a model more insidious because it gives the illusion of integrity. In the conquest model we invade or violate. In the conversion model we work very hard not simply to conquer but to get every assurance that our conquest of the victim is really giving her what she wants. In fact, a lot of excitement and adventure would go out of our lives if conquest were the only model. It is conversion that gives us our real kicks; it is the stuff of all our pornography, the stuff of Hollywood, the stuff of romance.

Our history is a combination of conquest and conversion. We conquered trees and converted them into a house, taking pride in having accomplished a difficult task. We conquered rivers and streams and converted them into lakes, marvelling in ourselves at the improvement we made on nature. We tramped with our conquering spaceboots on the fine ancient dust of the Moon and we sent our well-rehearsed statements of triumph back for a waiting world to hear. We'd like to think that much as the Moon resisted us, she really, down deep, wanted us—her masters—to tame her and to own her.

We did not ask permission of trees, river, Moon. We did not in any way recognize the part of the victim in the process. They were the conquered. We were the conquerer. The more "fight" they gave us and the more difficult the task, the more exhilarating was the contest and the more arrogant we became at winning over them. Many of us have heard it too often: "I like a woman who gives me a little fight." While there is satisfaction in conquering, the real rush comes if she resists and then gives in, if you make her want you, if you convert her, if the trees are big, if you fail the first few times to harness the river, if the Moon is hard to get to.

Since the middle ages scholars have been fond of classifying rhetoric into three bands: that which flows from the pulpit, that which is found at the bar of justice, and that which rings out on the senate floor. All three efforts demonstrate precisely a violence not just of conquest but also of conversion, whether it be conversion of the sinner, the jury, or the worthy opposition. Preachers, lawyers, and politicians may congratulate themselves that they are men of reason who have chosen civilized discourse above fighting. Yet where the intent is to change another, the difference between a persuasive metaphor and a violent artillery attack is obscure and certainly one of degree rather than of kind. Our rational discourse, presumably such an improvement over war and barbarism, turns out to be in itself a subtle form of Might Makes Right. Speech and rhetoric teachers have been training a competent breed of weapons specialists who are skilled in emotional manoeuvers, expert in intellectual logistics and, in their attack upon attitude and belief systems, blissfully ignorant of their violation of nature or her processes.

Somewhere in a dark corner of human history we made a serious evolutionary blunder. We altered ourselves from a species in tune with the Earth, with our home, into a species that began ruthlessly to control and convert its environment. At that point, when we began to seek to change any other entity, we violated the integrity of that person or thing and our own integrity as well.

Political speculations about the origin of alienation, theological agitations about the beginning of evil, psychological ruminations about the birth of "the other" and philosophical explorations of the mind—body split—all have shown us the futility of trying to determine the cause of our violence as a species. Was it our coming to consciousness? Or some leap from our subjective ego to the recognition of another subjective ego? The drive to civilization or the drive to death through civilization? Perhaps the creative urge or the birth of language itself or the first time someone claimed private property? Did it occur when men discovered that they had some role in conception and got so carried away that they organized the patriarchy? Is the violence inherent in the nature of the human being, a product of the natural urge to compete or of the hierarchical mindset? Did it occur from something so practical as the planning ahead for survival through the storing of surplus goods? Or from something so ontological as the realization of death and the planning ahead against its occurrence?

The evidence is plain that somehow our energy has gone haywire, that we are riding roughshod over the biosphere, that we have no species consciousness, that we produce, reproduce, and consume in a constantly expanding pattern that is rapidly depleting our natural resources and driving us to the destruction of each other and of the planet which sustains us. "Rape of the Earth" is not simply a metaphor, or if it is a metaphor it is one so strong that it brings into sharp relief both the reality of the female/male relationship in Western culture and the separation of ourselves as a species from the original source of our being. The earth seems now to be giving us clear and unmistakeable signals that she will not endure our rule over her much longer, that we are a renegade civilization, a dying civilization which may have passed up its opportunity for survival. We need to come to a halt and reawaken ourselves, to refresh and resource ourselves at the lost wells of our own origin. Already it may be too late.

II

To pose the value question, "Can it be an act of integrity to seek to change another person or another entity?" is to open the door to alternatives to persuasion. I will explore here a non-persuasive notion of communication and show how I believe our discipline has been moving toward that notion in the recent past. Finally I will draw connections between recent understandings of communication and the womanization of culture that I believe is necessary for the survival of the planet.

If we are not to attempt to change our world, then is the alternative to sit forever in a quiet and desperate passivity? Must we choose between being an invader, a violent persuader, and a patient Griselda twiddling our thumbs and curbing our energy in the hope that some miraculous process will do it all for us? Surely it is of value to seek to alter injustices, to change oppressive societal institutions. Is there a way to relate to each other, to other entities, in acts that participate in the changing of our world but which do not themselves recapitulate our heritage of violence? Is there a difference between wanting circumstances to change and wanting to change circumstances?

Mao Tse Tung in his essay "On Contradiction" gave us the metaphor of the egg and the stone. No one can change an egg into a chicken. If, however, there is the potential in the egg to be a chicken—what Mao called the "internal basis for change"—then there is the likelihood that in the right environment (moisture, temperature, the "external conditions for change") the egg will hatch. A stone, on the other hand, has no internal basis for hatching into a chicken and an eternity of sitting in the proper conditions of moisture and temperature will not make possible its transformation into a chicken.

If we think of communicative acts not as attempts to change others or even as attempts to inform or to help them, then perhaps we can understand Mao's metaphor.

Communication can be a deliberate creation or co-creation of an atmosphere in which people or things, if and only if they have the internal basis for change, may change themselves; it can be a milieu in which those who are ready to be persuaded may persuade themselves, may choose to hear or choose to learn. With this understanding we can begin to operate differently in all communicative circumstances, particularly those wherein *learning* and *conflict encounter* take place.

What might take place in the learning circumstance could be best understood as a mutual generation of energy for purposes of growth; what would take place in the conflict encounter is best described for lack of a better word as dialogue. In either case, persons entering the interaction would be certain

1 that no intent to enlighten or to persuade would be made but rather that each party would seek to contribute to an atmosphere in which change for both/all parties can take place;
2 that there are differences among those who participate—in the case of learning differences of degree and quality of knowing specific subject matter, and in the case of conflict genuine disagreements between/among people;
3 that though there are differences, the persons involved feel equal in power to each other;
4 that communication is a difficult achievement, something to be worked at, since the odds are great that moments of miscommunication will outnumber moments of communication;
5 that each participant is willing on the deepest level to yield her/his position entirely to the other(s).

If the circumstance is one of learning then instructors must genuinely prepare to learn, prepare to be changed with students in the mutually created setting. As we observe from changes already taking place in classrooms across the country, the number of words spoken by any one individual—teacher or student—in such an atmosphere is far less important than the manner and the intentionality with which they speak the words.

If the circumstance is one of conflict, then all that we are already learning about dialogue comes into play. Somehow the mind—body split experienced by rhetoric or speech communication as well as by other disciplines will have to be bridged in the process of dialogue. Some unity will have to occur there of personality differences with the principled advocacy of positions; some techniques of interpersonal clarification and openness will have to blend with the use of good reason in the controversy. We functioned from Socrates to the 1950s with reason as our standard; then, with the advent of sensitivity training and small group communication, we seemed almost to exchange the tyranny of the mind for the tyranny of the emotions. What we now know is that, in any conflict circumstance, there are positions and arguments, but there are as well the multi-levelled dynamics of human personalities at work.

It is at this point, when we address emerging notions of learning and dialogue that we appreciate the recent changes of the rhetoric and public address that have occurred within the discipline of rhetoric and public address. It is fair to say that until the 1950s speech-making has been practiced and taught on the conquest/conversion model, on a very male chauvinist model, one that not only implied but explicitly assumed that all the power was in the speaker, just as we believed at one point in history that all power was in the sperm. He stood before the crowd, one hero, one persuader. He believed that he did it all, and unfortunately, his audience believed the same thing. His was the message, his the act of converting his hearers; his was the enlightened truth which sought a womb/audience in which to deposit itself and grow. Little attention was paid to the listener, and even less to the circumstances or the environment of the persuasive process.

In the last decades, however, the listener has come into her own. By drawing our attention away from the masses transfixed by one orator and toward the interactions that transpire in our daily lives, by sitting more often in groups or in dyads and less often in lectures, we have come to realize that in its more common and more natural setting communication does not have to be an invasion of enemy territory but can at least be a two-way street. We have begun to admit the listener's presence, perhaps even her participation in the speechmaking process. And the field of *rhetoric*—persuasion— has broadened into the field of *communication*, a change which in itself is a symptom of the change in our concerns.

In recent semantic and communication theory we move closer to the concern for environment, for climate; particularly is this true in a general systems approach and transactional models. Though the term is only beginning to be used, it is important that the whole communication environment be understood as a *matrix*, a womb. A matrix is that within which or from which something takes form or begins. A matrix "produces" a seed (like the sperm) only we call it an egg. Yet the matrix is not simply a generating substance. It is also a nurturing substance, the atmosphere in which growth and change take place. In terms of communication it is an atmosphere in which meanings are generated and nurtured. We could even say "The meaning is the matrix."

It is a new thing that we do in this century: to turn again toward the wholeness of the communication process instead of separating ourselves out from it, to think in terms of an organic atmosphere that is the source of meanings instead of waiting for an outsider who will, like a god, give us the meanings. We are perhaps on the brink of understanding that we do not have to be persuaders, that we no longer need to intend to change others. We are not the speaker, the-one-with-the-truth, the-one-who-with- his-power-will-change-lives. We are the matrix, we are she-who-is-the-home-of-this- particular-human-interaction, we are a co-creator and co-sustainer of the atmosphere in whose infinity of possible transformations we will all change.

Modern communication theory has not yet articulated its own process of change. With all of its extensive research into human behavior, with all its imagination and creative models, modern communication theory still is concerned almost exclusively with the how and the *what* of communication, how it works and what its definition is. At best it asks questions about the role of values in attitude change and fails as yet to ask essential value questions about its own intent.

The conquest/conversion rhetoricians of the first 2400 years of our discipline constantly asked questions of value: can virtue be taught? Can we allow a dangerous enemy to speak to the masses? What does a lie do to the speaker's credibility? Should teachers of rhetoric take fees for teaching? They too failed to ask the crucial value question, "Can we with integrity intend to change another?" But at least they reflected on their actions in the light of ethics. We recall, though, that rhetoric has always found its home in the humanities where value questions are the norm. Modern communication theory participates more readily in the social sciences where questions of value hide under the search for objective reality. Until such theory begins to entertain those ethical questions or until communicators in the humanities challenge modern theory on just such questions, we will be little better off than with our commitment to the old conquest/conversion assumptions.

In what is called the second wave of feminism, the rise of the woman's movement in the sixties and seventies of this century, there are threads that may connect a society presently violent to a nonviolent past and to a nonviolent future. One of the threads is an understanding of communication as essentially the womanlike process we have been describing.

Feminism is at the very least the rejection of the conquest/conversion model of interaction and the development of new forms of relationship which allow for wholeness in the individual and differences among people and entities. At the same time it means some sense of how that infinite variety thrives within a unity. Feminism is an ideology of change which rises out of the experiences of women, out of the experiences of our bodies, our experiences of our conditioning both in our individual lives and over the centuries.

It is important to the field of communication that biologically and historically we women have been thought of and think of ourselves as receptacles, as listeners, as hearers, as holders, nurturers, as matrices, as environments and creators of environments. It is important to the field of communication that, though we women now begin to discover what the suppression of our violence has meant to us, violence has been associated almost exclusively with men in our culture. The change in the discipline of speech from the concentration on speaker/conqueror to an interest in atmosphere, in listening, in receiving, in a collective rather than in a competitive mode—that change suggests the womanization of that discipline.

Many of us in the speech field, women and men alike, will be uncomfortable with that idea: that communication, like the rest of the culture, must be womanized, that in order to be authentic, in order to be nonviolent communicators, we must all become more like women. We have all learned that though women are okay they are somehow lesser human beings. It is a blow to the ego to suggest that we may be like a woman. It will be hard for men to think of changing because never having been environments they need lots of practice in becoming so. It will be hard for women in the field to think of changing because though we have been environments, we've spent most of our professional careers trying not to be so, trying not to be women, trying instead to scale ourselves to the conquest/conversion model of the speechmaker, the speech teacher.

We have all diligently studied our Aristotle and learned how to persuade others, how to enlighten them. We have all enjoyed the rush of power that has come with that. How can we forsake all this and think of ourselves not as bearers of great messages but as vessels out of whose variety messages will emerge? We have been practising conquer-and-convert for centuries, struggling for survival in a self-perpetuating system of violence and power conflicts. There is reason, good reason, for us to be uncomfortable with such a "weak" and "yielding" model of communication. There is reason enough to be insecure about giving up our desire to change others since our entire identity has been bound up in our power to change others. When all we've done for centuries is to penetrate the environment with the truth we've been taught to believe is ours alone, then it is difficult to enjoy being just a listener, just a co-creator of an atmosphere. Yet that is precisely the task.

Feminism is a source, a wellspring, a matrix, an environment for the womanization of communication, for the womanization of Western civilization. It calls for an ancient and deep understanding and ultimately for a fundamental change of attitude and perspective. In its challenge to history and to the present social order feminism in this, its second wave, feminism this time around, in this century, is playing for keeps for all of us—for women, for men, for children, animals and plants and for the earth herself. The stakes are that high.

16.
BEYOND PERSUASION: A PROPOSAL FOR AN INVITATIONAL RHETORIC
Sonja K. Foss and Cindy L. Griffin

Editors' Note: *Most traditional rhetorical theories reflect a patriarchal bias in the positive value they accord to changing, and thus dominating, others. This essay presents an alternative—invitational rhetoric—which is grounded in the feminist principles of equality, immanent value, and self-determination. Its purpose is to offer an invitation to understanding, and its communicative modes are the offering of perspectives and the creation of the external conditions of safety, value, and freedom.*

Acknowledgment of the patriarchal bias that undergirds most theories of rhetoric is growing steadily in the communication discipline. As feminist scholars have begun to explicate the ways in which standard theories of rhetoric embody patriarchal perspectives, they have identified communicative modes that previously have not been recognized or theorized because they are grounded in alternative values (see, for example, Edson, 1985; Elshtain, 1982; Foss & Foss, 1991; Foss, Foss, & Trapp, 1991; Foss & Griffin, 1992; Gearhart, 1979; Griffin, 1993; Kramarae, 1989; Shepherd, 1992). Attention to non-patriarchal forms of communication, feminist scholars argue, expands the scope of rhetorical theory and enhances the discipline's ability to explain diverse communicative phenomena successfully.

One manifestation of the patriarchal bias that characterizes much of rhetorical theorizing is the definition of rhetoric as persuasion. As far back as the Western discipline of rhetoric has been explored, rhetoric has been defined as the conscious intent to change others. As Shepherd (1992) notes, in humanistic, social scientific, and critical perspectives on communication, "interaction processes have typically been characterized essentially and primarily in terms of persuasion, influence, and power" (p. 204). Every communicative encounter has been viewed "as primarily an attempt at persuasion or influence, or as a struggle over power" (p. 206). As natural as an equation of rhetoric with persuasion seems for scholars of rhetoric, this conception is only one perspective on rhetoric and one, we suggest, with a patriarchal bias.

Implicit in a conception of rhetoric as persuasion is the assumption that humans are on earth to alter the "environment and to influence the social affairs" of others. Rhetorical scholars "have taken as given that it is a proper and even necessary human

Sonja K. Foss and Cindy L. Griffin, "Beyond Persuasion: A Proposal for an Invitational Rhetoric." *Communication Monographs* 62 (Mar. 1995): 2–18.

function to attempt to change others" (Gearhart, 1979, p. 195). The desire to effect change is so pervasive that the many ways in which humans engage in activities designed for this purpose often go unnoticed:

> We conquered trees and converted them into a house, taking pride in having accomplished a difficult task. We conquered rivers and streams and converted them into lakes, marvelling in ourselves at the improvement we made on nature. We tramped with our conquering spaceboots on the fine ancient dust of the Moon and we sent our well-rehearsed statements of triumph back for a waiting world to hear.
>
> (Gearhart, 1979, p. 196)

Embedded in efforts to change others is a desire for control and domination, for the act of changing another establishes the power of the change agent over that other. In some instances, the power of the rhetor over another is overt, as it is, for example, in laws that exert control over women's bodies, such as those concerned with abortion. In securing the adherence of women to these laws, lawmakers have power over women and their lives. But even in cases where the strategies used are less coercive, rhetors who convince others to adopt their viewpoints exert control over part of those others' lives. A student who tells another student that she ought to take a particular course, for example, controls or influences the nature of another's life, if only for a few minutes, if the other enrolls in the course or even considers enrolling in it. We suggest that a strikingly large part of many individuals' lives is spent in such efforts to change others, even when the desired changes have absolutely no impact on the lives of the change agents. Whether a friend enrolls in a particular course, for example, often is irrelevant to a student's own life.

The reward gained from successful efforts to make others change is a "rush of power" (Gearhart, 1979, p. 201)—a feeling of self-worth that comes from controlling people and situations. The value of the self for rhetors in this rhetorical system comes from the rhetor's ability to demonstrate superior knowledge, skills, and qualifications— in other words, authority—in order to dominate the perspectives and knowledge of those in their audiences. The value of the self derives not from a recognition of the uniqueness and inherent value of each living being but from gaining control over others.

The act of changing others not only establishes the power of the rhetor over others but also devalues the lives and perspectives of those others. The belief systems and behaviors others have created for living in the world are considered by rhetors to be inadequate or inappropriate and thus in need of change. The speaker's role very often "may be best described as paternalistic" (Scott, 1991, p. 205) in that the rhetor adopts a " 'let me help you, let me enlighten you, let me show you the way' approach" (Gearhart, 1979, p. 195). Audience members are assumed to be naive and less expert than the rhetor if their views differ from the rhetor's own.

Rhetorical scholars have prided themselves on the eschewal of physical force and coercion and the use, in their place, of "language and metalanguage, with refined func-tions of the mind" (Gearhart, 1979, p. 195) to influence others and produce change.

Although these discursive strategies allow more choice to the audience than do the supposedly more heavy-handed strategies of physical coercion, they still infringe on others' rights to believe as they choose and to act in ways they believe are best for them. Even discursive strategies can constitute a kind of trespassing on the personal integrity of others when they convey the rhetor's belief that audience members have inadequacies that in some way can be corrected if they adhere to the viewpoint of the rhetor. Such strategies disallow, in other words, the possibility that audience members are content with the belief systems they have developed, function happily with them, and do not perceive a need to change.

The traditional conception of rhetoric, in summary, is characterized by efforts to change others and thus to gain control over them, self-worth derived from and measured by the power exerted over others, and a devaluation of the life worlds of others. This is a rhetoric of patriarchy, reflecting its values of change, competition, and domination. But these are not the only values on which a rhetorical system can be constructed, and we would like to propose as one alternative a feminist rhetoric.

Although definitions of *feminism* vary, feminists generally are united by a set of basic principles. We have chosen to focus on three of these principles—equality, immanent value, and self-determination—to serve as the starting place for a new rhetoric. These principles are ones that explicitly challenge the positive value the patriarchy accords to changing and thus dominating others.

Primary among the feminist principles on which our proposed rhetoric is based is a commitment to the creation of relationships of equality and to the elimination of the dominance and elitism that characterize most human relationships. As Wood (1994) aptly summarizes this principle, "I don't accept oppression and domination as worthy human values, and I don't believe differences must be ranked on a continuum of good and bad. I believe there are better, more humane and enriching ways to live" (p. 4). Efforts to dominate and gain power over others cannot be used to develop relationships of equality, so feminists seek to replace the "alienation, competition, and dehumanization" that characterize relationships of domination with "intimacy, mutuality, and camaraderie" (hooks, 1984, p. 34).

Yet another principle that undergirds most feminisms is a recognition of the immanent value of all living beings. The essence of this principle is that every being is a unique and necessary part of the pattern of the universe and thus has value. Immanent value derives from the simple principle that "your life is worth something. . . . You need only be what you are" (Starhawk, 1987, pp. 115–116). Worth cannot be determined by positioning individuals on a hierarchy so they can be ranked and compared or by attending to emblems of external achievement, for worth cannot be "earned, acquired, or proven" (Starhawk, 1987, p. 21). Concomitant with a recognition of the immanent value of another individual is the eschewal of forms of communication that seek to change that individual's unique perspective to that held by the rhetor.

Self-determination is a third principle that typically comprises a feminist world view. Grounded in a respect for others, self-determination allows individuals to make their own decisions about how they wish to live their lives. Self-determination involves the recognition that audience members are the authorities on their own lives and accords respect to others' capacity and right to constitute their worlds as they choose. As Johnson (1991) explains, this principle involves a trust that others are doing the best they can at the moment and simply need "to be unconditionally accepted as the experts on their own lives" (p. 162). When others are seen as experts who are making competent decisions about their lives, efforts by a rhetor to change those decisions are seen as a violation of their life worlds and the expertise they have developed.

Our purpose in this essay is to propose a definition and explication of a rhetoric built on the principles of equality, immanent value, and self-determination rather than on the attempt to control others through persuasive strategies designed to effect change. Although we believe that persuasion is often necessary, we believe an alternative exists that may be used in instances when changing and controlling others is not the rhetor's goal; we call this rhetoric *invitational rhetoric*. In what follows, we offer a description of this rhetoric, beginning with a discussion of its definition and purpose and then describing the communicative options available to rhetors who wish to use it. We conclude our essay with two examples of invitational rhetoric and a discussion of some implications of invitational rhetoric for rhetorical theory.

Although invitational rhetoric is constructed largely from feminist theory, the literature in which its principles and various dimensions have been theorized most thoroughly, we are not suggesting that only feminists have dealt with and developed its various components or that only feminists adhere to the principles on which it is based. Some dimensions of this rhetoric have been explicated by traditional rhetorical theorists, and we have incorporated their ideas into our description of this rhetoric. We also do not want to suggest that the rhetoric we propose describes how all women communicate or that it is or can be used only by women. Feminism "implies an understanding of inclusion with interests beyond women" (Wood, 1993, p. 39), and its aim is not to "privilege women over men" or "to benefit solely any specific group of women" (hooks, 1984, p. 26). The rhetoric we describe is a rhetoric used at various times by some women and some men, some feminists and some non-feminists. What makes it feminist is not its use by a particular population of rhetors but rather the grounding of its assumptions in feminist principles and theories. Our goal in offering this theory is to expand the array of communicative options available to all rhetors and to provide an impetus for more focused and systematic efforts to describe and assess rhetoric in all of its manifestations.

Definition

Invitational rhetoric is an invitation to understanding as a means to create a relationship rooted in equality, immanent value, and self-determination. Invitational rhetoric constitutes an invitation to the audience to enter the rhetor's world and to see it as the rhetor does. In presenting a particular perspective, the invitational rhetor does not judge or denigrate others' perspectives but is open to and tries to appreciate and validate those perspectives, even if they differ dramatically from the rhetor's own. Ideally, audience members accept the invitation offered by the rhetor by listening to and trying to understand the rhetor's perspective and then presenting their own. When this happens, rhetor and audience alike contribute to the thinking about an issue so that everyone involved gains a greater understanding of the issue in its subtlety, richness, and complexity. Ultimately, though, the result of invitational rhetoric is not just an understanding of an issue. Because of the nonhierarchical, nonjudgmental, nonadversarial framework established for the interaction, an understanding of the participants themselves occurs, an understanding that engenders appreciation, value, and a sense of equality.

The stance taken by invitational rhetors toward their audiences obviously is different from that assumed by traditional rhetors. Invitational rhetors do not believe they have the right to claim that their experiences or perspectives are superior to those of their audience members and refuse to impose their perspectives on them. Rhetors view the choices selected by audience members as right for them at that particular time, based on their own abilities to make those decisions. Absent are efforts to dominate another because the goal is the understanding and appreciation of another's perspective rather than the denigration of it simply because it is different from the rhetor's own. The result of the invitational rhetor's stance toward the audience is a relationship of equality, respect, and appreciation.

Invitational rhetoric is characterized, then, by the openness with which rhetors are able to approach their audiences. Burke (1969) suggests that rhetors typically adjust their conduct to the external resistance they expect in the audience or situation: "We in effect modify our own assertion in reply to its assertion" (p. 237). In invitational rhetoric, in contrast, resistance is not anticipated, and rhetors do not adapt their communication to expected resistance in the audience. Instead, they identify possible impediments to the creation of understanding and seek to minimize or neutralize them so they do not remain impediments.

Change may be the result of invitational rhetoric, but change is not its purpose. When change does occur as a result of understanding, it is different from the kind of change that typifies the persuasive interactions of traditional rhetoric. In the traditional model, change is defined as a shift in the audience in the direction requested by the rhetor, who then has gained some measure of power and control over the audience. In invitational rhetoric, change occurs in the audience or rhetor or both as a result of new understanding and insights gained in the exchange of ideas. As rhetors and audience members offer their ideas on an issue, they allow diverse positions to be compared in a process of discovery and questioning that may lead to transformation for themselves and others. Participants even may choose to be transformed because they are persuaded by something someone in the interaction says, but the insight that is persuasive is offered by a rhetor not to support the superiority of a particular perspective but to contribute to the understanding by all participants of the issue and of one another.

The internal processes by which transformation occurs also are different in invitational rhetoric. In traditional rhetoric, the change process often is accompanied by feelings of inadequacy, insecurity, pain, humiliation, guilt, embarrassment, or angry submission on the part of the audience as rhetors communicate the superiority of their positions and the deficiencies of those of the audience. In invitational rhetoric, on the other hand, rhetors recognize the valuable contributions audience members can make to the rhetors' own thinking and understanding, and they do not engage in strategies that may damage or sever the connection between them and their audiences. This does not mean that invitational rhetoric always is free of pain. In invitational rhetoric, there may be a wrenching loose of ideas as assumptions and positions are questioned as a result of an interaction, a process that may be uncomfortable. But because rhetors affirm the beliefs of and communicate respect for others, the changes that are made are likely to be accompanied by an appreciation for new perspectives gained and gratitude for the assistance provided by others in thinking about an issue.

Communicative Options

The process of engaging in invitational rhetoric assumes two primary rhetorical forms. One is offering perspectives, a mode by which rhetors put forward for consideration their perspectives; the second is the creation of external conditions that allow others to present their perspectives in an atmosphere of respect and equality.

Offering Perspectives

When rhetors do not seek to impose their positions on audience members in invitational rhetoric, the presentation and function of individual perspectives differ significantly from their nature and function in traditional rhetorics. Individual perspectives are articulated in invitational rhetoric as carefully, completely, and passionately as possible to give them full expression and to invite their careful consideration by the participants in the interaction. This articulation occurs not through persuasive argument but through offering—the giving of expression to a perspective without advocating its support or seeking its acceptance. Offering involves not probing or invading but giving, a process "of wrapping around the givee, of being available to her/him without insisting; our giving is a *presence,* an *offering,* an *opening*" (Gearhart, 1982, p. 198). In offering, rhetors tell what they currently know or understand; they present their vision of the world and show how it looks and works for them.

As a rhetorical form, offering may appear to be similar to some traditional rhetorical strategies, such as the use of personal narrative as a form of support for a rhetor's position. But narrative as offering functions differently from narrative as a means of support. It is presented in offering for the purpose of articulating a viewpoint but not as a means to increase the likelihood of the audience's adherence to that viewpoint. The offering of a personal narrative is, itself, the goal; the means and the ends are the same in offering. Offering is not based on a dichotomy of cause and effect, an action done in the present to affect the future. Instead, as Johnson (1989) explains, the "'means are the ends; . . . *how* we do something is *what* we get'" (p. 35). In this mode, then, a story is not told as a means of supporting or achieving some other end but as an end in itself—simply offering the perspective the story represents.

A critical dimension of the offering of a perspective, in whatever form it takes, is a willingness to yield. Not unlike Buber's (1965) notion of the "I–Thou" relationship, the basic movement of a willingness to yield is a turning toward the other. It involves meeting another's position "in its uniqueness, letting it have its impact" (p. xiv). Tracy (1987) explains the connection between the meeting of another's uniqueness and a willingness to yield: "To attend to the other as other, the different as different, is also to understand the different *as* possible" (p. 20). When they assume such a stance, rhetors communicate a willingness to call into question the beliefs they consider most inviolate and to relax their grip on those beliefs. The process is not unlike the self-risk that Natanson (1965) describes as the risking

> of the self's world of feeling, attitude, and the total subtle range of its affective and conative sensibility. . . . [W]hen I truly risk myself in arguing I open myself to the viable possibility that the consequence of an argument may be to make me *see* something of the structure of my immediate world.
>
> (p. 15)

Scott (1976) calls this self-risk "a grave risk: the risk of the self that resides in a value structure" (p. 105). Thus, the perspective presented through offering represents an initial, tentative commitment to that perspective—one subject to revision as a result of the interaction.

A few specific examples of offering may clarify the nature of this rhetorical form. Although much rarer than we would like, offering sometimes occurs in academic settings when faculty members and/or students gather to discuss a topic of mutual interest. When they enter the interaction with a goal not of converting others to their positions but of sharing what they know, extending one another's ideas, thinking critically about all the ideas offered, and coming to an understanding of the subject and of one another, they are engaged in offering. Offering also is marked by discursive forms such as "I tried this solution when that happened to me; I thought it worked well" or "What would happen if we introduced the idea of _____ into this problem?" rather than statements with forms such as "You really ought to do _____" or "Your idea is flawed because you failed to take into account _____."

Offering may occur not only in small-group settings but also in formal presentational contexts. A rhetor who presents her ideas at an academic colloquium, for example, engages in offering when she presents her ideas as valuable yet also as tentative. She acknowledges the fact that her work is in progress; thus, she is open to the ideas of others so she can continue to revise and improve it. She builds on and extends the work of others rather than tearing their ideas apart in an effort to establish the superiority of her own. In an offering mode, she provides explanations for the sources of her ideas rather than marshalling evidence to establish their superiority. Audience members, too, may engage in offering behavior. They do so when they ask questions and make comments designed not to show the stupidity or error of the perspective presented or to establish themselves as more powerful or expert than the presenter. Instead, their questions and suggestions are aimed at learning more about the presenter's ideas, understanding them more thoroughly, nurturing them, and offering additional ways of thinking about the subject for everyone involved in the interaction.

We have tried to write this essay using such features of the offering form. We present a *proposal* for an invitational rhetoric, for example, a word we chose deliberately to suggest that what we present here is only one of many equally legitimate perspectives possible. We suggest that invitational rhetoric is a viable form of interaction in many instances but do not assert that it is the only appropriate form of rhetoric and should be used in all situations or contexts. We acknowledge the importance and usefulness of traditional theories of rhetoric even as we propose an alternative to them, and we try to build on and extend the work of other theorists—both traditional and feminist—rather than characterizing their work as inaccurate or misguided. Although we are constrained somewhat by the format of a journal article, we see this essay as in progress and plan to continue to work on our ideas; the responses of some of our colleagues and the reviewers and editor of *Communication Monographs* already have helped us clarify and improve our description of this rhetoric. We have attempted, then, to model the offering of a perspective within the perimeters allowed by a framework of scholarly discourse.

Offering also may be seen in the nonverbal realm; a perspective may be offered in the clothing individuals wear, the places in which and how they live, and in all of the symbolic choices rhetors make that reveal their perspectives. This kind of offering is illustrated by Purple Saturday, sponsored by the Women's Caucus at Speech Communication Association (SCA) conventions. On Purple Saturday, the women attending the convention (and those men who wish to show their support for women) are asked to wear purple, a color of the early women's suffrage movement, to proclaim women's solidarity and presence in SCA. When women wear purple on Saturday at the convention, they are not trying to persuade others to become feminists, to accept feminist scholarship, or to value women. Instead, they are simply offering a perspective so that those who wish to learn more about feminist scholarship or to join in the celebration of feminism may do so. Although not designed to influence others to change in particular directions, such nonverbal offerings may have that effect; some who view the wearing of purple by others at a convention may choose, for example, to explore or engage in feminist research themselves.

Another form offering may take, particularly in a hostile situation or when a dominant perspective is very different from the one held by the rhetor, is re-sourcement (Gearhart, 1982). Re-sourcement is a response made by a rhetor according to a framework, assumptions, or principles other than those suggested in the precipitating message. In using re-sourcement, the rhetor deliberately draws energy from a new source—a source other than the individual or system that provided the initial frame for the issue. It is a means, then, of communicating a perspective that is different from that of the individual who produced the message to which the rhetor is responding. Re-sourcement is not unlike Burke's (1984) notion of perspective by incongruity, but in re-sourcement, the juxtaposition of two systems or frameworks is split between rhetor and audience, with one reflected in the original message, the other in the response.

Re-sourcement involves the two processes of disengagement from the framework, system, or principles embedded in the precipitating message and the creative development of a response so that the issue is framed differently. Rorty's (1986) description of the process of generating new vocabularies points to this two-part process: "The idea is to get a vocabulary which is (at the moment) incommensurable with the old in order to draw attention away from the issues stated in the old, and thereby help people to forget them" (p. 114). In Forget's (1989) words, this kind of communication is "a swerve, a leap to the other side, which lets us . . . deploy another logic or system" (p. 136).

Although a refusal to engage in conflict or interaction under the terms proposed by a rhetor sometimes is seen as a negative, ineffective form of communication because it is interpreted as disconfirmation (e.g., Veenendall & Feinstein, 1990) or as a kind of manipulation associated with passive-aggressive behavior, it can be a positive response to a situation. It allows rhetors to continue to value themselves as well as the audience because it communicates that they are not willing to allow the audience to violate their integrity. Re-sourcement also opens up possibilities for future rhetorical choices, providing more options for rhetors than were previously available. As later options, rhetors who use re-sourcement may articulate their positions through more traditional forms of offering or standard forms of persuasion.

An example of re-sourcement is provided by Starhawk (1987) in her description of an incident that followed the blockade of the Livermore Weapons Lab in California to protest its development of nuclear weapons. She and other women were arrested and held in a school gym, and during their confinement, a woman was chased into the gym by six guards. She dove into a cluster of women, and they held on to her as the guards pulled at her legs, trying to extract her from the group. The guards were on the verge of beating the women when one woman sat down and began to chant. As the other women followed suit, the guards' actions changed in response:

> They look bewildered. Something they are unprepared for, unprepared even to name, has arisen in our moment of common action. They do not know what to do. And so, after a moment, they withdraw. . . . In that moment in the jail, the power of domination and control met something outside its comprehension, a power rooted in another source.
>
> (p. 5)

The guards' message was framed in a context of opposition, violence, hostility, and fear; the women, in contrast, chose to respond with a message framed in terms of nonviolence and connection.

Re-sourcement in a discursive form is exemplified in a story told by Watzlawick, Weakland, and Fisch (1974) about a police officer who was

> issuing a citation for a minor traffic violation when a hostile crowd began to gather around him. By the time he had given the offender his ticket, the mood of the crowd was

ugly and the sergeant was not certain he would be able to get back to the relative safety
of his patrol car. It then occurred to him to announce in a loud voice: "You have just
witnessed the issuance of a traffic ticket by a member of your Oakland Police Department."
And while the bystanders were busy trying to fathom the deeper meaning of this all
too obvious communique, he got into his cruiser and drove off.

(pp. 108–109)

The initial message presented to the police officer was framed in the context of
opposition and hostility; he chose, however, to respond with a message grounded in
a framework of simple explanation, cooperation, and respect. Re-sourcement, as
a means of offering, allowed him to diffuse the situation and to communicate his
own perspective—that he was doing the job he was hired by the crowd members, as
taxpayers, to do.

External Conditions

Offering can occur whether or not an audience chooses to join with a rhetor in a
process of discovery and understanding. But if invitational rhetoric is to result in
mutual understanding of perspectives, it involves not only the offering of the rhetor's
perspective but the creation of an atmosphere in which audience members' perspectives also can be offered. We propose that to create such an environment, an invitational
rhetoric must create three external conditions in the interaction between rhetors and
audience members—safety, value, and freedom. These are states or prerequisites
required if the possibility of mutual understanding is to exist.

The condition of *safety* involves the creation of a feeling of security and freedom
from danger for the audience. Rhetoric contributes to a feeling of safety when it conveys
to audience members that the ideas and feelings they share with the rhetor will be
received with respect and care. When rhetoric establishes a safe context, the rhetor
makes no attempt to hurt, degrade, or belittle audience members or their beliefs, and
audience members do not fear rebuttal of or retribution for their most fundamental
beliefs. Even in a volatile situation such as that described by Starhawk, when the guards
were about to beat a woman seeking safe haven in a group of protesters, rhetoric
that promotes a feeling of safety can be created. In this case, the women did nothing
to endanger the guards or make them feel as though they would be hurt. They did
not fight them physically or argue against the guards' use of force; neither did they
engage in verbal abuse or ridicule the guards' training and beliefs about how to deal
with prisoners.

Rhetoric that contributes to a feeling of safety also provides some means for
audience members to order the world so it seems coherent and makes sense to
them. When audience members feel their sense of order is threatened or challenged,
they are more likely to cling to familiar ways of thinking and to be less open to
understanding the perspectives of others. When a safe environment is created, then,
audience members trust the rhetor and feel the rhetor is working with and not
against them.

The condition of *value is* the acknowledgment that audience members have intrinsic or immanent worth. This value is what Benhabib (1992) calls "*the principle of universal moral respect*"—"the right of all beings capable of speech and action to be participants" in the conversation (p. 29). Barrett (1991) describes this condition as "respectfully, affirming others" while at the same time "one affirms oneself" (p. 148).

Value is created when rhetors approach audience members as "unrepeatable individuals" and eschew "distancing, depersonalizing, or paternalistic attitudes" (Walker, 1989, pp. 22, 23). As a result, audience members feel their identities are not forced upon or chosen for them by rhetors. Rhetors do not attempt to fit audience members into any particular roles but face "the 'otherness of the other,' one might say to face their 'alterity,' their irreducible distinctness and difference from the self" (Benhabib, 1992, p. 167). Rhetors celebrate the unique and individual identities of audience members—what Benhabib (1992) describes as

> the actuality of my choices, namely to how I, as a finite, concrete, embodied individual, shape and fashion the circumstances of my birth and family, linguistic, cultural and gender identity into a coherent narrative that stands as my life's story.
>
> (pp. 161–162)

One way in which rhetoric may contribute to the acknowledgment and celebration of freely chosen, unique identities by audience members is through a process Gendlin (1978) calls "*absolute listening*" (p. 116), Morton (1985) describes as "hearing to speech" (p. 202), and Johnson (1987) terms "hearing into being" (p. 130). In such rhetoric, listeners do not interrupt, comfort, or insert anything of their own as others tell of their experiences. Such a stance contrasts with typical ways of listening, in which "we nearly always stop each other from getting very far inside. Our advice, reactions, encouragements, reassurances, and well-intentioned comments actually prevent people from feeling understood" (Gendlin, 1978, p. 116) and encourage them to direct their comments toward listeners' positions or orientations (Johnson, 1987). While speaking to listeners who do not insert themselves into the talk, individuals come to discover their own perspectives. Morton (1985) quotes a woman's description of her experience in the process of being heard to speech: "You didn't smother me. You gave it [my voice] space to shape itself. You gave it time to come full circle" (p. 205).

Value is conveyed to audience members when rhetors not only listen carefully to the perspectives of others but try to think from those perspectives. Benhabib's (1992) notion of the "reversibility of perspectives" (p. 145) is relevant here; it is the capacity to reverse perspectives and to reason from the standpoint of others, "making present to oneself what the perspectives of others involved are or could be" (p. 137). When value is created in a communicative situation, audience members feel rhetors see them as significant individuals and appreciate and attend to their uniqueness. They feel rhetors care about them, understand their ideas, and allow them to contribute in significant ways to the interaction.

Freedom, the power to choose or decide, is a third condition whose presence in an environment is a prerequisite for the possibility of mutual understanding. In invitational rhetoric, rhetors do not place restrictions on an interaction. Participants can bring any and all matters to the interaction for consideration; no subject matter is off limits, and all presuppositions can be challenged. The rhetor's ideas also are not privileged over those of the audience in invitational rhetoric. All the participants in the interaction are able, in Barrett's (1991) words, to "speak up, to speak out" (p. 148). Benhabib (1992) calls this *"the principle of egalitarian reciprocity"* (p. 29); within conversations, it suggests, "each has the same symmetrical rights to various speech acts, to initiate new topics, to ask for reflection about the presuppositions of the conversation, etc." (p. 29).

Freedom also is developed when a rhetor provides opportunities for others to develop and choose options from alternatives they, themselves, have created. Rather than presenting a predetermined set of options from which individuals may choose, a rhetor who wishes to facilitate freedom allows audience members to develop the options that seem appropriate to them, allowing for the richness and complexity of their unique subjective experiences. Perspectives are articulated as a means to widen options—to generate more ideas than either rhetors or audiences had initially—in contrast to traditional rhetoric, where rhetors seek to limit the options of audiences and encourage them to select the one they advocate.

Freedom of choice is made available to audiences, as well, in that, in invitational rhetoric, the audience's lack of acceptance of or adherence to the perspective articulated by the rhetor truly makes no difference to the rhetor. Some audience members will choose to try to understand the perspective of the rhetor, but others will not. Of those who do, some will choose to accept the perspective offered by the rhetor, but others will not. Either outcome—acceptance or rejection—is seen as perfectly acceptable by the invitational rhetor, who is not offended, disappointed, or angry if audience members choose not to adopt a particular perspective. Should the audience choose not to accept the vision articulated by the rhetor, the connection between the rhetor and the audience remains intact, and the audience still is valued and appreciated by the rhetor. The maintenance of the connection between rhetors and audiences is not dependent on rhetors' approval of the choices made by audience members. Rogers' (1962) notion of unconditional positive regard suggests the nature of the autonomy the rhetor accords the audience; the audience has the freedom to make choices without the possibility of losing the respect of the rhetor.

Illustrations

Invitational rhetoric offers an invitation to understanding—to enter another's world to better understand an issue and the individual who holds a particular perspective on it. Ultimately, its purpose is to provide the basis for the creation and maintenance of relationships of equality. Its primary communicative options are offering perspectives and the creation of the external conditions of safety, value, and freedom that enable audience members to present their perspectives to the rhetor. In this section, we present two examples of invitational rhetoric to clarify its primary features.

The first example is the acceptance speech given by Adrienne Rich when she was awarded the National Book Awards' prize for poetry in 1974 (Rich, Lorde, & Walker, 1974/1994). When Rich accepted the award, she read a statement that she had prepared with Alice Walker and Audre Lorde—both of whom also had been nominated for the prize. In the statement, the three women announced that they were accepting the award together: "We, Audre Lorde, Adrienne Rich, and Alice Walker, together accept this award in the name of all the women whose voices have gone and still go unheard in a patriarchal world" (p. 148).

The statement clearly articulated the women's own position: "We believe that we can enrich ourselves more in supporting and giving to each other than by competing against each other; and that poetry—if it *is* poetry—exists in a realm beyond ranking and comparison" (p. 148). They presented no arguments in favor of their belief, however, nor did they argue against the position held by representatives of the National Book Awards. Thus, they did not seek the adherence of others to their perspective but simply offered their own vision.

The speech illustrates re-sourcement as a form of offering in that the women communicated their differences with the hierarchical, competitive framework established by the National Book Awards simply by not communicating within the terms of that framework: "None of us could accept this money for herself" (p. 148). They chose to respond within a different framework—one based on support and cooperation—by accepting the prize in the name of all women: "We will share this prize among us, to be used as best we can for women" (p. 148).

The three external conditions of safety, value, and freedom required for others to present their perspectives were created by the speech. The rhetors communicated safety when they suggested that they regarded the perspective of the judges as a legitimate one that they would treat with respect and care. "We appreciate the good faith of the judges for this award" (p. 148), they stated.

They accorded value in very specific ways to many individuals, both those in their immediate audience and others:

> We dedicate this occasion to the struggle for self-determination of all women, of every color, identification, or derived class: the poet, the housewife, the lesbian, the mathematician, the mother, the dishwasher, the pregnant teenager, the teacher, the grandmother, the prostitute, the philosopher, the waitress, the women who will understand what we are doing here and those who will not understand yet.
>
> (pp. 148–149)

They not only recognized these diverse and unique individuals but credited them as sources for their own work, calling them "the silent women whose voices have been denied us, the articulate women who have given us strength to do our work" (p. 149).

The brevity of the speech precluded the opportunity for the extensive development of freedom for the audience, but it is evident in that Rich, Walker, and Lorde do not specify particular options for action for women; they leave open to women whatever routes of "self-determination" (p. 148) they, themselves, choose. Nor do they suggest

the kind of support women should give to each other or the particular contributions other women have made to them. Their ambiguity in these areas leaves
open options for the audience and does not confine the terms of the interaction they
initiated.

Feminist and animal-rights activist Sally Miller Gearhart (1993) provides a second
example of invitational rhetoric in her narration of her interaction with an anti-
abortion advocate. In the interaction, Gearhart used both traditional and invitational
rhetoric, so her narrative provides a useful contrast between the two and the kinds of
results each tends to produce. On a trip with a friend to upstate New York, Gearhart
encountered a man in the Kennedy airport "railing about all these women and
abortion rights." Because of her own pro-choice beliefs, Gearhart

> took him on. As a matter of fact, I took him on so loudly that we gathered a little crowd
> there in the Kennedy airport. I was screaming at him; I was trying to make him change. It
> was not successful, and it was pretty ugly, as a matter of fact. . . . They didn't have to actually
> physically separate us, but it was close to that.

An hour later, as she was boarding the shuttle bus to take her to Plattsburg, her
destination, Gearhart encountered the man again: "There was only one seat on that
bus, and guess who it was next to? . . . He looked at me and I looked at him as if to say,
'Oh, my God, what are we going to do?'" Rather than continue to engage the man as she
had in the airport, Gearhart decided to try something different—to engage in what we
suggest was invitational rhetoric: "I decided that what I would do was to try to approach
this man with something different . . . and so I began asking him about his life and
about the things that he did," seeking to understand his perspective and the reasons it
made sense to him. "In fact," Gearhart explains, "it was even worse than I had originally
thought. In fact, he was a chemist, and he had experimented on animals. He had grown
up as a hunter and, of course, all that is absolutely counter to the things that I believe."
But rather than attempting to convince him of the error of his ways, Gearhart continued
to listen to the man, and he did the same as she shared her own perspectives and
experiences with him.

The invitational rhetoric in which the two engaged brought Gearhart and the man
together, although neither one "had changed our original position." As the two crossed
paths for the third time in the parking lot, waiting for their respective rides, they started
walking toward each other. Gearhart finishes the story:

> I don't know which one of us did it first, but I guess maybe I flung open my arms and he
> flung open his arms and we came together in this terrific hug, both of us in tears, sobbing,
> crying like babies. I said, "You know, I don't know what has happened here, but my life has
> been totally changed after today." And he said, "My life is totally changed, too, and I don't
> know what's happened."

We suggest that what happened was that the two individuals had offered their
perspectives and listened to and acknowledged one another's perspectives in an

environment of safety, value, and freedom. Their communication thus invited understanding and brought them to a new place of awareness of and appreciation for one another. Gearhart's (1993) summary of the experience is an excellent summary of invitational rhetoric: "It's a way to disagree and at the same time not to hurt each other and to respect each other and to have, actually, something very close and tender."

We see the statement of Rich, Lorde, and Walker and Gearhart's interaction as invitational, then, in that both were rooted in the principles of equality, immanent value, and respect for others and validation of their perspectives. Rich, Lorde, and Walker offered a perspective and communicated its difference with that of the judges, but they neither sought adherence for it nor denigrated the different viewpoint of the judges. Gearhart also offered a perspective very different from that of her acquaintance and listened to one very different from her own without seeking adherence or pronouncing judgment. Each rhetor created conditions of safety, value, and freedom, contributing to an environment in which audience members were able to present their different perspectives. The result was an understanding on which relationships of equality and respect could be built.

Implications for Rhetorical Theory

The expansion of the notion of rhetoric to include invitational rhetoric has several implications for rhetorical theory. The introduction of invitational rhetoric into the scope of rhetorical theory challenges the presumption that has been granted to persuasion as the interactional goal in the rhetorical tradition. Identification and explication of a rhetoric not grounded in the intent to produce a desired change in others undermine the position of privilege accorded to efforts to influence in rhetoric. The existence of invitational rhetoric encourages the exploration of yet other rhetorics that do not involve this singular interactional goal.

A second implication is that invitational rhetoric may contribute to the efforts of communication scholars who are working to develop models for cooperative, non-adversarial, and ethical communication. Such a goal, for example, is espoused by Herrick (1992), in his discussion of the link between rhetoric and ethics, when he suggests "that a virtue approach to rhetorical ethics may provide the kind of flexible, yet directive, ethic needed" to maintain the democratic nature of a pluralistic social order (p. 147). Van Eemeren and Grootendorst (1992) also propose such a goal in their book on argumentation; their approach is designed to create an open and free exchange and responsible participation in cooperative, dialogic communication. The framework provided by invitational rhetoric may allow such theorists to achieve their laudatory missions more easily by contributing to a reconciliation of goals and means (Makau, in press). According to Herrick's and van Eemeren and Grootendorst's definitions of rhetoric as a process in which rhetors seek to secure the acceptance of their perspectives by others, rhetors tend to see their audiences as opponents and sometimes may be tempted to engage in questionable ethical practices to win their "battles" with them. Rules thus are required to contain the interaction that results from the use of such strategies. Invitational rhetoric may serve as a way to allow these scholars to develop models for interaction not characterized by the opposition and competition that make the achievement of their goal difficult.

The introduction of invitational rhetoric to the array of rhetorical forms available also serves a greater heuristic, inventive function than rhetoric previously has allowed. Traditional theories of rhetoric occur within preimposed or preconceived frameworks that are reflexive and reinforce the vocabularies and tenets of those frameworks. In rhetoric in which the rhetor seeks to impose change on others, an idea is adapted to the audience or is presented in ways that will be most persuasive to the audience; as a result, the idea stays lodged within the confines of the rhetorical system in which it was framed. Others may challenge the idea but only within the confines of the framework of the dispute already established. The inventive potential of rhetoric is restricted as the interaction converts the idea to the experience required by the framework.

Invitational rhetoric, on the other hand, aims at converting experience "to one of the many views which are indeterminately possible" (Holmberg, 1977, p. 237). As a result, much is open in invitational rhetoric that is not in traditional rhetorics— the potential of the audience to contribute to the generation of ideas is enhanced, the means used to present ideas are not those that limit the ideas to what is most persuasive for the audience, the view of the kind of environment that can be created in the interaction is expanded, and the ideas that can be considered multiply. The privileging of invention in invitational rhetoric allows for the development of interpretations, perspectives, courses of actions, and solutions to problems different from those allowed in traditional models of rhetoric. Rather than the discovery of how to make a case, invitational rhetoric employs invention to discover more cases, a process Daly (1984) describes as one of creating "an atmosphere in which further creativity may flourish. . . . [w]e become breathers/creators of free space. We are windy, stirring the stagnant spaces with life" (p. 18).

The inclusion of an invitational rhetoric in the array of rhetorics available suggests the need to revise and expand rhetorical constructs of various kinds to take into account the nature and function of this form. Invitational rhetoric suggests, for example, that the traditional view of the audience as an opponent ought to be questioned. It challenges the traditional conception of the notion of rhetorical strategies as means to particular ends in that in invitational rhetoric, the means constitute the ends. It suggests the need for a new schema of ethics to fit interactional goals other than inducement of others to adherence to the rhetor's own beliefs.

Finally, invitational rhetoric provides a mode of communication for women and other marginalized groups to use in their efforts to transform systems of domination and oppression. At first glance, invitational rhetoric may seem to be incapable of resisting and transforming oppressive systems such as patriarchy because the most it seems able to do is to create a space in which representatives of an oppressive system understand a different—in this case, a feminist—perspective but do not adopt it. Although invitational rhetoric is not designed to create a specific change, such as the transformation of systems of oppression into ones that value and nurture individuals, it may produce such an outcome. Invitational rhetoric may resist an oppressive system simply because it models an alternative to the system by being "itself an Other way of thinking/speaking" (Daly, 1978, p. xiii)—it presents an alternative feminist vision rooted in affirmation and respect and thus shows how an alternative looks and works. Invitational rhetoric thus may transform an oppressive system precisely because it does not engage that system on its own terms, using arguments developed from the system's framework or orientation. Such arguments usually are co-opted by the dominant system (Ferguson, 1984) and provide the impetus "to strengthen, refine, and embellish the original edifice," entrenching the system further (Johnson, 1989, pp. 16–17). Invitational rhetoric, in contrast, enables rhetors to disengage from the dominance and mastery so common to a system of oppression and to create a reality of equality and mutuality in its place, allowing for options and possibilities not available within the familiar, dominant framework.

Our interest in inserting invitational rhetoric into the scope of rhetorical theory is not meant to suggest that it is an ideal for which rhetors should strive or that it should or can be used in all situations. Invitational rhetoric is one of many useful and legitimate rhetorics, including persuasion, in which rhetors will want to be skilled. With the identification of the rhetorical mode of invitational rhetoric, however, rhetors will be able to recognize situations in which they seek not to persuade others but simply to create an environment that facilitates understanding, accords value and respect to others' perspectives, and contributes to the development of relationships of equality.

Sonja K. Foss is an associate professor of communication at Ohio State University.

Cindy L. Griffin is an assistant professor of speech communication at Colorado State University. A previous version of this essay was presented at the Speech Communication Association convention in Miami, Florida, in 1993. The authors wish to thank Sally Miller Gearhart, James F. Klumpp, Josina M. Makau, and Julia T. Wood for their contributions to the development of this essay.

References

Barrett, H. (1991). *Rhetoric and civility: Human development, narcissism, and the good audience.* New York: State University of New York Press.

Benhabib, S. (1992). *Situating the self: Gender, community and postmodernism in contemporary ethics.* New York: Routledge.

Buber, M. (1965). *Between man and man* (R.G. Smith, Trans.). New York: Macmillan.

Burke, K. (1984). *Attitudes toward history* (3rd ed.). Berkeley: University of California Press.

Burke, K. (1969). *A grammar of motives.* Berkeley: University of California Press.

Daly, M. (1978). *Gyn/ecology: The metaethics of radical feminism.* Boston: Beacon.

Daly, M. (1984). *Pure lust: Elemental feminist philosophy.* Boston: Beacon.

Edson, B.A. (1985). Bias in social movement theory: A view from a female-systems perspective. *Women's Studies in Communication, 8,* 34–45.

Elshtain, J.B. (1982). Feminist discourse and its discontents: Language, power, and meaning. *Signs, 7,* 603–621.

Ferguson, K.E. (1984). *The feminist case against bureaucracy.* Philadelphia: Temple University Press.

Ferguson, M. (1980). *The aquarian conspiracy: Personal and social transformation in the 1980s.* Los Angeles: J.P. Tarcher.

Forget, P. (1989). Argument(s). In D. Michelfelder & R. Palmer (Eds.), *Dialogue and deconstruction: The Gadamer-Derrida encounter* (pp. 129–149). Albany, NY: SUNY Press.

Foss, K.A., & Foss, S.K. (1991). *Women speak: The eloquence of women's lives.* Prospect Heights, IL: Waveland.

Foss, S.K., Foss, K.A., & Trapp, R. (1991). *Contemporary perspectives on rhetoric* (rev. ed.). Prospect Heights, IL: Waveland.

Foss, S.K., & Griffin, C.L. (1992). A feminist perspective on rhetorical theory: Toward a clarification of boundaries. *Western Journal of Communication, 56,* 330–349.

Gearhart, S.M. (1979). The womanization of rhetoric. *Women's Studies International Quarterly, 2,* 195–201.

Gearhart, S. (1982). Womanpower: Energy re-sourcement. In C. Spretnak (Ed.), *The politics of women's spirituality: Essays on the rise of spiritual power within the feminist movement* (pp. 194–206). Garden City, NY: Anchor.

Gearhart, S.M. (1993, January). [Videotaped interview with Sonja K. Foss and members of the Feminist Rhetorical Theory class, Ohio State University].

Gendlin, E.T. (1978). *Focusing.* New York: Everest.

Griffin, C.L. (1993). Women as communicators: Mary Daly's hagography as rhetoric. *Communication Monographs, 60,* 158–177.

Herrick, J.A. (1992). Rhetoric, ethics, and virtue. *Communication Studies, 43,* 133–149.

Holmberg, C. (1977). Dialectical rhetoric and rhetorical rhetoric. *Philosophy and Rhetoric, 10,* 232–243.

hooks, b. (1984). *Feminist theory: From margin to center.* Boston: South End.

Johnson, S. (1987). *Going out of our minds: The metaphysics of liberation.* Freedom, CA: Crossing.

Johnson, S. (1989). *Wildfire: Igniting the she/volution.* Albuquerque, NM: Wildfire.

Johnson, S. (1991). *The ship that sailed into the living room: Sex and intimacy reconsidered.* Estancia, NM: Wildfire.

Kramarae, C. (1989). Feminist theories of communication. In E. Barnouw (Ed.), *International encyclopedia of communications* (Vol. 2, pp. 157–160). New York: Oxford University Press.

Makau, J.M. (in press). [Review of *Argumentation, communication and fallacies: A pragma-dialectical perspective*]. *Philosophy and Rhetoric.*

Morton, N. (1985). *The journey is home.* Boston: Beacon.

Natanson, M. (1965). The claims of immediacy. In M. Natanson & H.W. Johnstone, Jr. (Eds.), *Philosophy, rhetoric and argumentation* (pp. 10–19). University Park: Pennsylvania State University Press.

Rich, A., Lorde, A., & Walker, A. (1994). A statement for voices unheard: A challenge to the National Book Awards. In S.K. Foss & K.A. Foss, *Inviting transformation: Presentational speaking for a changing world* (pp. 148–149). Prospect Heights, IL: Waveland. (Speech presented 1974)

Rogers, C.R. (1962). The interpersonal relationship: The core of guidance. *Harvard Educational Review, 32,* 416–429.

Rorty, R. (1986). Beyond realism and anti-realism. In L. Nagl & R. Heinrich (Eds.), *Wo steht die Analytische Philosophie heute?* (pp. 103–115). Vienna, Austria: Oldenbourg.

Scott, R.L. (1976). Dialogue and rhetoric. In J. Blankenship & H. Stelzner (Eds.), *Rhetoric and communication: Studies in the University of Illinois tradition* (pp. 99–109). Urbana: University of Illinois Press.

Scott, R.L. (1991). The necessary pluralism of any future history of rhetoric. *Pre/Text*, 12, 195–209.

Shepherd, G.J. (1992). Communication as influence: Definitional exclusion. *Communication Studies*, 43, 203–219.

Starhawk. (1987). *Truth or dare: Encounters with power, authority, and mystery.* San Francisco: Harper and Row.

Starhawk. (1988). *Dreaming the dark: Magic, sex and politics* (rev. ed.). Boston: Beacon.

Tracy, D. (1987). *Plurality and ambiguity: Hermeneutics, religion, hope.* San Francisco: Harper and Row.

van Eemeren, F.H., & Grootendorst, R. (1992). *Argumentation, communication and fallacies: A pragmadialectical perspective.* Hillsdale, NJ: Lawrence Erlbaum.

Veenendall, T.L., & Feinstein, M.C. (1990). *Let's talk about relationships.* Prospect Heights, IL: Waveland.

Walker, M.U. (1989). Moral understandings: Alternative "epistemology" for a feminist ethics. *Hypatia*, 4, 15–28.

Watzlawick, P., Weakland, J.H., & Fisch, R. (1974). *Change: Principles of problem formation and problem resolution.* New York: W.W. Norton.

Wood, J.T. (1993). Enlarging conceptual boundaries: A critique of research in interpersonal communication. In S.P. Bowen & N. Wyatt (Eds.), *Transforming visions: Feminist critiques in communication studies* (pp. 19–49). Cresskill, NJ: Hampton.

Wood, J.T. (1994). *Gendered lives: Communication, gender, and culture.* Belmont, CA: Wadsworth.

17.
BORDER CROSSINGS: INTERSECTIONS OF RHETORIC AND FEMINISM
Lisa Ede, Cheryl Glenn, and Andrea A. Lunsford[1]

Editors' Note: *This essay explores the intersections of rhetoric and feminism and the resulting transformations to both disciplines. Rhetoric offers feminism a vibrant process of inquiring, organizing, and thinking, while feminism offers rhetoric a reason to bridge differences, to include, and to empower. The rhetorical canons can emphasize the mutually heuristic nature of the border crossings between rhetoric and feminism. Although the canons are treated separately, they overlap and interact: arrangement, style, and delivery all assume a rethinking of invention and memory. Such careful attention to how these canons are deployed in feminist and rhetorical discourse urges continued interrogation and renewed responsibility for all discursive acts.*

> One quality or action is nobler than another if it is that of a naturally finer being: thus a man's will be nobler than a woman's.
>
> —Aristotle, *Rhetoric* I.9

> The work of *mestiza* consciousness is to break down the subject–object duality that keeps her a prisoner and to show in the flesh and through the images in her work how duality is transcended.
>
> —Gloria Anzaldúa, *Borderlands/La Frontera* 82

Standing at the Border

Western rhetoric began, or so one predominant disciplinary narrative tells us, as a response to disputes regarding property, regarding borders.[2] As language awareness became closely linked with the expedient workings of the newly democratic Syracuse, rhetoric flourished as a practical art, a vital part of civic life in this democracy fraught with a mass of litigation on property claims. Corax and Tisias, the heroes of this narrative, crossed borders to establish boundaries, pioneers armed only with an *enchiridion* of successful rhetorical practices.

After dedicating its early years to settling boundary disputes, rhetoric soon found itself submitting to the same kinds of boundarying. Unsettled by Plato's sound drubbing in the *Gorgias* and increasingly disarmed by philosophy's disvaluing, rhetoric has, for

Lisa Ede, Cheryl Glenn, and Andrea A. Lunsford. "Border Crossings: Intersections of Rhetoric and Feminism." *Rhetorica: The Journal of the International Society for the History of Rhetoric* XIII (Autumn 1995): 285–325.

much of its history, been viewed as either the codification of and instruction in discursive, persuasive practices or as a sophisticated system of tropes. But even within these bounds, rhetoric contained and remembered its power. In his *In Defence of Rhetoric,* Brian Vickers joins other twentieth-century scholars as he works to release that power and reemphasize rhetoric's central role in public discourse. As Vickers argues, the "conception of rhetoric as public debate in a society guaranteeing free speech, a debate in which both sides of the case are heard and those qualified to vote come to a decision binding on all parties, has much more to offer us . . . than Plato's equation of it with cosmetics, cookery, and other more disreputable arts designed, according to him, to satisfy base pleasures rather than promote knowledge."[3] Other scholars, such as Kenneth Burke, Samuel IJsseling, and Ernesto Grassi,[4] have interrogated philosophy's traditional disvaluing of rhetoric, exposing the willed misreadings that support such a view, and thus they have rehabilitated rhetoric's epistemic status and heuristic value across the disciplines. Rhetoric may well border other studies, but it is not necessarily circumscribed by them.

Thanks to both broad and deep shifts in our contemporary epistemological assumptions and practices—shifts that call into question what Jane Flax terms western culture's "Enlightenment story"—rhetoric's boundaries are no longer so clearly delimited or contested.[5] Indeed, as John Bender and David E. Wellbery note in *The Ends of Rhetoric: History, Theory, Practice,* "rhetorical inquiry, as it is thought and practiced today, occurs in an interdisciplinary matrix that touches on such fields as philosophy, linguistics, communication studies, psychoanalysis, cognitive science, sociology, anthropology, and political theory."[6] Each of us doubtless has his or her own response to Bender and Wellbery's list—and to the larger issue of appropriation that disciplinary border-crossing inevitably raises.[7] As teachers of writing and scholars of rhetoric, we note, for instance, the absence from this catalogue of both classics and composition studies, two fields of disciplinary inquiry whose borders often intersect with those of rhetoric. In this essay, however, we wish to focus on another disciplinary field whose borders have upon occasion intersected with those of rhetoric, but which still remain largely at the margins of rhetorical inquiry: feminism. More specifically, we explore the intersections of rhetoric and feminism—intersections that Gloria Anzaldúa might refer to as "the Borderlands/*La Frontera*."[8]

As a political movement—as resistance to patriarchal assumptions and practices—feminism is as old as, well, at least as old as Aphrodite. But as a self-conscious academic field of inquiry, feminism is more recent, its history having developed over the last thirty years. Although much feminist work is grounded in the humanities, considerable work in the social sciences and sciences has taken place.[9] Like rhetoric, feminism is both multidisciplinary—situated in multiple academic disciplines—and, in many instances at least, also interdisciplinary.[10] In spite of its multidisciplinarity and the inevitable accompanying methodological differences, the feminist project was, until the 1970s, marked by a strong degree of consensus. As Michele Barrett and Anne Phillips tell us in *Destabilizing Theory: Contemporary Feminist Debates,* "1970s feminism assumed that one could specify a *cause* of women's oppression. Feminists differed substantially (and fiercely) as to what this cause might be . . . but did not really question the notion of a cause itself. Nor was there any difficulty with the idea of *oppression,* which seemed to have self-evident application."[11]

Since that time, a number of factors have radically destabilized this consensus. African-American and third-world/postcolonial women writers have pointed out the extent to which feminism's claims for authority and representation rested upon racist and ethnocentric assumptions about women's nature and oppression; they have also charged feminism with ignoring the intersections of gender with race and class. Marianne Hirsch and Evelyn Fox Keller explored and documented such *Conflicts in Feminism* in their 1990 collection: Mary Childers and bell hooks held a "Conversation about Race and Class"; Elizabeth Abel asked (and answered) some cogent questions about "Race, Class, and Psychoanalysis"; and Jane Gallop, Hirsch, and Nancy K. Miller "Criticiz[ed] Feminist Criticism."[12] In addition, poststructuralist and postmodern theorists have also raised questions about many of feminism's traditional assumptions and practices. Theorists such as Carla Freccero, Amy Ling, Joan W. Scott, Elaine Showalter, and Gayatri Chakrovorty Spivak have characterized feminism (or certain strains of feminism) as relying upon individualist, rationalist, and universalist assumptions.[13] From such a perspective, feminism's traditional dream of freedom from oppression and equality for women appears complicitous with both Enlightenment and modernist narratives of individualism and progress.

As a result of such contemporary debates, those writing within feminism have increasingly been drawn to the term "feminisms," rather than "feminism," as a marker for their projects.[14] For purely stylistic reasons, we have chosen to use the singular form throughout this essay, yet we wish to acknowledge the extent to which feminism—like rhetoric, for that matter—is not only a construction but a place of contest and difference. Although both feminism and rhetoric have at times been represented as having continuous traditions and innocent encounters with others (peoples, disciplines, cultures), their situations are, of course, much more complex.

In "Towards a Transactional View of Rhetorical and Feminist Theory," Barbara A. Biesecker calls for "putting into contact the genius of Rhetoric and the (very different) genius of feminism."[15] In this essay, we attempt to respond to Biesecker's call as we inhabit and unsettle the conventionally understood borders between rhetoric and feminism. We hope that further engagement between these two disciplinary projects will be beneficial, but we cannot anticipate, much less predict, the consequences of ongoing dialogue—though we tend to agree with Biesecker, who suggests that the contact may "both uncramp the orthodoxy of rhetorical theory and advance the theory and practice of feminism."[16] We, too, see our project as encouraging the kind of border crossings that might allow both feminists and rhetoricians to reflect upon, and possibly even to reconsider, their disciplinary projects.

Canonical Mappings

Aristotle may well have been the first cartographer of western rhetoric; in the fourth century BCE, he charted the canons of invention, arrangement, and style for the edification and ease of his students. Together, his *Rhetoric* and Anaximenes' *Rhetorica ad Alexandrum* serve as baseline maps for the author of *Rhetorica ad Herennium* as well as for Cicero and Quintilian, all of whom added the dimensions of memory and delivery. Throughout the ages, then, this map of rhetoric has evolved. All maps are cultural artifacts that reveal value, and the value of the canons of invention, memory, arrangement, style, and delivery has remained uncontested—regardless of deviations in their forms and influence in varying historical eras. Whether studied separately or in truncated form, the canons today retain their "tendency toward completeness, interaction, and interdependence."[17]

As a result of their long history, the traditional rhetorical canons provide familiar guides for us as we attempt to explore the borderlands of rhetoric and feminism. We have chosen to use the canons to mark the sections of our essay not only because of their enthymematic familiarity, but also in order to emphasize the mutually heuristic nature of the border crossing that we envision for rhetoric and feminism. Feminist theories and practices pose interesting questions and challenges for traditional understandings of the canons. But the canons also help illuminate how much is at stake in feminism's scholarly and performative enterprise, providing a fertile context for exploring the radical nature and significance of contemporary feminist efforts.

As Burkean terministic screens, then, the canons provide a framework that enables us to gain new perspectives on both rhetoric and feminism by inhabiting their borders. But as is the case with all terministic screens, our framework entails certain limitations. Although the linearity of print demands that we treat the canons consecutively, we wish to call attention at the outset to their tendency to overlap and interact. As Kathleen Welch writes, in this regard the canons represent "the aspects of composing which work together in a recursive, synergistic, mutually dependent relationship,"[18] one we find particularly apt for the collaborative process we have enjoyed in composing this essay.

On Invention and Memory

[Invention] is the most important of all the divisions, and above all is used in every kind of pleading.

Cicero, *De inventione* 1.7.9

Now let us turn . . . to the custodian of all parts of rhetoric, memory.

Rhetorica ad Herennium 1.2.3

We begin our exploration by linking invention, the heart and soul of inquiry, with memory, the very substance of knowledge. Although these canons have, of course, traditionally been treated separately, with invention often relegated to the province of philosophy, and memory often ignored or deleted without comment, there seem to us to be compelling reasons for considering them together, not the least of which is the rich overlap between inquiring (*inventio*) and knowing (*memoria*), one that demonstrates interconnections and blurrings characteristic of all canonical boundaries. Sharon Crowley tells us that

> until the modern period, memory held a central place within rhetorical theory ... In ancient times even people who could write easily ... relied on their memories, not merely as storage facilities for particulars, but as structured heuristic systems. In other words, memory was not only a system of recollection ...; it was a means of invention.[19]

Even in the most traditional terms, then, the canon of invention leads the rhetor to search "in any given place [for] the available means of persuasion" and to use the topics and the *pisteis* to do so.[20] But additionally, the rhetor must surely rely heavily, in all searches, on *memoria*, for where else would the ancients have stored their commonplaces, their topics? Cicero tells us that the "structure of memory, like a wax tablet, employs places [*loci*] and in these gathers together images."[21] Thus memory ignites the process of invention. With the dominance of print over oral culture, however, memory became misremembered, and, eventually, associated not with the full powers of invention but with mere rote memorization.

Much important work of the last thirty-five years has sought to reclaim the canons of invention and memory for contemporary rhetoric. For invention, the work of James Kinneavy, Janice Lauer, Edward P. J. Corbett, Richard Young, Chaim Perelman and L. Olbrechts-Tyteca, and Burke has been particularly significant.[22] For memory, similar reclamation has been carried out by Mary Carruthers, Brian Stock, Fred Reynolds, Sharon Crowley, and Welch.[23] But even this contemporary work on invention and memory, though valuable, all too often focused on method, such as new ways of recovering information, locating topics, using heuristics, and building proofs, without acknowledging the degree to which these tools are themselves always situated within larger discursive and ideological systems that tend to valorize some methods while silently rejecting others.

From a postmodern perspective, invention and memory are hardly neutral methods but rather represent socially and historically constructed—and constructing—language games.[24] Like other games, more is at stake in acts of invention and memory than might first seem apparent, for invention and memory constrain and shape both who can know and what can be known. Consider, for instance, the frequent references (including our own) to such ancient Greek city-states as Syracuse as democracies. In order to identify Syracuse as a democracy—to remember this "fact" and to select it as an example and an "available means of persuasion"—the rhetor must accept as natural and commonsensical these city-states' exclusion of slaves and women from civic participation. Feminist efforts not only to remember these exclusions, but also to employ them in contemporary arguments about the nature and significance of western democracies, aim to expose the political and ideological assumptions that inevitably inform any act of invention or memory.

Before they could engage in this act of memory, invention, and argumentation— or at least before they could claim a public space for this engagement—feminists had to recognize, remember, and challenge traditional understandings of the rhetor, for until recently, the figure of the rhetor has been assumed to be masculine, unified, stable, autonomous, and capable of acting rationally on the world through language. Those who did not fit this pattern—women, people of color, poorly educated workers, those judged to be overly emotional or unstable—those people stood outside of the rhetorical situation, for they were considered neither capable of nor in need of remembering and inventing arguments. From a feminist vantage point, however, it is impossible to take the subjectivity of the rhetor for granted, impossible not to locate that subjectivity within the larger context of personal, social, economic, cultural, and ideological forces, impossible not to notice not only the context itself, but also who is absent from this context as well as what exclusionary forces (regarding knowledge and argument, for example) are at work there.

Equally challenged by this perspective is what counts as knowledge. In this regard, feminist theory has consistently challenged any public/private distinction, arguing that knowledge based in the personal, in lived experience, be valued and accepted as important and significant. In describing her own way of speaking and writing, of inventing, hooks says she must "incorporate . . . a sense of place, of not just who I am in the present but where I am coming from, the multiple voices within me. . . . When I say then that these words emerge from suffering, I refer to that personal struggle to name the location from which I came to voice."[25] Women have also sought to include the intuitive and paralogical, the thinking of the body, as valuable sources of knowing, as sites of invention. Lorde writes, "As women, we have come to distrust that power which rises from our deepest and nonrational knowledge. We have been warned against it all our lives by the male world, which values this depth of feeling enough to keep women around in order to exercise it in the service of men, but which fears this same depth too much to examine the possibilities of it within themselves."[26]

If in making these claims, contemporary feminists have implicitly sought to expand the canon of invention, they have often done so by linking it with memory, which Toni Morrison tells us is "a form of willed creation. It is not an effort to find out the way it really was. . . . The point is to dwell on the way it appeared and why it appeared in that particular way," which, she insists, is the province of *memoria*.[27] A brilliant example of Morrison's point about the relationship between invention and memory is readily available in the work of Isabel Allende, especially her *House of Spirits*. In this text, Allende weaves together past, present, and future events, resulting not in "individualistic autobiographical searchings [but in] revelations of traditions, re-collections of disseminated identities . . . [that] are a modern version of the Pythagorean arts of memory: retrospection to gain a vision for the future."[28] Hooks also comments on this intricate connection in a discussion of works such as the film *Freedom Charter* (which portrays the anti-apartheid movement in Africa) and Gloria Naylor's novel *Mama Day*. She notes that in these and other works, "fragments of memory are not simply represented as flat documentary but constructed . . . to move us into a different mode of articulation . . . [, a] remembering that serves to illuminate and transform the present."[29]

As this discussion indicates, as human beings we are both limited and empowered by our individual and collective memory and invention. This recognition spurred our interest in working collaboratively on this article, for we realized that any effort to inhabit the borderlands of feminism and rhetoric could only be enriched by such dialogue. We also quickly realized the centrality of invention and memory to conceptions of subjectivity and knowledge as well as to understandings of the other canons. We wish to emphasize, then, that the following discussions of arrangement, style, and delivery both assume and depend upon a rethinking of invention and memory—one that recognizes the role that both these canons play in current efforts to reconceptualize and reenact what it means to know, speak, and write.

On Arrangement

> A speech has two parts. You must state your case, and you must prove it.
>
> —Aristotle, *Rhetoric* III.13

Aristotle's cryptic injunction to arrange discourse into "two parts" was elaborated into a powerful, seven-part architectonic for the creation of ideas (*inventio*). Indeed, Cicero's adumbration and exploration of *exordium, narratio, partitio, confirmatio, reprehensio, digressio,* and *conclusio* established a highly flexible pattern for what Richard Enos calls "structuring compositions to the limits of the situation."[30] This structure has, in many respects, stood the test of 2500 years. Certainly it has worked well to realize the traditional ends of rhetoric: to deploy, in Aristotle's terms, "all the available means of persuasion,"[31] or in Burke's, to use "language as a symbolic means of inducing cooperation in beings that by nature respond to symbols."[32] In short, if speakers/writers wanted to "state a case and prove it," they would be hard pressed to find more effective ways of disposing their cases and proof than in this logical, linear chain aimed at persuasion.

Or so western writers have generally assumed. But what if what constitutes "your case" and "your proof" are not clear-cut, are instead themselves highly contested sites? And what if the traditional aim of persuasion, of winning over an audience, is also highly contested? What might such disruptions suggest for the venerable canon of arrangement? While few theorists of rhetoric or of feminism have addressed these questions directly and in quite these terms, many feminist scholars have approached them obliquely. In a widely-cited early article, for instance, Sally Miller Gearhart charges that rhetoric is based on a "conquest model" and that "any intent to persuade is an act of violence."[33] Over fifteen years later, Sonja Foss and Cindy Griffin elaborated Gearhart's claim, tracing the ways in which rhetoric's focus on winning has led to the dominance of several master narratives—of progress and exclusion, of subjection, of conversion.[34] All of these narratives, Foss and Griffin insist, invoke patterns of arrangement aimed at winning, at control.

Other scholars have noted the ways in which patterns of control are inscribed in seemingly innocuous conventions related to the arrangement of discourse, such as those governing endnote/footnote and works cited lists, all of which are relegated to the margins, to the periphery or very end of discourse. The text exerts its own univocal control, taking center stage and pushing beyond its borders the voices of others. Many women writers, such as Tillie Olsen, have sought to open up this textual space, to allow for the sharing of space and authority.[35] Perhaps no one on the contemporary scene has done so as consistently and consciously, however, as hooks. Early in her career, hooks chose to eschew the use of footnotes and to open up her text and her style to multiple voices. She has done so out of her belief that such discursive conventions are exclusionary, that they mark discourse "for highly educated, academic audiences only." Hooks aims instead to reach out, *sans* footnotes, to a very broad audience, "to speak simply with language that is accessible to as many folks as possible"—even if such practices lead critics to label her "anti-intellectual" and "unprofessional."[36]

But these narratives of control and exclusion, of subjection/winning, of conversion, no longer seem to encompass or to respond to many writers' goals. Consider the well-known case of literary critic Jane Tompkins, invited to contribute a critical response to the work of another scholar for the journal *New Literary History*. In traditional rhetorical terms, Tompkins' goal is clear: she should make her case, that the other scholar's essay is mistaken in its view of epistemology, and she should do so (as she puts it) by "using evidence, reasons, chains of inference, citations of authority, analogies, illustrations, and so on."[37] Tompkins does not want to do so, however, or to dispose her arguments in traditional form, for such a response ignores what she calls her "other voice," the one that is deeply in sympathy with the other scholar's goals, the one that wants to write about her feelings that the kind of academic discourse she is expected to write is a "straitjacket" she longs to throw off, the one that wants not to fight, not to "beat the other person down," not, in short, to *win*.[38] In rejecting the master narrative of triumphing over an opponent, Tompkins also eschews traditional patterns of arrangement, suggesting, at least indirectly, that the aim and the means of realizing the aim are inextricably linked. Instead, Tompkins opts for an alternation, and a dissonant juxtaposition, of her "two voices," concluding not on a note of victory or of traditional closure but of rage: "I can't strap myself psychically into an apparatus that will produce the right gestures when I begin to move. . . . This one time I've taken off the straitjacket, and it feels so good."[39]

Tompkins has not been alone in wishing to loosen the "straitjacket" of agonistic aims and patterns of discourse. Of the many feminists who have attempted to slip its holds (from Sappho to Mary Wollstonecraft and from Emily Dickinson to Lorde), we would like to call special attention to Margaret Fuller, the only woman admitted as an intellectual equal to the rarefied Transcendental Club of Ralph Waldo Emerson, Bronson Alcott, and other highly educated and influential mid-nineteenth-century Bostonians. In a detailed reading of Fuller's *Woman in the Nineteenth Century*, Annette Kolodny demonstrates the revolutionary nature of Fuller's rhetorical patterning.[40] In particular, Kolodny responds to Fuller's contemporary critic Orestes Brownson, who archly assessed Fuller's book to be "no book, but a long talk. . . . It has neither beginning, middle, nor end, and may be read backwards as well as forwards, and from the center outwards each way, without affecting the continuity of the thought or the succession of ideas. We see no reason why it should stop where it does, or why the lady might not keep on talking in the same strain till doomsday, unless prevented by want of breath."[41] Kolodny's essay demonstrates the epistemological and ideological grounds on which this judgment of incompetence rests. Fuller, herself thoroughly versed in classical and contemporary rhetoric and having developed a rhetoric class for women derived in part from a detailed and highly insightful reading of Richard Whately,[42] was perfectly capable of producing the rhetorical forms Brownson values. Rather, Kolodny shows, Fuller rejected the "authoritarianism of coercion and the manipulative strategies [of traditional forms] . . . endeavoring instead to create a collaborative process of assertion and response in which multiple voices could—and did—find a place." As Kolodny concludes, Fuller's use of a conversational and collaborative structural pattern, rather than one based on traditional ways of disposing an argument, led to her devaluation, one that still prevents our hearing the brilliant rhetorical lessons she had to teach. If we view Fuller from the perspective gained by standing on the borderlands of rhetoric and feminism, however, we may read her refusal to order her discourse in conventional ways not as a failure at winning a traditional argument but instead as a striking success at conducting "the inclusive, collaborative, and open-ended conversations"[43] she and many other women before and since have valued.

Learning to look anew at discourse that does not follow conventional patterns, that does not pursue a master narrative of subjection, can yield major insights for rhetoricians and theorists of rhetoric, as Kolodny has clearly shown. In the same way, we have much to gain by reexamining the traditional rhetorical drive toward closure, with its reliance on those structures that lead readers inevitably to an ending, that follow Aristotle's advice that discourse must have a beginning, a middle, and an end. In this regard, we also have much to gain by crisscrossing the borders of rhetoric and feminism, particularly in terms of long-standing feminist attempts to disrupt the linear orderliness of prose, to contain contradictions and anomalies, to resist closure. These goals have been pursued vigorously by Hélène Cixous, whose attempts at "writing the body" introduce disruptive forms that push against traditional patterns of discourse and closure.[44] Drawing on Cixous' work, Lynn Worsham argues that conventional standards of unity and coherence, standards that rely on linearity and closure, rest on a logic that is thoroughly masculine—but that alternative logics, those that value indeterminacy, nonclosure, and multiplicity of meanings, are also possible.[45]

Julia Kristeva is another theorist who has written extensively of alternative discursive possibilities. In "Women's Time," for example, Kristeva invokes a discursive attitude that could allow for, indeed invite, "parallel existence[s] . . . in the same historical time or even . . . interwoven one with the other."[46] This possibility of simultaneity and multiplicity offers, Suzanne Clark suggests, a "dialogic rhetoric,"[47] one based not on oppositions or conquest but on collaboration, relationality, and mutuality, one that "can interrupt the rigidities of language and open it to a subject in process, to the unsettling and nonlogical life of the body."[48] Kristeva's project, which resists the domination of sameness and order by offering a way to transform language from within, aims to provide a pathway through the crisis of modernity and away from the "colonizing discourse of mastery."[49] Ironically—especially in light of rhetoric's long association with democratic ideals—this discourse of mastery, so familiar to traditional rhetorical forms of arrangement and aim, is itself a great threat; in Kristeva's view, the future of political democracies will depend on their ability to include in material and practical as well as rhetorical ways all those within their borders. As Clark points out in a studied understatement, "There are high stakes involved in finding more inclusive forms of argument."[50]

If Cixous' and Kristeva's attempts to enact and to theorize alternative discursive possibilities are perhaps best known in academic circles, particularly in North America and Europe, many other writers are currently working to embody and arrange language in nontraditional and more inclusive ways. Within our own limited frame of reference, for example, we think in this regard of Lorde's open letter to Mary Daly, in which she explicitly rejects traditional hierarchical, linear patterns of argument in attempting a critique that is open, dialogic, accepting and, indeed, loving.[51] We also think of Patricia Williams' personalized and nonlinear analysis of the law in *The Alchemy of Race and Rights.*[52] And we think of Nobel prize winner Toni Morrison's remarkable use of nonlinear and multiplicitous orderings, and her refusal of closure, in *Beloved*[53]—and, more remarkably still, in her acceptance address for the Nobel award. Further examples abound, increasingly and importantly from third-world/postcolonial women writers such as Rigoberta Menchú, Marià Lugones, and Tey Diana Rebolledo.

As we hope these examples suggest, the borderlands of feminism and rhetoric offer provocative signposts toward a reexamination of the canon of arrangement. Drawing on rhetoric's (potential) plasticity, its attention to context, and its goal of finding discursive forms to meet the needs of particular audiences; and drawing on feminism's insights regarding the ideological freight and exclusionary result of many influential contemporary forms—as well as on women's long-standing attempts to create alternative discursive patternings—we may find our way toward a reimagined *dispositio,* one we may both theorize and enact.

On Style

The right thing in speaking really is that we should be satisfied not to annoy our hearers, without trying to delight them. . . . [N]evertheless the arts of language cannot help having a small but real importance, whatever it is we have to expound to others: the way in which a thing is said does affect its intelligibility. Not, however, so much as people think. All such arts are fanciful and meant to charm the hearer. Nobody uses fine language when teaching geometry.

—Aristotle, *Rhetoric* III.1

One has only to think of Aristotle's comments on style in the *Rhetoric* to be reminded of the extent to which style functions as a site of tension and contest within rhetoric. As readers will recall, in Book III Aristotle provides copious advice about style and delivery, but he does so with some ambivalence. For bordering Aristotle's emphasis on style—"it is not enough to know *what* we ought to say; we must also say it *as* we ought"[54]—is an anxiety about the extent to which language can be used to obscure and mislead, to play upon the emotions of the audience. As Aristotle notes, the speaker "must disguise his art and give the *impression* of speaking naturally and not artificially" (our emphasis).[55]

Inscribed in Aristotle's comments on style are a series of oppositions—between *res* and *verba,* reason and emotion, demonstration and persuasion, and fact and interpretation—that for centuries have troubled those working within the rhetorical tradition. An example from Corbett's *Classical Rhetoric for the Modern Student* provides a useful instance of one such difficulty. In this work, Corbett introduces his discussion of style by noting that "once arguments had been discovered, selected, and arranged, they had to be put into words. Words ... serve as the medium of communication between speakers or writers and their audience."[56] Corbett's definition of style is certainly conventional, but it nevertheless represents a potential dilemma for rhetoric. If ideas and arguments are separate from and prior to language, as Corbett's definition seems to suggest, then they are epistemologically foundational, and rhetoric, however necessary and helpful, is open to the charge of being "mere outward show for pleasing the hearer."[57] Aware of this potential difficulty, Corbett quickly modifies his opening statement, commenting that "one notion about style that needs to be erased at the outset is that style is simply 'the dress of thought.'"[58]

It is no accident, of course, that Corbett uses the derogatory—and gendered— phrase "dress of thought" to characterize undesirable views of rhetoric. As Susan Jarratt observes in *Rereading the Sophists: Classical Rhetoric Refigured*, "Both rhetoric and women ... [have been] trivialized by identification with sensuality, costume, and color—all of which are supposed to be manipulated in attempts to persuade through deception."[59] The history of rhetoric as a scholarly and pedagogical discipline, as well as a performative tradition, is marked by recurring tensions and oscillations as both theorists and rhetors have negotiated the relation of rhetoric, poetics, and logic—and in so doing have often challenged the centrality, and at times even the validity, of attention to style. Think of Plato's dismissal of rhetoric in the *Gorgias* as mere "pandering," akin to "cookery" and "beautyculture"[60]; of Ramus' bifurcation of invention and arrangement from style and delivery; and of the Royal Society's effort, reported by Thomas Spratt, to "reject all the amplifications, digressions, and swellings of style; to return back to the primitive purity, and shortness, when men deliver'd so many *things*, almost in an equal number of *words*."[61]

As feminists have noted, the "primitive purity" that the rejection of style entails has generally necessitated the exclusion of women from the rhetorical scene, for how could women, with their inferior reason and their involvement in the stylish, the embodied, and the material, hope to attain such rigorous rationality? But not only women have been excluded: inherent in rhetoric's internalized ambivalence about style is an anxiety about rhetoric's relationship with audience in general, particularly popular audiences. (For instance, Plato handily forces Gorgias to agree that "a popular audience means an ignorant audience."[62]) In her study of modernism and its unsettled relationship with "sentimental" literature—literature that transgresses modernist values both in its gendering and in its identification with popular audiences—Clark exposes the extent to which "modernism is both caught in and stabilized by a system of gendered binaries."[63] In such a situation, Clark asks, "What kind of subject or ethos may function [in discourse] with authority? What kind of relationship to the audience— what pathos—may be seen as legitimate?"[64]

Given rhetoric's own construction of (and construction within) similar binaries, these questions resonate with equal fullness for the rhetorical tradition, emphasizing that although rhetoric may desire to decenter style, style—as the material embodiment of the relationships among self, text, and world—resists such displacement. For though some writers (including a number of feminists) experience style primarily as technique, many others find that style raises powerful and difficult personal, political, and ethical issues. Acutely aware of the patriarchal nature of the western phallogocentric tradition, many feminist writers feel themselves to be in a double bind. In order to claim authority and agency, to function as subjects in the discursive arena and thus further feminism's emancipatory goals, some feminists choose (as we choose in this essay) to adhere to the stylistic conventions of traditional western discourse—conventions that sharply dichotomize the public and the private, that devalue personal experience in favor of "objective" facts, "rational" logic, and established authorities.

For many, however, Lorde's well-known dictum that "the master's tools will never dismantle the master's house" powerfully evokes the potential limitations of such an approach. For even when women employ the style of traditional argumentation, gender-related concerns and questions can and often do influence both the immediate and subsequent reception of their work. Consider, for instance, the case of Emma Goldman, the Russian-born American anarchist, lecturer, writer, and editor who achieved great notoriety in the United States from the 1890s to 1917. Although Goldman's politics were radical (she was a passionate anarchist and argued [among other things] in favor of free love and birth control), her argumentative style in many ways resembled "standard American rhetoric."[65] Nevertheless, Goldman often scandalized contemporary popular audiences, while intellectuals and critics—both then and now—have tended to dismiss her as sentimental and romantic.

Such a double bind was almost inevitable, Clark argues. As a speaker, Goldman's *ethos* and style of delivery violated the expectations of mass audiences, for Goldman "broke their most sacred codes of womanly behavior. She did not smile; she did not defer" as she uttered her passionately held and expressed ideas.[66] Goldman's more intellectual listeners and readers had different reservations; they found her lacking because her "language was not like the symbolist or modernist practice, not experimental."[67] In the "twentieth century . . . struggle over how emotion is to be regulated and distributed," modernism came down on the side of a refined aestheticism that favored irony and restraint, not passion.[68] Goldman resisted these (gendered) conventions, preferring to emulate such earlier American writers as Ralph Waldo Emerson— an unacceptable practice given modernism's critique of American romanticism. As a consequence, from a modernist perspective, Goldman occupied "the impossible position of the passionate woman."[69]

Goldman did succeed in creating a space for her words and ideas in her own time; and if she stirred controversy and strong response (a response that eventually led to her deportation to Russia), she "generated not only antagonists but also adherents."[70] Goldman's writing could not survive the critique of modernism, however, for her passion and her adherence to a once-revered Emersonian style was an embarrassment. Consequently, "under the regime of the new criticism, Goldman's connections to literary history became unspeakable, and forgotten."[71]

Mindful of the fate of Goldman and of the previously discussed Fuller, "the most forgotten major literary figure of her own times,"[72] a number of women have attempted to forge not only alternative styles but also alternative discourses. Perhaps one of the most radical such efforts is that of Daly, whose "coconjured" *Websters'* [sic]

First New Intergalactic Wickedary of the English Language[73] represents an attempt to "conceive of language itself as a fabric that was originally woven by women in conversation with one another."[74] In so doing, Daly often reclaims earlier meanings of words, giving back to the term "spinster," for instance, its significance as "a woman whose occupation is to spin."[75] Such projects are not without their own risks, however. After reading Daly's earlier *Gyn/Ecology: The Metaethics of Radical Feminism*[76] Lorde wrote "An Open Letter to Mary Daly," which questioned the sources of Daly's alternative vision for feminism, asking, among other things, why Daly's "goddess-images [are] only white, western-european, judeo-christian."[77] Lorde's letter is of interest not only for its suggestive treatment of arrangement, noted above, and its commentary on Daly's work, but also for its direct, dialogic, and invitational style. Rather than relying upon confrontational, agonistic strategies, Lorde employs personal disclosures, frequent addresses to readers, and questioning rather than critique or dismissal to convey her reservations about Daly's work. Lorde concludes her letter with these words:

> We first met at the MLA [Modern Language Association] panel, "The Transformation of Silence Into Language and Action." Shortly before that date, I had decided never again to speak to white women about their racism. I felt it was wasted energy, because of their destructive guilt and defensiveness, and because whatever I had to say might better be said by white women to one another, at far less emotional cost to the speaker, and probably with a better hearing. This letter attempts to break this silence.
>
> I would like not to have to destroy you in my consciousness. So as a sister Hag, I ask you to speak to my perceptions.
>
> Whether or not you do, Mary, again I thank you for what I have learned from you.
> This letter is in repayment.[78]

In this closing passage, Lorde fuses the public and the private, the personal and the political, using direct address, many first- and second-person pronouns, and personal reminiscence to demonstrate her gratitude and make connections that unsettle the traditional borders between speaker and listener.

We have already discussed the work of Cixous and Kristeva, continental writers who resist traditional western stylistic conventions of unity, coherence, linearity, and closure and whose texts challenge traditional distinctions between poetry and prose. In "If I Could Write This in Fire, I Would Write This in Fire," Jamaican Michelle Cliff similarly composes a text that offers stylistic explorations while occupying the borderlands between poetry and prose.[79] Her essay moves with poetic intensity from personal reflections to snatches of texts and remembered sayings, interweaving a sustained, though hardly traditional, critique of race relations in her country and abroad. In the closing paragraph, Cliff comments upon her writing and its relationship to her experience:

> There is no ending to this piece of writing. There is no way to end it. As I read back over it, I see that we/they/I may become confused in the mind of the reader: but these pronouns have always co-existed in my mind.... I am Jamaica is who I am. No matter how far I travel—how deep the ambivalence I feel about ever returning. And Jamaica is a place in which we/they/I connect and disconnect—change place.[80]

Other writers, such Anzaldúa and Sandra Cisneros,[81] portray the various stylistic borderings they inhabit by blending English, Spanish, and "Spanglish" throughout their fiction and essays; in so doing, they not only portray the multiple realities through which they live and write, but also provide opportunities for others to experience such multiplicities.

A number of feminists in the United States have enacted yet another form of stylistic resistance to conventional expectations. These (largely academic—and tenured) writers compose what literary critic Miller terms "personal criticism," criticism that engages, rather than distances, the writer's experiences.[82] Such criticism, Miller argues, represents an intervention into contemporary cultural and theoretical practices, and it does so at the level of style: "[B]y turning its authorial voice into spectacle, personal writing theorizes the stakes of its own performance ... Personal writing opens an inquiry on the cost of writing—critical writing or Theory—and its effects."[83]

Not all feminists agree with Miller's assessment of the value of the personal style or with Daly's effort to create a language free of patriarchal influence. In "Surviving to Speak New Language: Mary Daly and Adrienne Rich," Jane Hedley argues that Daly's efforts to construct a feminist discourse are ultimately totalizing, "*self*-contextualizing and autotelic to a quite remarkable degree."[84] Many postmodern feminists are also suspicious of efforts to develop more personally grounded forms of criticism, believing that such efforts reinscribe the western tradition's emphasis on individualism and authenticity, while feminists of color such as hooks and Trinh T. Minh-ha challenge the ease with which many white feminists have felt comfortable representing (or, from hooks's and Trinh's perspectives, ignoring or misrepresenting) the experiences of others. Even recent attempts on the part of feminists to acknowledge the extent to which feminism has ignored race and class and to affirm what Rich terms a "politics of location" often have the effect, critics such as hooks argue, of "recentering the white authorial presence."[85]

For these and other reasons, in contemporary feminism, few issues are as contentious as issues of style. While some feminists engage in agonistic arguments about the disadvantages and advantages of experimental efforts such as those of Kristeva and Cixous and of personal criticism as practiced by Tompkins and Miller, others focus their inquiry on the difficulty of writing itself. In *Woman, Native, Other,* for instance, Trinh calls for feminists to embrace "a practice of language which remains, through its signifying operations, a process constantly unsettling the identity of meaning and speaking/writing subject, a process never allowing I to fare without non-I."[86] In the context of such a practice, style marks the borderland where conflicting ideological, cultural, political, and other forces important to both rhetoric and feminism contend.

On Delivery

[Delivery] is, essentially, a matter of the right management of the voice to express the various emotions.... Those who bear [delivery] in mind ... usually win prizes in the dramatic contests; and just as in drama ... so it is in the contests of public life, owing to the defects of our political institutions.

—Aristotle, *Rhetoric* III.1

Aristotle's barest outline of the canon of delivery emphasized "the three things—volume of sound, modulation of pitch, and rhythm—that a speaker bears in mind." Fully aware of rhetoric as public display, as performance art, as the one-time demonstration before a judge and jury, Aristotle lamented rhetoric's "unworthy" yet necessary concern with the delivery of "appearances." After all, we should "fight our case with no help beyond the bare facts: nothing . . . should matter except the proof of these facts." But "owing to the defects of our hearers" (that is, to the defects of our humanness), "we must pay attention to the subject of delivery . . . because we cannot do without it."[87]

Theophrastus, Aristotle's successor as head of the Peripatetic School, later elaborated and codified this canon, dividing delivery into matters of voice and gesture—or action—and providing rules for each. His now-lost but influential *On Delivery* informed rhetoric throughout antiquity, as numerous texts attest. The author of *Rhetorica ad Herennium* details delivery's "exceptionally great usefulness,"[88] for example, and Cicero addresses delivery in *De oratore* as "the dominant factor in oratory; without delivery the best speaker cannot be of any account at all, and a moderate speaker with a trained delivery can often outdo the best of them."[89] Delivery is presented in *Brutus* as that element of rhetoric that "penetrates the mind, shapes, moulds, turns it,"[90] and in the *Orator* as a "sort of language of the body."[91] Quintilian notes that "the nature of the speech we have composed within our minds is not so important as the manner in which we produce it, since the emotion of each member of our audience will depend on the impression made upon his hearing."[92] And both Cicero and Quintilian took apparent pleasure in recounting Demosthenes' memorable response when asked to list the three most important components of rhetoric: "Delivery, delivery, delivery."[93]

Delivery remains vital to rhetoric, given that it is, indeed, the culmination of the composing process, the combination and culmination of all five canons. Whether written, oral, or visual/aural (electronic), each rhetorical act culminates in delivery. Just as the ancient teachers went to great lengths to teach their students rhetorical effectiveness, so, too, have all students, from antiquity to this postmodern era, hoped to inhabit rhetorical power. In writing this essay, for example, we aimed throughout at effective delivery. Just a glance at the lengthy annotated footnotes, the copious examples (our artistic and nonartistic proofs), and our use of time-honored sources indicates how thoroughly we three academic women have attempted to embody the traditional delivery medium of the professional academic essay. Our introduction with its aims of establishing good will, common ground, and good sense; our presentation of topic and explanation of methodology; the very linearity of our argument, in which we use the canons of rhetoric as organizing principles—all these strategies comprise the public performance, the appearance before and attention to a university-trained, international audience, all of whom have easy familiarity with the delivery system represented by an academic journal.[94]

But our ability to enter this arena of public academic discourse and to deliver our message is utterly dependent on one crucial item: access not only to the conventions regarding delivery but also to the system of delivery itself. Cicero conflates delivery with the "language of the body,"[95] making us particularly conscious of the privilege we enjoy since, as Biesecker (among others) notes, "Rhetoric is a discipline whose distinctive characteristic is its focus on *public* address, a realm to which women as a class have historically been denied access."[96] Indeed, for most of the history of rhetoric in the western world, women generally could not have entered the public arena as we have here. Most women have been closed out of a rhetorical tradition of vocal, public, and, therefore, privileged men, silenced by force and by means of their educations. Nevertheless, women have not been excluded entirely from effective communication.

Those whose work we will note here represent only a fraction of the largely as-yet unexplored number of women who have turned to alternative, often private, forms of delivery (in secondary sources, mystical visions, autobiographies, translations, letters, lists, prose-poems, teachings, humor, and recordings by educated males).[97] First of all, these women had to gain access to a medium of delivery; then they most often found themselves altering that medium in whatever ways would allow them to speak (through the writings of others, for example), even if those voices reached no attentive audience for centuries. Other women reached a highly educated audience only by translating, filtering their erudition through the words of men. Still others, those who took hold of a system designed for men, shaped the traditionally masculine medium of oral delivery to their own advantage and pushed the boundaries of platform rhetoric to include a broader listening audience. Although largely ignored until very recently, the rhetorical deliveries of these women have ultimately proved as powerful and long-lasting as traditionally masculine displays.[98]

By means of secondary sources, fifth-century BCE Aspasia of Miletus, for example, provides one of the earliest examples of women's use of alternative delivery methods: her work has been delivered to us by the way of men's writing, for none of Aspasia's work exists in primary sources.[99] Aspasia's reputation as both a rhetorician and philosopher, as well as the text of her various speeches, have been preserved by men.[100] Given the cultural constraints that limited her, Aspasia used the only media of delivery available—that is, media employed by men. The most important of her compositions may well be Pericles' Funeral Oration, a moving, patriotic epideictic that the Platonic Socrates recites from memory in the *Menexenus*.[101] Although we have no access to her original text, the Platonic version (an exaggerated encomium abounding with historical misstatements and anachronisms) aligns well with the Platonic Aspasia's opinions on the efficacy of rhetoric: "It is by means of speech finely spoken that deeds nobly done gain for their doers from the hearers the meed of memory and renown."[102] This version of Pericles' Funeral Oration also aligns with Aspasia's reputation as rhetorician, philosopher, and influential colleague in the Sophistic movement, a movement devoted to the analysis and creation of rhetoric—and of truth. Aspasia's oral text, delivered to us in the print medium of secondary sources, not only provides a compelling demonstration of rhetoric's potential to create belief, but perhaps just as important, her dispersed but still powerful text has at last reached an appreciative audience.[103]

In old age, illiterate medieval mystic Margery Burnham Kempe (1373—c.1439) used the oral system of delivery to dictate the story of her life to scribes. *The Book of*

Margery Kempe, left unidentified until five hundred years after it was written, recounts the trials and triumphs of her worldly and spiritual pilgrimages, gives voice to the silent, middle-class, uneducated woman, and appears to be the earliest extant autobiography in the English language.[104] Despite her lack of formal literacy and training, Kempe located herself within the particular discourse of Franciscan affective piety, where she could self-consciously author and own the story of her life, create her self, record her spiritual development, and, most importantly, validate her life and her mystical visions.[105] Kempe knew well the power of the written word, so she attached herself to the oral component of that written word, studying (listening to and memorizing) with a priest until she became literate—without being able to read and write (without being text-dependent). And her employment of an amanuensis enabled her to leave a written record of her oral deliveries, a written record intended, no doubt, for oral performance or delivery. Thus, her *Book* is Kempe's unique inscription of rhetorical practice and delivery. It demonstrates the way in which one woman, denied ready access to the print medium, refracted her oral discourse through a scribe and sent her message down to us.

Renaissance intellect Margaret More Roper (1504–44), daughter of Thomas More, delivers her rhetorical skill in her translation of Erasmus' *Devout treatise upon the Pater noster* (1524). Considered derivative, defective, and muted, the feminine art of translation posed no threat to the masculine art of composition—not even when the translation itself became a major intellectual influence. Roper's translation remains one of the earliest examples of the Englishing of Erasmian piety; in addition, it broke new ground as part of a broad campaign directed at the English-reading public in that it domesticated and disseminated Erasmus' view of the devotional life. Translations provided Roper an outlet for her rhetorical skills and a measure of intellectual and religious influence—but only because she chose decorously to conceal her voice and identity as a writer in the work of a known and accepted author, only because she delivered her thoughts through the words of men, within the constraints of womanly modesty, piety, and humility.

Like Kempe, Sojourner Truth (1797–1883) remained illiterate all her life, though she drew deep from the wellsprings of oral tradition, delivering her own words through her own body. This former slave commanded large audiences whenever she spoke to the two most crucial political and social issues of her day: slavery and suffrage. At a time when the science of voice, gesture, and elocution were all the rage in rhetorical circles, at a time when (white) women's presence at a pulpit, a podium, a platform, or the bar was often illegal (the presence of a black woman would have been unimaginable), Truth's rhetoric of practicality shot through the fog of belletristic display. Like Kempe, she, too, appropriated the medium of oral delivery to her own end. Indeed, in contrast to most contemporary oral delivery, Truth made use of simple, straightforward language in an attempt to reach the broadest possible audience, fusing her simple style with her simple delivery. As Suzanne Pullon Fitch notes, Truth's "use of the simple language of the uneducated, which she could weave into striking narrative and metaphors, her nearly six-foot frame that revealed the strength developed working as a farmhand and house maid, and her powerful low voice telling of her denied rights as a woman and an African-American made her one of the most forceful instruments of reform."[106] Truth's physical bearing, enhanced by her use of simple language and memorable stories, helped her reach her goal, that of a more inclusive audience engagement and participation.

How different the "plain style" delivery of this woman was from the formal rhetorical delivery so common among nineteenth-century American public speakers, nearly all of whom were males. So memorable (and perhaps threatening) was this alternative rhetorical display—in terms of her style, her delivery, her arrangement, and her subject—that one pro-slavery newspaper wrote: "She is a crazy, ignorant, repelling negress, and her guardians would do a Christian act to restrict her entirely to private life."[107] Yet this "ignorant" woman continued in the public sphere, exhorting note-taking college students to "put their notes in their heads"[108] and parlaying her illiteracy into stylized delivery: "You know, children, I don't read such small stuff as letters, I read men and nations. I can see through a millstone, though I can't see through a spelling-book. What a narrow idea a reading qualification is for a voter! I know and do what is right better than many big men who read."[109] On these and many other occasions, Truth clearly practiced Cicero's dictum for delivery as the "language of the body." Still, hers was an alternative delivery, the only practice available for an illiterate, slave-class, black woman, particularly a woman who wanted to transform hostile and separatist audiences with a rhetoric of inclusion.

Truth is only one in a long tradition of women who have attempted to appropriate conventional oral delivery to their own ends. If we turn to contemporary America for another example, we might well point to the former governor of Texas, Ann Willis Richards, who, like Truth, uses oral delivery—valorized speech and language—to seek out, speak, and listen to new voices. In the United States, Richards, perhaps best known for her 1988 keynote address to the Democratic National Convention, participates fully in public, political, argumentative, powerful rhetoric—rhetoric in our most traditional(ly masculine) sense.

But her participation is on her own terms, that of a woman, a feminist, who easily conflates the public with the private, inviting more and more people into her audience. If a commonplace in feminist theory is the link between where one stands—and delivers—in society and what one perceives, then feminist Richards self-consciously enters the political arena, perceiving with great clarity not only her own position but that of male privilege. Ever-mindful of her audience, Richards carefully avoids elitism, agonism, and paternalism, enacting, instead—in her platform delivery—a fierce "maternalism" that embraces her constituents. From the platform, she reads letters from the disempowered and downtrodden. From the platform, she testifies to the benefits of inclusion, cooperation, and connection, qualities often associated with the feminine. From the platform, she reaches out to all women who worry about their families and children, to all grandmothers who want life to promise steady improvements for their generations, to all feminists who join Richards in hoping that her granddaughter Lily may never believe "that there was a time when blacks could not drink from public water fountains, when Hispanic children were punished for speaking Spanish in the public schools and women couldn't vote."[110] She delivers all these messages with homely examples (a staple of platform rhetoric) and common sense (one of her favorite lines is, "Tell it so my Mama in Waco can understand it"). As she fuses her style with her delivery, she transforms her politics through her female body, and she speaks from the borderlands of women in politics—all to the advantage of her rhetorical power.

In addition to providing us an example of (traditionally masculine) delivery informed by feminine/feminist ethics, Richards also exemplifies an oral delivery inscribed in and by different media. With (seemingly) full access to all systems of delivery, Richards speaks aloud from her written text to a "live" audience as well as to the audiences who hear her on the radio, watch and listen to her on television, and read excerpts from her speech in the newspaper—a merger of electronic, written, and oral media.

With this electronic delivery comes electronic writing, a new means of delivering text and graphics that offers another productive space within which rhetoric and feminism may work. At least some electronic media, such as hypertext, seem to allow for feminist concerns of inclusion, participation, and dialogue, and here we find the potential, at least, to allow full audience engagement in the establishment of the text itself. For example, in hypertext software designed for MacIntosh platforms, Deena Larsen offers *Marble Springs*,[111] a hypothetical space in nineteenth-century Colorado populated by many women. Primarily a collection of poetry written by and about the women of Marble Springs and detailing their many contributions to the town's history and development, the texts of *Marble Springs* can be rewritten, revised, and added to by the hypertext user. Thus like all hypertext, and electronic media in general, *Marble Springs* holds out the promise of an inclusionary rhetoric. But like all systems of delivery, electronic rhetoric also harbors the threat of exclusion, as George Landow's dystopic vision of the fate of writers in such a world makes alarmingly clear.[112] If the electronic medium establishes itself as the major delivery system of the next century, then rhetoricians and feminists together must continue to examine the power relations of its rhetorical situation: Who gets to speak/write? Who gets to listen? Who gets to rewrite? How many of us will have material access to the electronic media and to all their concomitant delivery systems?

Just as the history of rhetoric cannot be written from rhetoric books alone, neither can the canon of delivery be theorized beyond the point of successful practice. As we hope this discussion has revealed, border-crossings between rhetoric and feminism can help us better to appreciate the power of past practices. In looking to present and future practices, we have suggested that when rhetoric and feminism come together, as in this interrogation of the canon of delivery, both are transformed. Rhetoric, a vibrant process of inquiring, organizing, and thinking, offers a theorized space to talk about delivery. And feminism offers a reason to "bridge differences (rather than to create them), to include (rather than to exclude), and to empower (rather than to seek power or weakness)."[113] So when our discussion of delivery includes theories and artifacts that represent both the traditions of agonism, confidence, and competitiveness as well as more recently embodied examples of inclusion, cooperation, and identification, and when we put these influential feminine voices in dialogue with traditionally masculine deliveries, we move beyond a rhetoric of masculine privilege to a transformed rhetorical practice. Standing on the borderlands of rhetoric and feminism allows us to imagine a much wider, much more inclusive range of successful deliveries and fruitful border-crossings.

Conclusion

> The duty of rhetoric is to deal with such matters as we deliberate upon without arts or systems to guide us.
>
> —Aristotle, *Rhetoric* 1.2

> Culture forms our beliefs. We perceive the version of reality that it communicates. Dominant paradigms, predefined concepts that exist as unquestionable, unchallengeable, are transmitted to us through the culture.
>
> —Gloria Anzaldúa, *Borderlands/La Frontera* 16

In taking this *excursus* among the rhetorical canons, we have been especially conscious of our central metaphor—the borderlands (*la frontera*) of rhetoric and feminism. For us, this metaphor has been most powerful in its nuanced indeterminacy, its quiet reminder that borderlands shift and overlap, that they are, as Anzaldúa notes, in "a constant state of transition."[114] Indeed, as our discussion of the rhetorical canons has demonstrated, their borders also inevitably blur. At one point in working on this essay, we found ourselves disagreeing, to cite just one instance, as to whether we should discuss as style or delivery the dissonance between Goldman's presentation of public self (her refusal to smile, to defer) and the gendered expectations of her popular lecture audiences. How can it be possible to separate style from delivery, we wondered, when both are so intimately connected with the rhetor's subjectivity and *ethos* and with the specifics of the particular rhetorical situation? We thus found relevant to our experience in composing this essay Trinh's insight that "despite our desperate, eternal attempts to separate, contain, and mend, categories always leak."[115] Such leakage is, we believe, not only inevitable but helpful, for it reminds us that categories—and their boundaries and borderlands—are "sites of historicized struggles."[116]

In some of these historical moments, rhetoric and feminism have had few if any intersections. As the headnote from Aristotle's *Rhetoric* that begins this essay indicates, rhetoric was constituted as a patriarchal, exclusionary discipline, and it remained so for centuries. When Aristotle, Cicero, Quintilian, and Augustine considered the nature and province of rhetoric, they did not imagine that women—or those gendered feminine by their race, class, psychology, or other characteristics—might wish or be able to employ what Aristotle terms "the available means of persuasion" to communicate their ideas. As our discussion indicates, however, those whom rhetoric has gendered as "Other" have, nevertheless, employed strategies that those working within the rhetorical tradition have recognized as "rhetoric" to form, shape, and express their ideas.

In our contemporary historical moment, feminism and rhetoric stand, along with a number of other disciplines, amid a rich and intricate landscape—a landscape that postmodern and poststructural critique has complicated with its skeptical probings. In such a landscape, congruences as well as dissimilarities between rhetoric and feminism appear. Both fields, for example, place high value on *process*, as the longevity and influence of the canons and feminism's persistent commitment to working through to an understanding rather than to (premature) closure both demonstrate. In both fields, this focus on process signals a larger commitment to linking theory with practice, to recognizing and valuing local and applied knowledges. And both fields share a long-standing concern for public values and the public good, for creating spaces within which human subjectivities, at least potentially, can be realized, celebrated, and expanded.

Both fields have also demonstrated, it goes without saying, that they are capable of both conscious and unconscious hierarchies and exclusions, that they are, as Burke so eloquently indicates, "rotten with perfection."[117] We have already discussed feminism's belated recognition of the extent to which its scholarly and political project excludes women of color. As feminist theory has gained academic respectability—as scholars who viewed themselves as radical in the 1970s and 1980s have become tenured professors in the 1990s—a number of feminists, such as Kolodny, have become concerned that "Respectability Is Eroding the Revolutionary Potential of Feminist Criticism."[118] And feminists have been forced to recognize that they can be as agonistic, as competitive, as the most traditionally masculinist academic. In Gallop, Hirsch, and Miller's "Criticizing Feminist Criticism," for instance, Miller describes a particular vehement public attack on her work and her resulting recognition that she had "learned to fear other women in a way [she] hadn't done until that point."[119]

At the level of practice, then, feminists have become increasingly aware of the need to develop an ethics of communication. Such an ethics would also address an urgent theoretical question of concern to many contemporary feminists: how to justify and forward feminism's scholarly and political project given postmodern and poststructural skepticism about traditional humanistic argumentation. Once aware, as Judith Butler notes, that "the subject who theorizes is constituted as a 'theorizing subject' by a set of exclusionary and selective procedures,"[120] feminists must acknowledge the interestedness and situatedness of their own discourse. As a consequence, they must address, rather than evade, the question of rhetoric.

In *Thinking Fragments*, for instance, Flax begins her last chapter with this statement:

> A fundamental and unresolved question pervading this book is how to justify—or even frame—theoretical and narrative choices (including my own) without recourse to "truth" or domination. I am convinced we can and should justify our choices to ourselves and others, but what forms these justifications can meaningfully assume is not clear to me.[121]

As a tradition that has for centuries concerned itself with the question of how rhetors can and should justify their choices, rhetoric has, we believe, much to offer contemporary feminist theory and practice. For as our discussion of the canons has, we hope, indicated, rhetoric offers a rich conceptual framework and terminology that could prove heuristic as feminists attempt to probe and articulate these and other concerns. As Susan Brown Carlton notes, rhetoric could enable feminists to reconstruct what many have experienced as a contentious "philosophical impasse as a map of rhetorical options available for voicing the feminist stance."[122]

Rhetoric would also benefit, we believe, if the borderlands between rhetoric and feminism were more fully explored. Mining the borders of feminism and rhetoric would seem to offer intriguing interconnections and new ratios among *logos, pathos,* and *ethos,* ones that would expand the province of rhetorical proof and hence speak to and with wider and more diverse audiences. In insisting on the value of the local, the personal, the private, the mythic, for example, Anzaldúa's discourse embodies a set of proofs that transcends dualisms by embracing multiple understandings. The complex processes of knowing that Anzaldúa's work enacts (and invites) resituate proofs so that, as Lata Mani observes, "The relation between experience and knowledge is now seen to be not one of correspondence but one fraught with history, contingency, and struggle."[123]

In addition, sustaining a position on the borderlands of rhetoric and feminism holds promise of more complex and multiplicitous understandings of human communication, of how meanings arise and are inscribed. From this vantage point, the angles of the rhetorical triangle—speaker, hearer, text—become shape-shifters, three-dimensional and elastic points of contact, of location. Discussing this elasticity in another context, Michele Wallace describes the movement involved in this way of apprehending the world not as one of fixed stances (as writer *or* reader, for example), but as self-consciously "travelling from one position to another, thinking one's way from one position to another" and back again.[124]

Perhaps most importantly, Anzaldúa's *mestiza* borderland consciousness may create a space for public discourse that is inclusive, that accepts difference and Others, as Kristeva, Spivak, and hooks insist it must, without colonizing and also without shutting down exchange. Such an effort calls for considerable self-reflectiveness, a self-reflectiveness that requires rhetors to "become accountable for . . . [their] own investments in cultural metaphors and values," as well as a willingness to experiment, to take risks.[125] It also calls, as hooks wisely observes, for the continuing recognition that "it is not just important what we speak about, but how and why we speak."[126] As this essay has argued, from a perspective that borders rhetoric and feminism, attention to "what we speak about" and "how and why we speak" urges all of us not only to continued exploration and interrogation but also to a renewed responsibility for our professional and personal discursive acts.

Notes

1 In addition to the many voices of rhetoricians and feminists that animate our text, we are particularly grateful to Danielle Mitchell, who graciously, expertly—and valiantly—helped us prepare this manuscript for publication. We also thank Jean Williams, Melissa Goldthwaithe, and Jennifer Cognard-Black for their heroic long-distance research. Finally, we thank Jon Olson for his careful and astute readings as this essay took shape.

  Please note that the alphabetical listing of our names represents one attempt to resist the privileging of a "first" author and indicates the degree to which the thinking about and writing of this essay have been equally shared and thoroughly collaborative throughout.

2 We are aware that many historians of rhetoric challenge the foundational stories of western rhetoric
   (Richard Enos, *Greek Rhetoric before Aristotle* [Prospect Heights, IL: Waveland, 1993]; Cheryl Glenn,
   Rhetoric Retold: Regendering the Tradition from Antiquity through the Renaissance [Carbondale:
   Southern Illinois University Press, forthcoming]; Susan Jarratt, *Rereading the Sophists: Classical
   Rhetoric Refigured* [Carbondale: Southern Illinois University Press, 1991]; Jasper Neel, *Plato,
   Derrida, and Writing* [Carbondale: Southern Illinois University Press, 1988]; Takis Poulakos,
   Rethinking the History of Rhetoric [Boulder: Westview, 1993]; C. Jan Swearingen, *Rhetoric and Irony*
   [New York: Oxford University Press, 1991]; Victor Vitanza, *Writing Histories of Rhetoric* [Carbondale:
   Southern Illinois University Press, 1994]; Kathleen Welch, *The Contemporary Reception of Classical
   Rhetoric* [Hillsdale, NJ: Erlbaum, 1990]; and many others).
       Jane Sutton, for example, counters this story with "a scene in history when the earth was young
   and the Amazon ruled, [allowing] no Tyrant to direct the affairs of society" ("The Taming of
   the *Polos/Polis*: Rhetoric as an Achievement without Woman," *Southern Communication Journal*
   57 [Winter 1992]: 99–100). Sutton goes on to relate the Amazon story to Aphrodite and to link
   rhetoric's beginning to Aphrodite's female entourage, thus offering an intriguing parallel between
   the Amazonian myth and the story of Corax and Tisias, in both of which the hero(ine)s slay
   the Tyrant.
3 (Oxford: Clarendon-Oxford, 1988), p. viii.
4 See Burke, *A Rhetoric of Motives* (Berkeley: University of California Press, 1950); IJsseling, *Rhetoric
   and Philosophy in Conflict: An Historical Survey*, trans. Paul Dumphy (The Hague: Martinus Nijhoff,
   1976); and Grassi, *Rhetoric and Philosophy: The Humanist Tradition* (University Park and London:
   The Pennsylvania State University Press, 1980).
5 In *Thinking Fragments: Psychoanalysis, Feminism, and Postmodernism in the Contemporary West*
   (Berkeley: University of California Press, 1990), pp. 30–31, Flax populates the "Enlightenment"
   story with "major themes and characters": (1) a coherent, stable self (the author); (2) a distinctive
   and privileged mode of story-telling—philosophy (the critic and judge)—and a particular notion
   of "truth" (the hero); (3) a distinctive political philosophy (the moral) that posits complex and
   necessary interconnections among reason, autonomy, and freedom; (4) a transparent medium of
   expression (language); (5) an optimistic and rationalist philosophy of human nature (character
   development); and (6) a philosophy of knowledge (an ideal form).
6 (Stanford: Stanford University Press, 1990), p. vii.
7 Dwight Conquergood ("Rethinking Ethnography: Toward a Critical Cultural Politics,"
   Communication Monographs 58 [June 1991]: 179–98) observes that boundaries and borderlands
   pose multiple possibilities, not all of which are positive. Using the situation of refugees as a trope
   for the multiple possibilities inherent in borders, he notes that "with displacement, upheaval,
   unmooring, come the terror and potentiality of flux, improvisation, and creative recombinations"
   (p. 185). We cite Conquergood's observations to acknowledge that the rhetorical "turn" in the
   humanities and social sciences brings potential dangers and losses, as well as opportunities.
8 As we crossed disciplinary borders in this essay, we appreciated the work (and implications thereof)
   of Gloria Anzaldúa. Her compelling *Borderlands/La Frontera: The New Mestiza* (San Francisco:
   Aunt Lute, 1987) brilliantly articulates the promises—and dangers—inherent in crossing borders:
   cultural, political, racial, ethnic, and sexual borders. Anzaldúa tells us that to survive the Borderlands,
   we must "live *sin fronteras* [without borders]" (p. 195). To be conscious of Borderlands is, according
   to Anzaldúa, to develop a new consciousness, a *mestiza* consciousness and tolerance of blurring,
   instability, struggle, contradictions, and ambiguity (pp. 77ff.)—the very fabric of full human
   consciousness itself.
       We are not the first, of course, to explore the intersections of rhetoric and feminism. Although
   we cannot hope to survey all such efforts, we will whenever possible acknowledge current feminist
   work in the history of rhetoric. Helpful introductions to this work include: Barbara Biesecker,
   "Coming to Terms with Recent Attempts to Write Women into the History of Rhetoric," *Philosophy
   and Rhetoric* 25 (1992): 140–61; Karyln Kohrs Campbell, *Man Cannot Speak for Her: A Critical
   Study of Early Feminist Rhetoric*, 2 vols. (New York: Greenwood, 1989); Cheryl Glenn, "Remapping
   Rhetorical Territory," *Rhetoric Review* 13 (Spring 1995): 287–303; and Andrea Lunsford, *Reclaiming
   Rhetorica* (Pittsburgh: University of Pittsburgh Press, 1995). Cf. note 2.

9 Of course, it is beyond the scope of our essay and abilities to list all the feminist scholarship (cf. notes 2 and 5) that recuperates and analyzes women's contributions in the broad history of culture-making, but we want to provide at least a bare sketch. Feminist cultural analyses continue to sweep through philosophy (Linda Lopez McAlister, "Some Remarks on Exploring the History of Women in Philosophy," *Hypatia* 4 [Spring 1989]: 1–5; Nancy Tuana, *The Less Noble Sex: Scientific, Religious, and Philosophical Conceptions of Woman's Nature* [Bloomington: Indiana University Press, 1993]; Mary Ellen Waithe, *A History of Women Philosophers*, 2 vols. to date [Dordrecht: Martinus Nijhoff, 1987—]); literature (Sandra M. Gilbert and Susan Gubar, *The Madwoman in the Attic* [New Haven: Yale University Press, 1979]; Peggy Kamuf, *Fictions of Feminine Desire* [Lincoln: University of Nebraska Press, 1982]; Nancy K. Miller, *The Poetics of Gender* [New York: Columbia University Press, 1986]); language (Dennis Baron, *Grammar and Gender* [New Haven: Yale University Press, 1986]; Cheris Kramerae, *Women and Men Speaking: Frameworks for Analysis* [Rowley, MA: Newberry, 1981]; Dale Spender, *Man Made Language* [London: Routledge, 1980]); writing (Elizabeth Abel, "Race, Class, and Psychoanalysis? Opening Questions," in *Conflicts in Feminism*, eds. Marianne Hirsch and Evelyn Fox Keller [New York: Routledge, 1990], pp. 184–204; Cynthia L. Caywood and Gillian R. Overing, *Teaching Writing: Pedagogy, Gender, and Equality* [Albany: State University of New York Press, 1987]; Lisa Ede and Andrea Lunsford, *Singular Texts/Plural Authors* [Carbondale: Southern Illinois University Press, 1990]); societal structure (Edwin Ardener, "The Problem Revisited," in *Perceiving Women*, ed. Shirley Ardener [London: Malaby, 1975], pp. 19–28; Jean Bethke Elshtain, *Public Man, Private Woman* [Princeton: Princeton University Press, 1987]; Jane Gardner, *Women in Roman Law and Society* [New York: St. Martin's Press, 1987]; bell hooks, *Yearning: Race, Gender, and Cultural Politics* [Boston: South End Press, 1990]; Joan Kelly, *Women, History, and Theory: The Essays of Joan Kelly* [Chicago: University of Chicago Press, 1984]); Christianity (Mary Daly, *The Church and the Second Sex* [New York: Harper-Colophon, 1968]; Rosemary Radford Ruether, *Religion and Sexism: Images of Woman in Jewish and Christian Traditions* [New York: Simon and Schuster, 1974]); history (Simone de Beauvoir, *The Second Sex* [1952; rpt. New York: Vintage-Random, 1976]; Gerda Lerner, *The Majority Finds Its Past* [New York: Oxford University Press, 1981]; Joan Wallach Scott, *Gender and the Politics of History* [New York: Columbia University Press, 1988]); education (Sara Munson Deats, *Gender and Academe: Feminist Pedagogy and Politics* [Latham, MD: Rowman, 1994]; Madeleine R. Grumet, *Bittermilk: Women and Teaching* [Amherst: University of Massachusetts Press, 1988]; Kathleen Weiler, *Women Teaching for Change* [New York: Bergin, 1988]); reading (David Bleich, *The Double Perspective: Language, Literature, and Social Relations* [New York: Oxford University Press, 1988]; Elizabeth Flynn and Patrocinio Schweikart, eds., *Gender and Reading* [Baltimore: Johns Hopkins University Press, 1986]); psychology (Nancy Chodorow, *The Reproduction of Mothering* [Berkeley: University of California Press, 1978]; Carol Gilligan, *In a Different Voice: Psychological Theory and Women's Development* [Cambridge: Harvard University Press, 1982]; Juliet Mitchell, *Psychoanalysis and Feminism* [New York: Pantheon, 1974]); gender (Judith Butler, *Gender Trouble: Feminism and the Subversion of Identity* [New York: Routledge, 1990]; Peter Brown, *Body and Society* [New York: Columbia University Press, 1988]; Thomas Laqueur, *Making Sex* [Cambridge: Harvard University Press, 1990]); and science (Donna Haraway, *Primate Visions: Gender, Race, and Nature in the World of Modern Science* [New York: Routledge, 1989]; Evelyn Fox Keller, *Reflections on Gender and Science* [New Haven: Yale University Press, 1985]; Sara Ruddick and Pamela Daniels, eds., *Working It Out: 23 Women Writers, Artists, Scientists, and Scholars Talk About Their Lives and Work* [New York: Pantheon, 1977])—all of which, including the many others unnamed here, help create a space for reconceiving the rhetorical tradition in terms of feminism.

10 For example, biologist Donna Haraway demonstrates the pandisciplinarity of feminist work in her *Primate Visions.*

11 (Stanford: Stanford University Press, 1992), p. 2.

12 The essays cited here are in Hirsch and Keller, *Conflicts in Feminism*, pp. 60–81, and 349–69, respectively.

13 Freccero, "Notes of a Post-Sex Wars Theorizer," in ibid., pp. 305–25; Ling, "I'm Here: An Asian American Woman's Response," in *Feminisms*, eds. Robyn R. Warhol and Diane Price Herndl

(New Brunswick, NJ: Rutgers University Press, 1991), pp. 738–45; Scott, "Deconstructing Equality-Versus-Difference: Or, the Uses of Poststructuralist Theory for Feminism," in Hirsch and Keller, *Conflicts in Feminism,* pp. 134–48; Showalter, "A Criticism of Our Own: Autonomy and Assimilation in Afro-American and Feminist Literary Theory," in Warhol and Herndl, *Feminisms,* pp. 168–92; and Spivak, "Three Women's Texts and a Critique of Imperialism," in ibid., pp. 798–814.

14 Warhol and Herndl's 1991 *Feminisms* argues for the regular use of the term, which acknowledges the diversity of motivation, method, and experience among feminist academics. In their introduction, the editors tell us that from the outside, "feminism may appear monolithic, unified, or singularly definable... [But, actually, there is a] multiplicity of approaches and assumptions inside the movement. While this variety can lead to conflict and competition, it can also be the source of movement, vitality, and genuine learning. Such diversity—if fostered, as it has been in some feminist thought—can be a model for cultural heterogeneity."

15 *Southern Communication Journal* 57 (Winter 1992): 88.

16 Ibid.

17 Kathleen Welch, "Reconfiguring Writing and Delivery in Secondary Orality," in *Rhetorical Memory and Delivery,* ed. John Frederick Reynolds (Hillsdale, NJ: Erlbaum, 1993), p. 17.

18 "The Platonic Paradox: Plato's Rhetoric in Contemporary Rhetoric and Composition Studies," *Written Communication* 5 (1988): 5–6.

19 "Modern Rhetoric and Memory," in Reynolds, *Rhetorical Memory and Delivery,* p. 35.

20 Aristotle, *The Rhetoric and the Poetics of Aristotle* (1954; rpt. New York: Modern Library, 1984), I.2.

21 *Partitiones Oratoriae,* trans. E. W. Sutton (Cambridge: Harvard University Press, 1979), p. 26.

22 Kinneavy, *A Theory of Discourse* (1971; rpt. New York: Norton, 1980); Lauer, "Heuristics and Composition," in *Contemporary Rhetoric: A Conceptual Background with Readings,* ed. W. Ross Winterowd (New York: Harcourt, 1975), pp. 79–90; Corbett, *Classical Rhetoric for the Modern Student* (1965; rpt. New York: Oxford University Press, 1990); Young, "Invention: A Topographical Survey," in *Teaching Composition: Ten Bibliographic Essays,* ed. Gary Tate (Fort Worth: Texas Christian University Press, 1976), pp. 1–44; Perelman and Olbrechts-Tyteca, *The New Rhetoric: A Treatise on Argumentation,* trans. John Wilkinson and Purcell Weaver (Notre Dame: University of Notre Dame Press, 1969); Burke, *A Rhetoric of Motives.*

23 Carruthers, *The Book of Memory: A Study of Memory in Medieval Culture* (Cambridge: Cambridge University Press, 1990); Stock, *Listening for the Text* (Baltimore: Johns Hopkins University Press, 1990); Reynolds, *Rhetorical Memory and Delivery;* Crowley, "Modern Rhetoric and Memory," in ibid., pp. 31–44; Welch, "Reconfiguring Writing and Delivery in Secondary Orality," in ibid., pp. 17–30.

24 The term "postmodern" is itself a contested construction, both broadly and within feminism. We have found Flax's analysis of the central characteristics of postmodernism persuasive. Flax represents postmodern theorists as "masters of suspicion" (*Thinking Fragments,* p. 31) who argue that mind, reason, and truth are all effects of discourse; that discourses are "local, heterogeneous, and incommensurable" (p. 36), and thus caught up in issues of power, struggle, and hierarchy; and that such once-privileged narratives as philosophy and history can best be viewed as stories that are as rhetorically grounded and interested as any other story.

25 "Choosing the Margins as Space of Radical Openness," *Framework* 36 (1989): 16.

26 "Uses of the Erotic: The Erotic as Power," in *Sister Outsider* (Freedom, CA: Crossing, 1984), pp. 53–54.

27 "Memory, Creation, and Writing," *Thought* 59 (1984): 385.

28 Michael M. J. Fischer, "Ethnicity and the Post-Modern Arts of Memory," in *Writing Culture: The Poetics and Politics of Ethnography; A School of American Research Advanced Seminar,* eds. James Clifford and George E. Marcus (Berkeley: University of California Press, 1986), p. 198.

29 *Yearning: Race, Gender, and Cultural Politics,* p. 147.

30 "Ciceronian *Dispositio* as an Architecture for Creativity in Composition: A Note for the Affirmative," *Rhetoric Review* 4 (Sept. 1985): 108.

31 *Rhetoric* 1.2.

32 *A Rhetoric of Motives,* p. 43.

33 "The Womanization of Rhetoric," *Women's Studies International Quarterly* 2 (1979): 195. Gearhart's claims are echoed in the work of those who have lately focused our attention on what Elspeth Stuckey calls "the violence of literacy." Writing itself is, as Derrida long ago observed, an act of displacement. Even the word itself is related etymologically to cutting/carving, to acts of violence.

34 "Beyond Persuasion: A Proposal for an Invitational Rhetoric," *Communication Monographs* 62 (Mar. 1995): 2–18.

35 Olsen's prose, with its frequent ellipses, fragments, and erasures, its insistent inclusion of other women's words, calls attention not only to alternative forms of arrangement, of course, but to her methods of invention and even more to her style, demonstrating once again how the canons inevitably blur when put into practice. For a view of Olsen's method and rationale for opening up textual space, see "One Out of Twelve: Writers Who Are Women in Our Century" (in *Silences* [New York: Delacorte, 1978], pp. 41–660), a revealing overview of twentieth-century women writers.

36 *Talking Back: Thinking Feminist, Thinking Black* (Boston: South End, 1989), p. 77.

37 "Me and My Shadow," *New Literary History* 19 (Autumn 1987): 172.

38 Ibid.

39 Ibid., p. 178.

40 "Margaret Fuller: Inventing a Feminist Discourse," in Lunsford, *Reclaiming Rhetorica*, pp. 137–66.

41 Ibid., pp. 139–40.

42 See *Elements of Rhetoric* (1828; rpt. in *The Rhetoric of Blair, Campbell, and Whately,* eds. James L. Golden and Edward P. J. Corbett [Carbondale: Southern Illinois University Press, 1990]).

43 "Margaret Fuller," p. 159.

44 "Laugh of the Medusa," in *The Signs Reader,* eds. Elizabeth Abel and Emily K. Abel (Chicago: University of Chicago Press, 1983), pp. 279–97.

45 "Writing Against Writing: The Predicament of *Ecriture Féminine* in Composition Studies," in *Contending With Words,* eds. Patricia Harkin and John Schilb (New York: Modern Language Assoc., 1991), pp. 82–104.

46 In Warhol and Herndl, *Feminisms,* p. 458.

47 "Julia Kristeva and the Woman as Stranger," in Lunsford, *Reclaiming Rhetorica*, p. 309.

48 Ibid., p. 308.

49 Ibid., p. 314.

50 Ibid., p. 305.

51 "An Open Letter to Mary Daly," in *Sister Outsider,* pp. 66–71.

52 (Cambridge: Harvard University Press, 1991).

53 (New York: Plume-New American, 1987).

54 *Rhetoric* III.1.

55 Ibid.

56 P. 380.

57 Aristotle, *Rhetoric* III.1.

58 *Classical Rhetoric for the Modern Student,* p. 381.

59 P. 65. Such "sensuality, costume, and color" have often found embodiment in a theory of figures and tropes as discursive excesses and linguistic means of manipulation, although another view holds tropes to be central to all language and meaning. (J. Hillis Miller is one prominent contemporary proponent of this view.) In any case, feminist theorists have begun to carry out further forays into tropology. Jane Sutton, for example, attempts a tropological argument that moves "metaphorically, metonymically, synecdochically, and ironically" to unseat traditional tropes that inscribe woman ("The Taming of the *Polos/Polis*," p. 97). In another intriguing and nontraditional analysis, Foss and Griffin compare the rhetorics of Burke and feminist writer-activist Starhawk, noting the differing ways in which the two theorists use (and do not use) certain tropes (see "A Feminist Perspective on Rhetorical Theory: Toward a Clarification of Boundaries," *Western Journal of Communication* 56 [Fall 1992]: 330–49).

60 Trans. Walter Hamilton (London: Penguin, 1960), p. 44.

61 Qtd. in Michael Mooney, *Vico in the Tradition of Rhetoric* (Princeton: Princeton University Press, 1985), pp. 58–59.

62 *Gorgias*, p. 37.

63 *Sentimental Modernism: Women Writers and the Revolution of the Word* (Bloomington: Indiana University Press, 1991), p. 8.

64 Ibid., p. 3.

65 Ibid., p. 52.

66 Ibid., p. 55.

67 Ibid., p. 53.

68 Ibid., p. 31.

69 Ibid., p. 47.

70 Ibid., p. 54.

71 Ibid., p. 65.

72 Ibid., p. 45.

73 (Boston: Beacon, 1987).

74 Jane Hedley, "Surviving to Speak New Language: Mary Daly and Adrienne Rich," *Hypatia* 7 (Spring 1992): 43. Similar efforts include Monique Wittig and Sande Zeig's *Lesbian Peoples: Material for a Dictionary* (New York: Avon, 1979); and Cheris Kramerae and Paula A. Treichler's *Amazons, Bluestockings, and Crones* (London: Pandora, 1992).

75 *Websters'*, p. 167.

76 (Boston: Beacon, 1978).

77 P. 67.

78 Ibid., p. 71.

79 In *Multi-Cultural Literacy: Opening the American Mind*, eds. Rick Simonson and Scott Walker (Saint Paul, MN: Graywolf Press, 1988), pp. 63–81.

80 Ibid., p. 81.

81 See Cisneros, *House on Mango Street* (New York: Random House, 1994).

82 Recent examples include Alice Kaplan's *French Lessons: A Memoir* (Chicago: University of Chicago Press, 1993); hooks's *Talking Back;* Tompkins' "Me and My Shadow," pp. 169–78; and Marianna Torgovnick's edited collection *Eloquent Obsessions: Writing Cultural Criticism* (Durham: Duke University Press, 1994).

83 *The Poetics of Gender* (New York: Columbia University Press, 1986), p. 24.

84 P. 47.

85 *Yearning*, p. 21.

86 (Bloomington: Indiana University Press, 1989), p. 76.

87 Aristotle, *Rhetoric* III.1

88 Trans. Harry Caplan (Cambridge: Harvard University Press, 1954), 3.11.19.

89 Trans. E. W. Sutton (Cambridge: Harvard University Press, 1979), 3.56.213.

90 Cicero, *Brutus, On the Nature of the Gods, On Divination, On Duties*, trans. Hubert M. Poteat (Chicago: University of Chicago Press, 1950), 28.142.

91 Cicero, *Brutus, Orator*, trans. G. L. Hendrickson and H. M. Hubbell, respectively (Cambridge: Harvard University Press, 1949), 17.55.

92 *Institutio Oratoria*, trans. H. E. Butler, 4 vols. (1920; rpt. London: Heinemann, 1969), 11.3.2.

93 Ibid., 11.3–6.

94 We have not, however, used only traditional strategies. For example, we have chosen to collaborate, a nontraditional academic way to write and publish, in order to share equally the work and the credit of this essay, following the feminist tradition of "connected knowing" recorded in Mary Field Belenky, Blythe McVicker Clinchy, Nancy Rule Goldberger, and Jill Mattuck Tarule's *Women's Ways of Knowing* (New York: Basic, 1986) and expanded in Inderpal Grewal and Caren Kaplan's *Scattered Hegemonies* (Minneapolis: University of Minnesota Press, 1994). As Grewal and Kaplan note, "We must work collaboratively in order to formulate transnational feminist alliances" (p. 1). Nontraditionally, then, we deliver the third collaboratively written essay in *Rhetorica* (two earlier pieces, both on the rhetoric of science, were contributed by J. E. McGuire and Trevor Melia). In another nontraditional move, we use postmodern feminist examples and methodology, and we depend on a number of women writers and speakers who may not be familiar to our non-American readers.

95 *Orator* 17.55.

96 "Toward a Transactional View of Rhetorical and Feminist Theory: Rereading Hélène Cixous's *The Laugh of the Medusa*," *Southern Communication Journal* 57 (Winter 1992): 87.

97 Nor can we here explore the delivery of silence, a traditionally undervalued feminine mode, given the western tendency to valorize speech and language. Elaine Hedges and Shelley Fisher Fishkin (*Listening to Silences* [New York: Oxford University Press, 1944]) have recently helped us understand the expressive, positive powers of silence when it denotes alertness and sensitivity, when it signifies attentiveness or stoicism, and particularly when it seeks out and listens to new voices. Such explorations remind us of how much more we may yet learn here.

98 Throughout this essay, our examples have come from women using literate (print) delivery systems. In this section, we concentrate mostly on women's use of the oral medium of delivery. We do not speak to issues of facial and bodily gestures, nor will we comment on voice-timbre; except for our example of Ann Richards, we have no access to the actual physical delivery of these women.

99 Nor, of course, does any of Socrates' work, but the historical tradition has readily accepted secondary accounts of his influence, teaching, and beliefs. The same cannot be said for any female counterpart.

100 Discussions of Aspasia's intellectual activity can be found in the works of Plato (437–328 BCE), Xenophon (fl. 450 BCE), Cicero (100–43 BCE), Athenaeus (fl. AD 200), and Plutarch (AD 46–c.120).

101 Plato, *Timaeus, Critias, Cleitophon, Menexenus, Epistles,* trans. R. G. Bury (1929; rpt. London: Heinemann-Loeb, 1981), 240e ff.

102 Ibid., 236e.

103 For a thorough account of Aspasia's contributions to rhetoric, see Glenn's "sex, lies, and manuscript: Refiguring Aspasia in the History of Rhetoric," *College Composition and Communication* 45 (1994): 180–99.

104 In 1934, Hope Emily Allen identified and helped Sanford Brown Meech edit the unique manuscript, long the possession of the W. Butler-Bowden estate. (Margery Kempe, *The Book* of *Margery Kempe,* eds. Hope Emily Allen and Sanford Brown Meech [London: Oxford University Press, 1940].)

105 See Glenn's "Reexamining *The Book of Margery Kempe:* A Rhetoric of Autobiography" (in Lunsford, *Reclaiming Rhetorica,* pp. 53–71) for a fuller argument regarding Kempe's significance as a rhetorician.

106 "Sojourner Truth," in *Women Speakers in the United States: 1800–1925; 1925–1993,* ed. Karyln Kohrs Campbell, 2 vols. (Westport, CN: Greenwood, 1993), 1: 421.

107 Qtd. in ibid., 1: 428.

108 Harriet Carter, "Sojourner Truth," *Chautauquan* 7 (May 1887): 479.

109 Elizabeth Cady Stanton, Susan B. Anthony, and Matilda Joslyn Gage, eds., *History of Woman Suffrage* (Salem, NH: Ayer, 1985), 2: 926.

110 Ibid., 2: 649.

111 Illus. Kathleen Turner Suarez (Cambridge: Eastgate System, 1993).

112 *Hypertext: The Convergence of Contemporary Theory and Technology* (Baltimore: Johns Hopkins University Press, 1992).

113 Jamie R. Barlowe, conversation among the contributors in the "Afterword," Lunsford, *Reclaiming Rhetorica,* p. 327.

114 *Borderlands/La Frontera,* p. 3.

115 *Woman, Native, Other,* p. 94.

116 Kaplan, *French Lessons,* p. 149.

117 *Language as Symbolic Action: Essays on Life, Literature, and Method* (Berkeley: University of California Press, 1966), p. 16.

118 *The Chronicle of Higher Education,* May 4, 1988, p. A52.

119 See *Conflicts in Feminism,* p. 352.

120 "Contingent Foundations: Feminism and the Question of 'Postmodernism,'" in *Feminists Theorize the Political* (New York: Routledge, 1992), p. 8.

121 P. 222.

122 "Voice and the Naming of Woman," in *Voices on Voice: Perspectims, Definitions, Inquiry,* ed. Kathleen Blake Yancey (Urbana, IL: NCTE, 1994), p. 240.

123 "Multiple Mediations: Feminist Scholarship in the Age of Multinational Reception," *Inscriptions* 5 (1989): 4.

124 "The Politics of Location: Cinema/Theory/Literature/Ethnicity/Sexuality/Me," *Framework* 36 (1989): 53.

125 Kaplan, *French Lessons*, p. 139.

126 *Yearning*, p. 151.

INDEX

Note: 'N' after a page number indicates a note.

Abel, Elizabeth 230
abolition, rhetoric of Black women regarding
    85–9, 90
absolute listening 219
Abzug, Bella 2
academic settings: cross-boundary discourse in
    131; ideology of individualism in 62; offering
    as rhetorical strategy in 215–16; as privileged
    111; public-private split in 182; voice in 130.
    See also cross-boundary discourse
activism: of first-wave feminists 2; of
    19th-century Black women 84–5; of
    second-wave feminists 2
Adisa, Opal Palmer 128, 130
Adjectives, use by women 42
Adverbs, use by women 42
Aeschines 72
affirmative action 51–2
afrafeminist methodology 8, 141–2
Afric-American Female Intelligence Society of
    Boston 90
African American women. *See* Black women
Alcoff, Linda 6, 109, 111–12
Allende, Isabel, *House of Spirits* 233
American Anti-Slavery Society 86
American Equal Rights Association (AERA) 91
American Missionary Association (AMA) 87
American National Baptist Convention 92
Anaxagoras 71
Anaximenes, *Rhetorica ad Alexandrum* 230–1
Annas, Pamela 178n2
Anzaldúa, Gloria E. 241, 249, 251n8;
    Borderlands/La Frontera 9
Aphrodite 250n2
areté 80n14
argumentation 23
Aristophanes: *Acharnians* 80n11;
    Thesmophoriazousae 117
Aristotle 62, 69–70, 76; on arrangement 234; on
    delivery 242; *Rhetoric* 231, 237–8; on style
    237–8; on women 76

Armstrong, Nancy 108
arrangement 234–7, 253n35
Aspasia of Miletus 1, 5, 8, 9, 117; as author of
    Pericles' Funeral Oration 71–4, 243; as
    courtesan 79n7; criticism of 80nn10–12; and
    delivery methods 243; as forgotten 77; and
    Heloise 80n17; influence of 75–7; in *Lives of
    the Noble Grecians and Romans* (Plutarch)
    68; overview of 67–8; and Pericles 68–9, 71,
    80n12; and Plato 75–6; reputation of, as
    rhetorician 68–9, 73; and Socrates 72–3,
    75–6; Sophistic training 73–4
Astell, Mary 9, 139
Athenaeus 72
Atkinson, Ti-Grace 30n2
attack metaphors 25
audiences: Campbell on 53; and delivery 242; as
    "feminine" 31n21; and invitational rhetoric
    212–20; and power dynamics 210–11, 223–4;
    and style 239
Auerbach, Nina 184–5, 187

Barker, Pat, *Blow Your House Down* 188–90
Barnett, Ferdinand 95
Barrett, H. 219, 220
Barrett, Michele, *Destabilizing Theory:
    Contemporary Feminist Debates* 229
Bartkowski, Frances 57
Bauer, Dale, "The Other 'F' Word: The Feminist
    in the Classroom" 10
Baumfree, Isabella. *See* Truth, Sojourner
Belenky, Mary 255n94; connected knowing 172;
    Women's Ways of Knowing 169, 170–1
Bender, John, *The Ends of Rhetoric: History,
    Theory, Practice* 229
Benhabib, S. 219, 220
Benston, Margaret 31n19
Bernstein, Basil 43
Berthoff, Ann 78, 168
Bethel Literary and Historical Association
    84

Biesecker, Barbara 243; "Coming to Terms with Recent Attempts to Write Women into the History of Rhetoric" 4, 67; on female tokenism 4; "Towards a Transactional View of Rhetorical and Feminist Theory" 230

Bitch Manifesto 25

Bitzer, Lloyd 28, 53

Bizzell, Patricia 161, 185, 187–8; "Feminist Methods of Research in the History of Rhetoric: What Difference Do They Make?" 7; on Gale's critique of Glenn and Jarratt 8; "Opportunities for Feminist Research in the History of Rhetoric" 66–7; *The Rhetorical Tradition* 7, 133–5; on Royster's afrafeminist methodology 8; on women speakers 119n6

Black Sash 13

Black women: on abolition of slavery 85–9, 90; communication of, vs. Black men 35; delivery methods of 244–5; on lynching 94–6; multiplicity of voices of 128–9; as 19th-century orators 84–100; on racial uplift 96–9; recovery of rhetorical practices 5–6; power of storytelling by 127–8; on women's rights 89–94. *See also* women of color

Blair, Carole 57–8, 77, 78, 79n5

boundaries: Conquergood on 250n7; of rhetoric 229–31; risks of crossing 251n8

Brandt, Paul 80n12

Britton, James 168

Broadcasting, women and 39

Brody, Miriam 161

Broughton, Virginia 92

Brown, William Wells 86

Brownmiller, Susan 2

Brownson, Orestes 236

Brummett, Barry 138

Buber, M. 215

Bunch-Weeks, Charlotte 30n1

Burgess, Parke 28

Burke, Kenneth 31n21, 54, 140, 161, 185, 213, 229, 232, 234, 248, 253n59 ; "Identification and Consubstantiality" 186; perspective by incongruity 216–17; *Rhetoric of Motives* 186, 190

Burroughs, Nannie Helen 84

Butler, Judith 248

Caffre people 35

Campbell, George 160

Campbell, Karlyn Kohrs 161; and canonical ideology of individualism 52, 54; hegemonic feminism of 63n19; *Man Cannot Speak for Her* 4, 49–50; "The Rhetoric of Women's Liberation: An Oxymoron" 3, 53; on women's liberation 3

The Cancer Journals (Lorde) 2

canon: affirmative action approach to expanding 51–2; Campbell as affirming ideology of 52; underlying logic of 52

Cantarella, Eva 79n7, 79n8, 80n11

Carlton, Susan Brown 248–9

Carruthers, Mary 232

Carter, Kathryn 50–1

Cary, Mary Ann Shadd 5, 85, 86, 87–8, 89, 90

Cathcart, Robert 29

Caywood, Cynthia 177–8n2

Chavez, Cesar 157

Cheney, Ednah 85

Chicano people, and identity 154–7

Chicano Spanish 151–4

Childers, Mary 230

Chodorow, Nancy: on male interactional patterns 174; relational identification 172, 174; *The Reproduction of Mothering* 169–70

Christian, Barbara 127

Christine de Pisan 9

Cicero 71, 72, 231; on arrangement 234; *De Inventione* 75–6; on delivery 242–3; on memory 232

Cisneros, Sandra 241

Cixous, Helene 118, 236, 241

Clark, Suzanne 181, 237, 239–40

classical antiquity, gender in 116–18

classical Athens: *areté* 80n14; funeral orations in 73; *hetaerae* (courtesans) of 79n8; men's role in 69–70; *polis* in 70; rhetoric in 70; Sophistic movement 73–4; women's role in 67, 69–70, 76–7, 80n9, 80n13. *See also* Aspasia of Miletus

class issues, feminism as overlooking 230

Cliff, Michelle 240

Clinchy, Blythe 254n94 ; *Women's Ways of Knowing* 169, 170–1

Cocks, Joan 105, 106, 107

Code Pink 13

Cole, Susan 79n7

collaboration 254n94

collaborative learning, gender and 178n2

Collins, Vicki Tolar 8, 139 colonialism 112

Colored National Convention 87

communication: logos, ethos, and pathos in 249; as exchange of energy 202; Kramer on women's 3; as matrix 206; non-persuasive notions of 204–6; sex-related differences in 34–43; stuttering 36–7; "womanization" of 207–8. *See also* language; women's speech

composition and writing studies: collaborative vs. one-to-one learning 177–8n2 ; feminist approaches to 10; and feminist studies 168–9, 177–8n2; gender manifested in student writing 171–5; and mothering 178n2; as process oriented 167–8; and silence 178n2; strategies for analyzing gender in 175–7; and women 168–9. *See also* pedagogy
connected knowing 172
Conquergood, Dwight 250n7
conquest/conversion model 202–3, 206–8, 235–6
consciousness raising 22–3, 27, 53; origins of 31n20; and women's speech 193. *See also* personal experiences
contact zones 125
Cook, Mary 92–3
Cooper, Anna Julia 5, 84, 94, 128
Cooper, Martha 57–8
Corax 228
Corbett, Edward P. J. 79n3, 232, 238
corridos 155–6
Courtney, William 79n7
Crockett, Harry J., Jr. 35–6
cross-boundary discourse: in academic settings 131; new paradigm as necessary for 129–30; and *The Souls of Black Folk* (Du Bois) 126–7; subjectivity in 122
cross-cultural misconduct 124–5
Crowhurst, Marion 168
Crowley, Sharon 232
Cudlipp, Edythe 30n1
Culler, Jonathan: "Reading as a Woman" 176–7; Showalter on 178n4
Culley, Margo, "The Politics of Nurturance" 182–83
cultural values: femininity as conflicting with 27; for men vs. women 20–1

Daeumer, Elisabeth 177–8n2
Dalai Lama 12
Daly, Mary 2, 224, 225, 237, 240
de Certeau, Michel 105, 106, 107, 114–15; *The Practice of Everyday Life* 60–1
Declaration of Sentiments 2
deconstruction 55, 110
de Lauretis, Teresa 51, 110
Delcourt, Marie 69
Deleuze, Gilles 115, 116
delivery 255n98; and access 243; alternative forms of 243–6; electronic forms of 246–7; intonation 38, 40, 242;

power dynamics of 247; private vs. public forms of 243; volume and pitch 39, 242
Democritus 80n10
Demosthenes 242
Derrida, Jacques 54–5, 57, 59–60, 253n33
The Dialectic of Sex: The Case for Feminist Revolution (Firestone) 2
dialogics 182–4
Diamond, Arlyn, "The Politics of Nurturance" 183–4
Dickinson, Anna 97
Dillard, J. L. 39
Diotima 9
discriminatory legislation: judicial opinions upholding 31n12; marriage laws 20; wage laws 21
Douglass, Frederick 86, 95, 97
Draine, Betsy 108
Dred Scott Decision 87
duBois, Page 6, 117, 118
Du Bois, W. E. B., *The Souls of Black Folk* 126–7
Dworkin, Andrea 2

economic issues: discriminatory wage laws 21; and "woman's place" 31n16; and women's role 31n19
Ede, Lisa 168; "Border Crossing: Intersections of Rhetoric and Feminism" 11
education, as persuasion 185
educational discourse: alternatives to persuasion in 205–6; maternal voice in 196; quantitative vs. qualitative measures 194–5; voices in, as "choral" 196. *See also* pedagogy
Edwards, Lee, "The Politics of Nurturance" 183–4
electronic media 246–7
Eliot, George 43
Elizabeth I 1
Ellmann, Mary 40, 42–3
Elshtain, Jean Bethke 80n15, 109
Emig, Janet 78, 168
emotions: and feminist historiography 138–9; function of, in scholarly work 8, 139; in Royster's research 140–3
Enheduanna 1
Enos, Richard 134, 135, 136, 234

Equal Rights Amendment 3
Erasmus 244–5
Erikson, Erik 30n9
essentialism 43, 110, 138, 140

ethics: and historiography 106; pedagogical 183; of rhetoric 207, 223–4. *See also* morality

eudaimonia 14

Felski, Rita 196

female tokenism 4, 50–1

The Feminine Mystique (Friedan) 2

femininity: as conflicting with societal values 21, 27; cost of deviance from 21; and writing 43

feminism: aims of 212; bias against terminology 10; and class issues 230; French 108; and individualism 230; principles of 211–12; and racial issues 230, 240–2, 248; rejection of conquest/conversion model 207–8; and rhetoric 11–12; as rhetorical criticism 186; student resistance to, in classroom 180–4

feminisms, use of term 230, 252n14

feminists, first-wave 2

feminists, second-wave 2–3

feminist studies, and composition and writing studies 168–9

feminist theory: and invention/memory 233–4; and persuasion as control 235; and rhetorical arrangement 234–7; and style 237–41

Ferreira-Buckley, Linda 135, 136

Fields, A. Belden 64n35

Fifteenth Amendment 91

film, women's voices in 193–4

Firestone, Shulamith 36, 41

First Congress of Colored Women 93

Fisch, R. 217–18

Fishkin, Shelley Fisher 255n97

Fitch, Suzanne Pullon 244

Flacéliere, Robert 79n8, 80n11

Flax, Jane 113, 229, 248, 250n5, 253n24

Flexner, Stuart 41, 42

Flower, Linda 168

Flynn, Elizabeth A. 107; "Composing as a Woman" 10

Fogarty, Daniel 160–1

Forget, P. 217

Fortune, T. Thomas 85

Foss, Karen 50

Foss, Sonja 50, 161, 234, 253n59; "Beyond Persuasion: A Proposal for Invitational Rhetoric" 11

Foucault, Michel 108, 115, 116; *The Archaeology of Knowledge* 55–6; on Derrida 57; *Madness and Civilization* 57; on resistance to power 58; space in works of 59; on subjectivity 56–9

Fourteenth Amendment 20

Frazer, J. G. 35

Freccero, Carla 230

Freedom Charter (film) 233

Freire, Paulo 181

French, Marilyn 2

Friedan, Betty 2

Fugitive Slave Act 86, 87

Fuller, Margaret 9, 235, 236, 240

funeral orations 73

Furley, Paul 35

Gale, Xin Liu 8, 135–9

Gallop, Jane 230, 248–9

Gandhi, Mahatma 12

Garner, Margaret 86–7

Garrison, William Lloyd 91

Gbowee, Leymah 13

Gearheart, Sally Miller 209–10, 214, 234 , 253n33; invitational rhetoric of 222–3; "Womanization of Rhetoric" 11

gender: and communication 34; and cultural values 27; effects of, in human development 169–71; manifested in student writing 171–5; norms of, for men vs. women 21; pedagogical strategies for analyzing 175–7; as social category 70

gendered analysis: of classical texts 116–18; definition of 107; of history, vs. women's history 107–10; Jarratt on 6. *See also* historiography

Gere, Anne Ruggles 161

Gerome, J. L., "Alcibiades and Aspasia" 66, 77

Giddings, Paula 98

Gilligan, Carol 10, 193; *In a Different Voice* 169, 170, 175, 176

Giroux, Henry 184

Glenn, Cheryl 135–9, 162; on Aspasia of Miletus 5; "Border Crossing: Intersections of Rhetoric and Feminism" 11; Gale on 8; "sex, lies, and manuscript: Refiguring Aspasia in the History of Rhetoric" 5

Goldberg, Philip 36

Goldberger, Nancy 254n94; *Women's Ways of Knowing* 169, 170–1

Goldman, Emma 239–40, 248

Gonchar, Ruth 29

Gorgias 75; *Encomium of Helen* 118

Grassi, Ernesto 229

Greenough, James B. 41

Greenwood, Grace 88

Gregg, Richard 24

Grewal, Inderpal 254n94

Griffin, Cindy L. 234, 253n59; "Beyond Persuasion: A Proposal for Invitational Rhetoric" 11

Griffin, Leland 28

Grimke, Angelina 85
Grootendorst, R. 223
Grumet, Madeleine R., on voice 10–11

Haas, Mary R. 35
Habermas, Jurgen 196
Hahn, Dan 29
Hairston, Maxine, "Breaking Our Bonds and Reaffirming Our Connections" 168–9
Haley, Alex, *Roots* 130
Hampton Negro Conference 98–9
Harper, Fenton 92
Harper, Frances 5, 84, 85, 86, 88–9, 92, 96–7
Hartsock, Nancy 6, 57, 112–13
Hauser, Gerard, *Introduction to Rhetorical Theory* 49
Heath, Shirley 168
Hedges, Elaine 255n97
Hedley, Jane 241
Heilbrun, Carolyn 2
Heloise 72, 80n17
Henry, Madeleine 136–9
Herndl, Diane Price 252n14
Hernstein, Richard J., *The Bell Curve: Intelligence and Class Structure in American Life* 124
Herrick, J.A. 223
Herzberg, Bruce 161; *The Rhetorical Tradition* 7, 133–5
Highgate, Edmonia G. 96, 97–8
Hirsch, Marianne 248–9; *Conflicts in Feminism* 230
historiography: feminist 106, 107; as interpretive act 106; location as ethical orientation 110–14; normative ethics of 106; representation 114–16; teaching feminist 118–19. *See also* gendered analysis; rhetoric, history of
Hitler, Adolf 31n21
Hoenigswald, Henry M. 37
Holbrook, Sue Ellen 161
Hollis, Karyn 161
Holmberg, C. 224
"home training" 125
hooks, bell 128–9, 211, 212, 230, 234, 235, 241, 249
Horner, Win 168
Howe, Florence, "Identity and Expression: A Writing Course for Women" 168
Hughes, Langston 127
hybrid people 129
hyperbole 42

identifications, realistic vs. idealistic 185–6
identity: Chicana/o 154–8; as "choral" 196–7; Foucault on 56–9; and poststructuralism 54–5; as social construction 186. *See also* subjectivity
IJsseling, Samuel 229
immanent value 211
individualism, ideology of: in academic settings 62; as basis of rhetorical canon 52–3; and Campbell 54; and feminism 230
International Women's Day 12
intonation 38, 40
invention and memory 231–4
invitational rhetoric. *See* rhetoric, invitational
Isocrates 70
"I-Thou" relationship 215

Jacks, John W 93
Jackson, Laura Riding 9
Jacobus, Mary 109
Jaggar, Alison 109, 113, 114
James, Henry 109
Jameson, Fredric 113–14
Janeway, Elizabeth 23, 30n9, 33n47
Jarratt, Susan 73,; Gale on 8, 136–9; on gendered analysis 6; on pedagogy 6–7; rejection of objectivity as goal 6; on rhetoric and women 238; "Speaking to the Past: Feminist Historiography in Rhetoric" 6
Jay, Gregory 184
Jehlen, Myra 77
Jespersen, Otto 35, 38, 40, 41, 42
Jimenez, Flaco 156
Johnson, Nan 161
Johnson, S. 212, 214–15, 219, 225
Jones, Jane E. Hitchcock 97
Jordan, Barbara 2
Jordan, Steve 156
Just, Roger 80n11

Kahl, Mary L. 79n5
Kaplan, Caren 255n94
Karman, Tawakkol 13
Keller, Evelyn Fox, *Conflicts in Feminism* 230
Kelly, Joan 79n5, 107, 108
Kempe, Margery 9, 244
Kempton, Sally 26; "Cutting Loose" 23–4
Kennedy, John F. 156
Kester, Judy 36
Keuls, Eva C. 80n10
King, Martin Luther, Jr. 12
Kingston, Maxine Hong 2

Kinneavy, James 232
Kirsch, Gesa 8
Kitto, H. D. F. 80n9
Kittredge, George L. 41
Kohlberg, Lawrence 170
Kolodny, Annette 160, 235–6, 248
Korzybski, Alfred 161
Kramer, Cheris: "Woman's Speech: Separate but Unequal" 3; on women's ways of communicating 3
Kristeva, Julia 9, 236, 241; "chora" 195–6
Kwanza 148–9

Labov, William 35, 43
Lacan, Jacques 54, 195–6
Lakoff, Robin 38, 42
Landow, George 246
Laney, Lucy 6, 96, 98–9
Langer, Suzanne K. 9
Langston, John M. 97–8
language: and accented English 150–1; and alternative discourses 240; Anzaldúa on 9; Chicano Spanish 153–4; as ideologically charged 185; "Spanglish" 241; transformation of silence into 147–9. *See also* communication; style
Laqueur, Thomas 70
Larsen, Deena, *Marble Springs* 246
Lauer, Janice 78, 232
Lennox, Sara, "The Politics of Nurturance" 183–4
Lerner, Gerda 6, 116–17
Levine, Lewis 35–6
Liberian Mass Action for Peace 13
Licht, Hans 80n12
Lincoln, C. Eric 92
Linearity, in Western style 234–7
Ling, Amy 230
Linguistic terrorism 154–5
listening 219
location: and feminist historiography 110–14; and positionality 111–12; and standpoint theory 112–14
Locke, John 161
Logan, Shirley Wilson: "Black Women on the Speaker's Platform, 1832–1899" 4; *With Pen and Voice: A Critical Anthology of African American Women* 5; and recovery of Black women's rhetoric 5–6; *"We Are Coming": The Persuasive Discourse of Nineteenth-Century African American Women* 5
Loraux, Nicole 73, 74, 79n7
Lorde, Audre 2, 127, 233, 239, 240–1, 221–2, 223; "Open Letter to Mary Daly" 3;

"Transformation of Silence into Language and Action" 9
Luce, Irigaray 118
Lugones, Maria 111, 237
Lukacs, Georg 112
Lunsford, Andrea 168; "Border Crossing: Intersections of Rhetoric and Feminism" 11; *Reclaiming Rhetorica: Women in the Rhetorical Tradition* 9
lynchings 94–6
Lysistrata 12

Mackin, James A., Jr. 73
Madres de la Plaza de Mayo 13
Maine Anti-Slavery Society 85, 88
Mamiya, Lawrence H. 92
Mani, Lata 249
Mao Tse Tung, "On Contradiction" 204
marginalization, and feminist historiography 110–14
marriage laws 20
Martin, Nancy 168
masculinity 21; and speech 42; and writing 43
material inequality 21. *See also* economic issues
Matthews, Victoria Earle 5, 84, 93
McArthur, Alexander 87
McIntosh, Peggy 111
McKane, Alice Woodby 85
Mead, Margaret 34, 43
Mejía, Miquel Aceves 155
memory. *See* invention and memory
men: in classical Athens 69–70; cultural values for, vs. women 20–1; interactional patterns of 174
Menander 80n10
Menchu, Rigoberta 237
Mendoza, Lydia 156
methods and methodology: afrafeminist 8, 141–2; Gale's critique of feminist 136–7; and postmodern theory 136–8; rhetorical 6–8, 135–9
Miller, J. Hillis 253n59
Miller, Maria 5
Miller, Nancy K. 230, 241, 248–9
Miller, Susan 161
Minh-ha, Trinh T. 241–2, 247
Mitchell, Juliet 31n14
Mohanty, Chandra Talpade 127
Moi, Toril, *Sexual/Textual Politics* 108
Morgan, Susan 108–9
Morrison, Toni 233–4; *Beloved* 237
Morton, N. 219
mothering 177–8n2

Mott, Lucretia 1
Murray, Charles, *The Bell Curve: Intelligence and Class Structure in American Life* 124

Natanson, Maurice 23, 26, 215
National Colored Labor Union 90
National Convention of Colored Men 97
Naylor, Gloria, *Mama Day* 233
Negrete, Jorge 155
nonverbal offering 216
nonviolent protest 12–13
North, Stephen 106
Nye, Andrea 80n17

Ober, Josiah, *Mass and Elite in Democratic Athens* 71
objectivity: Jarratt on 6; Royster's rejection of, as goal 7
offering 214–18
Olbrechts-Tyteca, Lucia 78, 232
Olbricht, Thomas 28
Olsen, Tillie 126, 234, 253n35
Ong, Rory 136–9
orators. *See* rhetors/orators
oratory. *See* rhetoric
organizational patterns 234–7, 253n35
O'Toole, Colleen 160
Our Bodies, Our Selves (Boston Women's Health) 2
Overing, Gillian 177–8n2
oxymoron, as metaphor for feminist rhetoric 29

Pachuco 152
Paine, Charles 183
Partridge, Eric 41–2
Peaden, Catherine 161
pedagogy: dialogics as strategy 182–4; of feminist historiography 118–19; Jarratt on 6–7; as oppressive act 201; as political 185; and "The Politics of Nurturance" 183–4; and rhetoric 10–11; and student resistance to feminism 180–4. *See also* composition and writing studies; educational discourse
Penn, I. Garland 95
Perelman, Chaim 232
Pericles: and Aspasia of Miletus 68–9, 71, 80n12; eloquence of 71; Funeral Oration 71–4, 243
Perl, Sondra 168
Perry, William, *Forms of Intellectual and Ethical Development in the College Years* 170–1
persuasion: alternatives to 204–6, 212, 223–4, 235–7; as contested aim of rhetoric 234–7; education as 185; vs. invitational rhetoric 213–14; leaderless 31n20; as violent act 11,

201–4, 209–11; and women's liberation 22, 28. *See also* rhetoric
Phelps, Louise Wetherbee 112
Phillips, Anne, *Destabilizing Theory: Contemporary Feminist Debates* 230
Philostratus 71
Piercy, Marge, *Woman on the Edge of Time* 176
Pinar, William 193
place. *See* location
Plato 71, 238; and Aspasia of Miletus 75–6; *Menexenus* 73, 74; *Phaedrus* 75, 117; on rhetoric 238
Plutarch 72, 80n11; *Lives of the Noble Grecians and Romans* 68
pocho 151, 152
Pogrebin, Letty Cottin 39
polis 70
Portuges, Catherine, "The Politics of Nurturance" 183–4
positionality 6, 111–12, 118–19
postmodern theory 136–8, 230; as contested construction 252n24; and invention and memory 232–3; and style 241
poststructuralism 54–9, 109, 230
power dynamics: of delivery 247; rejection of, in invitational rhetoric 212–16, 224; of rhetoric as persuasion 209–11, 223–4
practices and performances 8–9, 60. *See also* delivery
Pratt, Mary Louise 125
prostitution, in *Blow Your House Down* (Barker) 188–9
psychoanalysis 25; personal vs. social change as goal of 32n31
Purple Saturday 216

Quintilian 71, 231, 242

racial issues, feminism as overlooking 230, 240–2, 248
racial uplift, rhetoric of Black women regarding 96–9
Rackin, Phyllis 108
Radhakrishnan, R. 54
Ratcliffe, Krista 13
Rebolledo, Tey Diana 237
Rechy, John, *City of Night* 155
recovery and recuperation, of women in rhetoric 4–6
Reik, Theodor 41–2
relational identification 172, 174
Remond, Charles Lenox 86
Remond, John 86
Remond, Nancy 86

Remond, Sarah Parker 5, 86, 86–7, 90
research methods. *See* methods and
    methodology
re-sourcement 216–18, 221–2
Reynolds, Fred 232
rhetoric: arrangement 253n35; Biesecker on
    expanding definitions of 4–5; as body of
    identifications 186; boundaries of 229–31;
    canons 231; in classical Athens 70; conquest/
    conversion model of 202–3, 207–8, 235–6; as
    deceptive 74–5; delivery 242–7, 255n98;
    ethics of 207, 223–4; and first-wave feminists
    2; gendering, in classical antiquity 116–18; as
    inadequate to women's liberation 28–9;
    invention and memory 232–4; methods and
    methodology of 6–8; patriarchal bias of
    209–11, 248; pedagogical applications and
    implications 10–11; practices and
    performances of 8–9; recovery and
    recuperation of women in 4–6; and
    second-wave feminists 2; sophistic 114; style
    237–42; three types of 203; violence of 11,
    12; "womanization" of 207–8; women as
    overlooked in 1–2, 8–9; women's place in
    159–62. *See also* persuasion
rhetoric, feminist: goals of 13–14; as invitational
    11; stylistic features of 22–6; substantive
    features of 20–2; violating taboo as strategy
    of 25. *See also* women's speech
rhetoric, history of: and female tokenism 50–1;
    gender-sensitive 61–2; impact of feminist
    research in 135; restoration of women to
    66–7, 134–5; women as excluded from
    49–50, 66, 77–8, 79n3. *See also*
    historiography
rhetoric, invitational: and audiences 212–20;
    based on feminist principles 211–12;
    communicative options in 214–20; definition
    of 212–14; examples of 220–3; external
    conditions of 218–20; and freedom 219–20;
    implications of, for rhetorical theory 223–5;
    nonverbal offering 216; offering perspectives
    214–18; vs. persuasion 213–14; rejection of
    unequal power dynamics 212–17; and
    resistance to oppression 224–5;
    re-sourcement 216–18; and rhetors/orators
    212–20; and safety 218; and value 219
Rhetorica: A Journal of the History of Rhetoric 11
rhetorical analysis, of "Cutting Loose"
    (Kempton) 24
rhetorical listening 13
rhetorical strategies: attack metaphors 25;
    symbolic reversals 25–6 rhetors/orators:
    Black women of 19th century as 84–100; and

invitational rhetoric 212–20; as "masculine"
    31n21; nonverbal offerings 216; and power
    dynamics 210–11, 223–4; and re-sourcement
    216–18; subjectivity of 233, 249. *See also*
    specific individuals
Rich, Adrienne 2, 6, 167, 177; "'When We Dead
    Awaken': Writing as Re-Vision" 168; on
    female tokenism 50; invitational rhetoric of
    221–2, 223; "Notes toward a Politics of
    Location" 110–11
Richards, Ann 246
Richards, I. A. 161
Richardson, Marilyn 91
Riley, Denise 119n2
Rogers, Hester 139
Roper, Margaret Moore 244
Rorty, R. 217
Rosenblatt, Louise 9
Royster, Jacqueline Jones 8; afrafeminist
    methodology of 8; Bizzell on 8; and
    emotions in feminist research 140–3;
    rejection of objectivity as goal 7; on
    subjectivity as method 7; *Traces of a Stream*
    140; "When the First Voice You Hear Is Not
    Your Own" 7
Ruffin, Josephine St. Pierre 93
Runzo, Sandra 177–8n2

Sappho 1, 76, 118
Saturday Review cartoon 40–1
Schafer, Roy 196
Schaps, David 70, 80n13
scholarship, re-examining 78
Scott, Joan Wallach 107, 108, 118, 230
Scott, R.L 210, 215
self-determination 211–12
self-help clinics 27
Selma, Leydesdorff 118
semiotic discourse 195
sex differences: in communication 34–35 ; in
    oral comprehension and retention 37; and
    stuttering 36–7
Shaughnessy, Mina 78, 168
Shaw, Irwin, "The Girls in Their Summer
    Dresses" 175–6
Shepherd, G.J. 209
Shor, Ira 182
Showalter, Elaine 178n4, 230
Shuy, Roger 35, 36
silence: and composition and writing studies
    177–8n2 ; and International Women's Day
    12; and nonviolent protest 12–13;
    overcoming traditions of 151–3; powers of
    255n97; productive 13; and rhetorical

power 13; transformation of, into language and action 147–9; in women, as valued by male society 37–8, 66, 79n2. *See also* voice
Silverman, Kaja 193–6
Simons, Herbert 29
Sirleaf, Ellen Johnson 13
slang 41–2
slavery 85–9, 90
Smith, Ann 98
Smith, Barbara Hermstein 79n5
Smith, Lucy Wilmot 5, 92
Smith, Paul 58, 64–5n41, 119n4
Socrates 69, 72–3, 75–6
Sommers, Nancy 168
Sophists 73–4
Sophocles 76
space: Derrida's notion of 59–60; in Foucault's work 59
speak-outs 27
Spender, Dale 176
Spitzack, Carole 51–2
Spivak, Gayatri 6, 109, 182, 230; "Can the Subaltern Speak?" 112, 115–16; on deconstruction 55
Spratt, Thomas 238
Stallybrass, Peter 79n2
standpoint theory 6, 112–14
Stanger, Carol A. 177–8n2
Stanley, Julia 41
Stanton, Elizabeth Cady 2
Starhawk 211, 217, 218, 253n59
Steinem, Gloria 2, 30n2
Stevens, Wallace, "The Idea of Order At Key West" 192, 195
Stewart, Maria 5, 84, 85, 89, 90–1
Still, William 88, 96
Stock, Brian 232
Stone, Lucy 99
Stuckey, Elspeth 253n33
students, gender of, manifested in essays 171–5
stuttering 36–7
style: and audiences 239; dilemmas of, in traditional rhetoric 238–40; postmodern theory 241; and substance 26–7; of women's liberation as rhetorical movement 22–6. *See also* language
subjectivity: in cross-boundary discourse 122; Foucault on 56–9; invention and memory 234; and positionality 111–12; and poststructuralism 54–5; of rhetors/orators 233, 249; Royster on 7; and standpoint theory 112–14; and voice 123. *See also* identity

suffrage. *See* voting rights
Sui Kyi, Aung San 12
Sutherland, Christine Mason 8, 139
Sutton, Jane 250n2, 253n59
symbolic reversals 25–6, 33n47

taboo 25
tag-orders, in women's speech 38
tag-questions, in women's speech 38
Tarule, Jill 255n94; *Women's Ways of Knowing* 169, 170–1
Taylor Charles 13
techne 60–1
Terrell, Mary Church 5, 85
Tex-Mex music and film 155–6
Theophrastus 242
This Bridge Called my Back (Anzaldúa) 2
Thoreau, Henry David 131
Thucydides 74, 80n18
Thurman, Howard 128
Tilton, Theodore 98
Tisias 228
Titters (Stillman and Beatts) 2
tokenism. *See* female tokenism
Tompkins, Jane 235
Toward a Recognition of Androgyny (Heilbrun) 2
Tracy, D. 215
translation 244–5
"trespass vision" 126
tropology 253n59
Trudgill, Peter 36
Truth, Sojourner 5, 9, 84, 89, 245; "Ain't I a Woman" speech 91

U'Ren, Marjorie 38

van Eemeren, F.H. 223
Vernant, Jean-Pierre 79n6; *The Origins of Greek Thought* 70
Vickers, Brian, *In Defence of Rhetoric* 229
Vidal-Naquet, Pierre 80n13
Villa, Pancho 156
violence: in *Blow Your House Down* (Barker) 188–90; persuasion as 11, 201–4, 209–11; of traditional rhetoric 11, 12; of writing 253n33
voice: in academic settings 130; of Black women as ignored 127–8; and educational research 194–5; Gilligan on 193; Grumet on 10–11; in "The Idea of Order At Key West" (Stevens) 192, 195; maternal 195–6; multiplicity of 128, 196–7; and subjectivity 123. *See also* silence
voice-over narratives 193–4
volume and pitch 39

voting rights: and first-wave feminists 2; rhetoric of Black women regarding 90–4

wage equality 21
Waithe, Mary Ellen 79n7, 118
Walker, Alice 221–2, 223
Walker, David 90
Walker, M.U. 219
Wallace, Michele 249–50
Ward, Samuel 87
Warhol, Robyn R. 252n14
Watkins, William 86
Watzlawick, P. 217–18
Weakland, J.H. 217–18
Welch, Kathleen 231, 232
Wellbery, David E., *The Ends of Rhetoric: History, Theory, Practice* 229
Wells, Ida B. 5, 9, 84, 93, 94–6, 127, 140
Wertheimer, Molly Meijer 140
West, Cornel 129
Whately, Richard 235
Williams, Fannie Barrier 5, 93–4
Williams, Patricia 130, 237
Wollstonecraft, Mary 9
women: and alternative delivery methods 243–6; Aristotle on 76; in classical antiquity 116–18; in classical Athens 67, 69–70, 76–7, 80n9, 80n13; and composition and writing studies 168–9; cultural values for, vs. men 20–1; as excluded from rhetorical history 50, 66, 77–8, 79n3; legal inferiority of 20–1; and material inequality 21; as overlooked in rhetoric 1–2, 8–9; restoration of, to rhetorical history 66–7, 134–5; and rhetorical style 239–40; role of, in rhetorical tradition 159–62; as silenced 3, 9, 37–8, 66, 79n2. *See also* Black women
Women in Black 13
Women in White 13
women of color: as excluded from rhetorical discourse 240–2; as excluded from white feminist "goals"; as excluded from second-wave feminism 3. *See also* Black women
women's history, vs. gendered histories 107–10
Women's International Terrorist Conspiracy from Hell (W.I.T.C.H.) 25
women's liberation movement: Campbell on 3; "oxymoron" as metaphor for 29; as personal and political 27, 28; and persuasion 22, 28; as rhetorical movement 19; size of 30n1; stylistic features of 22–6; substantive features of 20–2; traditional rhetoric as inadequate to 28–9
women's rights, rhetoric of Black women regarding 89–94
Women's Rights Convention 2
women's speech: adjectives 42; adverbs 42; in classical antiquity 118; and consciousness raising 193; and cursing 41–2; in executives 39–40; hyperbole 42; intonation 38, 40; and slang 41–2; and Spanish-speaking traditions 151–3; stereotypes 37–8, 40; syntactic looseness of 40–1; tag-orders 38; tag-questions 38; volume and pitch 39. *See also* communication; rhetoric, feminist
Wood, J.T 211, 212
Wood, Marion 36
World's Congress of Representative Women 93, 95
Worsham, Lynn 236
writing: masculine vs. feminine modes of 43; as violent act 253n33; "as a woman" 119n2
writing studies. *See* composition and writing studies

Xenophon 72, 75

Yellin, Jean Fagan 89–90
Young, Richard 232

Zeitlin, Froma 6, 117